Abnormal Psychology

Abnormal Psychology

EDITED BY BILL PELZ

Contents

5. Self Analysis (or pseudo self-analysis)

About this Book

About this Book:

Your *Abnormal Psychology* textbook is a compilation of articles written by instructors for universities around the country. The entire compilation is provided free of charge online through a Creative Commons license. You can access or even copy all the material here, for your own reference, even after the semester ends.

Different Versions:

An electronic version is made available via https://courses.lumenlearning.com/suny-hccc-abnormalpsych/. Also, you may purchase a physical copy at the College Bookstore. The electronic version has access to multimedia content including video, PowerPoint, and interactive activities. The print version will have all the same reading material, but not include the multimedia content.

About the Author:

There are many different authors; look to the "Licenses and Attributions" section at the end of each chapter to identify contributors. This compilation was edited by Professor Bill Pelz at Herkimer County Community College/SUNY.

1. Abnormal Psychology: History, Theories, and Research Methods

Why Science

Scientific research has been one of the great drivers of progress in human history, and the dramatic changes we have seen during the past century are due primarily to scientific findings—modern medicine, electronics, automobiles and jets, birth control, and a host of other helpful inventions. Psychologists believe that scientific methods can be used in the behavioral domain to understand and improve the world. Although psychology trails the biological and physical sciences in terms of progress, we are optimistic based on discoveries to date that scientific psychology will make many important discoveries that can benefit humanity. This module outlines the characteristics of the science, and the promises it holds for understanding behavior. The ethics that guide psychological research are briefly described. It concludes with the reasons you should learn about scientific psychology.

Learning Objectives

- Describe how scientific research has changed the world.
- Describe the key characteristics of the scientific approach.
- Discuss a few of the benefits, as well as problems that have been created by science.
- Describe several ways that psychological science has improved the world.
- Describe a number of the ethical guidelines that psychologists follow.

Scientific Advances and World Progress

There are many people who have made positive contributions to humanity in modern times. Take a careful look at the names on the following list. Which of these individuals do you think has helped humanity the most?

1. Mother Teresa
2. Albert Schweitzer
3. Edward Jenner
4. Norman Borlaug
5. Fritz Haber

The usual response to this question is "Who on earth are Jenner, Borlaug, and Haber?" Many people know that Mother Teresa helped thousands of people living in the slums of Kolkata (Calcutta). Others recall that Albert Schweitzer opened his famous hospital in Africa and went on to earn the Nobel Peace Prize. The other three historical figures, on the other hand, are far less well known. Jenner, Borlaug, and Haber were scientists whose research discoveries saved millions, and even billions, of lives. Dr. Edward Jenner is often considered the "father of immunology" because he was among the first to conceive of and test vaccinations. His pioneering work led directly to the eradication of smallpox. Many other diseases have been greatly reduced because of vaccines discovered using science—measles, pertussis, diphtheria, tetanus, typhoid, cholera, polio, hepatitis—and all are the legacy of Jenner. Fritz Haber and Norman Borlaug saved more than a billion human lives. They created the "Green Revolution" by producing hybrid agricultural crops and synthetic fertilizer. Humanity can now produce food for the seven billion people on the planet, and the starvation that does occur is related to political and economic factors rather than our collective ability to produce food.

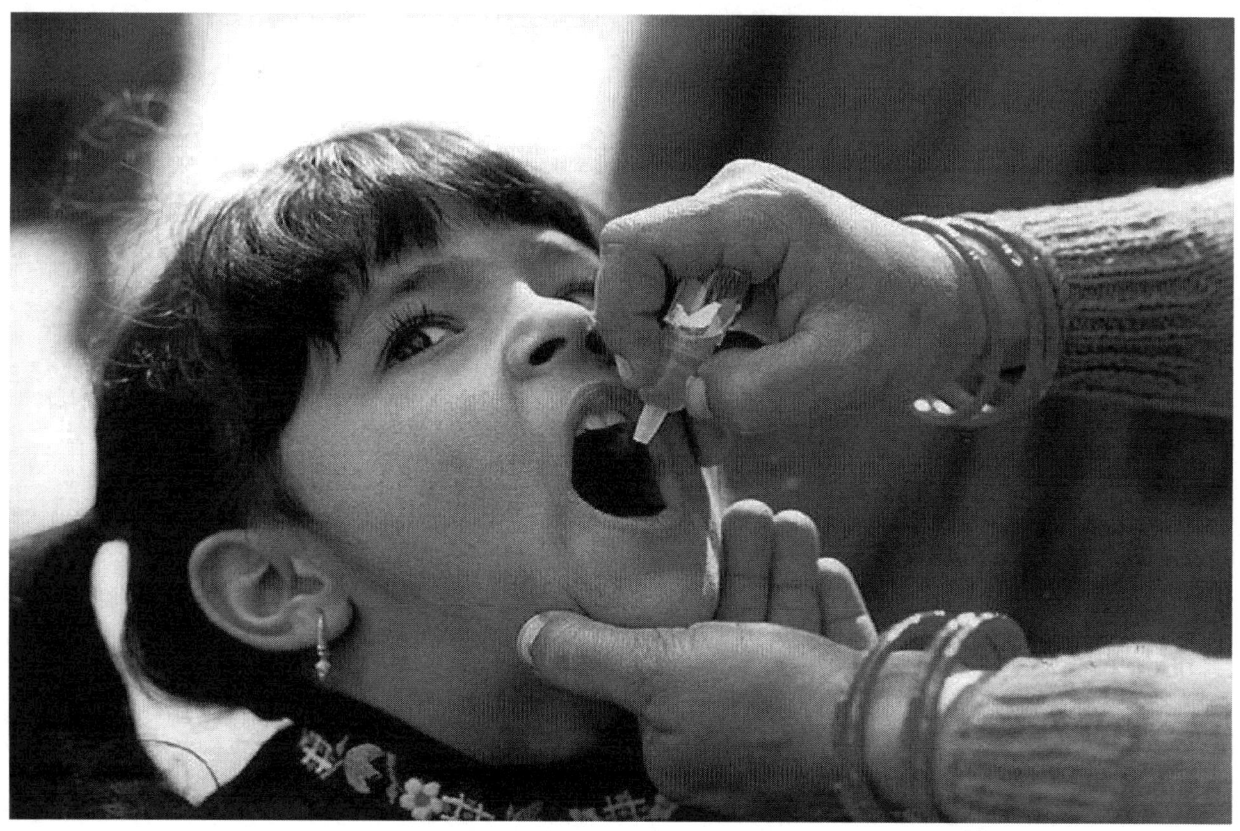

Due to the breakthrough work of Dr. Edward Jenner, millions of vaccinations are now administered around the world every year preventing the spread of many treatable diseases while saving the lives of people of all ages. [Image: CDC Global Health, https://goo.gl/hokiWz, CC BY 2.0, https://goo.gl/9uSnqN]

If you examine major social and technological changes over the past century most of them can be directly attributed to science. The world in 1914 was very different than the one we see today (Easterbrook, 2003). There were few cars and most people traveled by foot, horseback, or carriage. There were no radios, televisions, birth control pills, artificial hearts or antibiotics. Only a small portion of the world had telephones, refrigeration or electricity. These days we find that 80% of all households have television and 84% have electricity. It is estimated that three quarters of the world's population has access to a mobile phone! Life expectancy was 47 years in 1900 and 79 years in 2010. The percentage of hungry and malnourished people in the world has dropped substantially across the globe. Even average levels of I.Q. have risen dramatically over the past century due to better nutrition and schooling.

All of these medical advances and technological innovations are the direct result of scientific research and understanding. In the modern age it is easy to grow complacent about the advances of science but make no mistake about it—science has made fantastic discoveries, and continues to do so. These discoveries have completely changed our world.

What Is Science?

What is this process we call "science," which has so dramatically changed the world? Ancient people were more likely to believe in magical and supernatural explanations for natural phenomena such as solar eclipses or thunderstorms. By contrast, scientifically minded people try to figure out the natural world through testing and observation. Specifically, science is the use of systematic observation in order to acquire knowledge. For example, children in a science class might combine vinegar and baking soda to observe the bubbly chemical reaction. These empirical methods are wonderful ways to learn about the physical and biological world. Science is not magic—it will not solve all human problems, and might not answer all our questions about behavior. Nevertheless, it appears to be the most powerful method we have for acquiring knowledge about the observable world. The essential elements of science are as follows:

1. *Systematic observation is the core of science.* Scientists observe the world, in a very organized way. We often measure the phenomenon we are observing. We record our observations so that memory biases are less likely to enter in to our conclusions. We are systematic in that we try to observe under controlled conditions, and also systematically vary the conditions of our observations so that we can see variations in the phenomena and understand when they occur and do not occur.

Systematic observation is the core of science. [Image: Cvl Neuro, https://goo.gl/Avbju7, CC BY-SA 3.0, https://goo.gl/uhHola]

2. *Observation leads to hypotheses we can test.* When we develop **hypotheses** and **theories,** we state them in a way that can be tested. For example, you might make the claim that candles made of paraffin wax burn more slowly than do candles of the exact same size and shape made from bee's wax. This

claim can be readily tested by timing the burning speed of candles made from these materials.

3. *Science is democratic*. People in ancient times may have been willing to accept the views of their kings or pharaohs as absolute truth. These days, however, people are more likely to want to be able to form their own opinions and debate conclusions. Scientists are skeptical and have open discussions about their observations and theories. These debates often occur as scientists publish competing findings with the idea that the best data will win the argument.

4. *Science is cumulative*. We can learn the important truths discovered by earlier scientists and build on them. Any physics student today knows more about physics than Sir Isaac Newton did even though Newton was possibly the most brilliant physicist of all time. A crucial aspect of scientific progress is that after we learn of earlier advances, we can build upon them and move farther along the path of knowledge.

Psychology as a Science

Even in modern times many people are skeptical that psychology is really a science. To some degree this doubt stems from the fact that many psychological phenomena such as depression, intelligence, and prejudice do not seem to be directly observable in the same way that we can observe the changes in ocean tides or the speed of light. Because thoughts and feelings are invisible many early psychological researchers chose to focus on behavior. You might have noticed that some people act in a friendly and outgoing way while others appear to be shy and withdrawn. If you have made these types of observations then you are acting just like early psychologists who used behavior to draw inferences about various types of personality. By using behavioral measures and rating scales it is possible to measure thoughts and feelings. This is similar to how other researchers explore "invisible" phenomena such as the way that educators measure academic performance or economists measure quality of life.

One important pioneering researcher was Francis Galton, a cousin of Charles Darwin who lived in England during the late 1800s. Galton used patches of color to test people's ability to distinguish between them. He also invented the self-report questionnaire, in which people offered their own expressed judgments or opinions on various matters. Galton was able to use self-reports to examine—among other things—people's differing ability to accurately judge distances.

In 1875 Francis Galton did pioneering studies of twins to determine how much the similarities and differences in twins were affected by their life experiences. In the course of this work he coined the phrase "Nature versus Nurture". [Image: Xynn Tii Imagery, https://goo.gl/F1Wvu7, CC BY-NC-SA 2.0, https://goo.gl/Toc0ZF]

Although he lacked a modern understanding of genetics Galton also had the idea that scientists could look at the behaviors of identical and fraternal twins to estimate the degree to which genetic and social factors contribute to personality; a puzzling issue we currently refer to as the "nature-nurture question."

In modern times psychology has become more sophisticated. Researchers now use better measures, more sophisticated study designs and better statistical analyses to explore human nature. Simply take the example of studying the emotion of happiness. How would you go about studying happiness? One straightforward method is to simply ask people about their happiness and to have them use a numbered scale to indicate their feelings. There are, of course, several problems with this. People might lie about their happiness, might not be able to accurately report on their own happiness, or might not use the numerical scale in the same way. With these limitations in mind modern psychologists employ a wide range of methods to assess happiness. They use, for instance, "peer report measures" in which they ask close friends and family members about the happiness of a target individual. Researchers can then compare these ratings to the self-report ratings and check for discrepancies. Researchers also use memory measures, with the idea that dispositionally positive people have an easier time recalling pleasant events and negative people have an easier time recalling unpleasant events. Modern psychologists even use biological measures such as saliva cortisol samples (cortisol is a stress related hormone) or fMRI images of brain activation (the left pre-frontal cortex is one area of brain activity associated with good moods).

Despite our various methodological advances it is true that psychology is still a very young science. While physics and chemistry are hundreds of years old psychology is barely a hundred and fifty years old and most of our major findings have occurred only in the last 60 years. There are legitimate limits to psychological science but it is a science nonetheless.

Psychological Science is Useful

Psychological science is useful for creating interventions that help people live better lives. A growing body of research is concerned with determining which therapies are the most and least effective for the treatment of psychological disorders.

Cognitive Behavioral Therapy has shown to be effective in treating a variety of conditions, including depression. [Image: SalFalco, https://goo.gl/3knLoJ, CC BY-NC 2.0, https://goo.gl/HEXbAA]

For example, many studies have shown that cognitive behavioral therapy can help many people suffering from depression and anxiety disorders (Butler, Chapman, Forman, & Beck, 2006; Hoffman & Smits, 2008). In contrast, research reveals that some types of therapies actually might be harmful on average (Lilienfeld, 2007).

In organizational psychology, a number of psychological interventions have been found by researchers to produce greater productivity and satisfaction in the workplace (e.g., Guzzo, Jette, & Katzell, 1985). Human factor engineers have greatly increased the safety and utility of the products we use. For example, the human factors psychologist Alphonse Chapanis and other researchers redesigned the cockpit controls of aircraft to make them less confusing and easier to respond to, and this led to a decrease in pilot errors and crashes.

Forensic sciences have made courtroom decisions more valid. We all know of the famous cases of imprisoned persons who have been exonerated because of DNA evidence. Equally dramatic cases hinge on psychological findings. For instance, psychologist Elizabeth Loftus has conducted research demonstrating the limits and unreliability of eyewitness testimony and memory. Thus, psychological findings are having practical importance in the world outside the laboratory. Psychological science has experienced enough success to demonstrate that it works, but there remains a huge amount yet to be learned.

Ethics of Scientific Psychology

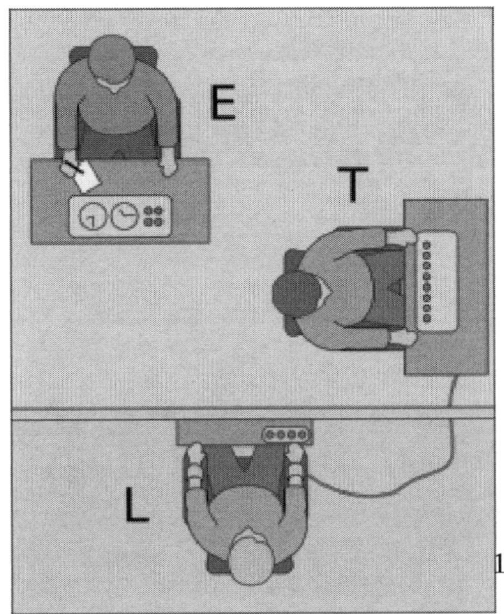

Diagram of the Milgram Experiment in which the "teacher" (T) was asked to deliver a (supposedly) painful electric shock to the "learner"(L). Would this experiment be approved by a review board today? [Image: Fred the Oyster, https://goo.gl/ZIbQz1, CC BY-SA 4.0, https://goo.gl/X3i0tq]

Psychology differs somewhat from the natural sciences such as chemistry in that researchers conduct studies with human research participants. Because of this there is a natural tendency to want to guard research participants against potential psychological harm. For example, it might be interesting to see how people handle ridicule but it might not be advisable to ridicule research participants.

Scientific psychologists follow a specific set of guidelines for research known as a code of ethics. There are extensive ethical guidelines for how human participants should be treated in psychological research (Diener & Crandall, 1978; Sales & Folkman, 2000). Following are a few highlights:

1. *Informed consent*. In general, people should know when they are involved in research, and understand what will happen to them during the study. They should then be given a free choice as to whether to participate.

2. *Confidentiality*. Information that researchers learn about individual participants should not be made public without the consent of the individual.

3. *Privacy*. Researchers should not make observations of people in private places such as their bedrooms without their knowledge and consent. Researchers should not seek confidential information from others, such as school authorities, without consent of the participant or his or her guardian.

4. *Benefits*. Researchers should consider the benefits of their proposed research and weigh these against potential risks to the participants. People who participate in psychological studies should be exposed to risk only if they fully understand these risks and only if the likely benefits clearly outweigh the risks.

5. *Deception*. Some researchers need to deceive participants in order to hide the true nature of the study. This is typically done to prevent participants from modifying their behavior in unnatural ways. Researchers are required to "debrief" their participants after they have completed the study. Debriefing is an opportunity to educate participants about the true nature of the study.

Why Learn About Scientific Psychology?

I once had a psychology professor who asked my class why we were taking a psychology course. Our responses give the range of reasons that people want to learn about psychology:

1. To understand ourselves

2. To understand other people and groups

3. To be better able to influence others, for example, in socializing children or motivating employees

4. To learn how to better help others and improve the world, for example, by doing effective psychotherapy

5. To learn a skill that will lead to a profession such as being a social worker or a professor

6. To learn how to evaluate the research claims you hear or read about

7. Because it is interesting, challenging, and fun! People want to learn about psychology because this is exciting in itself, regardless of other positive outcomes it might have. Why do we see movies? Because they are fun and exciting, and we need no other reason. Thus, one good reason to study psychology is that it can be rewarding in itself.

Conclusions

The science of psychology is an exciting adventure. Whether you will become a scientific psychologist, an applied psychologist, or an educated person who knows about psychological research, this field can influence your life and provide fun, rewards, and understanding. My hope is that you learn a lot from the modules in this e-text, and also that you enjoy the experience! I love learning about psychology and neuroscience, and hope you will too!

Outside Resources

Web: Science Heroes- A celebration of people who have made lifesaving discoveries.
http://www.scienceheroes.com/index.php?option=com_content&view=article&id=258&Itemid=27

Discussion Questions

1. Some claim that science has done more harm than good. What do you think?

2. Humanity is faced with many challenges and problems. Which of these are due to human behavior, and which are external to human actions?

3. If you were a research psychologist, what phenomena or behaviors would most interest you?

4. Will psychological scientists be able to help with the current challenges humanity faces, such as global warming, war, inequality, and mental illness?

5. What can science study and what is outside the realm of science? What questions are impossible for scientists to study?

6. Some claim that science will replace religion by providing sound knowledge instead of myths to explain the world. They claim that science is a much more reliable source of solutions to problems such as disease than is religion. What do you think? Will science replace religion, and should it?

7. Are there human behaviors that should not be studied? Are some things so sacred or dangerous that we should not study them?

Vocabulary

Empirical methods

Approaches to inquiry that are tied to actual measurement and observation.

Ethics

Professional guidelines that offer researchers a template for making decisions that protect research participants from potential harm and that help steer scientists away from conflicts of interest or other situations that might compromise the integrity of their research.

Hypotheses

A logical idea that can be tested.

Systematic observation

The careful observation of the natural world with the aim of better understanding it. Observations provide the basic data that allow scientists to track, tally, or otherwise organize information about the natural world.

Theories

Groups of closely related phenomena or observations.

References

- Butler, A. C., Chapman, J. E., Forman, E. M., & Beck, A. T. (2006). The empirical status of cognitive-behavioral therapy: A review of meta-analyses. *Clinical Psychology Review, 26*, 17–31.

- Diener, E., & Crandall, R. (1978). *Ethics in social and behavioral research*. Chicago, IL: University of Chicago Press.

- Easterbrook, G. (2003). *The progress paradox*. New York, NY: Random House.

- Guzzo, R. A., Jette, R. D., & Katzell, R. A. (1985). The effects of psychologically based intervention programs on worker productivity: A meta-analysis. *Personnel Psychology, 38*, 275.291.

- Hoffman, S. G., & Smits, J. A. J. (2008). Cognitive-behavioral therapy for adult anxiety disorders. *Journal of Clinical Psychiatry, 69*, 621–32.

- Lilienfeld, S. O. (2007). Psychological treatments that cause harm. *Perspectives on Psychological Science, 2*, 53–70.

- Moore, D. (2003). Public lukewarm on animal rights. Gallup News Service, May 21.

http://www.gallup.com/poll/8461/public-lukewarm-animal-rights.aspx

- Sales, B. D., & Folkman, S. (Eds.). (2000). *Ethics in research with human participants.* Washington, DC: American Psychological Association.

CC licensed content, Specific attribution

- Why Science. **Authored by**: Diener. **Provided by**: Noba Project. **Located at**: http://nobaproject.com/modules/why-science. **Project**: Achieving the Dream Course. **License**: *CC BY-NC-SA: Attribution-NonCommercial-ShareAlike*

Research Designs

Psychologists test research questions using a variety of methods. Most research relies on either correlations or experiments. With correlations, researchers measure variables as they naturally occur in people and compute the degree to which two variables go together. With experiments, researchers actively make changes in one variable and watch for changes in another variable. Experiments allow researchers to make causal inferences. Other types of methods include longitudinal and quasi-experimental designs. Many factors, including practical constraints, determine the type of methods researchers use. Often researchers survey people even though it would be better, but more expensive and time consuming, to track them longitudinally.

Learning Objectives

- Articulate the difference between correlational and experimental designs.
- Understand how to interpret correlations.
- Understand how experiments help us to infer causality.
- Understand how surveys relate to correlational and experimental research.
- Explain what a longitudinal study is.
- List a strength and weakness of different research designs.

Research Designs

In the early 1970's, a man named Uri Geller tricked the world: he convinced hundreds of thousands of people that he could bend spoons and slow watches using only the power of his mind. In fact, if you were in the audience, you would have likely believed he had psychic powers. Everything looked authentic—this man had to have paranormal abilities! So, why have you probably never heard of him before? Because when Uri was asked to perform his miracles in line with scientific experimentation, he was no longer able to do them. That is, even though it seemed like he was doing the impossible, when he was tested by science, he proved to be nothing more than a clever magician.

When we look at dinosaur bones to make educated guesses about extinct life, or systematically chart the heavens to learn about the relationships between stars and planets, or study magicians to figure out how they perform their tricks, we are forming observations—the foundation of science. Although we are all familiar with the saying "seeing is believing," conducting science is more than just what your eyes perceive. Science is the result of systematic and intentional study of the natural world. And psychology is no different. In the movie *Jerry Maguire*, Cuba Gooding, Jr. became famous for using the phrase, "Show me the money!" In psychology, as in all sciences, we might say, "Show me the data!"

One of the important steps in scientific inquiry is to test our research questions, otherwise known as hypotheses. However, there are many ways to test hypotheses in psychological research. Which method you choose will depend on the type of questions you are asking, as well as what resources are available to you. All methods have limitations, which is why the best research uses a variety of methods.

Most psychological research can be divided into two types: experimental and correlational research.

Experimental Research

If somebody gave you $20 that absolutely had to be spent today, how would you choose to spend it? Would you spend it on an item you've been eyeing for weeks, or would you donate the money to charity? Which option do you think would bring you the most happiness? If you're like most people, you'd choose to spend the money on yourself (duh, right?). Our intuition is that we'd be happier if we spent the money on ourselves.

At the Corner Perk Cafe customers routinely pay for the drinks of strangers. Is this the way to get the most happiness out of a cup of coffee? Elizabeth Dunn's research shows that spending money on others may affect our happiness differently than spending money on ourselves. [Image: The Island Packet, https://goo.gl/DMxA5n]

Knowing that our intuition can sometimes be wrong, Professor Elizabeth Dunn (2008) at the University of British Columbia set out to conduct an experiment on spending and happiness. She gave each of the participants in her experiment $20 and then told them they had to spend the money by the end of the day. Some of the participants were told they must spend the money on themselves, and some were told they must spend the money on others (either charity or a gift for someone). At the end of the day she measured participants' levels of happiness using a self-report questionnaire. (But wait, how do you measure something like happiness when you can't really see it? Psychologists measure many abstract concepts, such as happiness and intelligence, by beginning with operational definitions of the concepts. See the Noba modules on Intelligence [http://noba.to/ncb2h79v] and Happiness [http://noba.to/qnw7g32t], respectively, for more information on specific measurement strategies.)

In an experiment, researchers manipulate, or cause changes, in the independent variable, and observe or measure any impact of those changes in the dependent variable. The independent variable is the one under the experimenter's control, or the variable that is intentionally altered between groups. In the case of Dunn's experiment, the independent variable was whether participants spent the money on themselves or on others. The dependent variable is the variable that is not manipulated at all, or the one where the effect happens. One way to help remember this is that the dependent variable "depends" on what happens to the independent variable. In our example, the participants' happiness (the dependent variable in this experiment) depends on how the participants spend their money (the independent variable). Thus, any observed changes or group differences in happiness can be attributed to whom the money was spent on. What Dunn and her colleagues found was that, after all the spending had been done, the people who had spent the money on others were happier than those who had spent the money on themselves. In other words, spending on others causes us to be happier than spending on ourselves. Do you find this surprising?

But wait! Doesn't happiness depend on a lot of different factors—for instance, a person's upbringing or life circumstances? What if some people had happy childhoods and that's why they're happier? Or what if some people dropped their toast that morning and it fell jam-side down and ruined their whole day? It is correct to recognize that these factors and many more can easily affect a person's level of happiness. So how can we accurately conclude that spending money on others causes happiness, as in the case of Dunn's experiment?

The most important thing about experiments is random assignment. Participants don't get to pick which condition they are in (e.g., participants didn't choose whether they were supposed to spend the money on themselves versus others). The experimenter assigns them to a particular condition based on the flip of a coin or the roll of a die or any other random method. Why do researchers do this? With Dunn's study, there is the obvious reason: you can imagine which condition most people would choose to be in, if given the choice. But another equally important reason is that random assignment makes it so the groups, on average, are similar on all characteristics except what the experimenter manipulates.

By randomly assigning people to conditions (self-spending versus other-spending), some people with happy childhoods should end up in each condition. Likewise, some people who had dropped their toast that morning (or experienced some other disappointment) should end up in each condition. As a result, the distribution of all these factors will generally be consistent across the two groups, and this means that on average the two groups will be relatively equivalent on all these factors. Random assignment is critical to experimentation because if the only difference between the two groups is the independent variable, we can infer that the independent variable is the cause of any observable difference (e.g., in the amount of happiness they feel at the end of the day).

Here's another example of the importance of random assignment: Let's say your class is going to form two basketball teams, and you get to be the captain of one team. The class is to be divided evenly between the two teams. If you get to pick the players for your team first, whom will you pick? You'll probably pick the tallest members of the class or the most athletic. You probably won't pick the short, uncoordinated people, unless there are no other options. As a result, your team will be taller and more athletic than the other team. But what if we want the teams to be fair? How can we do this when we have people of varying height and ability? All we have to do is randomly assign players to the two teams. Most likely, some tall and some short people will end up on your team, and some tall and some short people will end up on the other team. The average height of the teams will be approximately the same. That is the power of random assignment!

Other considerations

In addition to using random assignment, you should avoid introducing confounds into your experiments. Confounds are things that could undermine your ability to draw causal inferences. For example, if you wanted to test if a new happy pill will make people happier, you could randomly assign participants to take the happy pill or not (the independent variable) and compare these two groups on their self-reported happiness (the dependent variable). However, if some participants know they are getting the happy pill, they might develop expectations that influence their self-reported happiness. This is sometimes known as a placebo effect. Sometimes a person just knowing that he or she is receiving special treatment or something new is enough to actually cause changes in behavior or perception: In other words, even if the participants in the happy pill condition were to report being happier, we wouldn't know if the pill was actually making them happier or if it was the placebo effect—an example of a confound. A related idea is participant demand. This occurs when participants try to behave in a way they think the experimenter wants them to behave. Placebo effects and participant demand often occur unintentionally. Even experimenter expectations can influence the outcome of a study. For example, if the experimenter knows who took the happy pill and who did not, and the dependent variable is the experimenter's observations of people's happiness, then the experimenter might perceive improvements in the happy pill group that are not really there.

One way to prevent these confounds from affecting the results of a study is to use a double-blind procedure. In a double-blind procedure, neither the participant nor the experimenter knows which condition the participant is in. For example, when participants are given the happy pill or the fake pill, they don't know which one they are receiving. This way the participants shouldn't experience the placebo effect, and will be unable to behave as the researcher expects (participant demand). Likewise, the researcher doesn't know which pill each participant is taking (at least in the beginning—later, the researcher will get the results for data-analysis purposes), which means the researcher's expectations can't influence his or her observations. Therefore, because both parties are "blind" to the condition, neither will be able to behave in a way that introduces a confound. At the end of the day, the only difference between groups will be which pills the participants received, allowing the researcher to determine if the happy pill actually caused people to be happier.

Correlational Designs

When scientists passively observe and measure phenomena it is called correlational research. Here, we do not intervene and change behavior, as we do in experiments. In correlational research, we identify patterns of relationships, but we usually cannot infer what causes what. Importantly, with correlational research, you can examine only two variables at a time, no more and no less.

So, what if you wanted to test whether spending on others is related to happiness, but you don't have $20 to give to each participant? You could use a correlational design—which is exactly what Professor Dunn did, too. She asked people how much of their income they spent on others or donated to charity, and later she asked them how happy they were. Do you think these two variables were related? Yes, they were! The more money people reported spending on others, the happier they were.

More details about the correlation

To find out how well two variables correspond, we can plot the relation between the two scores on what is known as a scatterplot (Figure 1). In the scatterplot, each dot represents a data point. (In this case it's individuals, but it could be some other unit.) Importantly, each dot provides us with two pieces of information—in this case, information about how good the person rated the past month (x-axis) and how happy the person felt in the past month (y-axis). Which variable is plotted on which axis does not matter.

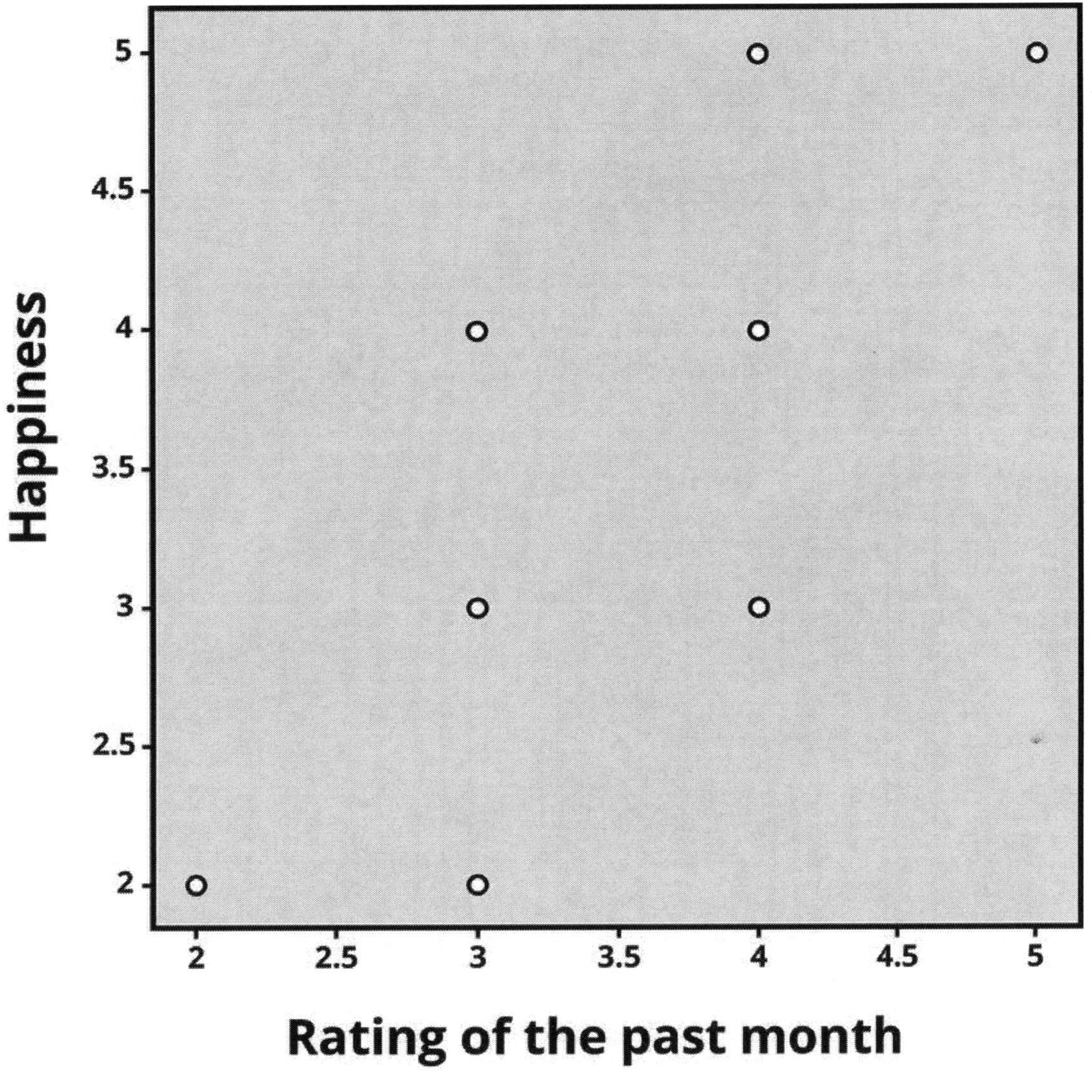

Figure 1. Scatterplot of the association between happiness and ratings of the past month, a positive correlation (r = .81). Each dot represents an individual.

The association between two variables can be summarized statistically using the correlation coefficient (abbreviated as *r*). A correlationcoefficient provides information about the direction and strength of the association between two variables. For the example above, the direction of the association is positive. This means that people who perceived the past month as being good reported feeling more happy, whereas people who perceived the month as being bad reported feeling less happy.

With a positive correlation, the two variables go up or down together. In a scatterplot, the dots form a pattern that extends from the bottom left to the upper right (just as they do in Figure 1). The *r* value for a positive correlation is indicated by a positive number (although, the positive sign is usually omitted). Here, the *r* value is .81.

A negative correlation is one in which the two variables move in opposite directions. That is, as one variable goes up, the other goes down. Figure 2 shows the association between the average height of males in a country (y-axis) and the pathogen prevalence (or commonness of disease; x-axis) of that country. In this scatterplot, each dot represents a country. Notice how the dots extend from the top left to the bottom right. What does this mean in real-world terms? It means that people are shorter in parts of the world where there is more disease. The *r* value for a negative correlation is indicated by a negative number—that is, it has a minus (–) sign in front of it. Here, it is –.83.

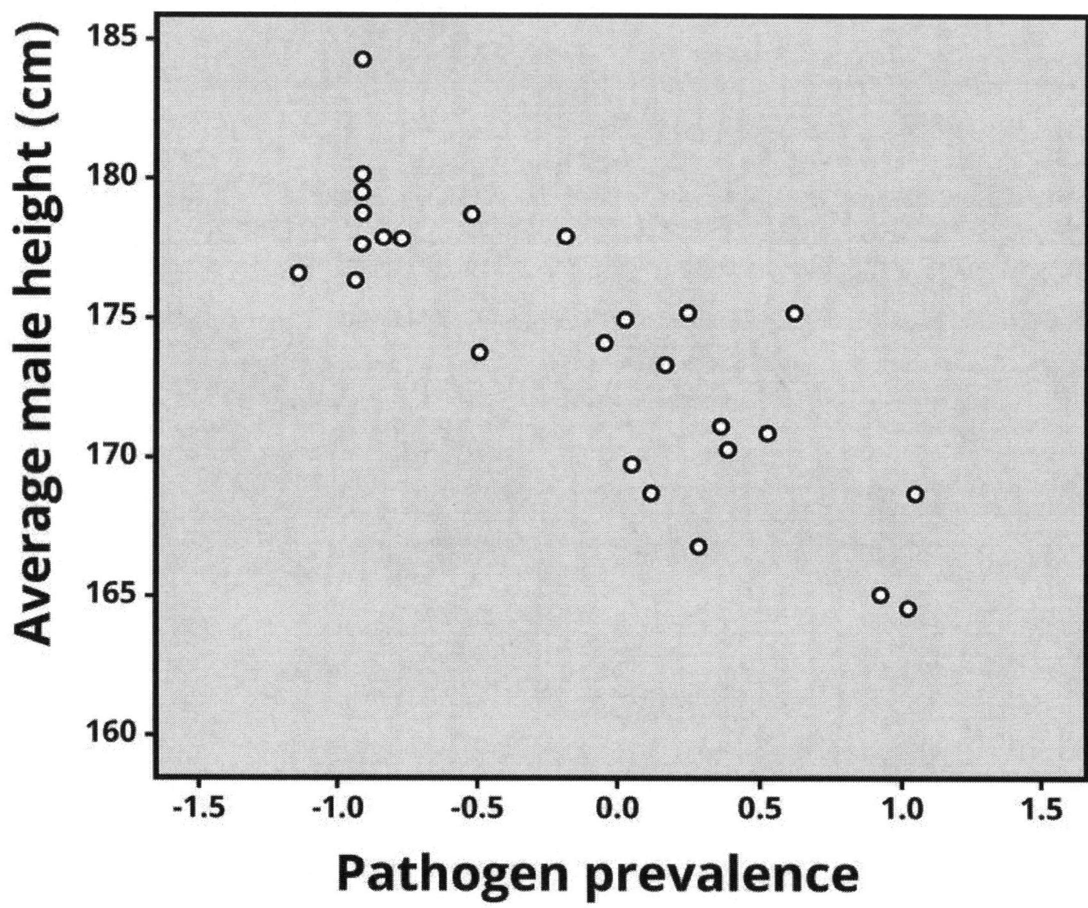

Figure 2. Scatterplot showing the association between average male height and pathogen prevalence, a negative correlation (r = –.83). Each dot represents a country. (Chiao, 2009)

The strength of a correlation has to do with how well the two variables align. Recall that in Professor Dunn's correlational study, spending on others positively correlated with happiness: The more money people reported spending on others, the happier they reported to be. At this point you may be thinking to yourself, I know a very generous person who gave away lots of money to other people but is miserable! Or maybe you know of a very stingy person who is happy as can be. Yes, there might be exceptions. If an association has many exceptions, it is considered a weak correlation. If an association has few or no exceptions, it is considered a strong correlation.

A strong correlation is one in which the two variables always, or almost always, go together. In the example of happiness and how good the month has been, the association is strong. The stronger a correlation is, the tighter the dots in the scatterplot will be arranged along a sloped line.

The *r* value of a strong correlation will have a high absolute value. In other words, you disregard whether there is a negative sign in front of the r value, and just consider the size of the numerical value itself. If the absolute value is large, it is a strong correlation. A weak correlation is one in which the two variables correspond some of the time, but not most of the time. Figure 3 shows the relation between valuing happiness and grade point average (GPA). People who valued happiness more tended to earn slightly lower grades, but there were lots of exceptions to this. The *r* value for a weak correlation will have a low absolute value. If two variables are so weakly related as to be unrelated, we say they are uncorrelated, and the *r* value will be zero or very close to zero. In the previous example, is the correlation between height and pathogen prevalence strong? Compared to Figure 3, the dots in Figure 2 are tighter and less dispersed. The absolute value of −.83 is large. Therefore, it is a strong negative correlation.

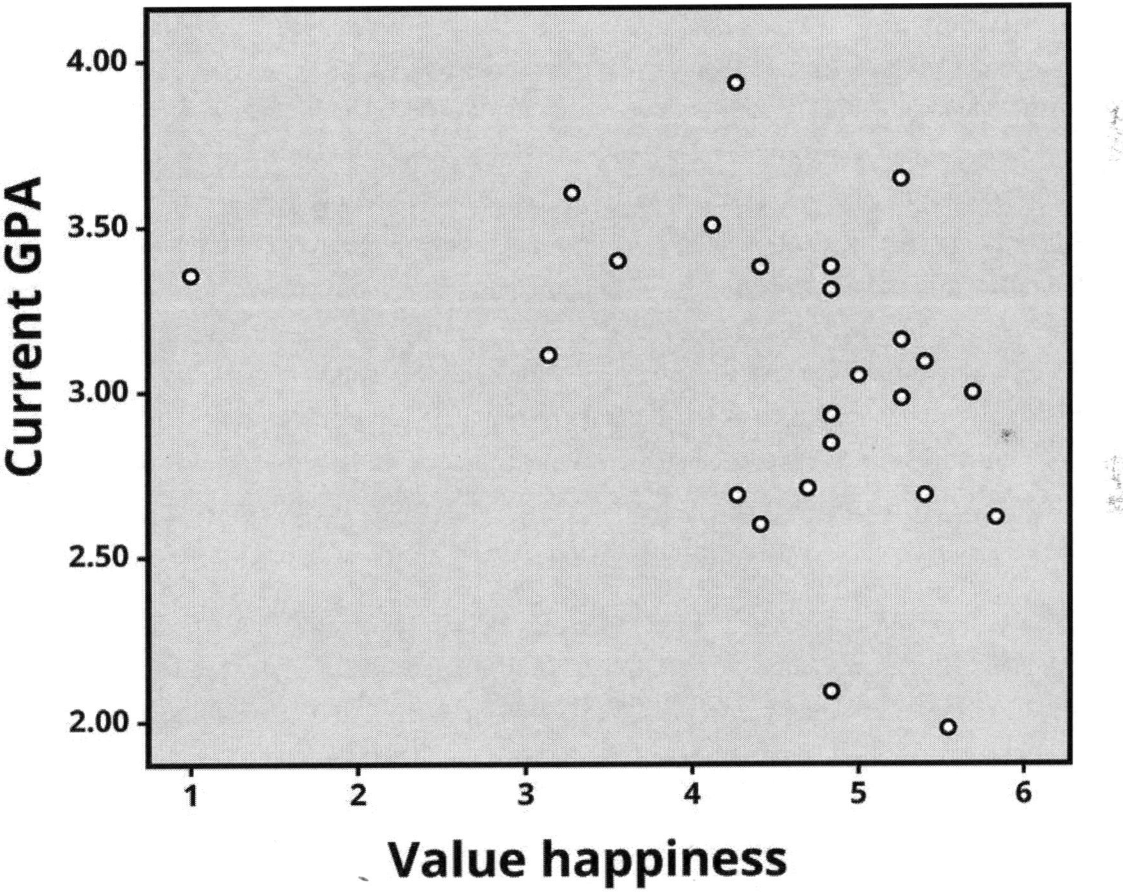

Figure 3. Scatterplot showing the association between valuing happiness and GPA, a weak negative correlation (r = −.32). Each dot represents an individual.

Can you guess the strength and direction of the correlation between age and year of birth? If you said this is a strong negative correlation, you are correct! Older people always have lower years of birth than younger people (e.g., 1950 vs. 1995), but at the same time, the older people will have a higher age (e.g., 65 vs. 20). In fact, this is a perfect correlation because there are no exceptions to this pattern. I challenge you to find a 10-year-old born before 2003! You can't.

Problems with the correlation

If generosity and happiness are positively correlated, should we conclude that being generous causes happiness? Similarly, if height and pathogen prevalence are negatively correlated, should we conclude that disease causes shortness? From a correlation alone, we can't be certain. For example, in the first case it may be that happiness causes generosity, or that generosity causes happiness. Or, a third variable might cause both happiness *and*generosity, creating the illusion of a direct link between the two. For example, wealth could be the third variable that causes both greater happiness and greater generosity. This is why correlation does not mean causation—an often repeated phrase among psychologists.

Qualitative Designs

Just as correlational research allows us to study topics we can't experimentally manipulate (e.g., whether you have a large or small income), there are other types of research designs that allow us to investigate these harder-to-study topics. Qualitative designs, including participant observation, case studies, and narrative analysis are examples of such methodologies. Although something as simple as "observation" may seem like it would be a part of all research methods, participant observation is a distinct methodology that involves the researcher embedding him- or herself into a group in order to study its dynamics. For example, Festinger, Riecken, and Shacter (1956) were very interested in the psychology of a particular cult. However, this cult was very secretive and wouldn't grant interviews to outside members. So, in order to study these people, Festinger and his colleagues pretended to be cult members, allowing them access to the behavior and psychology of the cult. Despite this example, it should be noted that the people being observed in a participant observation study usually know that the researcher is there to study them.

Another qualitative method for research is the case study, which involves an intensive examination of specific individuals or specific contexts. Sigmund Freud, the father of psychoanalysis, was famous for using this type of methodology; however, more current examples of case studies usually involve brain injuries. For instance, imagine that researchers want to know how a very specific brain injury affects people's experience of happiness. Obviously, the researchers can't conduct experimental research that involves inflicting this type of injury on people. At the same time, there are too few people who have this type of injury to conduct correlational research. In such an instance, the researcher may examine only one person with this brain injury, but in doing so, the researcher will put the participant through a very extensive round of tests. Hopefully what is learned from this one person can be applied to others; however, even with thorough tests, there is the chance that something unique about this individual (other than the brain injury) will affect his or her happiness. But with such a limited number of possible participants, a case study is really the only type of methodology suitable for researching this brain injury.

The final qualitative method to be discussed in this section is narrative analysis. Narrative analysis centers around the study of stories and personal accounts of people, groups, or cultures. In this methodology, rather than engaging with participants directly, or quantifying their responses or behaviors, researchers will analyze the themes, structure, and dialogue of each person's narrative. That is, a researcher will examine people's personal testimonies in order to learn more about the psychology of those individuals or groups. These stories may be written, audio-recorded, or video-recorded, and allow the researcher not only to study *what* the participant says but *how* he or she says it. Every person has a unique perspective on the world, and studying the way he or she conveys a story can provide insight into that perspective.

Quasi-Experimental Designs

What if you want to study the effects of marriage on a variable? For example, does marriage make people happier? Can you randomly assign some people to get married and others to remain single? Of course not. So how can you study these important variables? You can use a quasi-experimental design.

What is a reasonable way to study the effects of marriage on happiness? [Image: Nina Matthews Photography, https://goo.gl/IcmLqg, CC BY-NC-SA, https://goo.gl/HSisdg]

A quasi-experimental design is similar to experimental research, except that random assignment to conditions is not used. Instead, we rely on existing group memberships (e.g., married vs. single). We treat these as the independent variables, even though we don't assign people to the conditions and don't manipulate the variables. As a result, with quasi-experimental designs causal inference is more difficult. For example, married people might differ on a variety of characteristics from unmarried people. If we find that married participants are happier than single participants, it will be hard to say that marriage causes happiness, because the people who got married might have already been happier than the people who have remained single.

Because experimental and quasi-experimental designs can seem pretty similar, let's take another example to distinguish them. Imagine you want to know who is a better professor: Dr. Smith or Dr. Khan. To judge their ability, you're going to look at their students' final grades. Here, the independent variable is the professor (Dr. Smith vs. Dr. Khan) and the dependent variable is the students' grades. In an experimental design, you would randomly assign students to one of the two professors and then compare the students' final grades. However, in real life, researchers can't randomly force students to take one professor over the other; instead, the researchers would just have to use the preexisting classes and study them as-is (quasi-experimental design). Again, the key difference is random assignment to the conditions of the independent variable. Although the quasi-experimental design (where the students choose which professor they want) may seem random, it's most likely not. For example, maybe students heard Dr. Smith sets low expectations, so slackers prefer this class, whereas Dr. Khan sets higher expectations, so smarter students prefer that one. This now introduces a confounding variable (student intelligence) that will almost certainly have an effect on students' final grades, regardless of how skilled the professor is. So, even though a quasi-experimental design is similar to an experimental design (i.e., it has a manipulated independent variable), because there's no random assignment, you can't reasonably draw the same conclusions that you would with an experimental design.

Longitudinal Studies

Another powerful research design is the longitudinal study. Longitudinal studies track the same people over time. Some longitudinal studies last a few weeks, some a few months, some a year or more. Some studies that have contributed a lot to psychology followed the same people over decades. For example, one study followed more than 20,000 Germans for two decades. From these longitudinal data, psychologist Rich Lucas (2003) was able to determine that people who end up getting married indeed start off a bit happier than their peers who never marry. Longitudinal studies like this provide valuable evidence for testing many theories in psychology, but they can be quite costly to conduct, especially if they follow many people for many years.

Surveys

Surveys provide researchers with some significant advantages in gathering data. They make it possible to reach large numbers of people while keeping costs to the researchers and the time commitments of participants relatively low.

A survey is a way of gathering information, using old-fashioned questionnaires or the Internet. Compared to a study conducted in a psychology laboratory, surveys can reach a larger number of participants at a much lower cost. Although surveys are typically used for correlational research, this is not always the case. An experiment can be carried out using surveys as well. For example, King and Napa (1998) presented participants with different types of stimuli on paper: either a survey completed by a happy person or a survey completed by an unhappy person. They wanted to see whether happy people were judged as more likely to get into heaven compared to unhappy people. Can you figure out the independent and dependent variables in this study? Can you guess what the results were? Happy people (vs. unhappy people; the independent variable) were judged as more likely to go to heaven (the dependent variable) compared to unhappy people!

Likewise, correlational research can be conducted without the use of surveys. For instance, psychologists LeeAnn Harker and Dacher Keltner (2001) examined the smile intensity of women's college yearbook photos. Smiling in the photos was correlated with being married 10 years later!

Tradeoffs in Research

Even though there are serious limitations to correlational and quasi-experimental research, they are not poor cousins to experiments and longitudinal designs. In addition to selecting a method that is appropriate to the question, many practical concerns may influence the decision to use one method over another. One of these factors is simply resource availability—how much time and money do you have to invest in the research? (Tip: If you're doing a senior honor's thesis, do not embark on a lengthy longitudinal study unless you are prepared to delay graduation!) Often, we survey people even though it would be more precise—but much more difficult—to track them longitudinally. Especially in the case of exploratory research, it may make sense to opt for a cheaper and faster method first. Then, if results from the initial study are promising, the researcher can follow up with a more intensive method.

Beyond these practical concerns, another consideration in selecting a research design is the ethics of the study. For example, in cases of brain injury or other neurological abnormalities, it would be unethical for researchers to inflict these impairments on healthy participants. Nonetheless, studying people with these injuries can provide great insight into human psychology (e.g., if we learn that damage to a particular region of the brain interferes with emotions, we may be able to develop treatments for emotional irregularities). In addition to brain injuries, there are numerous other areas of research that could be useful in understanding the human mind but which pose challenges to a true experimental design—such as the experiences of war, long-term isolation, abusive parenting, or prolonged drug use. However, none of these are conditions we could ethically experimentally manipulate and randomly assign people to. Therefore, ethical considerations are another crucial factor in determining an appropriate research design.

Research Methods: Why You Need Them

Just look at any major news outlet and you'll find research routinely being reported. Sometimes the journalist understands the research methodology, sometimes not (e.g., correlational evidence is often incorrectly represented as causal evidence). Often, the media are quick to draw a conclusion for you. After reading this module, you should recognize that the strength of a scientific finding lies in the strength of its methodology. Therefore, in order to be a savvy consumer of research, you need to understand the pros and cons of different methods and the distinctions among them. Plus, understanding how psychologists systematically go about answering research questions will help you to solve problems in other domains, both personal and professional, not just in psychology.

Outside Resources

Article: Harker and Keltner study of yearbook photographs and marriage
http://psycnet.apa.org/journals/psp/80/1/112/
Article: Rich Lucas's longitudinal study on the effects of marriage on happiness
http://psycnet.apa.org/journals/psp/84/3/527/
Article: Spending money on others promotes happiness. Elizabeth Dunn's research
https://www.sciencemag.org/content/319/5870/1687.abstract
Article: What makes a life good?
http://psycnet.apa.org/journals/psp/75/1/156/

Discussion Questions

1. What are some key differences between experimental and correlational research?

2. Why might researchers sometimes use methods other than experiments?

3. How do surveys relate to correlational and experimental designs?

Vocabulary

Confounds
Factors that undermine the ability to draw causal inferences from an experiment.
Correlation
Measures the association between two variables, or how they go together.
Dependent variable
The variable the researcher measures but does not manipulate in an experiment.
Experimenter expectations
When the experimenter's expectations influence the outcome of a study.
Independent variable
The variable the researcher manipulates and controls in an experiment.
Longitudinal study
A study that follows the same group of individuals over time.
Operational definitions
How researchers specifically measure a concept.

Participant demand

When participants behave in a way that they think the experimenter wants them to behave.

Placebo effect

When receiving special treatment or something new affects human behavior.

Quasi-experimental design

An experiment that does not require random assignment to conditions.

Random assignment

Assigning participants to receive different conditions of an experiment by chance.

References

- Chiao, J. (2009). Culture–gene coevolution of individualism – collectivism and the serotonin transporter gene. *Proceedings of the Royal Society B, 277,* 529-537. doi: 10.1098/rspb.2009.1650

- Dunn, E. W., Aknin, L. B., & Norton, M. I. (2008). Spending money on others promotes happiness. Science, 319(5870), 1687–1688. doi:10.1126/science.1150952

- Festinger, L., Riecken, H.W., & Schachter, S. (1956). When prophecy fails. Minneapolis, MN: University of Minnesota Press.

- Harker, L. A., & Keltner, D. (2001). Expressions of positive emotion in women\'s college yearbook pictures and their relationship to personality and life outcomes across adulthood. Journal of Personality and Social Psychology, 80, 112–124.

- King, L. A., & Napa, C. K. (1998). What makes a life good? Journal of Personality and Social Psychology, 75, 156–165.

- Lucas, R. E., Clark, A. E., Georgellis, Y., & Diener, E. (2003). Re-examining adaptation and the set-point model of happiness: Reactions to changes in marital status. Journal of Personality and Social Psychology, 84, 527–539.

History of Mental Illness

This module is divided into three parts. The first is a brief introduction to various criteria we use to define or distinguish between normality and abnormality. The second, largest part is a history of mental illness from the Stone Age to the 20th century, with a special emphasis on the recurrence of three causal explanations for mental illness; supernatural, somatogenic, and psychogenic factors. This part briefly touches upon trephination, the Greek theory of hysteria within the context of the four bodily humors, witch hunts, asylums, moral treatment, mesmerism, catharsis, the mental hygiene movement, deinstitutionalization, community mental health services, and managed care. The third part concludes with a brief description of the issue of diagnosis.

Learning Objectives

- Identify what the criteria used to distinguish normality from abnormality are.

- Understand the difference among the three main etiological theories of mental illness.

- Describe specific beliefs or events in history that exemplify each of these etiological theories (e.g., hysteria, humorism, witch hunts, asylums, moral treatments).

- Explain the differences in treatment facilities for the mentally ill (e.g., mental hospitals, asylums, community mental health centers).

- Describe the features of the "moral treatment" approach used by Chiarughi, Pinel, and Tuke.

- Describe the reform efforts of Dix and Beers and the outcomes of their work.

- Describe Kräpelin's classification of mental illness and the current DSM system.

History of Mental Illness

References to mental illness can be found throughout history. The evolution of mental illness, however, has not been linear or progressive but rather cyclical. Whether a behavior is considered normal or abnormal depends on the context surrounding the behavior and thus changes as a function of a particular time and culture. In the past, uncommon behavior or behavior that deviated from the sociocultural norms and expectations of a specific culture and period has been used as a way to silence or control certain individuals or groups. As a result, a less cultural relativist view of abnormal behavior has focused instead on whether behavior poses a threat to oneself or others or causes so much pain and suffering that it interferes with one's work responsibilities or with one's relationships with family and friends.

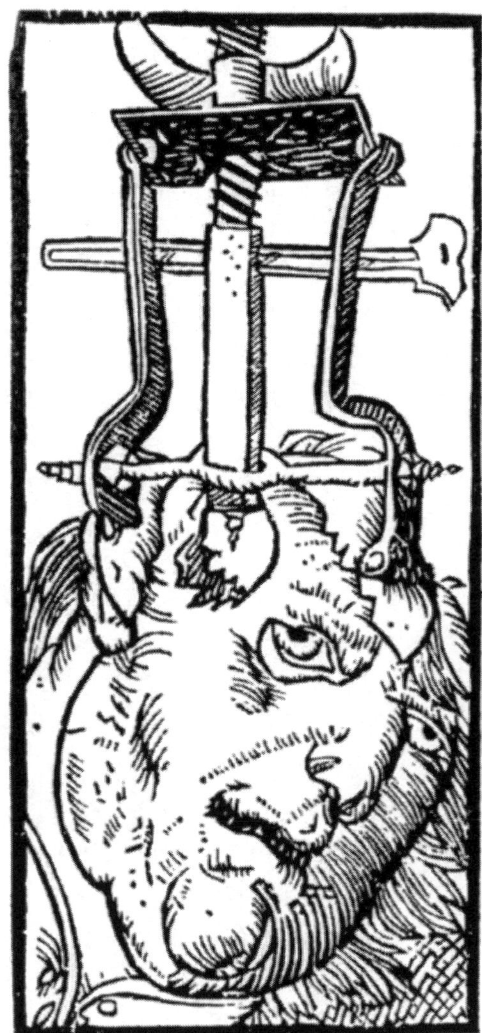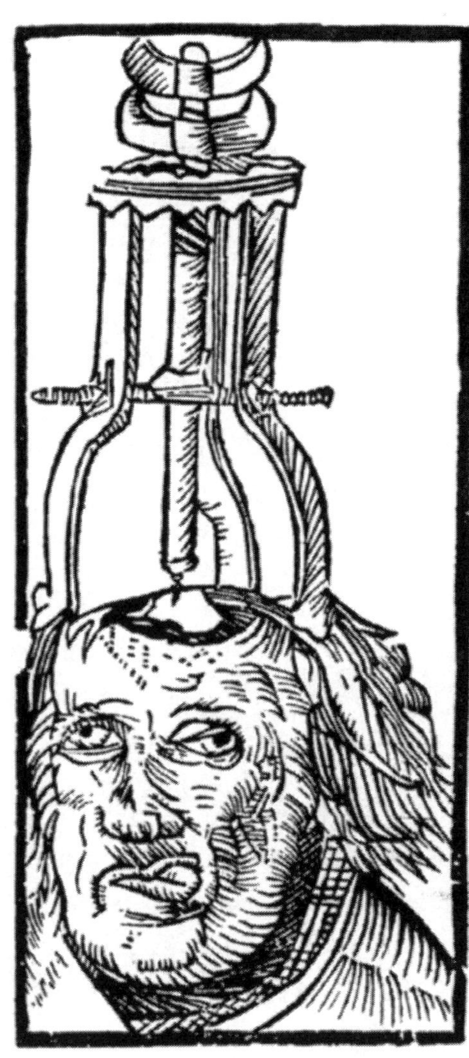

Engravings from 1525 showing trephination. It was believed that drilling holes in the skull could cure mental disorders. [Image: Peter Treveris, CC0 Public Domain, https://goo.gl/m25gce]

Throughout history there have been three general theories of the etiology of mental illness: supernatural, somatogenic, and psychogenic. Supernatural theories attribute mental illness to possession by evil or demonic spirits, displeasure of gods, eclipses, planetary gravitation, curses, and sin. Somatogenic theories identify disturbances in physical functioning resulting from either illness, genetic inheritance, or brain damage or imbalance. Psychogenic theories focus on traumatic or stressful experiences, maladaptive learned associations and cognitions, or distorted perceptions. Etiological theories of mental illness determine the care and treatment mentally ill individuals receive. As we will see below, an individual believed to be possessed by the devil will be viewed and treated differently from an individual believed to be suffering from an excess of yellow bile. Their treatments will also differ, from exorcism to blood-letting. The theories, however, remain the same. They coexist as well as recycle over time.

Trephination is an example of the earliest supernatural explanation for mental illness. Examination of prehistoric skulls and cave art from as early as 6500 BC has identified surgical drilling of holes in skulls to treat head injuries and epilepsy as well as to allow evil spirits trapped within the skull to be released (Restak, 2000). Around 2700 BC, Chinese medicine's concept of complementary positive and negative bodily forces ("yin and yang") attributed mental (and physical) illness to an imbalance between these forces. As such, a harmonious life that allowed for the proper balance of yin and yang and movement of vital air was essential (Tseng, 1973).

Mesopotamian and Egyptian papyri from 1900 BC describe women suffering from mental illness resulting from a wandering uterus (later named hysteria by the Greeks): The uterus could become dislodged and attached to parts of the body like the liver or chest cavity, preventing their proper functioning or producing varied and sometimes painful symptoms. As a result, the Egyptians, and later the Greeks, also employed a somatogenic treatment of strong smelling substances to guide the uterus back to its proper location (pleasant odors to lure and unpleasant ones to dispel).

Throughout classical antiquity we see a return to supernatural theories of demonic possession or godly displeasure to account for abnormal behavior that was beyond the person's control. Temple attendance with religious healing ceremonies and incantations to the gods were employed to assist in the healing process. Hebrews saw madness as punishment from God, so treatment consisted of confessing sins and repenting. Physicians were also believed to be able to comfort and cure madness, however.

Greek physicians rejected supernatural explanations of mental disorders. It was around 400 BC that Hippocrates (460–370 BC) attempted to separate superstition and religion from medicine by systematizing the belief that a deficiency in or especially an excess of one of the four essential bodily fluids (i.e., humors)—blood, yellow bile, black bile, and phlegm—was responsible for physical and mental illness. For example, someone who was too temperamental suffered from too much blood and thus blood-letting would be the necessary treatment. Hippocrates classified mental illness into one of four categories—epilepsy, mania, melancholia, and brain fever—and like other prominent physicians and philosophers of his time, he did not believe mental illness was shameful or that mentally ill individuals should be held accountable for their behavior. Mentally ill individuals were cared for at home by family members and the state shared no responsibility for their care. Humorism remained a recurrent somatogenic theory up until the 19th century.

While Greek physician Galen (AD 130–201) rejected the notion of a uterus having an animistic soul, he agreed with the notion that an imbalance of the four bodily fluids could cause mental illness. He also opened the door for psychogenic explanations for mental illness, however, by allowing for the experience of psychological stress as a potential cause of abnormality. Galen's psychogenic theories were ignored for centuries, however, as physicians attributed mental illness to physical causes throughout most of the millennium.

By the late Middle Ages, economic and political turmoil threatened the power of the Roman Catholic church. Between the 11th and 15th centuries, supernatural theories of mental disorders again dominated Europe, fueled by natural disasters like plagues and famines that lay people interpreted as brought about by the devil. Superstition, astrology, and alchemy took hold, and common treatments included prayer rites, relic touching, confessions, and atonement. Beginning in the 13th century the mentally ill, especially women, began to be persecuted as witches who were possessed. At the height of the witch hunts during the 15th through 17th centuries, with the Protestant Reformation having

Many of Hippocrates' medical theories are no longer practiced today. However, he pioneered medicine as an empirical practice and came up with the "Hippocratic oath," which all doctors must swear to before joining the profession (i.e., the promise to never intentionally harm a patient). [Image: Wellcome Images, https://goo.gl/dX21yj, CC BY 4.0, https://goo.gl/FJIuOM]

plunged Europe into religious strife, two Dominican monks wrote the *Malleus Maleficarum* (1486) as the ultimate manual to guide witch hunts. Johann Weyer and Reginald Scot tried to convince people in the mid- to late-16th century that accused witches were actually women with mental illnesses and that mental illness was not due to demonic possession but to faulty metabolism and disease, but the Church's Inquisition banned both of their writings. Witch-hunting did not decline until the 17th and 18th centuries, after more than 100,000 presumed witches had been burned at the stake (Schoeneman, 1977; Zilboorg & Henry, 1941).

Modern treatments of mental illness are most associated with the establishment of hospitals and asylumsbeginning in the 16th century. Such institutions' mission was to house and confine the mentally ill, the poor, the homeless, the unemployed, and the criminal. War and economic depression produced vast numbers of undesirables and these were separated from society and sent to these institutions. Two of the most well-known institutions, St. Mary of Bethlehem in London, known as Bedlam, and the Hôpital Général of Paris—which included La Salpêtrière, La Pitié, and La Bicêtre—began housing mentally ill patients in the mid-16th and 17th centuries. As confinement laws focused on protecting the public *from* the mentally ill, governments became responsible for housing and feeding undesirables in exchange for their personal liberty. Most inmates were institutionalized against their will, lived in filth and chained to walls, and were commonly exhibited to the public for a fee. Mental illness was nonetheless viewed somatogenically, so treatments were similar to those for physical illnesses: purges, bleedings, and emetics.

While inhumane by today's standards, the view of insanity at the time likened the mentally ill to animals (i.e., animalism) who did not have the capacity to reason, could not control themselves, were capable of violence without provocation, did not have the same physical sensitivity to pain or temperature, and could live in miserable conditions without complaint. As such, instilling fear was believed to be the best way to restore a disordered mind to reason.

By the 18th century, protests rose over the conditions under which the mentally ill lived, and the 18th and 19th centuries saw the growth of a more humanitarian view of mental illness. In 1785 Italian physician Vincenzo Chiarughi (1759–1820) removed the chains of patients at his St. Boniface hospital in Florence, Italy, and encouraged good hygiene and recreational and occupational training. More well known, French physician Philippe Pinel (1745–1826) and former patient Jean-Baptise Pussin created a "traitement moral" at La Bicêtre and the Salpêtrière in 1793 and 1795 that also included unshackling patients, moving them to well-aired, well-lit rooms, and encouraging purposeful activity and freedom to move about the grounds (Micale, 1985).

In England, humanitarian reforms rose from religious concerns. William Tuke (1732–1822) urged the Yorkshire Society of (Quaker) Friends to establish the York Retreat in 1796, where patients were guests, not prisoners, and where the standard of care depended on dignity and courtesy as well as the therapeutic and moral value of physical work (Bell, 1980).

Dorothea Dix worked to change the negative perceptions of people with mental illness and helped create institutions where they could receive compassionate care. [Image: State Archives of North Carolina, https://goo.gl/wRgGsi, no known copyright restrictions]

While America had asylums for the mentally ill—such as the Pennsylvania Hospital in Philadelphia and the Williamsburg Hospital, established in 1756 and 1773—the somatogenic theory of mental illness of the time—promoted especially by the father of America psychiatry, Benjamin Rush (1745–1813)—had led to treatments such as blood-letting, gyrators, and tranquilizer chairs. When Tuke's York Retreat became the model for half of the new private asylums established in the United States, however, psychogenic treatments such as compassionate care and physical labor became the hallmarks of the new American asylums, such as the Friends Asylum in Frankford, Pennsylvania, and the Bloomingdale Asylum in New York City, established in 1817 and 1821 (Grob, 1994).

Moral treatment had to be abandoned in America in the second half of the 19th century, however, when these asylums became overcrowded and custodial in nature and could no longer provide the space nor attention necessary. When retired school teacher Dorothea Dix discovered the negligence that resulted from such conditions, she advocated for the establishment of state hospitals. Between 1840 and1880, she helped establish over 30 mental institutions in the United States and Canada (Viney & Zorich, 1982). By the late 19th century, moral treatment had given way to the mental hygiene movement, founded by former patient Clifford Beers with the publication of his 1908 memoir *A Mind That Found Itself.* Riding on Pasteur's breakthrough germ theory of the 1860s and 1870s and especially on the early 20th century discoveries of vaccines for cholera, syphilis, and typhus, the mental hygiene movement reverted to a somatogenic theory of mental illness.

European psychiatry in the late 18th century and throughout the 19th century, however, struggled between somatogenic and psychogenic explanations of mental illness, particularly hysteria, which caused physical symptoms such as blindness or paralysis with no apparent physiological explanation. Franz Anton Mesmer (1734–1815), influenced by contemporary discoveries in electricity, attributed hysterical symptoms to imbalances in a universal magnetic fluid found in individuals, rather than to a wandering uterus (Forrest, 1999). James Braid (1795–1860) shifted this belief in mesmerism to one in hypnosis, thereby proposing a psychogenic treatment for the removal of symptoms. At the time, famed Salpetriere Hospital neurologist Jean-Martin Charcot (1825–1893), and Ambroise Auguste Liébault (1823–1904) and Hyppolyte Bernheim (1840–1919) of the Nancy School in France, were engaged in a bitter etiological battle over hysteria, with Charcot maintaining that the hypnotic suggestibility underlying hysteria was a neurological condition while Liébault and Bernheim believed it to be a general trait that varied in the population. Josef Breuer (1842–1925) and Sigmund Freud (1856–1939) would resolve this dispute in favor of a psychogenic explanation for mental illness by treating hysteria through hypnosis, which eventually led to the cathartic method that became the precursor for psychoanalysis during the first half of the 20th century.

Psychoanalysis was the dominant psychogenic treatment for mental illness during the first half of the 20th century, providing the launching pad for the more than 400 different schools of psychotherapy found today (Magnavita, 2006). Most of these schools cluster around broader behavioral, cognitive, cognitive-behavioral, psychodynamic, and client-centered approaches to psychotherapy applied in individual, marital, family, or group formats. Negligible differences have been found among all these approaches, however; their efficacy in treating mental illness is due to factors shared among all of the approaches (not particular elements specific to each approach): the therapist-patient alliance, the therapist's allegiance to the therapy, therapist competence, and placebo effects (Luborsky et al., 2002; Messer & Wampold, 2002).

In contrast, the leading somatogenic treatment for mental illness can be found in the establishment of the first psychotropic medications in the mid-20th century. Restraints, electro-convulsive shock therapy, and lobotomies continued to be employed in American state institutions until the 1970s, but they quickly made way for a burgeoning pharmaceutical industry that has viewed and treated mental illness as a chemical imbalance in the brain.

Both etiological theories coexist today in what the psychological discipline holds as the biopsychosocial model of explaining human behavior. While individuals may be born with a genetic predisposition for a certain psychological disorder, certain psychological stressors need to be present for them to develop the disorder. Sociocultural factors such as sociopolitical or economic unrest, poor living conditions, or problematic interpersonal relationships are also viewed as contributing factors. However much we want to believe that we are above the treatments described above, or that the present is always the most enlightened time, let us not forget that our thinking today continues to reflect the same underlying somatogenic and psychogenic theories of mental illness discussed throughout this cursory 9,000-year history.

Diagnosis of Mental Illness

Progress in the treatment of mental illness necessarily implies improvements in the diagnosis of mental illness. A standardized diagnostic classification system with agreed-upon definitions of psychological disorders creates a shared language among mental-health providers and aids in clinical research. While diagnoses were recognized as far back as the Greeks, it was not until 1883 that German psychiatrist Emil Kräpelin (1856–1926) published a comprehensive system of psychological disorders that centered around a pattern of symptoms (i.e., syndrome) suggestive of an underlying physiological cause. Other clinicians also suggested popular classification systems but the need for a single, shared system paved the way for the American Psychiatric Association's 1952 publication of the first *Diagnostic and Statistical Manual* (DSM).

Up until the 1970's, homosexuality was included in the DSM as a psychological disorder. Thankfully, society and clinical understanding changed to recognize it didn't belong. [Image: Rene Walter, https://goo.gl/CcJAA1, CC BY-NC-SA 2.0, https://goo.gl/TocOZF]

The DSM has undergone various revisions (in 1968, 1980, 1987, 1994, 2000, 2013), and it is the 1980 DSM-III version that began a multiaxial classification system that took into account the entire individual rather than just the specific problem behavior. Axes I and II contain the clinical diagnoses, including mental retardation and personality disorders. Axes III and IV list any relevant medical conditions or psychosocial or environmental stressors, respectively. Axis V provides a global assessment of the individual's level of functioning. The most recent version — the DSM-5– has combined the first three axes and removed the last two. These revisions reflect an attempt to help clinicians streamline diagnosis and work better with other diagnostic systems such as health diagnoses outlined by the World Health Organization.

While the DSM has provided a necessary shared language for clinicians, aided in clinical research, and allowed clinicians to be reimbursed by insurance companies for their services, it is not without criticism. The DSM is based on clinical and research findings from Western culture, primarily the United States. It is also a medicalized categorical classification system that assumes disordered behavior does not differ in degree but in kind, as opposed to a dimensional classification system that would plot disordered behavior along a continuum. Finally, the number of diagnosable disorders has tripled since it was first published in 1952, so that almost half of Americans will have a diagnosable disorder in their lifetime, contributing to the continued concern of labeling and stigmatizing mentally ill individuals. These concerns appear to be relevant even in the DSM-5 version that came out in May of 2013.

Outside Resources

Video: An introduction to and overview of psychology, from its origins in the nineteenth century to current study of the brain's biochemistry.
http://www.learner.org/series/discoveringpsychology/01/e01expand.html
Video: The BBC provides an overview of ancient Greek approaches to health and medicine.
https://www.tes.com/teaching-resource/ancient-greek-approaches-to-health-and-medicine-6176019
Web: Images from the History of Medicine. Search \"mental illness\"
http://ihm.nlm.nih.gov/luna/servlet/view/all
Web: Science Museum Brought to Life
http://www.sciencemuseum.org.uk/broughttolife/themes/menalhealthandillness.aspx
Web: The Social Psychology Network provides a number of links and resources.
https://www.socialpsychology.org/history.htm
Web: The UCL Center for the History of Medicine
http://www.ucl.ac.uk/histmed/
Web: The Wellcome Library. Search \"mental illness\".
http://wellcomelibrary.org/
Web: US National Library of Medicine
http://vsearch.nlm.nih.gov/vivisimo/cgi-bin/query-meta?query=mental+illness&v:project=nlm-main-website

Discussion Questions

1. What does it mean to say that someone is mentally ill? What criteria are usually considered to determine whether someone is mentally ill?

2. Describe the difference between supernatural, somatogenic, and psychogenic theories of mental illness and how subscribing to a particular etiological theory determines the type of treatment used.

3. How did the Greeks describe hysteria and what treatment did they prescribe?

4. Describe humorism and how it explained mental illness.

5. Describe how the witch hunts came about and their relationship to mental illness.

6. Describe the development of treatment facilities for the mentally insane, from asylums to community mental health centers.

7. Describe the humane treatment of the mentally ill brought about by Chiarughi, Pinel, and Tuke in the late 18th and early 19th centuries and how it differed from the care provided in the centuries preceding it.

8. Describe William Tuke's treatment of the mentally ill at the York Retreat within the context of the Quaker Society of Friends. What influence did Tuke's treatment have in other parts of the world?

9. What are the 20th-century treatments resulting from the psychogenic and somatogenic theories of mental illness?

10. Describe why a classification system is important and how the leading classification system used in the United States works. Describe some concerns with regard to this system.

Vocabulary

Animism

The belief that everyone and everything had a "soul" and that mental illness was due to animistic causes, for example, evil spirits controlling an individual and his/her behavior.

Asylum

A place of refuge or safety established to confine and care for the mentally ill; forerunners of the mental hospital or psychiatric facility.

Biopsychosocial model

A model in which the interaction of biological, psychological, and sociocultural factors is seen as influencing the development of the individual.

Cathartic method

A therapeutic procedure introduced by Breuer and developed further by Freud in the late 19th century whereby a patient gains insight and emotional relief from recalling and reliving traumatic events.

Cultural relativism

The idea that cultural norms and values of a society can only be understood on their own terms or in their own context.

Etiology

The causal description of all of the factors that contribute to the development of a disorder or illness.

Humorism (or humoralism)

A belief held by ancient Greek and Roman physicians (and until the 19th century) that an excess or deficiency in any of the four bodily fluids, or humors—blood, black bile, yellow bile, and phlegm—directly affected their health and temperament.

Hysteria

Term used by the ancient Greeks and Egyptians to describe a disorder believed to be caused by a woman's uterus wandering throughout the body and interfering with other organs (today referred to as conversion disorder, in which psychological problems are expressed in physical form).

Maladaptive

Term referring to behaviors that cause people who have them physical or emotional harm, prevent them from functioning in daily life, and/or indicate that they have lost touch with reality and/or cannot control their thoughts and behavior (also called dysfunctional).

Mesmerism

Derived from Franz Anton Mesmer in the late 18th century, an early version of hypnotism in which Mesmer claimed that hysterical symptoms could be treated through animal magnetism emanating from Mesmer's body and permeating the universe (and later through magnets); later explained in terms of high suggestibility in individuals.

Psychogenesis

Developing from psychological origins.

Somatogenesis

Developing from physical/bodily origins.

Supernatural

Developing from origins beyond the visible observable universe.

Syndrome

Involving a particular group of signs and symptoms.

"Traitement moral" (moral treatment)

A therapeutic regimen of improved nutrition, living conditions, and rewards for productive behavior that has been attributed to Philippe Pinel during the French Revolution, when he released mentally ill patients from their restraints and treated them with compassion and dignity rather than with contempt and denigration.

Trephination

The drilling of a hole in the skull, presumably as a way of treating psychological disorders.

References

- Bell, L. V. (1980). *Treating the mentally ill: From colonial times to the present.* New York: Praeger.

- Forrest, D. (1999). *Hypnotism: A history.* New York: Penguin.

- Grob, G. N. (1994). *The mad among us: A history of the care of America's mentally ill.* New York: Free Press.

- Luborsky, L., Rosenthal, R., Diguer, L., Andrusyna, T. P., Berman, J. S., Levitt, J. T., . . . Krause, E. D. (2002). The dodo bird verdict is alive and well—mostly. *Clinical Psychology: Science and Practice, 9,* 2–12.

- Messer, S. B., & Wampold, B. E. (2002). Let's face facts: Common factors are more potent than specific therapy ingredients. *Clinical Psychology: Science and Practice, 9*(1), 21–25.

- Micale, M. S. (1985). The Salpêtrière in the age of Charcot: An institutional perspective on medical history in the late nineteenth century. *Journal of Contemporary History, 20,* 703–731.

- Restak, R. (2000). *Mysteries of the mind.* Washington, DC: National Geographic Society.

- Schoeneman, T. J. (1977). The role of mental illness in the European witch hunts of the sixteenth and seventeenth centuries: An assessment. *Journal of the History of the Behavioral Sciences, 13*(4), 337–351.

- Tseng, W. (1973). The development of psychiatric concepts in traditional Chinese medicine. *Archives of General Psychiatry, 29,* 569–575.

- Viney, W., & Zorich, S. (1982). Contributions to the history of psychology: XXIX. Dorothea Dix and the history of psychology. *Psychological Reports, 50,* 211–218.

- Zilboorg, G., & Henry, G. W. (1941). *A history of medical psychology.* New York: W. W. Norton.

2. Assessment and Classification of Psychological Disorders

Mental Health Assessment

Link to Psychiatric Assessment in Wikipedia: https://en.wikipedia.org/wiki/Psychiatric_assessment

CC licensed content, Shared previously

- Link to Wikipedia article on Psychiatric Assessment. **Located at**: https://en.wikipedia.org/wiki/Psychiatric_assessment. **Project**: Abnormal Psychology Textbook. **License**: *CC BY: Attribution*

Classification of Mental Disorders

Link to Wikipedia: https://en.wikipedia.org/wiki/Classification_of_mental_disorders

Take this Mental Health Assessment

Link to Mental Health Assessment: https://www.psychologytoday.com/us/tests/health/mental-health-assessment

Psychological Disorders

Link to Sparknotes: http://www.sparknotes.com/psychology/psych101/disorders/

3. Psychological Disorders

ADHD and Behavioral Disorders in Children

Attention-Deficit/Hyperactivity Disorder (ADHD) is a psychiatric disorder that is most often diagnosed in school-aged children. Many children with ADHD find it difficult to focus on tasks and follow instructions, and these characteristics can lead to problems in school and at home. How children with ADHD are diagnosed and treated is a topic of controversy, and many people, including scientists and nonscientists alike, hold strong beliefs about what ADHD is and how people with the disorder should be treated. This module will familiarize the reader with the scientific literature on ADHD. First, we will review how ADHD is diagnosed in children, with a focus on how mental health professionals distinguish between ADHD and normal behavior problems in childhood. Second, we will describe what is known about the causes of ADHD. Third, we will describe the treatments that are used to help children with ADHD and their families. The module will conclude with a brief discussion of how we expect that the diagnosis and treatment of ADHD will change over the coming decades.

Learning Objectives

- Distinguish childhood behavior disorders from phases of typical child development.
- Describe the factors contributing to Attention-Deficit/Hyperactivity Disorder (ADHD)
- Understand the controversies surrounding the legitimacy and treatment of childhood behavior disorders
- Describe the empirically supported treatments for Attention-Deficit/Hyperactivity Disorder (ADHD)

Introduction

Although we commonly think of children as "little bundles of energy", one of the defining characteristics of children diagnosed with ADHD is that they are perpetually in motion even during times when they are expected to be still. [Image: Chicago's North Shore Conventions & Visitors Bureau, https://goo.gl/U2ZI18, CC BY 2.0, https://goo.gl/9uSnqN]

Childhood is a stage of life characterized by rapid and profound development. Starting at birth, children develop the skills necessary to function in the world around them at a rate that is faster than any other time in life. This is no small accomplishment! By the end of their first decade of life, most children have mastered the complex cognitive operations required to comply with rules, such as stopping themselves from acting impulsively, paying attention to parents and teachers in the face of distraction, and sitting still despite boredom. Indeed, acquiring self-control is an important developmental task for children (Mischel, Shoda, & Rodriguez, 1989), because they are expected to comply with directions from adults, stay on task at school, and play appropriately with peers. For children with Attention-Deficit/Hyperactivity Disorder (ADHD), however, exercising self-control is a unique challenge. These children, oftentimes despite their best intentions, struggle to comply with adults' instructions, and they are often labeled as "problem children" and "rule breakers." Historically, people viewed these children as willfully noncompliant due to moral or motivational defect (Still, 1902). However, scientists now know that the noncompliance observed in children with ADHD can be explained by a number of factors, including neurological dysfunction.

The goal of this module is to review the classification, causes, consequences, and treatment of ADHD. ADHD is somewhat unique among the psychiatric disorders in that most people hold strong opinions about the disorder, perhaps due to its more controversial qualities. When applicable, we will discuss some of the controversial beliefs held by social critics and laypeople, as well as scientists who study the disorder. Our hope is that a discussion of these controversies will allow you to reach your own conclusions about the legitimacy of the disorder.

Why Diagnose Children's Behavior Problems?

When a family is referred to a mental health professional for help dealing with their child's problematic behaviors, the clinician's first goal is to identify the nature and cause of the child's problems. Accurately diagnosing children's behavior problems is an important step in the intervention process, because a child's diagnosis can guide clinical decision making. Childhood behavior problems often arise from different causes, require different methods for treating, and have different developmental courses. Arriving at a diagnosis will allow the clinician to make inferences about how each child will respond to different treatments and provide predictive information to the family about how the disorder will affect the child as he or she develops.

Despite the utility of the current diagnostic system, the practice of diagnosing children's behavior problems is controversial. Many adults feel strongly that labeling children as "disordered" is stigmatizing and harmful to children's self-concept. There is some truth in this concern. One study found that children have more negative attitudes toward a play partner if they are led to believe that their partner has ADHD, regardless of whether or not their partner actually has the disorder (Harris, Milich, Corbitt, Hoover, & Brady, 1992). Others have criticized the use of the diagnostic system because they believe it pathologizes normal behavior in children. Despite these criticisms, the diagnostic system has played a central role in research and treatment of child behavior disorders, and it is unlikely to change substantially in the near future. This section will describe ADHD as a diagnostic category and discuss controversies surrounding the legitimacy of this disorder.

On the one hand, diagnosing a child with ADHD can help him or her get beneficial treatment; however, the diagnosis can also have potentially negative effects on peer relationships and how children perceive themselves. [Image: gibsonsgolfer, https://goo.gl/WWZfbQ, CC BY-NC 2.0, https://goo.gl/FIlc2e]

ADHD is the most commonly diagnosed childhood behavior disorder. It affects 3% to 7% of children in the United States (American Psychiatric Association, 2000), and approximately 65% of children diagnosed with ADHD will continue to experience symptoms as adults (Faraone, Biederman, & Mick, 2006). The core symptoms of ADHD are organized into two clusters, including clusters of hyperactivity/impulsivity and inattention. The hyperactive symptom cluster describes children who are perpetually in motion even during times when they are expected to be still, such as during class or in the car. The impulsive symptom cluster describes difficulty in delaying response and acting without considering the repercussions of behavior. Hyperactive and impulsive symptoms are closely related, and boys are more likely than girls to experience symptoms from this cluster (Hartung & Widiger, 1998). Inattentive symptoms describe difficulty with organization and task follow-through, as well as a tendency to be distracted by external stimuli. Two children diagnosed with ADHD can have very different symptom presentations. In fact, children can be diagnosed with different subtypes of the disorder (i.e., Combined Type, Predominantly Inattentive Type, or Predominantly Hyperactive-Impulsive Type) according to the number of symptoms they have in each cluster.

Are These Diagnoses Valid?

Many laypeople and social critics argue that ADHD is not a "real" disorder. These individuals claim that children with ADHD are only "disordered" because parents and school officials have trouble managing their behavior. These criticisms raise an interesting question about what constitutes a psychiatric disorder in children: How do scientists distinguish between clinically significant ADHD symptoms and normal instances of childhood impulsivity, hyperactivity, and inattention? After all, many 4-year-old boys are hyperactive and cannot focus on a task for very long. To address this issue, several criteria are used to distinguish between normal and disordered behavior:

1. The symptoms must significantly impair the child's functioning in important life domains (e.g., school, home).

2. The symptoms must be inappropriate for the child's developmental level.

One goal of this module will be to examine whether ADHD meets the criteria of a "true" disorder. The first criterion states that children with ADHD should show impairment in major functional domains. This is certainly true for children with ADHD. These children have lower academic achievement compared with their peers. They are more likely to repeat a grade or be suspended and less likely to graduate from high school (Loe & Feldman, 2007). Children with ADHD are often unpopular among their peers, and many of these children are actively disliked and socially rejected (Landau, Milich, & Diener, 1998). Children with ADHD are likely to experience comorbid psychological problems such as learning disorders, depression, anxiety, and oppositional defiant disorder. As they grow up, adolescents and adults with ADHD are at risk to abuse alcohol and other drugs (Molina & Pelham, 2003) and experience other adverse outcomes (see Focus Topic 1). In sum, there is sufficient evidence to conclude that children diagnosed with ADHD are significantly impaired by their symptoms.

Focus Topic 1: Adult outcomes of children with ADHD

Children with ADHD often continue to experience symptoms of the disorder as adults. Historically, this fact was not recognized by the medical community; instead, they believed that children "matured out" of their symptoms as they entered adulthood. Fortunately, opinions have changed over time, and it is now generally accepted that ADHD can be present among adults. A recent prevalence estimate suggests that 4.4% of adults in the United States meet criteria for ADHD (Kessler et al., 2006). This study also found that the majority of adults with ADHD are not receiving treatment for their disorder. Adult ADHD, if left untreated, can cause numerous negative outcomes, including:

- Depression and poor self-concept, personality disorder, and other psychiatric comorbidity (Kessler et al., 2006)

- Substance abuse (Molina & Pelham, 2003)

- Poor work performance, termination from jobs, chronic unemployment, and poor academic achievement (Barkley, Fischer, Smallish, & Fletcher, 2006)

- Divorce and problems with interpersonal relationships (Biederman et al., 2006)

- High-risk sexual behaviors and early parenthood (Barkley et al., 2006; Flory, Molina, Pelham, Gnagy, & Smith, 2006)

- Impairments in driving ability (Weafer, Fillmore, & Milich, 2009)

- Obesity (Cortese et al., 2008)

Despite the list of negative outcomes associated with adult ADHD, adults with the disorder are not doomed to live unfulfilling lives of limited accomplishment. Many adults with ADHD have benefited from treatment and are able to overcome their symptoms. For example, pharmacological treatment of adult ADHD has been shown to reduce risk of criminal behavior (Lichtenstein et al., 2012). Others have succeeded by avoiding careers in which their symptoms would be particularly problematic (e.g., those with heavy organizational demands). In any case, it is important that people with ADHD are identified and treated early, because early treatment predicts more positive outcomes in adulthood (Kessler et al., 2006).

It is also important to determine that a child's symptoms are not caused by normal patterns of development. Many of the behaviors that are diagnostic of ADHD in some children would be considered developmentally appropriate for a younger child. This is true for many psychological and psychiatric disorders in childhood. For example, bedwetting is quite common in 3-year-old children; at this age, most children have not gained control over nighttime urination. For this reason, a 3-year-old child who wets the bed would not be diagnosed with enuresis (i.e., the clinical term for chronic bedwetting), because his or her behavior is developmentally appropriate. Bedwetting in an 8-year-old child, however, is developmentally *inappropriate*. At this age, children are expected to remain dry overnight, and failure to master this skill would prevent children from sleeping over at friends' houses or attending overnight camps. A similar example of developmentally appropriate versus inappropriate hyperactivity and noncompliance is provided in Focus Topic 2.

Focus Topic 2: Two children referred for problems with noncompliance and hyperactivity

Case 1 – Michael

Michael, a 4-year-old boy, was referred to a child psychologist to be evaluated for ADHD. His parents reported that Michael would not comply with their instructions. They also complained that Michael would not remain seated during "quality time" with his father. The evaluating psychologist interviewed the family, and by all accounts Michael was noncompliant and often left his seat. Specifically, when Michael's mother asked him to prepare his preschool lunch, Michael would leave the kitchen and play with his toys soon after opening his lunch box. Further, the psychologist found that quality time involved Michael and his father sitting down for several hours to watch movies. In other settings, such as preschool, Michael was compliant with his teacher's request and no more active than his peers.

In this case, Michael's parents held unrealistic expectations for a child at Michael's developmental level. The psychologist would likely educate Michael's parents about normative child development rather than diagnosing Michael with ADHD.

Case 2 – Jake

Jake, a 10-year-old boy, was referred to the same psychologist as Michael. Jake's mother was concerned because Jake was not getting ready for school on time. Jake also had trouble remaining seated during dinner, which interrupted mealtime for the rest of the family. The psychologist found that in the morning, Jake would complete one or two steps of his routine before he became distracted and switched activities, despite his mother's constant reminders. During dinnertime, Jake would leave his seat between 10 and 15 times over the course of the meal. Jake's teachers were worried because Jake was only able to complete 50% of his homework. Further, his classmates would not pick Jake for team sports during recess because he often became distracted and wondered off during the game.

In this case, Jake's symptoms would not be considered developmentally appropriate for a 10-year-old child. Further, his symptoms caused him to experience impairment at home and school. Unlike Michael, Jake probably would be diagnosed with ADHD.

Why Do Some Children Develop Behavior Disorders?

The reasons that some children develop ADHD are complex, and it is generally recognized that a single cause is insufficient to explain why an individual child does or does not have the disorder. Researchers have attempted to identify risk factors that predispose a child to develop ADHD. These risk factors range in scope from genetic (e.g., specific gene polymorphisms) to familial (e.g., poor parenting) to cultural (e.g., low socioeconomic status). This section will identify some of the risk factors that are thought to contribute to ADHD. It will conclude by reviewing some of the more controversial ideas about the causes of ADHD, such as poor parenting and children's diets, and review some of the evidence pertaining to these causes.

Studies of twins have shown that genetics are primarily responsible for ADHD. [Image: donnierayjones, https://goo.gl/dgPvFx, CC BY 2.0, https://goo.gl/9uSnqN]

Most experts believe that genetic and neurophysiological factors cause the majority of ADHD cases. Indeed, ADHD is primarily a genetic disorder—twin studies find that whether or not a child develops ADHD is due in large part (75%) to genetic variations (Faraone et al., 2005). Further, children with a family history of ADHD are more likely to develop ADHD themselves (Faraone & Biederman, 1994). Specific genes that have been associated with ADHD are linked to neurotransmitters such as dopamine and serotonin. In addition, neuroimagining studies have found that children with ADHD show reduced brain volume in some regions of the brain, such as the pre-frontal cortex, the corpus callosum, the anterior cingulate cortex, the basal ganglia, and the cerebellum (Seidman, Valera, & Makris, 2005). Among their other functions, these regions of the brain are implicated in organization, impulse control, and motor activity, so the reduced volume of these structures in children with ADHD may cause some of their symptoms.

Although genetics appear to be a main cause of ADHD, recent studies have shown that environmental risk factors may cause a minority of ADHD cases. Many of these environmental risk factors increase the risk for ADHD by disrupting early development and compromising the integrity of the central nervous system. Environmental influences such as low birth weight, malnutrition, and maternal alcohol and nicotine use during pregnancy can increase the likelihood that a child will develop ADHD (Mick, Biederman, Faraone, Sayer, & Kleinman, 2002). Additionally, recent studies have shown that exposure to environmental toxins, such as lead and pesticides, early in a child's life may also increase risk of developing ADHD (Nigg, 2006).

Controversies on Causes of ADHD

Controversial explanations for the development of ADHD have risen and fallen in popularity since the 1960s. Some of these ideas arise from cultural folklore, others can be traced to "specialists" trying to market an easy fix for ADHD based on their proposed cause. Some other ideas contain a kernel of truth but have been falsely cast as causing the majority of ADHD cases.

Some critics have proposed that poor parenting is a major cause of ADHD. This explanation is popular because it is intuitively appealing—one can imagine how a child who is not being disciplined at home may be noncompliant in other settings. Although it is true that parents of children with ADHD use discipline less consistently, and a lack of structure and discipline in the home can exacerbate symptoms in children with ADHD (Campbell, 2002), it is unlikely that poor parenting alone causes ADHD in the first place. To the contrary, research suggests that the noncompliance and impulsivity on the child's part can cause caregivers to use discipline less effectively.

In a classic series of studies, Cunningham and Barkley (1979) showed that mothers of children with ADHD were less attentive to their children and imposed more structure to their playtime relative to mothers of typically devel-oping children. However, these researchers also showed that when the children were given stimulant medication, their compliance increased and their mothers' parenting behavior improved to the point where it was comparable to that of the mothers of children without ADHD (Barkley & Cunningham, 1979). This research suggests that instead of poor parenting causing children to develop ADHD, it is the stressful effects of managing an impulsive child that causes parenting problems in their caregivers. One can imagine how raising a child with ADHD could be stressful for parents. In fact, one study showed that a brief interaction with an impulsive and noncompliant child caused parents to increase their alcohol consumption—presumably these parents were drinking to cope with the stress of dealing with the impulsive child (Pelham et al., 1997). It is, therefore, important to consider the rec-iprocal effects of noncompliant children on parenting behavior, rather than assuming that parenting ability has a unidirectional effect on child behavior.

It is still a common belief that giving sugar to kids makes them hyperactive; however, a critical review of the research showed that such a belief is nothing more than a myth. [Image: courosa, https://goo.gl/0NerUI, CC BY-NC-SA 2.0, https://goo.gl/HEXbAA]

Other purported causes of ADHD are dietary. For example, it was long believed that excessive sugar intake can cause children to become hyperactive. This myth is largely disproven (Milich, Wolraich, & Lindgren, 1986). However, other diet-oriented explanations for ADHD, such as sensitivity to certain food additives, have been proposed (Feingold, 1976). These theories have received a bit more support than the sugar hypothesis (Pelsser et al., 2011). In fact, the possibility that certain food additives may cause hyperactivity in children led to a ban on several artificial food colorings in the United Kingdom, although the Food and Drug Administration rejected similar measures in the United States. Even if artificial food dyes do cause hyperactivity in a subgroup of children, research does not support these food additives as a primary cause of ADHD. Further, research support for elimination diets as a treatment for ADHD has been inconsistent at best.

In sum, scientists are still working to determine what causes children to develop ADHD, and despite substantial progress over the past four decades, there are still many unanswered questions. In most cases, ADHD is probably caused by a combination of genetic and environmental factors. For example, a child with a genetic predisposition to ADHD may develop the disorder after his or her mother uses tobacco during her pregnancy, whereas a child without the genetic predisposition may not develop the disorder in the same environment. Fortunately, the causes of ADHD are relatively unimportant for the families of children with ADHD who wish to receive treatment, because what caused the disorder for an individual child generally does not influence how it is treated.

Methods of Treating ADHD in Children

There are several types of evidence-based treatment available to families of children with ADHD. The type of treatment that might be used depends on many factors, including the child's diagnosis and treatment history, as well as parent preference. To treat children with less severe noncompliance problems, parents can be trained to systematically use contingency management (i.e., rewards and punishments) to manage their children's behavior more effectively (Kazdin, 2005). For the children with ADHD, however, more intensive treatments often are necessary.

Medication

Some critics of medicating as a possible attempt to mitigate the effects of ADHD, are concerned that the medications to treat ADHD might be over-prescribed. [Image: Tony Webster, https://goo.gl/qo2xNB, CC BY 2.0, https://goo.gl/9uSnqN]

The most common method of treating ADHD is to prescribe stimulant medications such as Adderall™. These medications treat many of the core symptoms of ADHD—treated children will show improved impulse control, time-on-task, and compliance with adults, and decreased hyperactivity and disruptive behavior. However, there are also negative side effects to stimulant medication, such as growth and appetite suppression, increased blood pressure, insomnia, and changes in mood (Barkley, 2006). Although these side effects can be unpleasant for children, they can often be avoided with careful monitoring and dosage adjustments.

Opinions differ on whether stimulants should be used to treat children with ADHD. Proponents argue that stimulants are relatively safe and effective, and that untreated ADHD poses a much greater risk to children (Barkley, 2006). Critics argue that because many stimulant medications are similar to illicit drugs, such as cocaine and methamphetamine, long-term use may cause cardiovascular problems or predispose children to abuse illicit drugs. However, longitudinal studies have shown that people taking these medications are not more likely to experience cardiovascular problems or to abuse drugs (Biederman, Wilens, Mick, Spencer, & Faraone, 1999; Cooper et al., 2011). On the other hand, it is not entirely clear how long-term stimulant treatment can affect the brain, particularly in adults who have been medicated for ADHD since childhood.

Finally, critics of psychostimulant medication have proposed that stimulants are increasingly being used to manage energetic but otherwise healthy children. It is true that the percentage of children prescribed stimulant medication has increased since the 1980s. This increase in use is not unique to stimulant medication, however. Prescription rates have similarly increased for most types of psychiatric medication (Olfson, Marcus, Weissman, & Jensen, 2002). As parents and teachers become more aware of ADHD, one would expect that more children with ADHD will be identified and treated with stimulant medication. Further, the percentage of children in the United States being treated with stimulant medication is lower than the estimated prevalence of children with ADHD in the general population (Nigg, 2006).

Parent Management Training

Parenting children with ADHD can be challenging. Parents of these children are understandably frustrated by their children's misbehavior. Standard discipline tactics, such as warnings and privilege removal, can feel ineffective for children with ADHD. This often leads to ineffective parenting, such as yelling at or ridiculing the child with ADHD. This cycle can leave parents feeling hopeless and children with ADHD feeling alienated from their family. Fortunately, parent management training can provide parents with a number of tools to cope with and effectively manage their child's impulsive and oppositional behavior. Parent management training teaches parents to use immediate, consistent, and powerful consequences (i.e., rewards and punishment), because children with ADHD respond well to these types of behavioral contingencies (Luman, Oosterlaan, & Sergeant, 2005). Other, more intensive, psychosocial treatments use similar behavioral principles in summer camp–based settings (Pelham, Fabiano, Gnagy, Greiner, & Hoza, 2004), and school-based intervention programs are becoming more popular. A description of a school-based intervention program for ADHD is described in Focus Topic 3.

Focus Topic 3: Treating ADHD in Schools

Succeeding at school is one of the most difficult challenges faced by children with ADHD and their parents. Teachers expect students to attend to lessons, complete lengthy assignments, and comply with rules for approximately seven hours every day. One can imagine how a child with hyperactive and inattentive behaviors would struggle under these demands, and this mismatch can lead to frustration for the student and his or her teacher. Disruptions caused by the child with ADHD can also distract and frustrate peers. Succeeding at school is an important goal for children, so researchers have developed and validated intervention strategies based on behavioral principles of contingency management that can help children with ADHD adhere to rules in the classroom (described in DuPaul & Stoner, 2003). Illustrative characteristics of an effective school-based contingency management system are described below:

Token reinforcement program

This program allows a student to earn tokens (points, stars, etc.) by meeting behavioral goals and not breaking rules. These tokens act as secondary reinforcers because they can be redeemed for privileges or goods. Parents and teachers work with the students to identify problem behaviors and create concrete behavioral goals. For example, if a student is disruptive during silent reading time, then a goal might be for him or her to remain seated for at least 80% of reading time. Token reinforcement programs are most effective when tokens are provided for appropriate behavior and removed for inappropriate behavior.

Time out

Time out can be an effective punishment when used correctly. Teachers should place a student in time out only when they fail to respond to token removal or if they engage in a severely disruptive behavior (e.g., physical aggression). When placed in time out, the student should not have access to any type of reinforcement (e.g., toys, social interaction), and the teacher should monitor their behavior throughout time out.

Daily report card

The teacher keeps track of whether or not the student meets his or her goals and records this information on a report card. This information is sent home with the student each day so parents can integrate the student's performance at school into a home-based contingency management program.

Educational services and accommodations

Students with ADHD often show deficits in specific academic skills (e.g., reading skills, math skills), and these deficits can be improved through direct intervention. Students with ADHD may spend several hours each week working one-on-one with an educator to improve their academic skills. Environmental accommodations can also help a student with ADHD be successful. For example, a student who has difficulty focusing during a test can be allowed extra time in a low-distraction setting.

What Works Best? The Multimodal Treatment Study

Recently, a large-scale study, the Multimodal Treatment Study (MTA) of Children with ADHD, compared pharmacological and behavioral treatment of ADHD (MTA Cooperative Group, 1999). This study compared the outcomes of children with ADHD in four different treatment conditions, including standard community care, intensive behavioral treatment, stimulant medication management, and the combination of intensive behavioral treatment and stimulant medication. In terms of core symptom relief, stimulant medication was the most effective treatment, and combined treatment was no more effective than stimulant medication alone (MTA Cooperative Group, 1999). Behavioral treatment was advantageous in other ways, however. For example, children who received combined treatment were less disruptive at school than children receiving stimulant medication alone (Hinshaw et al., 2000). Other studies have found that children who receive behavioral treatment require lower doses of stimulant medication to achieve the desired outcomes (Pelham et al., 2005). This is important because children are better able to tolerate lower doses of stimulant medication. Further, parents report being more satisfied with treatment when behavioral management is included as a component in the program (Jensen et al., 2001). In sum, stimulant medication and behavioral treatment each have advantages and disadvantages that complement the other, and the best outcomes likely occur when both forms of treatment are used to improve children's behavior.

The Future of ADHD

It is difficult to predict the future; however, based on trends in research and public discourse, we can predict how the field may change as time progresses. This section will discuss two areas of research and public policy that will shape how we understand and treat ADHD in the coming decades.

Controlling Access to Stimulant Medication

It is no secret that many of the drugs used to treat ADHD are popular drugs of abuse among high school and college students, and this problem seems to be getting worse. The rate of illicit stimulant use has steadily risen over the past several decades (Teter, McCabe, Cranford, Boyd, & Guthrie, 2005), and it is probably not a coincidence that prescription rates for stimulant medication have increased during the same time period (Setlik, Bond, & Ho, 2009). Students who abuse stimulants often report doing so because they act as an academic performance enhancer by boosting alertness and concentration. Although they may enhance performance in the short term, nonmedical use of these drugs can lead to dependence and other adverse health consequences, especially when taken in ways other than prescribed (e.g., crushed and snorted) (Volkow & Swanson, 2003). Stimulants can be particularly dangerous when they are taken without supervision from a physician, because this may lead to adverse drug interactions or side effects. Because this increase in prescription stimulant abuse represents a threat to public health, an important goal for policy makers will be to reduce the availability of prescription stimulants to those who would use them for nonmedical reasons.

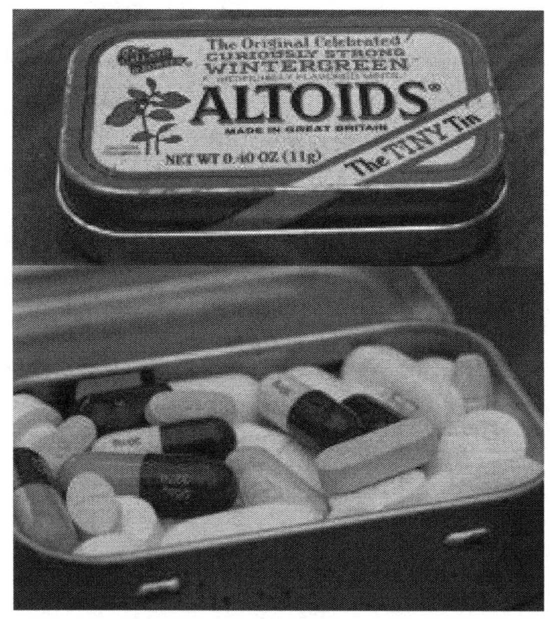

Prescription stimulant abuse among young people is a growing concern. [Image: Jesse! S?, https://goo.gl/GlFyCg,CC BY 2.0, https://goo.gl/v4Y0Zv]

One of the first steps for addressing prescription stimulant abuse will be understanding how illicit users gain access to medication. Probably the most common method of obtaining stimulants is through drug diversion. The majority of college students who abuse stimulants report obtaining them from peers with valid prescriptions (McCabe & Boyd, 2005). Another way that would-be abusers may gain access to medication is by malingering(i.e., faking)symptoms of ADHD (Quinn, 2003). These individuals will knowingly exaggerate their symptoms to a physician in order to obtain a prescription. Other sources of illicit prescription drugs have been identified (e.g., pharmacy websites) (Califano, 2004), but more research is needed to understand how much these sources contribute to the problem. As we gain an understanding of how people gain access to illicit medication, policy makers and researchers can make efforts to curtail the rate of stimulant misuse. For example, because drug diversion is a major source of illicit stimulants, policymakers have enacted prescription monitoring programs to keep track of patient's prescription-seeking behavior (Office of Drug Control Policy, 2011), and, in some cases, patients are required to pass drug screens before receiving their prescriptions. To address malingering, researchers are working to develop psychological tests that can identify individuals who are faking symptoms (Jasinski et al., 2011). Finally, pharmacologists are working to develop stimulant medications that do not carry the same risk of abuse as the currently available drugs (e.g., lisdexamfetamine) (Biederman et al., 2007).

Although all of these measures will reduce illicit users' access to stimulant medication, it is important to consider how the policies will affect access among people who need these medications to treat their ADHD symptoms. Prescription tracking programs may reduce physicians' willingness to prescribe stimulants out of fear of being investigated by law enforcement. Patients with ADHD with comorbid substance abuse problems may be denied access to stimulant medication because they are considered high risk for drug diversion. Similarly, lengthy psychological evaluations to assess for malingering and mandated drug screenings may be prohibitively expensive for less affluent individuals with ADHD. These measures to reduce illicit drug use are necessary from a public health perspective, but as we move forward and enact policies to reduce stimulant abuse, it will be equally important to consider impact of such legislation on patients' access to treatment.

The Role of Neuroscience and Behavioral Genetics in Understanding ADHD

Much of the research on ADHD has been conducted to answer several deceptively complex questions: What causes ADHD? How are people with ADHD different from their typically developing peers? How can ADHD be prevented or treated? Historically, our tools for answering these questions was limited to observing outward human behavior, and our ability to ask questions about the physiology of ADHD was severely limited by the technology of the time. In the past two decades, however, rapid advances in technology (e.g., functional magnetic resonance imaging, genetic analysis) have allowed us to probe the physiological bases of human behavior. An exciting application of this technology is that we are able to extend our understanding of ADHD beyond basic behavior; we are learning about the underlying neurophysiology and genetics of the disorder. As we gain a fuller understanding of ADHD, we may be able to apply this knowledge to improve prevention and treatment of the disorder. Knowledge of the underlying physiology of ADHD may guide efforts to develop new nonstimulant medications, which may not carry the side effects or abuse potential of traditional stimulants. Similarly, these advances may improve our ability to diagnose ADHD. Although it is extremely unlikely that a perfectly accurate genetic or neuroimaging test for ADHD will ever be developed (Thome et al., 2012), such procedures could be used in conjunction with behavioral evaluation and questionnaires to improve diagnostic accuracy. Finally, identifying genetic traits that predispose children to develop ADHD may allow physicians to use targeted prevention programs that could reduce the chances that children at risk for developing the disorder will experience symptoms.

Discussion Questions

1. Does ADHD meet the definition of a psychiatric disorder?

2. Explain the difference between developmentally appropriate and developmentally inappropriate behavior problems.

3. Do you believe that it is ethical to prescribe stimulant medication to children? Why or why not? What are the risks associated with withholding stimulant medication from children with ADHD?

4. How should society balance the need to treat individuals with ADHD using stimulants with public health concerns about the abuse of these same medications?

Vocabulary

Contingency management

A reward or punishment that systematically follows a behavior. Parents can use contingencies to modify their children's behavior.

Drug diversion

When a drug that is prescribed to treat a medical condition is given to another individual who seeks to use the drug illicitly.

Malingering

Fabrication or exaggeration of medical symptoms to achieve secondary gain (e.g., receive medication, avoid school).

Oppositional defiant disorder

A childhood behavior disorder that is characterized by stubbornness, hostility, and behavioral defiance. This disorder is highly comorbid with ADHD.

Parent management training

A treatment for childhood behavior problems that teaches parents how to use contingencies to more effectively manage their children's behavior.

Pathologizes

To define a trait or collection of traits as medically or psychologically unhealthy or abnormal.

References

- American Psychiatric Association. (2000). *Diagnostic and statistical manual of mental disorders* (4th ed., text revision.). Washing DC: Author.

- Barkley, R. A. (2006). *Attention-deficit/hyperactivity disorder: A handbook for diagnosis and treatment* (3rd ed.). New York, NY: Guilford Press.

- Barkley, R. A., & Cunningham, C. E. (1979). Effects of methylphenidate on the mother-child interactions of hyperactive children. *Archives of General Psychiatry, 36*, 201–208.

- Barkley, R. A., Fischer, M., Smallish, L., & Fletcher, K. (2006). Young adult outcome of hyperactive children: Adaptive functioning in major life activities. *Journal of the American Academy of Child and Adolescent Psychiatry, 45*, 192–202.

- Biederman, J., Boellner, S. W., Childress, A., Lopez, F. A., Krishnan, S., & Zhang, Y. X. (2007). Lisdexamfetamine dimesylate and mixed amphetamine salts extended-release in children with ADHD: A double-blind, placebo-controlled, crossover analog classroom study. *Biological Psychiatry, 62*, 970–976.

- Biederman, J., Faraone, S. V., Spencer, T. J., Mick, E., Monuteaux, M. C., & Aleardi, M. (2006). Functional impairments in adults with self-reports of diagnosed ADHD: A controlled study of 1,001 adults in the community. *Journal of Clinical Psychiatry, 67*, 524–540.

• Biederman, J., Wilens, T., Mick, E., Spencer, T., & Faraone, S. V. (1999). Pharmacotherapy of attention-deficit/hyperactivity disorder reduces risk for substance use disorder. *Pediatrics, 104*, 20.

• Califano, J. (2004). *You've got drugs! Prescription drug pushers on the Internet. A CASA white paper.* The National Center on Addiction and Substance Abuse. New York, NY: Columbia University.

• Campbell, S. B. (2002). *Behavior problems in preschool children.* (2nd ed.). New York, NY: Guilford Press.

• Cooper, W. O., Habel, L. A., Sox, C. M., Chan, K. A., Arbogast, P. G., Cheetham, C., … Ray, W. A. (2011). ADHD drugs and serious cardiovascular events in children and young adults. *New England Journal of Medicine, 365*, 1896–1904.

• Cortese, S., Angriman, M., Maffeis, C., Isnard, P., Konofal, E., Lecendreux, M., … Mouren, M. C. (2008). Attention-deficit/hyperactivity disorder (ADHD) and obesity: A systematic review of the literature. *Critical Reviews in Food Science and Nutrition*, 48, 524–537.

• Cunningham, C. E., & Barkley, R. A. (1979). Interactions of normal and hyperactive children with their mothers in free play and structured tasks. *Child Development, 50*, 217–224.

• Faraone, S. V., & Biederman, J. (1994). Is attention-deficit hyperactivity disorder familial? *Harvard Review of Psychiatry, 1*, 271–287.

• Faraone, S. V., Biederman, J., & Mick, E. (2006). The age-dependent decline of attention deficit hyperactivity disorder: A meta-analysis of follow-up studies. *Psychological Medicine, 36*, 159–165.

• Faraone, S. V., Perlis, R. H., Doyle, A. E., Smoller, J. W., Goralnick, J. J., Holmgren, M. A., & Sklar, P. (2005). Molecular genetics of attention-deficit/hyperactivity disorder. *Biological Psychiatry, 57*, 1313–1323.

• Feingold, B. F. (1976). Hyperkinesis and learning disabilities linked to the ingestion of artificial food colors and flavors. *Journal of Learning Disabilities*, 9, 551–559.

• Flory, K., Molina, B. S. G., Pelham, W. E., Gnagy, E., & Smith, B. (2006). Childhood ADHD predicts risky sexual behavior in young adulthood. *Journal of Clinical Child and Adolescent Psychology*, 35, 571–577.

• Harris, M. J., Milich, R., Corbitt, E. M., Hoover, D. W., & Brady, M. (1992). Self-fulfilling effects of stigmatizing information on children's social interactions. Journal of *Personality and Social Psychology, 63*, 41–50.

• Hartung, C. M., & Widiger, T. A. (1998). Gender differences in the diagnosis of mental disorders: Conclusions and controversies of the DSM-IV. *Psychological Bulletin, 123*, 260–278.

• Hinshaw, S. P., Owens, E. B., Wells, K. C., Kraemer, H. C., Abikoff, H. B., Arnold, E. L., … Wigal, T. (2000). Family processes and treatment outcome in the MTA: Negative/ineffective parenting practices in relation to multimodal treatment. *Journal of Abnormal Child Psychology, 28*, 555–568.

- Jasinski, L. J., Harp, J. P., Berry, D. T. R., Shandera-Ochsner, A. L., Mason, L. H., & Ranseen, J. D. (2011). Using symptom validity tests to detect malingered ADHD in college students. *Clinical Neuropsychologist, 25*, 1415–1428.

- Jensen, P. S., Hinshaw, S. P., Swanson, J. M., Greenhill, L. L., Conners, C. K., Arnold, L. E., … Wigal, T. (2001). Findings from the NIMH Multimodal Treatment Study of ADHD (MTA): Implications and applications for primary care providers. *Developmental and Behavioral Pediatrics, 22*, 60-73.

- Kazdin, A. E. (2005). *Parent management training: Treatment for oppositional, aggressive, and antisocial behavior in children and adolescents.* New York, NY: Oxford University Press.

- Kessler, R. C., Adler, L., Barkley, R., Biederman, J., Conners, C. K., Demler, O., … Zaslavsky, A. M. (2006). The prevalence and correlates of adult ADHD in the United States: Results from the National Comorbidity Survey Replication. *American Journal of Psychiatry*, 163, 716–723.

- Landau, S., Milich, R., & Diener, M. B. (1998). Peer relations of children with attention-deficit hyperactivity disorder. *Reading & Writing Quarterly, 14*, 83–105.

- Lichtenstein, P., Halldner, L., Zetterqvist, J., Sjölander, A., Serlachius, E., Fazel, S., … Larsson, H. (2012). Medication for attention deficit-hyperactivity disorder and criminality. *New England Journal of Medicine*, 367, 2006–2014.

- Loe, I. M., & Feldman, H. M. (2007). Academic and educational outcomes of children with ADHD. *Ambulatory Pediatrics, 7*, 82–90.

- Luman, M., Oosterlaan, J., & Sergeant, J. A. (2005). The impact of reinforcement contingencies on AD/HD: A review and theoretical appraisal. *Clinical Psychology Review, 25*, 183–213.

- MTA Cooperative Group (1999). A 14-month randomized clinical trial of treatment strategies for attention-deficit/hyperactivity disorder. *Archives of General Psychiatry, 56*, 1073–1086.

- McCabe, S. E., & Boyd, C. J. (2005). Sources of prescription drugs for illicit use. *Addictive Behaviors, 30*, 1342–1350.

- Mick, E., Biederman, J., Faraone, S. V., Sayer, J., & Kleinman, S. (2002). Case-control study of attention-deficit hyperactivity disorder and maternal smoking, alcohol use, and drug use during pregnancy. *Journal of the American Academy of Child and Adolescent Psychiatry, 41*, 378–385.

- Milich, R., Wolraich, M., & Lindgren, S. (1986). Sugar and hyperactivity: A critical review of empirical findings. *Clinical Psychology Review, 6*, 493–513.

- Mischel, W., Shoda, Y., & Rodriguez, M. L. (1989). Delay of gratification in children. *Science, 244*, 933–938.

- Molina, B. S. G., & Pelham, W. E. (2003). Childhood predictors of adolescent substance use in a longitudinal study of children with ADHD. *Journal of Abnormal Psychology, 112*, 497–507.

- Nigg, J. T. (2006). *What causes ADHD? Understanding what goes wrong and why.* New York, NY: The Guilford Press.

- Office of Drug Control Policy (2011). *Epidemic: Responding to America's prescription drug abuse cri-*

sis. Retrieved from http://www.whitehouse.gov/sites/default/files/ondcp/issues-content/prescription-drugs/rx_abuse_plan_0.pdf

- Olfson, M., Marcus, S. C., Weissman, M. M., & Jensen, P. S. (2002). National trends in the use of psychotropic medications by children. *Journal of the American Academy of Child and Adolescent Psychiatry, 41*, 514–521.

- Pelham, W. E., Burrows-MacLean, L., Gnagy, E. M., Fabiano, G. A., Coles, E. K., Tresco, K. E., … Hoffman, M. T. (2005). Transdermal methylphenidate, behavioral, and combined treatment for children with ADHD. *Experimental and Clinical Psychopharmacology, 13*, 111–126.

- Pelham, W. E., Fabiano, G. A., Gnagy, E. M., Greiner, A. R., & Hoza, B. (2004). Intensive treatment: Summer treatment program for children with ADHD. In E. D. Hibbs, & P. S. Jensen (Eds.), *Psychosocial treatments for children and adolescent disorders: Empirically based strategies for clinical practice* (pp. 311–340). Washington, DC: American Psychological Association Press.

- Pelham, W. E., Lang, A. R., Atkeson, B., Murphy, D. A., Gnagy, E. M., Greiner, A. R., … Greenslade, K. E. (1997). Effects of deviant child behavior on parental distress and alcohol consumption in laboratory interactions. *Journal of Abnormal Child Psychology, 25*, 413–424.

- Pelsser, L. M., Frankena, K., Toorman, J., Savelkoul, H. F., Dubois, A. E., Pereira, R. R., … Buitelaar, J. K. (2011). Effects of a restricted elimination diet on the behaviour of children with attention-deficit hyperactivity disorder (INCA study): A randomised controlled trial. *Lancet, 377*, 494–503.

- Quinn, C. A. (2003). Detection of malingering in assessment of adult ADHD. *Archives of Clinical Neuropsychology, 18(4)*, 379–395.

- Seidman, L. J., Valera, E. M., & Makris, N. (2005). Structural brain imaging of attention-deficit/hyperactivity disorder. *Biological Psychiatry, 57*, 1263–1272.

- Setlik, J., Bond, G. R., & Ho, M. (2009). Adolescent prescription ADHD medication abuse Is rising along with prescriptions for these medications. *Pediatrics, 124*, 875–880.

- Still, G. F. (1902). Some abnormal psychical conditions in children: The Goulstonian lectures. *Lancet, 1*, 1008–1012.

- Teter, C. J., McCabe, S. E., Cranford, J. A., Boyd, C. J., & Guthrie, S. K. (2005). Prevalence and motives for illicit use of prescription stimulants in an undergraduate student sample. *Journal of American College Health, 53*, 253–262.

- Thome, J., Ehlis, A. C., Fallgatter, A. J., Krauel, K., Lange, K. W., Riederer, P., … Gerlach, M. (2012). Biomarkers for attention-deficit/hyperactivity disorder (ADHD). A consensus report of the WFSBP task for on biological markers and the World Federation of ADHD. *World Journal of Biological Psychiatry, 13*, 379–400.

- Volkow, N. D., & Swanson, J. M. (2003). Variables that affect the clinical use and abuse of methylphenidate in the treatment of ADHD. *American Journal of Psychiatry, 160*, 1909–1918.

- Weafer, J., Fillmore, M. T., & Milich, R. (2008). Simulated driving performance of adults with ADHD:

Comparisons with alcohol intoxication. *Experimental and Clinical Psychopharmacology*, 16, 251–263.

CC licensed content, Shared previously

Autism: Insights from the Study of the Social Brain

People with autism spectrum disorder (ASD) suffer from a profound social disability. Social neuroscience is the study of the parts of the brain that support social interactions or the "social brain." This module provides an overview of ASD and focuses on understanding how social brain dysfunction leads to ASD. Our increasing understanding of the social brain and its dysfunction in ASD will allow us to better identify the genes that cause ASD and will help us to create and pick out treatments to better match individuals. Because social brain systems emerge in infancy, social neuroscience can help us to figure out how to diagnose ASD even before the symptoms of ASD are clearly present. This is a hopeful time because social brain systems remain malleable well into adulthood and thus open to creative new interventions that are informed by state-of-the-art science.

Learning Objectives

- Know the basic symptoms of ASD.

- Distinguish components of the social brain and understand their dysfunction in ASD.

- Appreciate how social neuroscience may facilitate the diagnosis and treatment of ASD.

Defining Autism Spectrum Disorder

Autism Spectrum Disorder (ASD) is a developmental disorder that usually emerges in the first three years and persists throughout the individual's life. Though the key symptoms of ASD fall into three general categories (see below), each person with ASD exhibits symptoms in these domains in different ways and to varying degrees. This *phenotypic heterogeneity* reflects the high degree of variability in the genes underlying ASD (Geschwind & Levitt, 2007). Though we have identified genetic differences associated with individual cases of ASD, each accounts for only a small number of the actual cases, suggesting that no single genetic cause will apply in the majority of people with ASD. There is currently no biological test for ASD.

Autism is in the category of *pervasive developmental disorders*, which includes Asperger's disorder, childhood disintegrative disorder, autistic disorder, and pervasive developmental disorder – not otherwise specified. These disorders, together, are labeled *autism spectrum disorder* (ASD). ASD is defined by the presence of profound difficulties in social interactions and communication combined with the presence of repetitive or restricted interests, cognitions and behaviors. The diagnostic process involves a combination of parental report and clinical observation. Children with significant impairments across the social/communication domain who also exhibit repetitive behaviors can qualify for the ASD diagnosis. There is wide variability in the precise symptom profile an individual may exhibit.

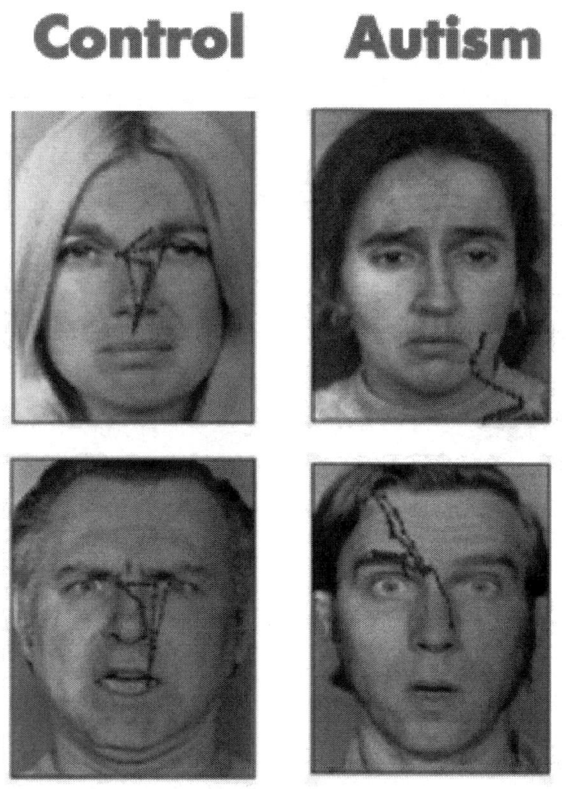

Figure 1. The red lines indicate the scan paths (collection of eye movements) used by people with (right column) and without (left column) autism to explore faces. Modified from Pelphrey et al., (2002).

Since Kanner first described ASD in 1943, important commonalities in symptom presentation have been used to compile criteria for the diagnosis of ASD. These diagnostic criteria have evolved during the past 70 years and continue to evolve (e.g., see the recent changes to the diagnostic criteria on the American Psychiatric Association's website, http://www.dsm5.org/), yet impaired social functioning remains a required symptom for an ASD diagnosis. Deficits in social functioning are present in varying degrees for simple behaviors such as eye contact, and complex behaviors like navigating the give and take of a group conversation for individuals of all functioning levels (i.e. high or low IQ). Moreover, difficulties with social information processing occur in both visual (e.g., Pelphrey et al., 2002) and auditory (e.g., Dawson, Meltzoff, Osterling, Rinaldi, & Brown, 1998) sensory modalities.

Consider the results of an eye tracking study in which Pelphrey and colleagues (2002) observed that individuals with autism did not make use of the eyes when judging facial expressions of emotion (see right panels of Figure 1). While repetitive behaviors or language deficits are seen in other disorders (e.g., obsessive-compulsive disorder and specific language impairment, respectively), basic social deficits of this nature are unique to ASD. Onset of the social deficits appears to precede difficulties in other domains (Osterling, Dawson, & Munson, 2002) and may emerge as early as 6 months of age (Maestro et al., 2002).

Defining the Social Brain

Within the past few decades, research has elucidated specific brain circuits that support perception of humans and other species. This *social perception* refers to "the initial stages in the processing of information that culminates in the accurate analysis of the dispositions and intentions of other individuals" (Allison, Puce, & McCarthy, 2000). Basic social perception is a critical building block for more sophisticated social behaviors, such as thinking about the motives and emotions of others. Brothers (1990) first suggested the notion of a social brain,a set of interconnected neuroanatomical structures that process social information, enabling the recognition of other individuals and the evaluation their mental states (e.g., intentions, dispositions, desires, and beliefs).

The social brain is hypothesized to consist of the amygdala, the orbital frontal cortex (OFC), fusiform gyrus (FG), and the posterior superior temporal sulcus (STS) region, among other structures. Though all areas work in coordination to support social processing, each appears to serve a distinct role. The amygdala helps us recognize the emotional states of others (e.g., Morris et al., 1996) and also to experience and regulate our own emotions (e.g., LeDoux, 1992). The OFC supports the "reward" feelings we have when we are around other people (e.g., Rolls, 2000). The FG, located at the bottom of the surface of the temporal lobes detects faces and supports face recognition (e.g., Puce, Allison, Asgari, Gore, & McCarthy, 1996). The posterior STS region recognizes the biological motion, including eye, hand and other body movements, and helps to interpret and predict the actions and intentions of others (e.g., Pelphrey, Morris, Michelich, Allison, & McCarthy, 2005).

Current Understanding of Social Perception in ASD

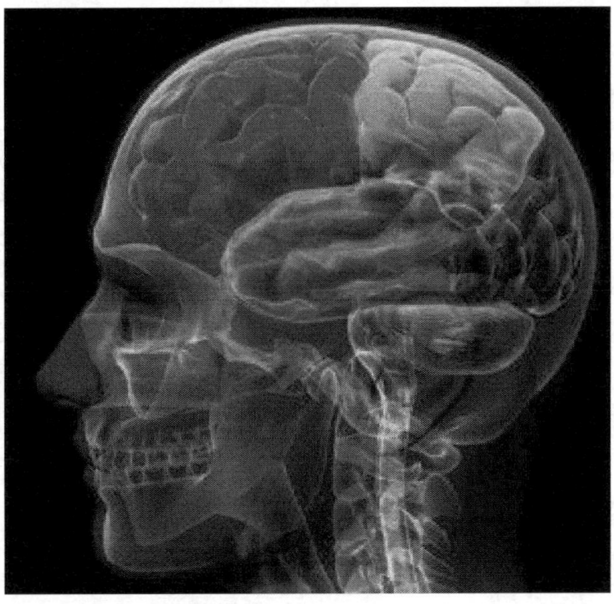

The social brain is of great research interest because the social difficulties characteristic of ASD are thought to relate closely to the functioning of this brain network. Functional magnetic resonance imaging (fMRI) and event-related potentials (ERP)are complementary brain imaging methods used to study activity in the brain across the lifespan. Each method measures a distinct facet of brain activity and contributes unique information to our understanding of brain function.

FMRI uses powerful magnets to measure the levels of oxygen within the brain, which vary according to changes in neural activity. As the neurons in specific brain regions "work harder", they require more oxygen. FMRI detects the brain regions that exhibit a relative increase in blood flow (and oxygen levels) while people listen to or view social stimuli in the MRI scanner. The areas of the brain most crucial for different social processes are thus identified, with spatial information being accurate to the millimeter.

In contrast, ERP provides direct measurements of the firing of groups of neurons in the cortex. Non-invasive sensors on the scalp record the small electrical currents created by this neuronal activity while the subject views stimuli or listens to specific kinds of information. While fMRI provides information about *where* brain activity occurs, ERP specifies *when* by detailing the timing of processing at the millisecond pace at which it unfolds.

ERP and fMRI are complementary, with fMRI providing excellent *spatial resolution* and ERP offering outstanding *temporal resolution*. Together, this information is critical to understanding the nature of social perception in ASD. To date, the most thoroughly investigated areas of the social brain in ASD are the superior temporal sulcus (STS), which underlies the perception and interpretation of biological motion, and the fusiform gyrus (FG), which supports face perception. Heightened sensitivity to biological motion (for humans, motion such as walking) serves an essential role in the development of humans and other highly social species. Emerging in the first days of life, the ability to detect biological motion helps to orient vulnerable young to critical sources of sustenance, support, and learning, and develops independent of visual experience with biological motion (e.g., Simion, Regolin, & Bulf, 2008). This inborn "life detector" serves as a foundation for the subsequent development of more complex social behaviors (Johnson, 2006).

From very early in life, children with ASD display reduced sensitivity to biological motion (Klin, Lin, Gorrindo, Ramsay, & Jones, 2009). Individuals with ASD have reduced activity in the STS during biological motion perception. Similarly, people at increased genetic risk for ASD but who do not develop symptoms of the disorder (i.e. unaffected siblings of individuals with ASD) show increased activity in this region, which is hypothesized to be a compensatory mechanism to offset genetic vulnerability (Kaiser et al., 2010).In typical development, preferential attention to faces and the ability to recognize individual faces emerge in the first days of life (e.g., Goren, Sarty, & Wu, 1975). The special way in which the brain responds to faces usually emerges by three months of age (e.g., de Haan, Johnson, & Halit, 2003) and continues throughout the lifespan (e.g., Bentin et al., 1996). Children with ASD, however, tend to show decreased attention to human faces by six to 12 months (Osterling & Dawson, 1994). Children with ASD also show reduced activity in the FG when viewing faces

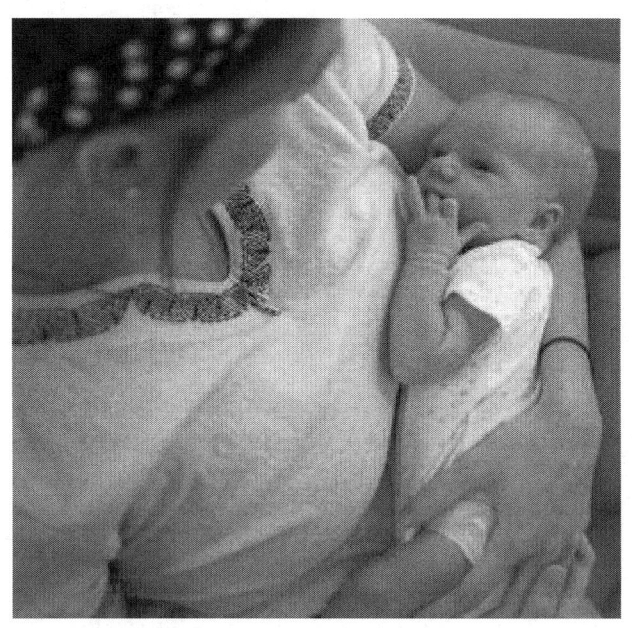

From an evolutionary standpoint, it was incredibly important for our survival to maintain social relationships. Therefore, it makes sense that we would be able to recognize faces within the first few days of our infancy. [Image: donnierayjones, https://goo.gl/obrI2x, CC BY 2.0, https://goo.gl/v4Y0Zv]

(e.g., Schultz et al., 2000). Slowed processing of faces (McPartland, Dawson, Webb, Panagiotides, & Carver, 2004) is a characteristic of people with ASD that is shared by parents of children with ASD (Dawson, Webb, &

McPartland, 2005) and infants at increased risk for developing ASD because of having a sibling with ASD (McCleery, Akshoomoff, Dobkins, & Carver, 2009). Behavioral and attentional differences in face perception and recognition are evident in children and adults with ASD as well (e.g., Hobson, 1986).

Exploring Diversity in ASD

Because of the limited quality of the behavioral methods used to diagnose ASD and current clinical diagnostic practice, which permits similar diagnoses despite distinct symptom profiles (McPartland, Webb, Keehn, & Dawson, 2011), it is possible that the group of children currently referred to as having ASD may actually represent different syndromes with distinct causes. Examination of the social brain may well reveal diagnostically meaningful subgroups of children with ASD. Measurements of the "where" and "when" of brain activity during social processing tasks provide reliable sources of the detailed information needed to profile children with ASD with greater accuracy. These profiles, in turn, may help to inform treatment of ASD by helping us to match specific treatments to specific profiles.

The integration of imaging methods is critical for this endeavor. Using face perception as an example, the combination of fMRI and ERP could identify who, of those individuals with ASD, shows anomalies in the FG and then determine the stage of information processing at which these impairments occur. Because different processing stages often reflect discrete cognitive processes, this level of understanding could encourage treatments that address specific processing deficits at the neural level.

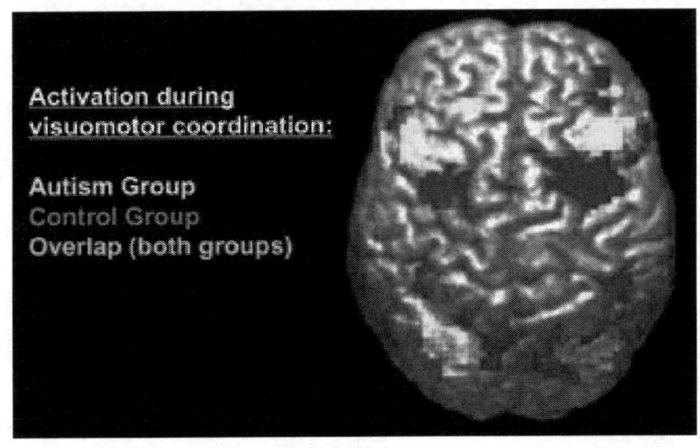

Trying to diagnose the precise autism disorder can be difficult; many cases share similar symptoms. However, burgeoning technology, like the fMRI, allows clinicians a glimpse into the patient's brain and thus a better understanding of his or her disorder. [Image: Ralph-Axel Müller, https://goo.gl/WwxCV1, CC BY 2.5, https://goo.gl/0QtWcf]

For example, differences observed in the early processing stages might reflect problems with low-level visual perception, while later differences would indicate problems with higher-order processes, such as emotion recognition. These same principles can be applied to the broader network of social brain regions and, combined with measures of behavioral functioning, could offer a comprehensive profile of brain-behavior performance for a given individual. A fundamental goal for this kind of subgroup approach is to improve the ability to tailor treatments to the individual.

Another objective is to improve the power of other scientific tools. Most studies of individuals with ASD compare groups of individuals, for example, individuals on with ASD compared to typically developing peers. However, studies have also attempted to compare children across the autism spectrum by group according to differential diagnosis (e.g., Asperger's disorder versus autistic disorder), or by other behavioral or cognitive characteristics (e.g., cognitively able versus intellectually disabled or anxious versus non-anxious). Yet, the power of a scientific study to detect these kinds of significant, meaningful, individual differences is only as strong as the accuracy of the factor used to define the compared groups.

The identification of distinct subgroups within the autism spectrum according to information about the brain would allow for a more accurate and detailed exposition of the individual differences seen in those with ASD. This is especially critical for the success of investigations into the genetic basis of ASD. As mentioned before, the genes discovered thus far account for only a small portion of ASD cases. If meaningful, quantitative distinctions in individuals with ASD are identified; a more focused examination into the genetic causes specific to each subgroup could then be pursued. Moreover, distinct findings from neuroimaging, or *biomarkers*, can help guide genetic research. Endophenotypes, or characteristics that are not immediately available to observation but that reflect an underlying genetic liability for disease, expose the most basic components of a complex psychiatric disorder and are more stable across the lifespan than observable behavior (Gottesman & Shields, 1973). By describing the key characteristics of ASD in these objective ways, neuroimaging research will facilitate identification of genetic contributions to ASD.

Atypical Brain Development Before the Emergence of Atypical Behavior

Because autism is a developmental disorder, it is particularly important to diagnose and treat ASD early in life. Early deficits in attention to biological motion, for instance, derail subsequent experiences in attending to higher level social information, thereby driving development toward more severe dysfunction and stimulating deficits in additional domains of functioning, such as language development. The lack of reliable predictors of the condition during the first year of life has been a major impediment to the effective treatment of ASD. Without early predictors, and in the absence of a firm diagnosis until behavioral symptoms emerge, treatment is often delayed for two or more years, eclipsing a crucial period in which intervention may be particularly successful in ameliorating some of the social and communicative impairments seen in ASD.

In response to the great need for sensitive (able to identify subtle cases) and specific (able to distinguish autism from other disorders) early indicators of ASD, such as biomarkers, many research groups from around the world have been studying patterns of infant development using prospective longitudinal studies of infant siblings of children with ASD and a comparison group of infant siblings without familial risks. Such designs gather longitudinal information about developmental trajectories across the first three years of life for both groups followed by clinical diagnosis at approximately 36 months.

These studies are problematic in that many of the social features of autism do not emerge in typical development until after 12 months of age, and it is not certain that these symptoms will manifest during the limited periods of observation involved in clinical evaluations or in pediatricians' offices. Moreover, across development, but especially during infancy, behavior is widely variable and often unreliable, and at present, behavioral observation is the only means to detect symptoms of ASD and to confirm a diagnosis. This is quite problematic because, even highly sophisticated behavioral methods, such as eye tracking (see Figure 1), do not necessarily reveal reliable differences in infants with ASD (Ozonoff et al., 2010). However, measuring the brain activity associated with social perception can detect differences that do not appear in behavior until much later. The identification of bio-markers utilizing the imaging methods we have described offers promise for earlier detection of atypical social development.

ERP measures of brain response predict subsequent development of autism in infants as young as six months old who showed normal patterns of visual fix-ation (as measured by eye tracking) (Elsabbagh et al., 2012). This suggests the great promise of brain imag-ing for earlier recognition of ASD. With earlier detec-tion, treatments could move from addressing existing symptoms to preventing their emergence by altering the course of abnormal brain development and steer-ing it toward normality.

Hope for Improved Outcomes

The brain imaging research described above offers hope for the future of ASD treatment. Many of the functions of the social brain demonstrate signifi-cant *plasticity*, meaning that their functioning can be affected by experience over time. In contrast to theo-ries that suggest difficulty processing complex infor-

If autism is diagnosed early enough, treatments have developed to the point that children with ASD can learn and grow to have more intensive social interactions. [Image: hepingting, https://goo.gl/TIoAcY, CC BY-SA 2.0, https://goo.gl/rxiUsF]

mation or communicating across large expanses of cortex (Minshew & Williams, 2007), this malleability of the social brain is a positive prognosticator for the development of treatment. The brains of people with ASD are not wired to process optimally social information. But this does not mean that these systems are irretrievably *broken*. Given the observed plasticity of the social brain, remediation of these difficulties may be possible with appropri-ate and timely intervention.

Outside Resources

Web: American Psychiatric Association's website for the 5th edition of the *Diagnostic and Statistical Man-ual of Mental Disorders*
http://www.dsm5.org
Web: Autism Science Foundation – organization supporting autism research by providing funding and other assistance to scientists and organizations conducting, facilitating, publicizing and disseminating autism research. The organization also provides information about autism to the general public and serves to increase awareness of autism spectrum disorders and the needs of individuals and families affected by autism.
http://www.autismsciencefoundation.org/

Web: Autism Speaks – Autism science and advocacy organization

http://www.autismspeaks.org/

Discussion Questions

1. How can neuroimaging inform our understanding of the causes of autism?

2. What are the ways in which neuroimaging, including fMRI and ERP, may benefit efforts to diagnosis and treat autism?

3. How can an understanding of the social brain help us to understand ASD?

4. What are the core symptoms of ASD, and why is the social brain of particular interest?

5. What are some of the components of the social brain, and what functions do they serve?

Vocabulary

Endophenotypes

A characteristic that reflects a genetic liability for disease and a more basic component of a complex clinical presentation. Endophenotypes are less developmentally malleable than overt behavior.

Event-related potentials (ERP)

Measures the firing of groups of neurons in the cortex. As a person views or listens to specific types of information, neuronal activity creates small electrical currents that can be recorded from non-invasive sensors placed on the scalp. ERP provides excellent information about the timing of processing, clarifying brain activity at the millisecond pace at which it unfolds.

Functional magnetic resonance imaging (fMRI)

Entails the use of powerful magnets to measure the levels of oxygen within the brain that vary with changes in neural activity. That is, as the neurons in specific brain regions "work harder" when performing a specific task, they require more oxygen. By having people listen to or view social percepts in an MRI scanner, fMRI specifies the brain regions that evidence a relative increase in blood flow. In this way, fMRI provides excellent spatial information, pinpointing with millimeter accuracy, the brain regions most critical for different social processes.

Social brain

The set of neuroanatomical structures that allows us to understand the actions and intentions of other people.

References

- Allison, T., Puce, A., & McCarthy, G. (2000). Social perception from visual cues: Role of the STS region. *Trends in Cognitive Science, 4*(7), 267–278.

- Bentin, S., Allison, T., Puce, A., Perez, E., et al. (1996). Electrophysiological studies of face perception in humans. *Journal of Cognitive Neuroscience, 8*(6), 551–565.

- Brothers, L. (1990). The social brain: A project for integrating primate behavior and neurophysiology in a new domain. *Concepts in Neuroscience, 1*, 27–51.

• Dawson, G., Meltzoff, A. N., Osterling, J., Rinaldi, J., & Brown, E. (1998). Children with autism fail to orient to naturally occurring social stimuli. *Journal of Autism & Developmental Disorders, 28*(6), 479–485.

• Dawson, G., Webb, S. J., & McPartland, J. (2005). Understanding the nature of face processing impairment in autism: Insights from behavioral and electrophysiological studies. *Developmental Neuropsychology, 27*(3), 403–424.

• Elsabbagh, M., Mercure, E., Hudry, K., Chandler, S., Pasco, G., Charman, T., et al. (2012). Infant neural sensitivity to dynamic eye gaze is associated with later emerging autism. *Current Biology, 22*(4), 338–342.

• Geschwind, D. H., & Levitt, P. (2007). Autism spectrum disorders: Developmental disconnection syndromes. *Current Opinion in Neurobiology, 17*(1), 103–111.

• Goren, C. C., Sarty, M., & Wu, P. Y. (1975). Visual following and pattern discrimination of face-like stimuli by newborn infants. *Pediatrics, 56*(4), 544–549.

• Gottesman I. I., & Shields, J. (1973) Genetic theorizing and schizophrenia. *British Journal of Psychiatry, 122*, 15–30.

• Hobson, R. (1986). The autistic child's appraisal of expressions of emotion. *Journal of Child Psychology and Psychiatry, 27*(3), 321–342.

• Johnson, M. H. (2006). Biological motion: A perceptual life detector? *Current Biology, 16*(10), R376–377.

• Kaiser, M. D., Hudac, C. M., Shultz, S., Lee, S. M., Cheung, C., Berken, A. M., et al. (2010). Neural signatures of autism. *Proceedings of the National Academy of Sciences of the United States of America, 107*(49), 21223–21228.

• Kanner, L. (1943). Autistic disturbances of affective contact. *Nervous Child, 2*, 217–250.

• Klin, A., Lin, D. J., Gorrindo, P., Ramsay, G., & Jones, W. (2009). Two-year-olds with autism orient to non-social contingencies rather than biological motion. *Nature, 459*(7244), 257–261.

• Maestro, S., Muratori, F., Cavallaro, M. C., Pei, F., Stern, D., Golse, B., et al. (2002). Attentional skills during the first 6 months of age in autism spectrum disorder. *Journal of the American Academy of Child and Adolescent Psychiatry, 41*(10), 1239–1245.

• McCleery, J. P., Akshoomoff, N., Dobkins, K. R., & Carver, L. J. (2009). Atypical face versus object processing and hemispheric asymmetries in 10-month-old infants at risk for autism. *Biological Psychiatry, 66*(10), 950–957.

• McPartland, J. C., Dawson, G., Webb, S. J., Panagiotides, H., & Carver, L. J. (2004). Event-related brain potentials reveal anomalies in temporal processing of faces in autism spectrum disorder. *Journal of Child Psychology and Psychiatry, 45*(7), 1235–1245.

• McPartland, J. C., Webb, S. J., Keehn, B., & Dawson, G. (2011). Patterns of visual attention to faces and objects in autism spectrum disorder. *Journal of Autism and Develop Disorders, 41*(2), 148–157.

- Minshew, N. J., & Williams, D. L. (2007). The new neurobiology of autism: Cortex, connectivity, and neuronal organization. *Archives of Neurology, 64*(7), 945–950.

- Osterling, J., & Dawson, G. (1994). Early recognition of children with autism: A study of first birthday home videotapes. *Journal of Autism and Developmental Disorders, 24*, 247-257.

- Osterling, J. A., Dawson, G., & Munson, J. A. (2002). Early recognition of 1-year-old infants with autism spectrum disorder versus mental retardation. *Development & Psychopathology, 14*(2), 239–251.

- Ozonoff, S., Iosif, A. M., Baguio, F., Cook, I. C., Hill, M. M., Hutman, T., et al. (2010). A prospective study of the emergence of early behavioral signs of autism. *Journal of the American Academy of Child and Adolescent Psychiatry, 49*(3), 256–266.

- Pelphrey, K. A., Sasson, N. J., Reznick, J. S., Paul, G., Goldman, B. D., & Piven, J. (2002). Visual scanning of faces in autism. *Journal of Autism & Developmental Disorders, 32*(4), 249–261.

- Schultz, R. T., Gauthier, I., Klin, A., Fulbright, R. K., Anderson, A. W., Volkmar, F., et al. (2000). Abnormal ventral temporal cortical activity during face discrimination among individuals with autism and Asperger syndrome. *Archives of General Psychiatry, 57*(4), 331–340.

- Simion, F., Regolin, L., & Bulf, H. (2008). A predisposition for biological motion in the newborn baby. *Proceedings of the National Academy of Sciences, 105*(2), 809–813.

- de Haan, M., Johnson, M. H., & Halit, H. (2003). Development of face-sensitive event-related potentials during infancy: A review. *International Journal of Psychophysiology, 51*(1), 45–58.

Anxiety and Related Disorders

Anxiety is a natural part of life and, at normal levels, helps us to function at our best. However, for people with anxiety disorders, anxiety is overwhelming and hard to control. Anxiety disorders develop out of a blend of biological (genetic) and psychological factors that, when combined with stress, may lead to the development of ailments. Primary anxiety-related diagnoses include generalized anxiety disorder, panic disorder, specific phobia, social anxiety disorder (social phobia), post traumatic stress disorder, and obsessive-compulsive disorder. In this module, we summarize the main clinical features of each of these disorders and discuss their similarities and differences with everyday experiences of anxiety.

Learning Objectives

- Understand the relationship between anxiety and anxiety disorders.

- Identify key vulnerabilities for developing anxiety and related disorders.

- Identify main diagnostic features of specific anxiety-related disorders.

- Differentiate between disordered and non-disordered functioning.

Introduction

What is anxiety? Most of us feel some anxiety almost every day of our lives. Maybe you have an important test coming up for school. Or maybe there's that big game next Saturday, or that first date with someone new you are hoping to impress. Anxiety can be defined as a negative mood state that is accompanied by bodily symptoms such as increased heart rate, muscle tension, a sense of unease, and apprehension about the future (APA, 2013; Barlow, 2002).

Anxiety is what motivates us to plan for the future, and in this sense, anxiety is actually a good thing. It's that nagging feeling that motivates us to study for that test, practice harder for that game, or be at our very best on that date. But some people experience anxiety so intensely that it is no longer helpful or useful. They may become so overwhelmed and distracted by anxiety that they actually fail their test, fumble the ball, or spend the whole date fidgeting and avoiding eye contact. If anxiety begins to interfere in the person's life in a significant way, it is considered a disorder.

Anxiety and closely related disorders emerge from "triple vulnerabilities,"a combination of biological, psychological, and specific factors that increase our risk for developing a disorder (Barlow, 2002; Suárez, Bennett, Goldstein, & Barlow, 2009). Biological vulnerabilities refer to specific genetic and neurobiological factors that might predispose someone to develop anxiety disorders. No single gene directly causes anxiety or panic, but our genes may make us more susceptible to anxiety and influence how our brains react to stress (Drabant et al., 2012; Gelernter & Stein, 2009; Smoller, Block, & Young, 2009). Psychological vulnerabilities refer to the influences that our early experiences have on how we view the world. If we were confronted with unpredictable stressors or traumatic experiences at younger ages, we may come to view the world as unpredictable and uncontrollable, even dangerous (Chorpita & Barlow, 1998; Gunnar & Fisher, 2006). Specific vulnerabilities refer to how our experiences lead us to focus and channel our anxiety (Suárez et al., 2009). If we learned that physical illness is dangerous, maybe through witnessing our family's reaction whenever anyone got sick, we may focus our anxiety on physical sensations. If we learned that disapproval from others has negative, even dangerous consequences, such as being yelled at or severely punished for even the slightest offense, we might focus our anxiety on social evaluation. If we learn that the "other shoe might drop" at any moment, we may focus our anxiety on worries about the future. None of these vulnerabilities directly causes anxiety disorders on its own—instead, when all of these vulnerabilities are present, and we experience some triggering life stress, an anxiety disorder may be the result (Barlow, 2002; Suárez et al., 2009). In the next sections, we will briefly explore each of the major anxiety based disorders, found in the fifth edition of the *Diagnostic and Statistical Manual of Mental Disorders* (DSM-5) (APA, 2013).

While everyone may experience some level of anxiety at one time or another, those with anxiety disorders experience it consistently and so intensely that it has a significantly negative impact on their quality of life. [Image: Bada Bing, https://goo.gl/aawyLi, CC BY-NC-SA 2.0, https://goo.gl/Toc0ZF]

Generalized Anxiety Disorder

Most of us worry some of the time, and this worry can actually be useful in helping us to plan for the future or make sure we remember to do something important. Most of us can set aside our worries when we need to focus on other things or stop worrying altogether whenever a problem has passed. However, for someone with generalized anxiety disorder (GAD), these worries become difficult, or even impossible, to turn off. They may find themselves worrying excessively about a number of different things, both minor and catastrophic. Their worries also come with a host of other symptoms such as muscle tension, fatigue, agitation or restlessness, irritability, difficulties with sleep (either falling asleep, staying asleep, or both), or difficulty concentrating.The *DSM-5* criteria specify that at least six months of excessive anxiety and worry of this type must be ongoing, happening more days than not for a good proportion of the day, to receive a diagnosis of GAD. About 5.7% of the population has met criteria for GAD at some point during their lifetime (Kessler, Berglund, et al., 2005), making it one of the most common anxiety disorders (see Table 1).

Disorder	1-Year Prevalence Rates [1]	Lifetime Prevalence Rates [2]	Prevalence by Gender	Median Age of Onset
Generalized Anxiety Disorder	3.1%	5.7%	67% female	31 yrs.
OCD	1%	1.6%	55% female	19 yrs.
Panic Disorder	2.7%	4.7%	67% female	24 yrs.
PTSD	3.5%	6.8%	52% female[3]	23 yrs.
Social Anxiety	6.8%	12.1%	50% female	13 yrs.
Specific Phobia	8.7%	12.5%	60% - 90% female [4]	7-9 yrs.

Table 1: Prevalence rates for major anxiety disorders. [1] Kessler et al. (2005), [2]Kessler, Chiu, Demler, Merikangas, & Walters (2005), [3]Kessler, Sonnega, Bromet, Hughes, & Nelson (1995), [4]Craske et al. (1996).

What makes a person with GAD worry more than the average person? Research shows that individuals with GAD are more sensitive and vigilant toward possible threats than people who are not anxious (Aikins & Craske, 2001; Barlow, 2002; Bradley, Mogg, White, Groom, & de Bono, 1999). This may be related to early stressful experiences, which can lead to a view of the world as an unpredictable, uncontrollable, and even dangerous place. Some have suggested that people with GAD worry as a way to gain some control over these otherwise uncontrollable or unpredictable experiences and against uncertain outcomes (Dugas, Gagnon, Ladouceur, & Freeston, 1998). By repeatedly going through all of the possible "What if?" scenarios in their mind, the person might feel like they are less vulnerable to an unexpected outcome, giving them the sense that they have *some* control over the situation (Wells, 2002). Others have suggested people with GAD worry as a way to avoid feeling distressed (Borkovec, Alcaine, & Behar, 2004). For example, Borkovec and Hu (1990) found that those who worried when confronted with a stressful situation had less physiological arousal than those who didn't worry, maybe because the worry "distracted" them in some way.

The problem is, all of this "what if?"-ing doesn't get the person any closer to a solution or an answer and, in fact, might take them away from important things they should be paying attention to in the moment, such as finishing an important project. Many of the catastrophic outcomes people with GAD worry about are very unlikely to happen, so when the catastrophic event doesn't materialize, the act of worrying gets reinforced (Borkovec, Hazlett-Stevens, & Diaz, 1999). For example, if a mother spends all night worrying about whether her teenage daughter will get home safe from a night out and the daughter returns home without incident, the mother could easily attribute her daughter's safe return to her successful "vigil." What the mother hasn't learned is that her daughter would have returned home just as safe if she had been focusing on the movie she was watching with her husband, rather than being preoccupied with worries. In this way, the cycle of worry is perpetuated, and, subsequently, people with GAD often miss out on many otherwise enjoyable events in their lives.

Panic Disorder and Agoraphobia

Have you ever gotten into a near-accident or been taken by surprise in some way? You may have felt a flood of physical sensations, such as a racing heart, shortness of breath, or tingling sensations. This alarm reaction is called the "fight or flight" response (Cannon, 1929) and is your body's natural reaction to fear, preparing you to either fight or escape in response to threat or danger. It's likely you weren't too concerned with these sensations, because you knew what was causing them. But imagine if this alarm reaction came "out of the blue," for no apparent reason, or in a situation in which you didn't expect to be anxious or fearful. This is called an "unexpected" panic attack or a false alarm. Because there is no apparent reason or cue for the alarm reaction, you might react to the sensations with intense fear, maybe thinking you are having a heart attack, or going crazy, or even dying. You might begin to associate the physical sensations you felt during this attack with this fear and may start to go out of your way to avoid having those sensations again.

Panic disorder is a debilitating condition that leaves sufferers with acute anxiety that persists long after a specific panic attack has subsided. When this anxiety leads to deliberate avoidance of particular places and situations a person may be given a diagnosis of agoraphobia. [Image: Nate Steiner, https://goo.gl/dUYWDf, Public Domain]

Unexpected panic attacks such as these are at the heart of panic disorder (PD). However, to receive a diagnosis of PD, the person must not only have unexpected panic attacks but also must experience continued intense anxiety and avoidance related to the attack for at least one month, causing significant distress or interference in their lives. People with panic disorder tend to interpret even normal physical sensations in a catastrophic way, which triggers more anxiety and, ironically, more physical sensations, creating a vicious cycle of panic (Clark, 1986, 1996). The person may begin to avoid a number of situations or activities that produce the same physiological arousal that was present during the beginnings of a panic attack. For example, someone who experienced a racing heart during a panic attack might avoid exercise or caffeine. Someone who experienced choking sensations might avoid wearing high-necked sweaters or necklaces. Avoidance of these internal bodily or somatic cues for panic has been termed interoceptive avoidance (Barlow & Craske, 2007; Brown, White, & Barlow, 2005; Craske & Barlow, 2008; Shear et al., 1997).

The individual may also have experienced an overwhelming urge to escape during the unexpected panic attack. This can lead to a sense that certain places or situations—particularly situations where escape might not be possible—are not "safe." These situations become external cues for panic. If the person begins to avoid several places or situations, or still endures these situations but does so with a significant amount of apprehension and anxiety, then the person also has agoraphobia (Barlow, 2002; Craske & Barlow, 1988; Craske & Barlow, 2008). Agoraphobia can cause significant disruption to a person's life, causing them to go out of their way to avoid situations, such as adding hours to a commute to avoid taking the train or only ordering take-out to avoid having to enter a grocery store. In one tragic case seen by our clinic, a woman suffering from agoraphobia had not left her apartment for 20 years and had spent the past 10 years confined to one small area of her apartment, away from the view of the outside. In some cases, agoraphobia develops in the absence of panic attacks and therefor is a separate disorder in DSM-5. But agoraphobia often accompanies panic disorder.

About 4.7% of the population has met criteria for PD or agoraphobia over their lifetime (Kessler, Chiu, Demler, Merikangas, & Walters, 2005; Kessler et al., 2006) (see Table 1). In all of these cases of panic disorder, what was once an adaptive natural alarm reaction now becomes a learned, and much feared, false alarm.

Specific Phobia

The majority of us might have certain things we fear, such as bees, or needles, or heights (Myers et al., 1984). But what if this fear is so consuming that you can't go out on a summer's day, or get vaccines needed to go on a special trip, or visit your doctor in her new office on the 26th floor? To meet criteria for a diagnosis of specific phobia, there must be an irrational fear of a specific object or situation that substantially interferes with the person's ability to function. For example, a patient at our clinic turned down a prestigious and coveted artist residency because it required spending time near a wooded area, bound to have insects. Another patient purposely left her house two hours early each morning so she could walk past her neighbor's fenced yard before they let their dog out in the morning.

The list of possible phobias is staggering, but four major subtypes of specific phobia are recognized: blood-injury-injection (BII) type, situational type (such as planes, elevators, or enclosed places), natural environment type for events one may encounter in nature (for example, heights, storms, and water), and animal type.

A fifth category "other" includes phobias that do not fit any of the four major subtypes (for example, fears of choking, vomiting, or contracting an illness). Most phobic reactions cause a surge of activity in the sympathetic nervous system and increased heart rate and blood pressure, maybe even a panic attack. However, people with BII type phobias usually experience a marked *drop* in heart rate and blood pressure and may even faint. In this way, those

Elevators can be a trigger for sufferers of claustrophobia or agoraphobia. [Image: srgpicker, CC BY-NC-SA 2.0, https://goo.gl/Toc0ZF]

with BII phobias almost always differ in their physiological reaction from people with other types of phobia (Barlow & Liebowitz, 1995; Craske, Antony, & Barlow, 2006; Hofmann, Alpers, & Pauli, 2009; Ost, 1992). BII phobia also runs in families more strongly than any phobic disorder we know (Antony & Barlow, 2002; Page & Martin, 1998). Specific phobia is one of the most common psychological disorders in the United States, with 12.5% of the population reporting a lifetime history of fears significant enough to be considered a "phobia" (Arrindell et al., 2003; Kessler, Berglund, et al., 2005) (see Table 1). Most people who suffer from specific phobia tend to have multiple phobias of several types (Hofmann, Lehman, & Barlow, 1997).

Social Anxiety Disorder (Social Phobia)

Many people consider themselves shy, and most people find social evaluation uncomfortable at best, or giving a speech somewhat mortifying. Yet, only a small proportion of the population fear these types of situations significantly enough to merit a diagnosis of social anxiety disorder (SAD) (APA, 2013). SAD is more than exaggerated shyness (Bogels et al., 2010; Schneier et al., 1996). To receive a diagnosis of SAD, the fear and anxiety associated with social situations must be so strong that the person avoids them entirely, or if avoidance is not possible, the person endures them with a great deal of distress. Further, the fear and avoidance of social situations must get in the way of the person's daily life, or seriously limit their academic or occupational functioning. For example, a patient at our clinic compromised her perfect 4.0 grade point average because she could not complete a required oral presentation in one of her classes, causing her to fail the course. Fears of negative evaluation might make someone repeatedly turn down invitations to social events or avoid having conversations with people, leading to greater and greater isolation.

The specific social situations that trigger anxiety and fear range from one-on-one interactions, such as starting or maintaining a conversation; to performance-based situations, such as giving a speech or performing on stage; to assertiveness, such as asking someone to change disruptive or undesirable behaviors. Fear of social evaluation might even extend to such things as using public restrooms, eating in a restaurant, filling out forms in a public place, or even reading on a train. Any type of situation that could potentially draw attention to the person can become a feared social situation. For example, one patient of ours went out of her way to avoid any situation in which she might have to use a public restroom for fear that someone would hear her in the bathroom stall and think she was disgusting. If the fear is limited to performance-based situations, such as public speaking, a diagnosis of SAD performance only is assigned.

What causes someone to fear social situations to such a large extent? The person may have learned growing up that social evaluation in particular can be dangerous, creating a specific psychological vulnerability to develop social anxiety (Bruch & Heimberg, 1994; Lieb et al., 2000; Rapee & Melville, 1997). For example, the person's caregivers may have harshly criticized and punished them for even the smallest mistake, maybe even punishing them physically.

Social trauma in childhood may have long-lasting effects.
[Image: ihtatho, https://goo.gl/dTzrdj, CC BY-NC 2.0,
https://goo.gl/VnKlK8]

Or, someone might have experienced a social trauma that had lasting effects, such as being bullied or humiliated. Interestingly, one group of researchers found that 92% of adults in their study sample with social phobia experienced severe teasing and bullying in childhood, compared with only 35% to 50% among people with other anxiety disorders (McCabe, Antony, Summerfeldt, Liss, & Swinson, 2003). Someone else might react so strongly to the anxiety provoked by a social situation that they have an unexpected panic attack. This panic attack then becomes associated (conditioned response) with the social situation, causing the person to fear they will panic the next time they are in that situation. This is not considered PD, however, because the person's fear is more focused on social evaluation than having unexpected panic attacks, and the fear of having an attack is limited to social situations. As many as 12.1% of the general population suffer from social phobia at some point in their lives (Kessler, Berglund, et al., 2005), making it one of the most common anxiety disorders, second only to specific phobia (see Table 1).

Posttraumatic Stress Disorder

With stories of war, natural disasters, and physical and sexual assault dominating the news, it is clear that trauma is a reality for many people. Many individual traumas that occur every day never even make the headlines, such as a car accident, domestic abuse, or the death of a loved one. Yet, while many people face traumatic events, not everyone who faces a trauma develops a disorder. Some, with the help of family and friends, are able to recover and continue on with their lives (Friedman, 2009). For some, however, the months and years following a trauma are filled with intrusive reminders of the event, a sense of intense fear that another traumatic event might occur, or a sense of isolation and emotional numbing. They may engage in a host of behaviors intended to protect themselves from being vulnerable or unsafe, such as constantly scanning their surroundings to look for signs of potential danger, never sitting with their back to the door, or never allowing themselves to be anywhere alone. This lasting reaction to trauma is what characterizes posttraumatic stress disorder (PTSD).

A diagnosis of PTSD begins with the traumatic event itself. An individual must have been exposed to an event that involves actual or threatened death, serious injury, or sexual violence. To receive a diagnosis of PTSD, exposure to the event must include either directly experiencing the event, witnessing the event happening to someone else, learning that the event occurred to a close relative or friend, or having repeated or extreme exposure to details of the event (such as in the case of first responders). The person subsequently re-experiences the event through both intrusive memories and nightmares. Some memories may come back so vividly that the person feels like they are experiencing the event all over again, what is known as having a flashback. The individual may avoid anything that reminds them of the trauma, including conversations, places, or even specific types of people. They may feel emotionally numb or restricted in their ability to feel, which may interfere in their interpersonal relationships. The person may not be able to remember certain aspects of what happened during the event. They may feel a sense of a foreshortened future, that they will never marry, have a family, or live a long, full life. They may be jumpy or easily startled, hypervigilant to their surroundings, and quick to anger. The prevalence of PTSD among the population as a whole is relatively low, with 6.8% having experienced PTSD at some point in their life (Kessler, Berglund, et al., 2005) (see Table 1). Combat and sexual assault are the most common precipitating traumas (Kessler, Sonnega, Bromet, Hughes, & Nelson, 1995). Whereas PTSD was previously categorized as an Anxiety Disorder, in the most recent version of the DSM (DSM-5; APA, 2013) it has been reclassified under the more specific category of Trauma- and Stressor-Related Disorders.

A person with PTSD is particularly sensitive to both internal and external cues that serve as reminders of their traumatic experience. For example, as we saw in PD, the physical sensations of arousal present during the initial trauma can become threatening in and of themselves, becoming a powerful reminder of the event. Someone might avoid watching intense or emotional movies in order to prevent the experience of emotional arousal. Avoidance of conversations, reminders, or even of the experience of emotion itself may also be an attempt to avoid triggering internal cues. External stimuli that were present during the trauma can also become strong triggers. For example, if a woman is raped by a man wearing a red t-shirt, she may develop a strong alarm reaction to the sight of red shirts, or perhaps even more indiscriminately to anything with a similar color red. A combat veteran who experienced a strong smell of gasoline during a roadside bomb attack may have an intense alarm reaction when pumping gas back at home. Individuals with a psychological vulnerability toward viewing the world as uncontrollable and unpredictable may particularly struggle with the possibility of additional future, unpredictable traumatic events, fueling their need for hypervigilance and avoidance, and perpetuating the symptoms of PTSD.

Obsessive-Compulsive Disorder

Have you ever had a strange thought pop into your mind, such as picturing the stranger next to you naked? Or maybe you walked past a crooked picture on the wall and couldn't resist straightening it. Most people have occasional strange thoughts and may even engage in some "compulsive" behaviors, especially when they are stressed (Boyer & Liénard, 2008; Fullana et al., 2009). But for most people, these thoughts are nothing more than a passing oddity, and the behaviors are done (or not done) without a second thought. For someone with obsessive-compulsive disorder (OCD), however, these thoughts and compulsive behaviors don't just come and go. Instead, strange or unusual thoughts are taken to mean something much more important and real, maybe even something dangerous or frightening. The urge to engage in some behavior, such as straightening a picture, can become so intense that it is nearly impossible *not* to carry it out, or causes significant anxiety if it can't be carried out. Further, someone with OCD might become preoccupied with the possibility that the behavior wasn't carried out to completion and feel compelled to repeat the behavior again and again, maybe several times before they are "satisfied."

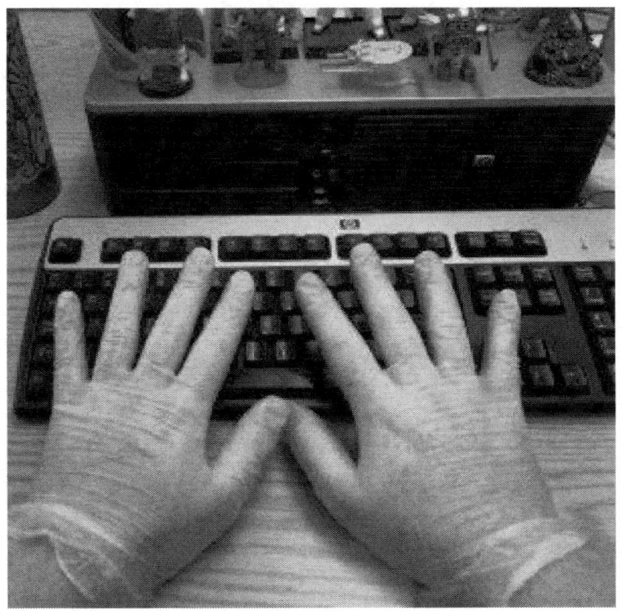

People suffering from OCD may have an irrational fear of germs and "becoming contaminated". [Image: benchilada, https://goo.gl/qemgDm, CC BY-NC-SA 2.0, https://goo.gl/Toc0ZF]

To receive a diagnosis of OCD, a person must experience obsessive thoughts and/or compulsions that seem irrational or nonsensical, but that keep coming into their mind. Some examples of obsessions include doubting thoughts (such as doubting a door is locked or an appliance is turned off), thoughts of contamination (such as thinking that touching almost anything might give you cancer), or aggressive thoughts or images that are unprovoked or nonsensical. Compulsions may be carried out in an attempt to neutralize some of these thoughts, providing temporary relief from the anxiety the obsessions cause, or they may be nonsensical in and of themselves. Either way, compulsions are distinct in that they must be repetitive or excessive, the person feels "driven" to carry out the behavior, and the person feels a great deal of distress if they can't engage in the behavior. Some examples of compulsive behaviors are repetitive washing (often in response to contamination obsessions), repetitive checking (locks, door handles, appliances often in response to doubting obsessions), ordering and arranging things to ensure symmetry, or doing things according to a specific ritual or sequence (such as getting dressed or ready for bed in a specific order). To meet diagnostic criteria for OCD, engaging in obsessions and/or compulsions must take up a significant amount of the person's time, at least an hour per day, and must cause significant distress or impairment in functioning. About 1.6% of the population has met criteria for OCD over the course of a lifetime (Kessler, Berglund, et al., 2005) (see Table 1). Whereas OCD was previously categorized as an Anxiety Disorder, in the most recent version of the DSM (DSM-5; APA, 2013) it has been reclassified under the more specific category of Obsessive-Compulsive and Related Disorders.

People with OCD often confuse having an intrusive thought with their potential for carrying out the thought. Whereas most people when they have a strange or frightening thought are able to let it go, a person with OCD may become "stuck" on the thought and be intensely afraid that they might somehow lose control and act on it. Or worse, they believe that having the thought is just as bad as doing it. This is called thought-action fusion. For example, one patient of ours was plagued by thoughts that she would cause harm to her young daughter. She experienced intrusive images of throwing hot coffee in her daughter's face or pushing her face underwater when she was giving her a bath. These images were so terrifying to the patient that she would no longer allow herself any physical contact with her daughter and would leave her daughter in the care of a babysitter if her husband or another family was not available to "supervise" her. In reality, the last thing she wanted to do was harm her daughter, and she had no intention or desire to act on the aggressive thoughts and images, nor does anybody with OCD act on these thoughts, but these thoughts were so horrifying to her that she made every attempt to prevent herself from the potential of carrying them out, even if it meant not being able to hold, cradle, or cuddle her daughter. These are the types of struggles people with OCD face every day.

Treatments for Anxiety and Related Disorders

Many successful treatments for anxiety and related disorders have been developed over the years. Medications (anti-anxiety drugs and antidepressants) have been found to be beneficial for disorders other than specific phobia, but relapse rates are high once medications are stopped (Heimberg et al., 1998; Hollon et al., 2005), and some classes of medications (minor tranquilizers or benzodiazepines) can be habit forming.

Exposure-based CBT aims to help patients recognize and change problematic thoughts and behaviors in real-life situations. A person with a fear of elevators would be encouraged to practice exposure exercises that might involve approaching or riding elevators to attempt to overcome their anxiety. [Image: Mag3737, https://goo.gl/j9L5AQ, CC BY-NC-SA 2.0, https://goo.gl/Toc0ZF]

Exposure-based cognitive behavioral therapies (CBT) are effective psychosocial treatments for anxiety disorders, and many show greater treatment effects than medication in the long term (Barlow, Allen, & Basden, 2007; Barlow, Gorman, Shear, & Woods, 2000). In CBT, patients are taught skills to help identify and change problematic thought processes, beliefs, and behaviors that tend to worsen symptoms of anxiety, and practice applying these skills to real-life situations through exposure exercises. Patients learn how the automatic "appraisals" or thoughts they have about a situation affect both how they feel and how they behave. Similarly, patients learn how engaging in certain behaviors, such as avoiding situations, tends to strengthen the belief that the situation is something to be feared. A key aspect of CBT is exposure exercises, in which the patient learns to gradually approach situations they find fearful or distressing, in order to challenge their beliefs and learn new, less fearful associations about these situations.

Typically 50% to 80% of patients receiving drugs or CBT will show a good initial response, with the effect of CBT more durable. Newer developments in the treatment of anxiety disorders are focusing on novel interventions, such as the use of certain medications to enhance learning during CBT (Otto et al., 2010), and transdiagnostic treatments targeting core, underlying vulnerabilities (Barlow et al., 2011). As we advance our understanding of anxiety and related disorders, so too will our treatments advance, with the hopes that for the many people suffering from these disorders, anxiety can once again become something useful and adaptive, rather than something debilitating.

1. Kessler et al. (2005).

2. Kessler, Chiu, Demler, Merikangas, & Walters (2005).

3. Kessler, Sonnega, Bromet, Hughes, & Nelson (1995).

4. Craske et al. (1996).

Outside Resources

American Psychological Association (APA)
http://www.apa.org/topics/anxiety/index.aspx
National Institutes of Mental Health (NIMH)
http://www.nimh.nih.gov/health/topics/anxiety-disorders/index.shtml
Web: Anxiety and Depression Association of America (ADAA)
http://www.adaa.org/
Web: Center for Anxiety and Related Disorders (CARD)
http://www.bu.edu/card/

Discussion Questions

1. Name and describe the three main vulnerabilities contributing to the development of anxiety and related disorders. Do you think these disorders could develop out of biological factors alone? Could these disorders develop out of learning experiences alone?

2. Many of the symptoms in anxiety and related disorders overlap with experiences most people have. What features differentiate someone with a disorder versus someone without?

3. What is an "alarm reaction?" If someone experiences an alarm reaction when they are about to give a speech in front of a room full of people, would you consider this a "true alarm" or a "false alarm?"

4. Many people are shy. What differentiates someone who is shy from someone with social anxiety disorder? Do you think shyness should be considered an anxiety disorder?

5. Is anxiety ever helpful? What about worry?

Vocabulary

Agoraphobia
A sort of anxiety disorder distinguished by feelings that a place is uncomfortable or may be unsafe because it is significantly open or crowded.
Anxiety
A mood state characterized by negative affect, muscle tension, and physical arousal in which a person apprehensively anticipates future danger or misfortune.
Biological vulnerability
A specific genetic and neurobiological factor that might predispose someone to develop anxiety disorders.
Conditioned response
A learned reaction following classical conditioning, or the process by which an event that automatically elicits a response is repeatedly paired with another neutral stimulus (conditioned stimulus), resulting in the ability of the neutral stimulus to elicit the same response on its own.

External cues

Stimuli in the outside world that serve as triggers for anxiety or as reminders of past traumatic events.

Fight or flight response

A biological reaction to alarming stressors that prepares the body to resist or escape a threat.

Flashback

Sudden, intense re-experiencing of a previous event, usually trauma-related.

Generalized anxiety disorder (GAD)

Excessive worry about everyday things that is at a level that is out of proportion to the specific causes of worry.

Internal bodily or somatic cues

Physical sensations that serve as triggers for anxiety or as reminders of past traumatic events.

Interoceptive avoidance

Avoidance of situations or activities that produce sensations of physical arousal similar to those occurring during a panic attack or intense fear response.

Obsessive-compulsive disorder (OCD)

A disorder characterized by the desire to engage in certain behaviors excessively or compulsively in hopes of reducing anxiety. Behaviors include things such as cleaning, repeatedly opening and closing doors, hoarding, and obsessing over certain thoughts.

Panic disorder (PD)

A condition marked by regular strong panic attacks, and which may include significant levels of worry about future attacks.

Posttraumatic stress disorder (PTSD)

A sense of intense fear, triggered by memories of a past traumatic event, that another traumatic event might occur. PTSD may include feelings of isolation and emotional numbing.

Psychological vulnerabilities

Influences that our early experiences have on how we view the world.

Reinforced response

Following the process of operant conditioning, the strengthening of a response following either the delivery of a desired consequence (positive reinforcement) or escape from an aversive consequence.

SAD performance only

Social anxiety disorder which is limited to certain situations that the sufferer perceives as requiring some type of performance.

Social anxiety disorder (SAD)

A condition marked by acute fear of social situations which lead to worry and diminished day to day functioning.

Specific vulnerabilities

How our experiences lead us to focus and channel our anxiety.

Thought-action fusion

The tendency to overestimate the relationship between a thought and an action, such that one mistakenly believes a "bad" thought is the equivalent of a "bad" action.

References

- APA. (2013). *Diagnostic and statistical manual of mental disorders (5th ed.)*. Washington, D.C.: American Psychiatric Association.

- Aikins, D. E., & Craske, M. G. (2001). Cognitive theories of generalized anxiety disorder. *Psychiatric Clinics of North America, 24*(1), 57-74, vi.

- Antony, M. M., & Barlow, D. H. (2002). Specific phobias. In D. H. Barlow (Ed.), *Anxiety and its disorders: The nature and treatment of anxiety and panic* (2nd ed.). New York, NY: Guilford Press.

- Arrindell, W. A., Eisemann, M., Richter, J., Oei, T. P., Caballo, V. E., van der Ende, J., . . . Cultural Clinical Psychology Study, Group. (2003). Phobic anxiety in 11 nations. Part I: Dimensional constancy of the five-factor model. *Behaviour Research and Therapy, 41*(4), 461-479.

- Barlow, D. H. (2002). *Anxiety and its disorders: The nature and treatment of anxiety and panic* (2nd ed.). New York: Guilford Press.

- Barlow, D. H., & Craske, M. G. (2007). *Mastery of your anxiety and panic* (4th ed.). New York, NY: Oxford University Press.

- Barlow, D. H., & Liebowitz, M. R. (1995). Specific and social phobias. In H. I. Kaplan & B. J. Sadock (Eds.), *Comprehensive textbook of psychiatry: VI* (pp. 1204-1217). Baltimore, MD: Williams & Wilkins.

- Barlow, D. H., Allen, L.B., & Basden, S. (2007). Pscyhological treatments for panic disorders, phobias, and generalized anxiety disorder. In P.E. Nathan & J.M. Gorman (Eds.), *A guide to treatments that work* (3rd ed.). New York, NY: Oxford University Press.

- Barlow, D. H., Ellard, K. K., Fairholme, C. P., Farchione, T. J., Boisseau, C. L., Allen, L. B., & Ehrenreich-May, J. (2011). *Unified Protocol for the Transdiagnostic Treatment of Emotional Disorders (Workbook)*. New York, NY: Oxford University Press.

- Barlow, D. H., Gorman, J. M., Shear, M. K., & Woods, S. W. (2000). Cognitive-behavioral therapy, imipramine, or their combination for panic disorder: A randomized controlled trial. *Journal of the American Medical Association*, 283(19), 2529-2536.

- Bogels, S. M., Alden, L., Beidel, D. C., Clark, L. A., Pine, D. S., Stein, M. B., & Voncken, M. (2010). Social anxiety disorder: questions and answers for the DSM-V. *Depression and Anxiety, 27*(2), 168-189. doi: 10.1002/da.20670

- Borkovec, T. D., & Hu, S. (1990). The effect of worry on cardiovascular response to phobic imagery. *Behaviour Research and Therapy, 28*(1), 69-73.

- Borkovec, T. D., Alcaine, O.M., & Behar, E. (2004). Avoidance theory of worry and generalized anxiety disorder. In R.G. Heimberg, Turk C.L. & D.S. Mennin (Eds.), *Generalized Anxiety Disorder: Advances in research and practice* (pp. 77-108). New York, NY: Guilford Press.

- Borkovec, T. D., Hazlett-Stevens, H., & Diaz, M.L. (1999). The role of positive beliefs about worry in generalized anxiety disorder and its treatment. *Clinical Psychology and Pscyhotherapy, 6*, 69-73.

- Boyer, P., & Liénard, P. (2008). Ritual behavior in obsessive and normal individuals: Moderating anxiety and reorganizing the flow of action. *Current Directions in Psychological Science, 17*(4), 291-294.

- Bradley, B. P., Mogg, K., White, J., Groom, C., & de Bono, J. (1999). Attentional bias for emotional faces in generalized anxiety disorder. *British Journal of Clinical Psychology, 38 (Pt 3)*, 267-278.

- Brown, T.A., White, K.S., & Barlow, D.H. (2005). A psychometric reanalysis of the Albany Panic and Phobia Questionnaire. *Behaviour Research and Therapy, 43*, 337-355.

- Bruch, M. A., & Heimberg, R. G. (1994). Differences in perceptions of parental and personal characteristics between generalized and non-generalized social phobics. *Journal of Anxiety Disorders, 8*, 155-168.

- Cannon, W.B. (1929). *Bodily changes in pain, hunger, fear and rage*. Oxford, UK: Appleton.

- Chorpita, B. F., & Barlow, D. H. (1998). The development of anxiety: the role of control in the early environment. *Psychological Bulletin, 124*(1), 3-21.

- Clark, D. M. (1996). Panic disorder: From theory to therapy. In P. Salkovskis (Ed.), *Fronteirs of cognitive therapy*(pp. 318-344). New York, NY: Guilford Press.

- Clark, D. M. (1986). A cognitive approach to panic. *Behaviour Research and Therapy, 24*(4), 461-470.

- Craske, M. G., & Barlow, D. H. (1988). A review of the relationship between panic and avoidance. *Clinical Pscyhology Review, 8*, 667-685.

- Craske, M. G., & Barlow, D.H. (2008). *Panic disorder and agoraphobia*. New York, NY: Guilford Press.

- Craske, M. G., Antony, M. M., & Barlow, D. H. (2006). *Mastering your fears and phobias: Therapist guide*. New York, NY: Oxford University Press.

- Drabant, E. M., Ramel, W., Edge, M. D., Hyde, L. W., Kuo, J. R., Goldin, P. R., . . . Gross, J. J. (2012). Neural mechanisms underlying 5-HTTLPR-related sensitivity to acute stress. *American Journal of Psychiatry, 169(4)*, 397-405. doi: 10.1176/appi.ajp.2011.10111699

- Dugas, M. J., Gagnon, F., Ladouceur, R., & Freeston, M. H. (1998). Generalized anxiety disorder: a preliminary test of a conceptual model. *Behaviour Research and Therapy, 36*(2), 215-226.

- Friedman, M. J. (2009). Phenomenology of postraumatic stress disorder and acute stress disorder. In M. M. Anthony & M. B. Stein (Eds.), *Oxford Handbook of Anxiety and Related Disorders*. New York, NY: Oxford University Press.

- Fullana, M. A., Mataix-Cols, D., Caspi, A., Harrington, H., Grisham, J. R., Moffitt, T. E., & Poulton, R. (2009). Obsessions and compulsions in the community: prevalence, interference, help-seeking, developmental stability, and co-occurring psychiatric conditions. *American Journal of Psychiatry, 166(3)*, 329-336. doi: 10.1176/appi.ajp.2008.08071006

- Gelernter, J., & Stein, M. B. (2009). Heritability and genetics of anxiety disorders. In M.M. Antony &

M.B. Stein (Eds.), *Oxford handbook of anxiety and related disorders*. New York, NY: Oxford University Press.

- Gunnar, M. R., & Fisher, P. A. (2006). Bringing basic research on early experience and stress neurobiology to bear on preventive interventions for neglected and maltreated children. *Developmental Psychopathology, 18*(3), 651-677.

- Heimberg, R. G., Liebowitz, M. R., Hope, D. A., Schneier, F. R., Holt, C. S., Welkowitz, L. A., . . . Klein, D. F. (1998). Cognitive behavioral group therapy vs phenelzine therapy for social phobia: 12-week outcome. *Archives of General Psychiatry, 55*(12), 1133-1141.

- Hofmann, S. G., Alpers, G. W., & Pauli, P. (2009). Phenomenology of panic and phobic disorders. In M. M. Antony & M. B. Stein (Eds.), *Oxford handbook of anxiety and related disorders* (pp. 34-46). New York, NY: Oxford University Press.

- Hofmann, S. G., Lehman, C. L., & Barlow, D. H. (1997). How specific are specific phobias? *Journal of Behavior Therapy and Experimental Psychiatry, 28*(3), 233-240.

- Hollon, S. D., DeRubeis, R. J., Shelton, R. C., Amsterdam, J. D., Salomon, R. M., O'Reardon, J. P., . . . Gallop, R. (2005). Prevention of relapse following cognitive therapy vs medications in moderate to severe depression. *Archives of General Psychiatry, 62*(4), 417-422. doi: 10.1001/archpsyc.62.4.417

- Kessler, R. C., Berglund, P., Demler, O., Jin, R., Merikangas, K. R., & Walters, E. E. (2005). Lifetime prevalence and age-of-onset distributions of DSM-IV disorders in the National Comorbidity Survey Replication. *Archives of General Psychiatry, 62*(6), 593-602. doi: 10.1001/archpsyc.62.6.593

- Kessler, R. C., Chiu, W. T., Demler, O., Merikangas, K. R., & Walters, E. E. (2005). Prevalence, severity, and comorbidity of 12-month DSM-IV disorders in the National Comorbidity Survey Replication. *Archives of General Psychiatry, 62*(6), 617-627. doi: 10.1001/archpsyc.62.6.617

- Kessler, R. C., Chiu, W. T., Jin, R., Ruscio, A. M., Shear, K., & Walters, E. E. (2006). The epidemiology of panic attacks, panic disorder, and agoraphobia in the National Comorbidity Survey Replication. *Archives of General Psychiatry, 63*(4), 415-424. doi: 10.1001/archpsyc.63.4.415

- Kessler, R. C., Sonnega, A., Bromet, E., Hughes, M., & Nelson, C. B. (1995). Posttraumatic stress disorder in the National Comorbidity Survey. *Archives of General Psychiatry, 52*(12), 1048-1060.

- Lieb, R., Wittchen, H. U., Hofler, M., Fuetsch, M., Stein, M. B., & Merikangas, K. R. (2000). Parental psychopathology, parenting styles, and the risk of social phobia in offspring: a prospective-longitudinal community study. *Archives of General Psychiatry, 57*(9), 859-866.

- McCabe, R. E., Antony, M. M., Summerfeldt, L. J., Liss, A., & Swinson, R. P. (2003). Preliminary examination of the relationship between anxiety disorders in adults and self-reported history of teasing or bullying experiences. *Cognitive Behavior Therapy, 32*(4), 187-193. doi: 10.1080/16506070310005051

- Myers, J. K., Weissman, M. M., Tischler, C. E., Holzer, C. E., Orvaschel, H., Anthony, J. C., . . . Stoltzman, R. (1984). Six-month prevalence of psychiatric disorders in three communities. *Archives of General Psychiatry, 41*, 959-967.

- Ost, L. G. (1992). Blood and injection phobia: background and cognitive, physiological, and behavioral variables. *Journal of Abnormal Psychology, 101*(1), 68-74.

- Otto, M. W., Tolin, D. F., Simon, N. M., Pearlson, G. D., Basden, S., Meunier, S. A., . . . Pollack, M. H. (2010). Efficacy of d-cycloserine for enhancing response to cognitive-behavior therapy for panic disorder. *Biological Psychiatry, 67*(4), 365-370. doi: 10.1016/j.biopsych.2009.07.036

- Page, A. C., & Martin, N. G. (1998). Testing a genetic structure of blood-injury-injection fears. American *Journal of Medical Genetics, 81*(5), 377-384.

- Rapee, R. M., & Melville, L. F. (1997). Recall of family factors in social phobia and panic disorder: comparison of mother and offspring reports. *Depress Anxiety, 5*(1), 7-11.

- Schneier, F. R., Leibowitz, M. R., Beidel, D. C., J., Fyer A., George, M. S., Heimberg, R. G., . . . Versiani, M. (1996). Social Phobia. In T. A. Widiger, A. J. Frances, H. A. Pincus, R. Ross, M. B. First & W. W. Davis (Eds.), *DSM-IV sourcebook* (Vol. 2, pp. 507-548). Washington, D.C.: American Psychiatric Association.

- Shear, M. K., Brown, T. A., Barlow, D. H., Money, R., Sholomskas, D. E., Woods, S. W., . . . Papp, L. A. (1997). Multicenter collaborative panic disorder severity scale. *American Journal of Psychiatry, 154*(11), 1571-1575.

- Smoller, J. W., Block, S. R., & Young, M. M. (2009). Genetics of anxiety disorders: the complex road from DSM to DNA. *Depression and Anxiety, 26*(11), 965-975. doi: 10.1002/da.20623

- Suárez, L, Bennett, S., Goldstein, C., & Barlow, D.H. (2009). Understanding anxiety disorders from a "triple vulnerabilities" framework. In M.M. Antony & M.B. Stein (Eds.), *Oxford Handbook of anxiety and related disorders* (pp. 153-172). New York, NY: Oxford University Press.

- Wells, A. (2002). GAD, metacognition, and mindfulness: An information processing analysis. Clinical *Psychology Science and Practice, 9*, 95-100.

CC licensed content, Shared previously

Social Anxiety

Social anxiety occurs when we are overly concerned about being humiliated, embarrassed, evaluated, or rejected by others in social situations. Everyone experiences social anxiety some of the time, but for a minority of people, the frequency and intensity of social anxiety is intense enough to interfere with meaningful activities (e.g., relationships, academics, career aspirations). When a person's level of social anxiety is excessive, social interactions are either dreaded or avoided, social cues and emotions are difficult to understand, and positive thoughts and emotions are rare, then that person may be diagnosed with social anxiety disorder (or social phobia). There are effective treatments—with both medications and psychotherapy–for this problem. Unfortunately, only a small proportion of people with social anxiety disorder actually seek treatment.

Learning Objectives

- Distinguish social anxiety from social anxiety disorder.

- Identify commonly feared social situations.

- Know the prevalence and treatment rates of social anxiety disorder.

- Understand how social anxiety influences thoughts, feelings, and behaviors.

- Identify effective treatments for social anxiety disorder.

Introduction

A public speaker waits backstage before her name is called. She visualizes what will happen in a few moments: the audience will cheer as she walks out and then turn silent, with all eyes on her. She imagines this will cause her to feel uncomfortable and, instead of standing balanced, she will lean to one side, not quite sure what to do with her hands. And when her mouth opens, instead of words, guttural sounds will emerge from a parched throat before her mind goes blank. In front of friends, family, and strangers, she is paralyzed with fear and embarrassment. Physically, in the moments leading up to the performance, she sweats, trembles, has difficulty breathing, notices a racing heartbeat, and feels nauseated. When someone asks her a question, she loses her voice or its pitch rises a few octaves. She attempts to hide her anxiety by tensing her muscles or telling herself to breathe and stay calm. Behaviorally, she seeks ways to escape the audience's gaze (e.g., by playing a video and asking the audience questions), and she tries to get through the performance as quickly as possible (e.g., rushing off the stage). Later, she works hard to avoid similar situations, passing up future speaking opportunities.

Welcome to the often terrifying world of social anxiety.

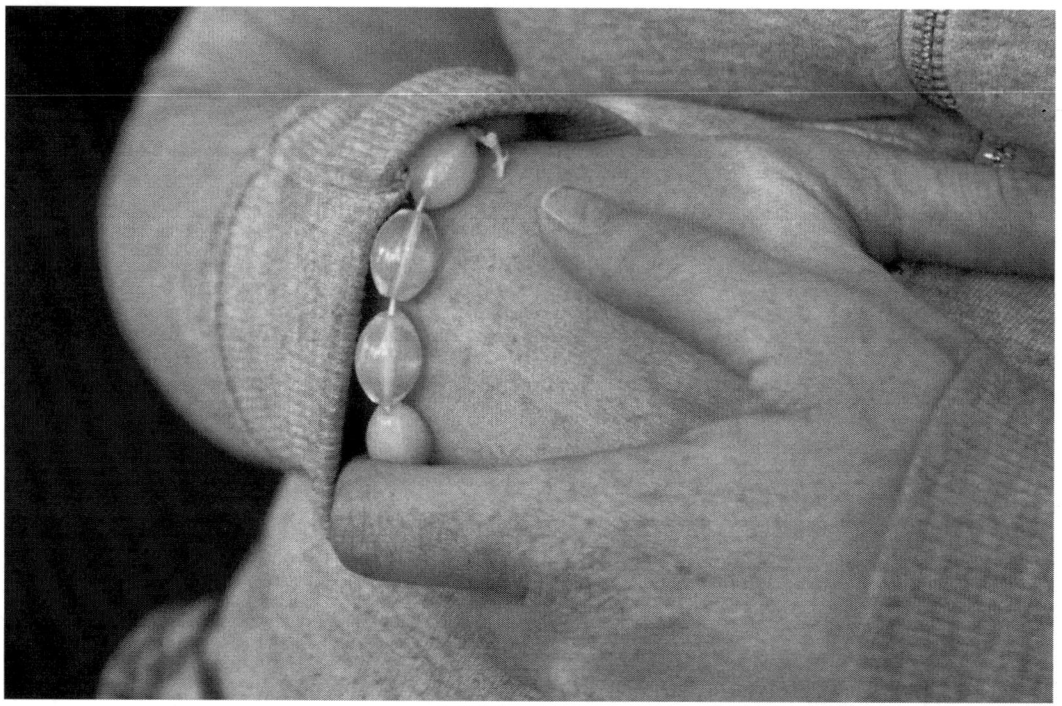

Social anxiety can be accompanied by physical manifestations such as shaking hands or a racing heartbeat. [Image: Kai Schreiber, https://goo.gl/XLYZHn, CC BY-SA 2.0, https://goo.gl/rxiUsF]

People have a fundamental need to feel like they belong and are liked, so it is painful when we feel rejected or left out by those who matter to us. In response, we often become acutely aware of the impression we make on others, and we avoid doing things that may cause others to be upset with us. Social anxiety is the *excessive*concern about being in social situations where scrutiny is likely. When people are socially anxious, they become overly concerned about embarrassing themselves, and they tend to reveal these signs of discomfort through sweating or blushing; they worry that their character flaws will be exposed and result in rejection. See Figure 1 for examples of situations that commonly evoke social anxiety.

The term anxiety describes a general apprehension about possible future danger, rather than a reaction to an immediate threat (i.e., fear). Nevertheless, like fear, the experience of social anxiety may involve *physical, emotional,* and *behavioral* symptoms like those described in the example above.

Nearly everyone experiences some social anxiety at one point or another. It is particularly common before performing in front of an audience or meeting new people on one's own, and this is normal. Social anxiety provides information about the demands required of us to handle an ongoing challenge (Frijda, 1996). It lets us know that the situation is meaningful, and the impression we make on other people may be important to our social standing. Most people are able to "power through" the situation, eventually feeling more comfortable and learning that it was not as bad as expected. This is a fundamentally important point: people think that their anxiety leading up to a situation (anticipatory feelings) will only increase further in the actual situation, when, in fact, our anxiety tends to peak in the moments before a situation.

Sometimes, people experience more than the "normal" amount of anxiety. For people with excessive social anxiety, their anxiety often arises in a broader array of situations, is more intense, and does not subside as quickly. For those people, negative social outcomes are viewed as highly probable and costly, and their attention during social interactions tends to be inwardly directed (e.g., "Did my comment sound stupid? Can she tell that I'm sweating?"). This running internal commentary prevents people from focusing on the situation at hand, and even simple social interactions may become overwhelming (Bögels & Mansell, 2004).

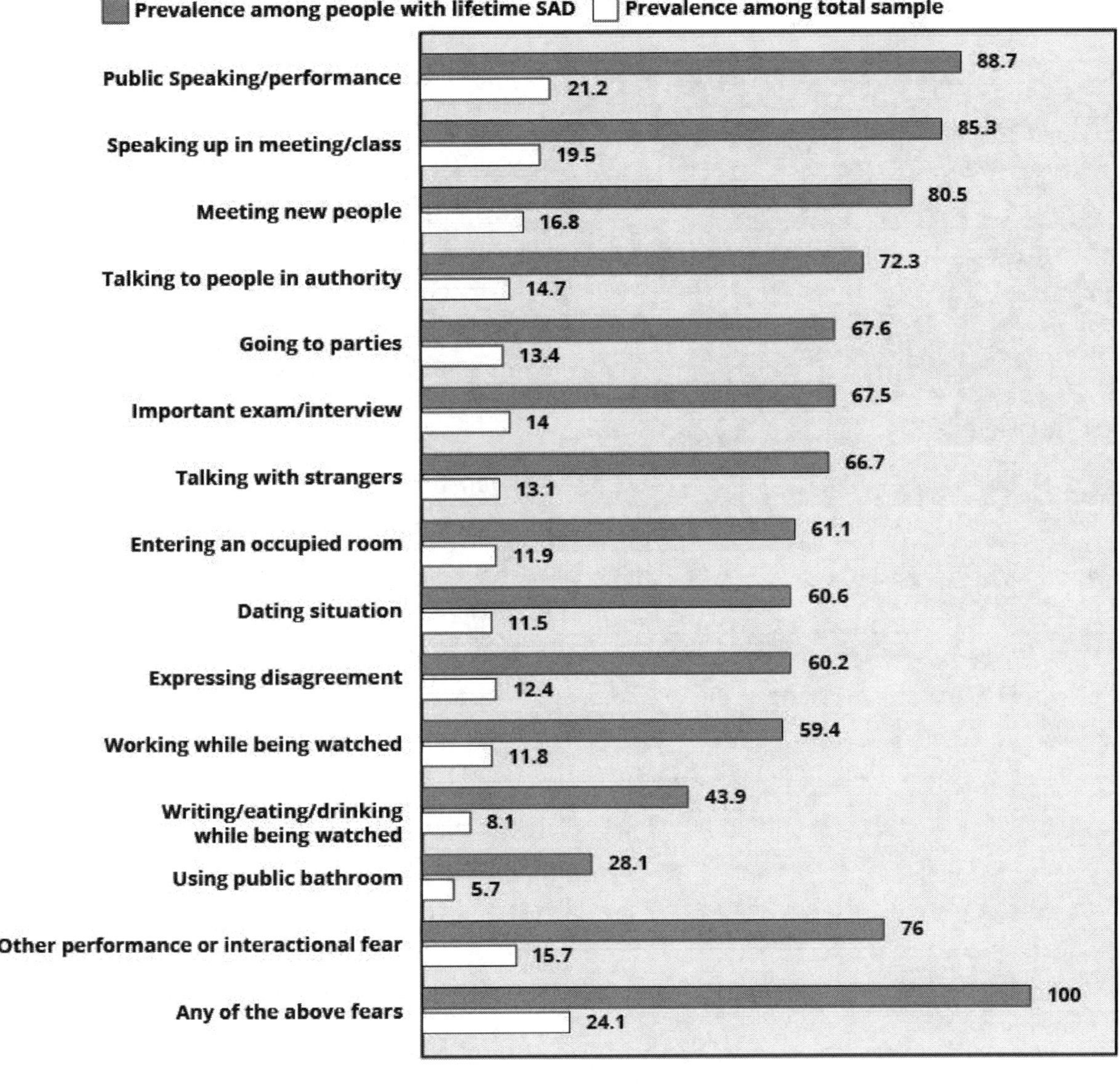

Figure 1: Lifetime Prevalence of Social Fears. Source: Ruscio, et al., 2008

Social Anxiety Disorder

When social anxiety and avoidance interfere with a person's ability to function in important roles (e.g., as a student, worker, friend), the condition is called social anxiety disorder (SAD), also known as social phobia (American Psychiatric Association, 2013). In the United States, SAD affects approximately 12.1% of people in their lifetimes and 7.1% of adults in a given year (Ruscio et al., 2008). About 1 of every 4 people report at least one significant social fear in their lifetimes—most commonly, public speaking (see Figure 1). To be diagnosed with SAD, a person must report an impairing fear of multiple social situations that has persisted for at least six months. Most people with SAD fear eight or more distinct social situations such as initiating a conversation with a stranger, maintaining conversations, going on a first date, going to a work party/function, talking with an authority figure, talking in front of a group of people, and eating in front of other people (Ruscio et al., 2008).

Fear of public performance is the most common of all social fears. [Image: Brisbane City Council, https://goo.gl/QakNCF, CC BY 2.0, https://goo.gl/BRvSA7]

SAD is one of the most common anxiety disorders recognized by the American Psychiatric Association's *Diagnostic and Statistical Manual of Mental Disorders* (DSM-5; APA, 2013). SAD affects men and women about equally, and the majority of people with SAD report that their fears began in early adolescence, typically around age 13 (Kessler et al., 2005). Unfortunately, this condition tends to be chronic and few people recover on their own without an intervention.

Despite the availability of effective treatments, few people seek help for their social fears (see Figure 2). In an epidemiological study, only 5.4% of people with SAD (and no other psychiatric disorders) ever received mental health treatment (Schneier, Johnson, Hornig, Liebowitz, & Weissman, 1992). There are several explanations for why people with SAD avoid treatment—for starters, the fear of being evaluated by a therapist and the stigma of seeking psychological services. Thus, the very features of the disorder may prevent a person from seeking treatment for it. Another explanation is that many physicians, teachers, parents, and peers do not believe that social anxiety disorder is a real condition and, instead, view it as nothing more than extreme shyness or inhibition. Finally, health care providers are often ill-equipped to assess SAD and may not be aware of evidence-based treatments (Kashdan, Christopher Frueh, Knapp, Hebert, & Magruder, 2006), and clients often do not know enough about social fears to discuss them with their doctors. Sadly, 60% to 80% of people with SAD suffer from symptoms for at least two decades (Ruscio et al., 2008). Thus, it is important to understand not only what social anxiety is but also what perpetuates social fears.

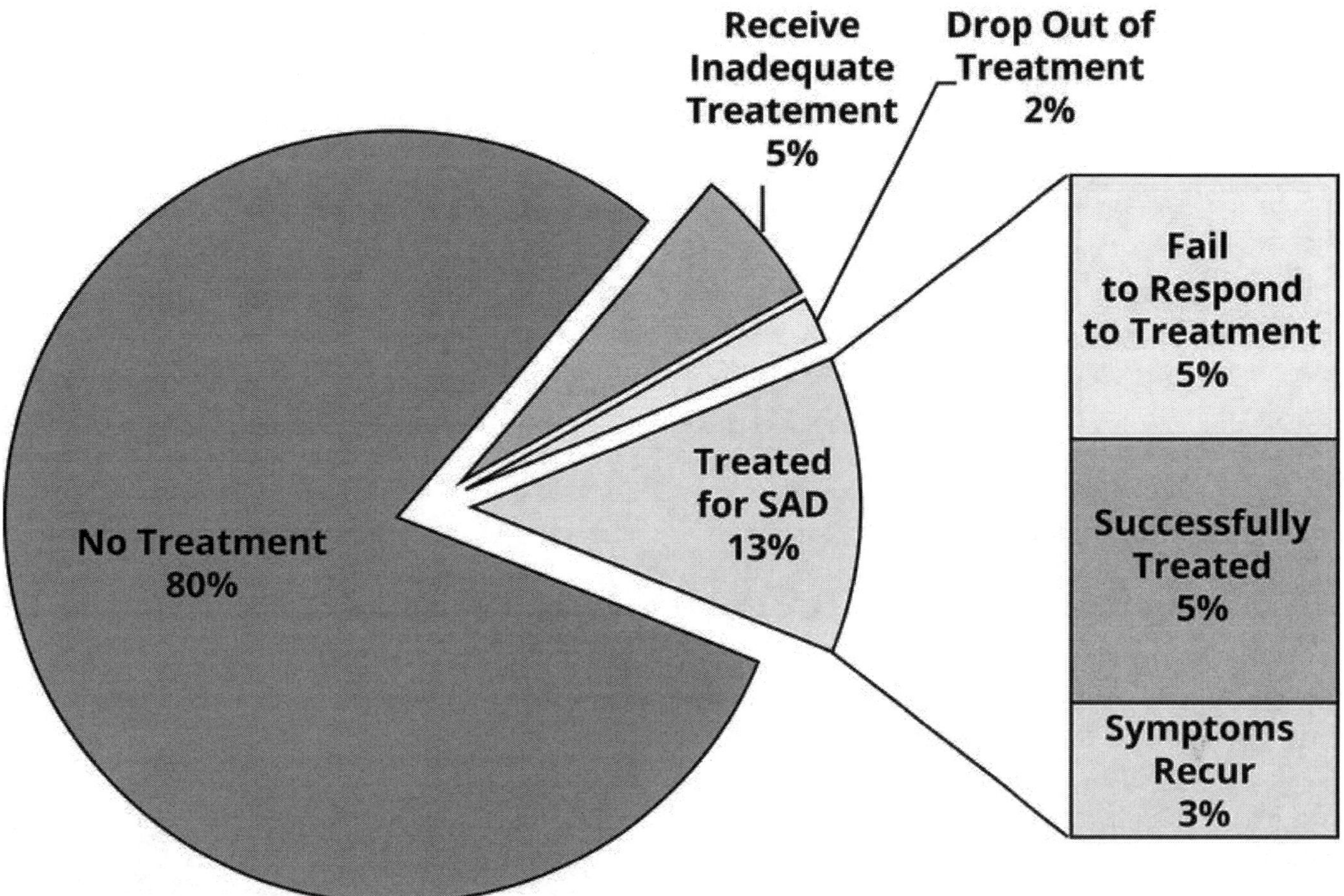

Figure 2: Treatment rate of adults with SAD based on data from Coles, et al., 2004; Feske and Chambless, 2005; Kessler, et al., 2005; and Ruscio, et al., 2008

Fear of Evaluation

A central component of the social anxiety experience is how a person thinks about him- or herself, about others, and about social situations. According to the self-presentation theory of social anxiety (Leary & Kowalski, 1995), people feel socially anxious when they wish to make a good impression on others but doubt their ability to do so. People with excessive social anxiety are likely to view themselves as having more flaws or deficits, compared to those who rarely feel social anxiety (Clark & Wells, 1995); thus, for SAD sufferers, social interactions may seem like dangerous places where flaws can be observed and scrutinized (Moscovitch, 2009).

At first, researchers believed that the core feature of SAD was a fear of negative evaluation —being preoccupied with the possibility of being unfavorably judged or rejected by others (Watson & Friend, 1969). Recent evidence has suggested that people with SAD are actually concerned with both positive and negative evaluation. Fear of positive evaluation is the dread associated with success and public favorable evaluation, raising the expectations for subsequent social interactions. The fear of being positively evaluated is particularly relevant when a social comparison occurs, such as when a person gets a promotion at work (Weeks, Heimberg, Rodebaugh, & Norton, 2008; Weeks, Heimberg, & Rodebaugh, 2008). Both of these fears of evaluation contribute to social anxiety (Weeks, Heimberg, Rodebaugh, Goldin, & Gross, 2012).

Why might socially anxious people dread being praised? Gilbert's (2001) evolutionary theory suggests that social anxiety is a mechanism that evolved to facilitate group cohesion. When in society there are people of different social ranks, a person lower on the social hierarchy (e.g., an entry-level employee) would experience anxiety when interacting with higher-ranking group members (e.g., bosses). Such anxiety would lead a person to display submissive behavior (e.g., avoiding eye contact) and prompt them to avoid doing anything that could cause conflict. Anything that increases social status—such as receiving a promotion or dating an attractive romantic partner—can cause tension and conflict with others of higher status. Whereas fear of negative evaluation is relevant to other psychological conditions, such as depression and eating disorders, fear of positive evaluation is unique to SAD (Fergus et al., 2009; Weeks, Heimberg, Rodebaugh, et al., 2008). Furthermore, when people are successfully treated for SAD, this fear of positive evaluation declines (Weeks et al., 2012).

Biased Attention and Interpretation

If you were to observe what people with SAD pay attention to in a social interaction, you would find that they are quick to recognize any signs of social threats. For instance, they are faster at detecting angry faces in a crowd (see Gilboa-Schechtman, Foa, & Amir, 1999). Imagine looking at the audience as you give a speech and the first faces you notice are scowling back!

At the same time, SAD sufferers' attention is biased *away* from positive, rewarding information (see Taylor, Bomyea, & Amir, 2010). This means that people with SAD are unlikely to notice the smiling, nodding faces in the crowd, and they fail to pick up the subtle hints that somebody wants to spend more time with them or to be asked out on a romantic date. These interpretation and attention biases are obstacles to starting and maintaining social relationships. When you attend to only negativity, you start to believe that you are unlovable and that the world is a hostile, unfriendly place.

Complete the following sentence: "As I passed a group of people in the hall, they burst out in laughter, because . . ."

People with SAD are more likely to complete the sentence with a statement suggesting that there is something wrong with their behavior or appearance (e.g., "they thought I looked ridiculous") as opposed to a neutral explanation (e.g., "one of them made a joke"). The problem is that when you assume people are attacking you, you feel more self-conscious and are less likely to stay in a situation and to interact with that group of people or others in the future. Our thoughts influence our behavior, and the negative interpretations and predictions of people with SAD only serve to feed their social avoidance patterns (Amir, Beard, & Bower, 2005).

People with SAD may apply interpretation biases to social situations that cause them to accentuate perceived negative interactions while failing to take notice of positive interactions. [Image: hobvias sudoneighm, https://goo.gl/q46fPn, CC BY 2.0, https://goo.gl/BRvSA7]

Deficient Positive Experiences

The strongest predictor of a happy, meaningful, long-lasting life is the presence of satisfying, healthy relationships (Berscheid & Reis, 1998). Thus, the fact that people with SAD frequently avoid social interactions—even those with the potential for fun or intimacy—means that they miss out on an important source of positive experiences.

By studying people's day-to-day experiences, researchers have discovered several positivity deficits in the lives of socially anxious people. For example, Kashdan and Collins (2010) gave participants portable electronic devices that randomly prompted them to describe what they were feeling and doing multiple times per day for several weeks. During such random assessments, socially anxious people reported less intense positive emotions (e.g., joy, happiness, calm), regardless of whether they were around other people (whereas, less anxious people report more intense positive emotions when socializing). Socially anxious people experience less frequent positive emotions even when spending time with close friends and family members (Brown, Silvia, Myin-Germeys, & Kwapil, 2007; Vittengl & Holt, 1998). In fact, even in the most intimate of situations—during sexual encounters with romantic partners—socially anxious people report less intense pleasure and less intimacy (Kashdan, Adams, et al., 2011). All of these findings highlight the vast reach of excessive social anxiety in people's lives and how it detracts from the relationships and activities that hold the greatest promise for happiness and meaning in life (Kashdan, Weeks, & Savostyanova, 2011).

Individuals with SAD may suffer from "positivity deficits" that limit the frequency or intensity of positive emotions such as joy or calm. [Image: Jan Jespersen, https://goo.gl/ohXejY, CC BY-NC 2.0, https://goo.gl/VnKlK8]

Problematic Emotion Regulation

A possible explanation for the distress and diminished positive experiences seen in SAD is that the sufferers' ability to respond to and manage their emotions is impaired. Emotion regulation refers to how people recognize, interpret, experience, and attempt to alter emotional states (Gross, 1998). One symptom of SAD is the concern that the anxiety will be visible to others (APA, 2013). Given this concern, socially anxious people spend considerable time and effort preparing for and avoiding anxiety-related thoughts, sensations, and behaviors. They engage in safety behaviors, such as rehearsing exactly what to say in a conversation, asking questions of others to deflect attention from themselves, and holding a drink or food to have an excuse to pause before responding to a question (Clark & Wells, 1995). Because there is only so much we can pay attention to in a given moment, excessive self-focused attention detracts from a person's ability to be mindful in a social encounter. In effect, by devoting effort to controlling emotions and minimizing the potential for rejection, a person paradoxically increases the likelihood of misunderstanding others or appearing aloof. Such encounters are also less enjoyable and possess less potential for deepening relationships.

Socially anxious people believe that openly expressing emotions is likely to have negative consequences (Juretic & Zivcic-Becirevic, 2013). In turn, they are more apt to suppress or hide their negative emotions (Spokas, Luterek, & Heimberg, 2009) and avoid anything that is distressing (Kashdan, Morina, & Priebe, 2009). Emotion suppression is often ineffective: the more we try not to think about something, the more we end up thinking about it (Richards & Gross, 1999). Unfortunately, people with SAD report being less skilled at using more effective emotion regulation strategies, such as finding alternative, constructive ways of thinking about a situation (Werner, Goldin, Ball, Heimberg, & Gross, 2011).

Socially anxious people also respond to positive emotions in an unexpected way. Whereas most people not only enjoy positive emotions but also seek them out and attempt to savor them, socially anxious people often fear intense positive emotions (Turk, Heimberg, Luterek, Mennin, & Fresco, 2005). When positive emotions arise, just like negative emotions, SAD sufferers make efforts to suppress them (Eisner, Johnson, & Carver, 2009; Farmer & Kashdan, 2012). Why downplay positive emotions? It is possible that avoiding public displays of positive emotions is another way that people with SAD can avoid scrutiny (e.g., not laughing because others might not find a joke funny) and prevent the wrath of powerful others (e.g., not expressing excitement about a personal triumph because others might be envious) (Weeks et al., 2008). A recent study sampled the day-to-day social interactions of people with and without SAD to uncover what distinguishes these two groups. What the researchers found was that the amount of social anxiety felt during social interactions was less important in distinguishing people with SAD from healthy adults than the intense effort put into avoid feeling anxious and infrequent positive emotions when spending time with other people (Kashdan et al., 2013).

The ego depletion model (Muraven & Baumeister, 2000) proposes that people have a limited capacity for physical and mental self-control (e.g., physical endurance, attention). When we perform tasks that require significant effort and energy (e.g., suppressing emotions), we deplete these self-control resources, leaving us with less capacity to focus on subsequent tasks or to make good decisions (Vohs, Baumeister, & Ciarocco, 2005). When depleted or mentally exhausted, we tend to opt for whatever is immediately rewarding as opposed to pursuing meaningful goals (Hayes, Luoma, Bond, Masuda, & Lillis, 2006). For socially anxious people, what is immediately rewarding tends to be escaping or avoiding social situations in order to minimize the potential for unpleasant feelings. In other words, the way people with high social anxiety control their emotions not only makes their social situations less pleasant in the moment but also limits their capacity for pursuing rewarding opportunities afterward. Consistent with this, Farmer and Kashdan (2012) demonstrated that over the course of two weeks, when socially anxious people used more emotion suppression, they experienced fewer pleasant social events and less intense positive emotions on the following day. Taken together, this research suggests that socially anxious people respond to their emotions in ways that have far-reaching effects on their well-being, likely maintaining fears associated with social anxiety.

Treatments

Although SAD tends to be a chronic condition if left untreated (Wittchen, Fuetsch, Sonntag, Müller, & Liebowitz, 2000), the good news is that there are effective treatments that reduce social fears. Currently, there are two gold-standard treatments for SAD: cognitive behavioral therapy (CBT) and pharmacotherapy (Gould, Buckminster, Pollack, & Otto, 1997). The frontrunner among psychotherapy options, CBT, is an approach mental health professionals (e.g., licensed clinical psychologists) use to help people with SAD learn to think, behave, and feel differently so that they can feel more comfortable in social situations and improve their quality of life (Heimberg & Becker, 2002).

The most effective strategy to treat SAD is exposure (Feske & Chambless, 1995)—where clients repeatedly confront their feared situations without the use of safety behaviors, starting with situations that are only slightly anxiety provoking (e.g., imagining a conversation with an attractive stranger) and gradually working their way up to more frightening situations (e.g., starting conversations with trained actors during therapy sections). Additional exposures are then assigned between sessions so that people can experiment with feared situations in their daily lives (e.g., saying hello to a passing pedestrian). As another example, someone who avoids riding elevators due to fear of interacting with other riders might start out by taking an elevator during off-peak hours, then during popular times, and then practicing talking with a stranger while riding an elevator, and so on. After taking part in these exposures, people learn that feared social situations are not as probable or dangerous as previously believed.

The exposure strategy encourages people with SAD to gradually build up their exposure to feared situations – like having conversations in public – without safety behaviors. [Image: torbakhopper, https://goo.gl/BqeFh2, CC BY-NC-ND 2.0, https://goo.gl/bhtmIY]

Cognitive techniques form the other component of CBT. These are strategies therapists use to help people develop more realistic and helpful thoughts and expectations about social situations. For example, people with SAD often have unrealistic beliefs that contribute to anxiety (e.g., "Everyone can see that I'm sweating"). The therapist helps them challenge such thoughts and develop more helpful expectations about situations (e.g., from "If I pause while speaking, then everyone will think I'm stupid" to "It is OK to pause; the silence may seem longer to me than to others"). These techniques are most effective in combination with behavioral techniques that help clients test out some of their assumptions in real situations (Taylor, 1996). For instance, a behavioral experiment might involve giving a cashier the wrong change (making a mistake), to test whether the feared consequence ("the cashier will laugh at me") actually arises and, if so, whether it is as painful as expected.

Pharmacotherapy for SAD involves using medications to reduce people's anxiety level so that they are able to stop avoiding situations and enjoy a better quality of life. The current first-line prescribed medications are selective serotonin re-uptake inhibitors (SSRIs), such as escitalopram, paroxetine, and sertraline, as well as serotonin norepinephrine reuptake inhibitors (SNRIs) like venlafaxine (Bandelow et al., 2012). Both of these medications are typically used as antidepressants that act on the neurotransmitter serotonin, which plays a big role in how the amygdala responds to possibly threatening information. SNRIs also act on norepinephrine at higher doses. These medications have few side effects and also are likely to improve symptoms of other anxiety or depression symptoms that often co-occur with SAD. Other classes of medications with some evidence of helpfulness for SAD symptoms include benzodiazepines and monoamine oxidase inhibitors, though these medications often produce a number of negative side effects (Blanco, Bragdon, Schneier, & Liebowitz, 2013).

Both approaches—CBT and medications—are moderately helpful at reducing social anxiety symptoms in approximately 60% of clients; however, the majority of people with SAD do not fully remit, and many experience a return of symptoms after treatment ends (Fedoroff & Taylor, 2001). Notably, CBT tends to have more lasting effects, and there is some modest evidence for possible added benefit when combining medications with psychotherapy (Blanco et al., 2010). It is obvious, though, that existing treatments are insufficient.

Current recommended treatments may not address some of the deficits discussed earlier. Specifically, people may avoid fewer social situations, but they might still have fewer, less intense positive life experiences. Researchers are constantly improving available treatments via new techniques and medications. Some new developments in the treatment of SAD include the encouragement of mindful awareness (vs. self-focus) and acceptance (vs. avoidance) of experiences (Dalrymple & Herbert, 2007; Goldin & Gross, 2010). As new treatments develop, it will be important to see whether these treatments not only improve SAD symptoms but also help sufferers achieve greater happiness, meaning in life, and success.

Conclusions

In this module, we discussed the normal experience of social anxiety as well as the clinically impairing distress suffered by people with SAD. It is important to remember that nearly every psychological experience and characteristic you will read about exists on a continuum. What appears to distinguish people with SAD from healthy adults is not the presence of intense social anxiety but the unwillingness to experience anxious thoughts, feelings, and sensations, and the immense effort put into avoiding this discomfort. Other problems linked to excessive social anxiety include infrequent positive events, diminished positive experiences, and a tendency to view benign and even positive social situations as threatening. Together, these symptoms prevent people from initiating and maintaining healthy social relationships, and lead to deficient well-being. When social fears become overwhelming, it is important to remember that effective treatments are available to improve one's quality of life.

Outside Resources

Institution: Andrew Kukes Foundation for Social Anxiety
http://akfsa.org/
Institution: Anxiety and Depression Association of America
http://www.adaa.org/

Video: Social Anxiety Documentary – Afraid of People

- https://youtu.be/gmEJEfy5f50

Web: CalmClinic

http://www.calmclinic.com/

Web: Which Celebrities Suffer with Social Anxiety?

https://www.verywell.com/which-celebrities-suffer-with-social-anxiety-3024283

Discussion Questions

1. What differentiates people who are shy from those with social anxiety disorder?

2. Because the most effective treatment for social anxiety disorder is exposure to feared situations, what kinds of exposures would you devise for someone who fears talking in front of an audience? Engaging in small talk? Writing or eating in front of others? Speaking up in a small group? Talking to strangers?

3. Why might social anxiety disorder typically begin in late childhood/early adolescence?

4. How does culture influence fears of negative and positive evaluation? After all, social groups differ in their adherence to a vertical social hierarchy.

5. What may be some reasons people with severe social anxiety might not seek or receive treatment? How would you remove these obstacles?

Vocabulary

Amygdala

A brain structure in the limbic system involved in fear reactivity and implicated in the biological basis for social anxiety disorder.

Anxiety

A state of worry or apprehension about future events or possible danger that usually involves negative thoughts, unpleasant physical sensations, and/or a desire to avoid harm.

Cognitive behavioral therapy (CBT)

Psychotherapy approach that incorporates cognitive techniques (targeting unhelpful thoughts) and behavioral techniques (changing behaviors) to improve psychological symptoms.

Ego depletion

The idea that people have a limited pool of mental resources for self-control (e.g., regulating emotions, willpower), and this pool can be used up (depleted).

Emotion regulation

The ability to recognize emotional experiences and respond to situations by engaging in strategies to manage emotions as necessary.

Exposure treatment

A technique used in behavior therapy that involves a patient repeatedly confronting a feared situation, without danger, to reduce anxiety.

Fear of negative evaluation

The preoccupation with and dread of the possibility of being judged negatively by others.

Fear of positive evaluation

The dread associated with favorable public evaluation or acknowledgment of success, particularly when it involves social comparison.

Pharmacotherapy

A treatment approach that involves using medications to alter a person's neural functioning to reduce psychological symptoms.

Safety behaviors

Actions people take to reduce likelihood of embarrassment or minimizing anxiety in a situation (e.g., not making eye contact, planning what to say).

Selective serotonin re-uptake inhibitors (SSRIs)

A class of antidepressant medications often used to treat SAD that increase the concentration of the neurotransmitter serotonin in the brain.

Serotonin norepinephrine reuptake inhibitors (SNRIs)

A class of antidepressant medications often used to treat SAD that increase the concentration of serotonin and norepinephrine in the brain.

Social anxiety

Excessive anticipation and distress about social situations in which one may be evaluated negatively, rejected, or scrutinized.

Social anxiety disorder (SAD)

An anxiety disorder marked by severe and persistent social anxiety and avoidance that interferes with a person's ability to fulfill their roles in important life domains.

References

- American Psychiatric Association. (2013). *Diagnostic and statistical manual of mental disorders* (5th ed.). Arlington, VA: American Psychiatric Publishing.

- Amir, N., Beard, C., & Bower, E. (2005). Interpretation bias and social anxiety. *Cognitive Therapy and Research, 29*(4), 433–443. doi:10.1007/s10608-005-2834-5

- Bandelow, B., Sher, L., Bunevicius, R., Hollander, E., Kasper, S., Zohar, J., … WFSBP Task Force on Anxiety Disorders, OCD and PTSD. (2012). Guidelines for the pharmacological treatment of anxiety disorders, obsessive–compulsive disorder and posttraumatic stress disorder in primary care. *International Journal of Psychiatry in Clinical Practice, 16*(2), 77–84. doi:10.3109/13651501.2012.667114

- Berscheid, E., & Reis, H. T. (1998). Attraction and close relationships. In D. T. Gilbert, S. T. Fiske, & G. Lindzey (Eds.), *The handbook of social psychology* (4th ed., Vols. 1 and 2, pp. 193–281). New York, NY: McGraw-Hill.

- Blanco, C., Bragdon, L. B., Schneier, F. R., & Liebowitz, M. R. (2013). The evidence-based pharmacotherapy of social anxiety disorder. *The International Journal of Neuropsychopharmacology, 16*(01), 235–249. doi:10.1017/S1461145712000119

- Blanco, C., Heimberg, R. G., Schneier, F. R., Fresco, D. M., Chen, H., Turk, C. L., … Liebowitz, M. R. (2010). A placebo-controlled trial of phenelzine, cognitive behavioral group therapy, and their combination for social anxiety disorder. *Archives of General Psychiatry, 67*(3), 286–295. doi:10.1001/archgenpsychiatry.2010.11

- Brown, L. H., Silvia, P. J., Myin-Germeys, I., & Kwapil, T. R. (2007). When the need to belong goes wrong: the expression of social anhedonia and social anxiety in daily life. *Psychological Science, 18,* 778–782. doi:10.1111/j.1467-9280.2007.01978.x

- Bögels, S. M., & Mansell, W. (2004). Attention processes in the maintenance and treatment of social phobia: hypervigilance, avoidance and self-focused attention. *Clinical Psychology Review, 24*(7), 827–856. doi:10.1016/j.cpr.2004.06.005

- Clark, D. M., & Wells, A. (1995). A cognitive model of social phobia. In *Social phobia: Diagnosis, assessment, and treatment* (pp. 69–93). New York: Guilford Press.

- Dalrymple, K. L., & Herbert, J. D. (2007). Acceptance and commitment therapy for generalized social anxiety disorder: A pilot study. *Behavior Modification, 31,* 543–568. doi:10.1177/0145445507302037

- Eisner, L. R., Johnson, S. L., & Carver, C. S. (2009). Positive affect regulation in anxiety disorders. *Journal of Anxiety Disorders, 23*(5), 645–649. doi:10.1016/j.janxdis.2009.02.001

- Farmer, A. S., & Kashdan, T. B. (2012). Social anxiety and emotion regulation in daily life: Spillover effects on positive and negative social events. *Cognitive Behaviour Therapy, 41,* 152–162. doi:10.1080/16506073.2012.666561

- Fedoroff, I. C., & Taylor, S. (2001). Psychological and pharmacological treatments of social phobia: A meta-analysis. *Journal of Clinical Psychopharmacology, 21*(3), 311–324. doi:10.1097/00004714-200106000-00011

- Fergus, T. A., Valentiner, D. P., McGrath, P. B., Stephenson, K., Gier, S., & Jencius, S. (2009). The Fear of Positive Evaluation Scale: Psychometric properties in a clinical sample. *Journal of Anxiety Disorders, 23*(8), 1177–1183. doi:10.1016/j.janxdis.2009.07.024

- Feske, U., & Chambless, D. L. (1995). Cognitive behavioral versus exposure only treatment for social phobia: A meta-analysis. *Behavior Therapy, 26*(4), 695–720. doi:10.1016/S0005-7894(05)80040-1

- Frijda, N. H. (1996). Passions: Emotion and socially consequential behavior. In *Emotion: Interdisciplinary perspectives* (pp. 1–27). Hillsdale, NJ: Lawrence Erlbaum Associates, Inc.

- Gilbert, P. (2001). Evolution and social anxiety: The role of attraction, social competition, and social hierarchies. *Psychiatric Clinics of North America, 24*(4), 723–751. doi:10.1016/S0193-953X(05)70260-4

- Goldin, P. R., & Gross, J. J. (2010). Effects of mindfulness-based stress reduction (MBSR) on emotion regulation in social anxiety disorder. *Emotion, 10*(1), 83–91. doi:10.1037/a0018441

- Gould, R. A., Buckminster, S., Pollack, M. H., & Otto, M. W. (1997). Cognitive-behavioral and pharmacological treatment for social phobia: A meta-analysis. *Clinical Psychology: Science and Practice, 4*(4), 291–306. doi:10.1111/j.1468-2850.1997.tb00123.x

- Gross, J. J. (1998). The emerging field of emotion regulation: An integrative review. *Review of General Psychology, 2*(3), 271–299. doi:10.1037/1089-2680.2.3.271

- Hayes, S. C., Luoma, J. B., Bond, F. W., Masuda, A., & Lillis, J. (2006). Acceptance and commitment therapy: Model, processes and outcomes. *Behaviour Research and Therapy, 44*(1), 1–25. doi:10.1016/j.brat.2005.06.006

- Heimberg, R. G., & Becker, R. E. (2002). *Treatment of social fears and phobias*. New York, NY: Guilford Press

- Juretic, J., & Zivcic-Becirevic, I. (2013). Social anxiety, beliefs about expressing emotions and experiencing positive emotions. In F. Durbano (Ed.), *New insights into anxiety disorders*. Rijeka, Croatia: InTech.

- Kashdan, T. B., & Collins, R. L. (2010). Social anxiety and the experience of positive emotion and anger in everyday life: An ecological momentary assessment approach. *Anxiety, Stress & Coping, 23*(3), 259–272. doi:10.1080/10615800802641950

- Kashdan, T. B., Adams, L., Savostyanova, A., Ferssizidis, P., McKnight, P. E., & Nezlek, J. B. (2011). Effects of social anxiety and depressive symptoms on the frequency and quality of sexual activity: A daily process approach. *Behaviour Research and Therapy, 49,* 352–360. doi:10.1016/j.brat.2011.03.004

- Kashdan, T. B., Christopher Frueh, B., Knapp, R. G., Hebert, R., & Magruder, K. M. (2006). Social anxiety disorder in veterans affairs primary care clinics. *Behaviour Research and Therapy, 44*(2), 233–247. doi:10.1016/j.brat.2005.02.002

- Kashdan, T. B., Farmer, A. S., Adams, L. M., Ferssizidis, P., McKnight, P. E., & Nezlek, J. B. (2013). Distinguishing healthy adults from people with social anxiety disorder: Evidence for the value of experiential avoidance and positive emotions in everyday social interactions. *Journal of Abnormal Psychology, 122*(3), 645–655. doi:10.1037/a0032733

- Kashdan, T. B., Morina, N., & Priebe, S. (2009). Post-traumatic stress disorder, social anxiety disorder, and depression in survivors of the Kosovo War: Experiential avoidance as a contributor to distress and quality of life. *Journal of Anxiety Disorders, 23,* 185–196. doi:10.1016/j.janxdis.2008.06.006

- Kashdan, T. B., Weeks, J. W., & Savostyanova, A. A. (2011). Whether, how, and when social anxiety shapes positive experiences and events: A self-regulatory framework and treatment implications. *Clinical Psychology Review, 31,* 786–799. doi:10.1016/j.cpr.2011.03.012

- Kessler, R. C., Berglund, P., Demler, O., Jin, R., Merikangas, K. R., & Walters, E. E. (2005). Lifetime prevalence and age-of-onset distributions of DSM-IV disorders in the National Comorbidity Survey Replication. *Archives of General Psychiatry, 62*(6), 593–602. doi:10.1001/archpsyc.62.6.593

- Leary, M. R., & Kowalski, R. M. (1995). *Social anxiety* (Vol. xii). New York, NY: Guilford Press.

- Moscovitch, D. A. (2009). What is the core fear in social phobia? A new model to facilitate individualized case conceptualization and treatment. *Cognitive and Behavioral Practice, 16,* 123–134. doi:10.1016/j.cbpra.2008.04.002

- Muraven, M., & Baumeister, R. F. (2000). Self-regulation and depletion of limited resources: Does self-control resemble a muscle? *Psychological Bulletin, 126*(2), 247–259. doi:10.1037/0033-2909.126.2.247

- Richards, J. M., & Gross, J. J. (1999). Composure at any cost? The cognitive consequences of emotion suppression. *Personality and Social Psychology Bulletin, 25*(8), 1033–1044. doi:10.1177/01461672992511010

- Ruscio, A. M., Brown, T. A., Chiu, W. T., Sareen, J., Stein, M. B., & Kessler, R. C. (2008). Social fears and social phobia in the USA: Results from the National Comorbidity Survey Replication. *Psychological Medicine, 38*(1), 15–28. doi:10.1017/S0033291707001699

- Schneier, F. R., Johnson, J., Hornig, C. D., Liebowitz, M. R., & Weissman, M. M. (1992). Social phobia: Comorbidity and morbidity in an epidemiologic sample. *Archives of General Psychiatry, 49*(4), 282–288. doi:10.1001/archpsyc.1992.01820040034004

- Spokas, M., Luterek, J. A., & Heimberg, R. G. (2009). Social anxiety and emotional suppression: The mediating role of beliefs. *Journal of Behavior Therapy and Experimental Psychiatry, 40,* 283–291. doi:10.1016/j.jbtep.2008.12.004

- Taylor, C. T., Bomyea, J., & Amir, N. (2010). Attentional bias away from positive social information mediates the link between social anxiety and anxiety vulnerability to a social stressor. *Journal of Anxiety Disorders, 24*(4), 403–408. doi:10.1016/j.janxdis.2010.02.004

- Taylor, S. (1996). Meta-analysis of cognitive-behavioral treatments for social phobia. *Journal of Behavior Therapy and Experimental Psychiatry, 27*(1), 1–9.

- Turk, C. L., Heimberg, R. G., Luterek, J. A., Mennin, D. S., & Fresco, D. M. (2005). Emotion dysregulation in generalized anxiety disorder: A comparison with social anxiety disorder. *Cognitive Therapy and Research, 29*(1), 89–106. doi:10.1007/s10608-005-1651-1

- Vittengl, J. R., & Holt, C. S. (1998). A time-series diary study of mood and social interaction. *Motivation and Emotion, 22*(3), 255–275.

- Vohs, K. D., Baumeister, R. F., & Ciarocco, N. J. (2005). Self-regulation and self-presentation: Regulatory resource depletion impairs impression management and effortful self-presentation depletes regulatory resources. *Journal of Personality and Social Psychology, 88,* 632–657. doi:10.1037/0022-3514.88.4.632

- Watson, D., & Friend, R. (1969). Measurement of social-evaluative anxiety. *Journal of Consulting and Clinical Psychology, 33,* 448–457. doi:10.1037/h0027806

- Weeks, J. W., Heimberg, R. G., & Rodebaugh, T. L. (2008). The Fear of Positive Evaluation Scale: Assessing a proposed cognitive component of social anxiety. *Journal of Anxiety Disorders, 22*(1), 44–55. doi:10.1016/j.janxdis.2007.08.002

- Weeks, J. W., Heimberg, R. G., Rodebaugh, T. L., & Norton, P. J. (2008). Exploring the relationship between fear of positive evaluation and social anxiety. *Journal of Anxiety Disorders, 22*, 386–400. doi:10.1016/j.janxdis.2007.04.009

- Weeks, J. W., Heimberg, R. G., Rodebaugh, T. L., Goldin, P. R., & Gross, J. J. (2012). Psychometric evaluation of the Fear of Positive Evaluation Scale in patients with social anxiety disorder. *Psychological Assessment, 24*(2), 301–312. doi:10.1037/a0025723

- Werner, K., Goldin, P., Ball, T., Heimberg, R., & Gross, J. (2011). Assessing emotion regulation in social anxiety disorder: The emotion regulation interview. *Journal of Psychopathology and Behavioral Assessment, 33*(3), 346–354. doi:10.1007/s10862-011-9225-x

- Wittchen, H. U., Fuetsch, M., Sonntag, H., Müller, N., & Liebowitz, M. (2000). Disability and quality of life in pure and comorbid social phobia. Findings from a controlled study. *European Psychiatry, 15*(1), 46–58. doi:10.1016/S0924-9338(00)00211-X

- ilboa-Schechtman, E., Foa, E. B., & Amir, N. (1999). Attentional biases for facial expressions in social phobia: The face-in-the-crowd paradigm. *Cognition & Emotion, 13*(3), 305–318. doi:10.1080/026999399379294

CC licensed content, Shared previously

Dissociative Disorders

In psychopathology, dissociation happens when thoughts, feelings, and experiences of our consciousness and memory do not collaborate well with each other. This module provides an overview of dissociative disorders, including the definitions of dissociation, its origins and competing theories, and their relation to traumatic experiences and sleep problems.

Learning Objectives

- Define the basic terminology and historical origins of dissociative symptoms and dissociative disorders.
- Describe the posttraumatic model of dissociation and the sleep-dissociation model, and the controversies and debate between these competing theories.
- What is the innovative angle of the sleep-dissociation model?
- How can the two models be combined into one conceptual scheme?

Introduction

Think about the last time you were daydreaming. Perhaps it was while you were driving or attending class. Some portion of your attention was on the activity at hand, but most of your conscious mind was wrapped up in fantasy. Now imagine that you could not control your daydreams. What if they intruded your waking consciousness unannounced, causing you to lose track of reality or experience the loss of time. Imagine how difficult it would be for you. This is similar to what people who suffer from dissociative disorders may experience. Of the many disorders listed in the *Diagnostic and Statistical Manual of Mental Disorders* (DSM-5) (American Psychiatric Association, 2013), dissociative disorders rank as among the most puzzling and controversial. Dissociative disorders encompass an array of symptoms ranging from memory loss (amnesia) for autobiographical events, to changes in identity and the experience of everyday reality (American Psychiatric Association, 2013).

Is it real?

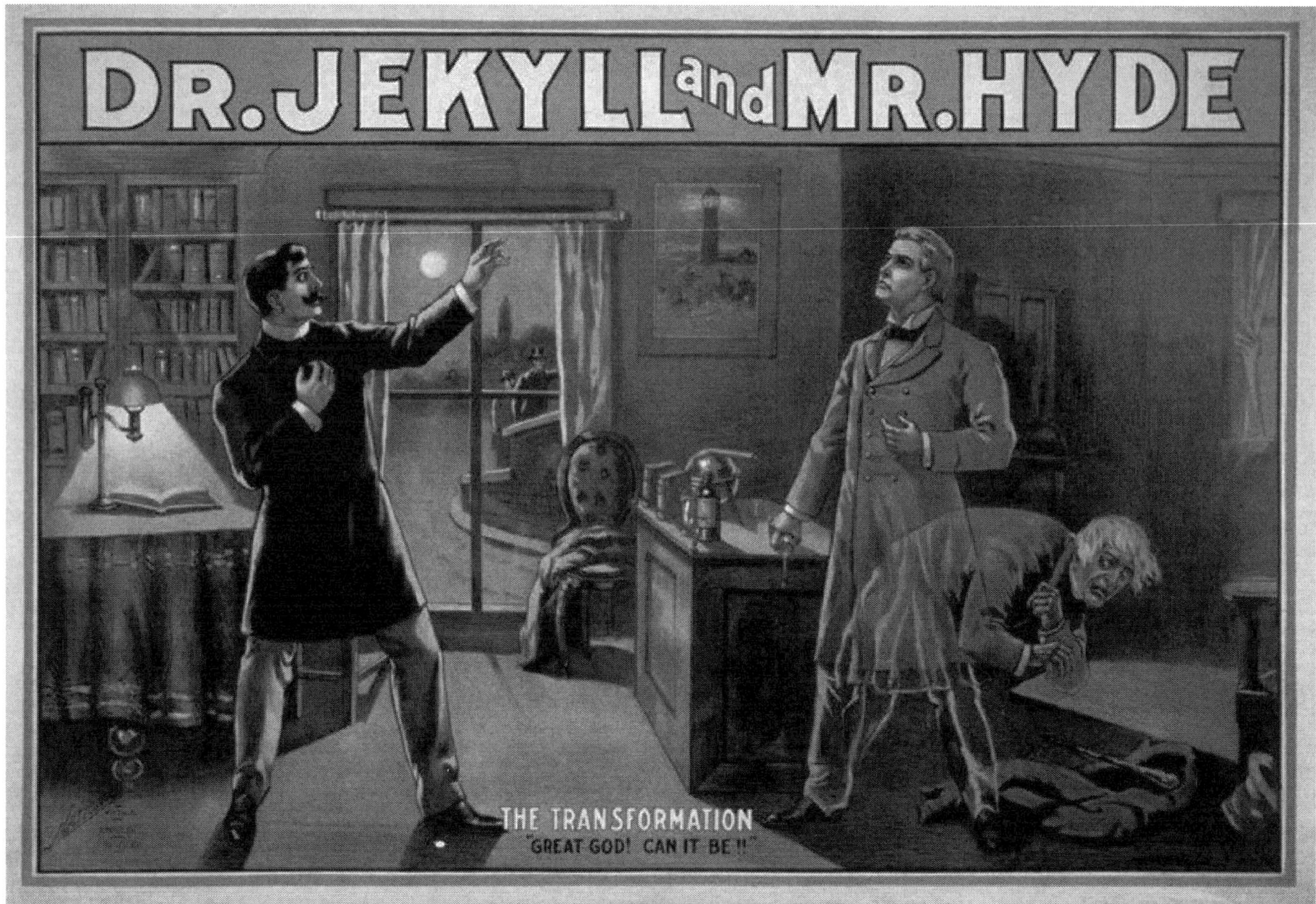

Dissociative disorders are often exaggerated when portrayed in television, books and movies; however, there is concrete evidence that people do suffer from these disorders. [Image: Library of Congress, https://goo.gl/BrTchp, CC BY-NC 3.0, https://goo.gl/osSgSv]

Let's start with a little history. Multiple personality disorder, or dissociative identity disorder—as it is known now—used to be a mere curiosity. This is a disorder in which people present with more than one personality. For example, at times they might act and identify as an adult while at other times they might identify and behave like a child. The disorder was rarely diagnosed until the 1980s. That's when multiple personality disorder became an official diagnosis in the DSM-III. From then on, the numbers of "multiples" increased rapidly. In the 1990s, there were hundreds of people diagnosed with multiple personality in every major city in the United States (Hacking, 1995). How could this "epidemic" be explained?

One possible explanation might be the media attention that was given to the disorder. It all started with the book *The Three Faces of Eve* (Thigpen & Cleckley, 1957). This book, and later the movie, was one of the first to speak of multiple personality disorder. However, it wasn't until years later, when the fictional "as told to" book of *Sybil* (Schreiber, 1973) became known worldwide, that the prototype of what it was like to be a "multiple personality" was born. Sybil tells the story of how a clinician—Cornelia Wilbur—unravels the different personalities of her patient Sybil during a long course of treatment (over 2,500 office hours!). She was one of the first to relate multiple personality to childhood sexual abuse. Probably, this relation between childhood abuse and dissociation has fueled the increase of numbers of multiples from that time on. It motivated therapists to actively seek for clues of childhood abuse in their dissociative patients. This suited well within the mindset of the 1980s, as childhood abuse was a sensitive issue then in psychology as well as in politics (Hacking, 1995).

From then on, many movies and books were made on the subject of multiple personality, and nowadays, we see patients with dissociative identity disorder as guests visiting the Oprah Winfrey show, as if they were our modern-day circus acts.

Defining dissociation

The DSM-5 defines dissociation as "a disruption and/or discontinuity in the normal integration of consciousness, memory, identity, emotion, perception, body representation, motor control and behavior" (American Psychiatric Association, 2013, p. 291). A distinction is often made between dissociative *states* and dissociative *traits* (e.g., Bremner, 2010; Bremner & Brett, 1997). State dissociation is viewed as a transient symptom, which lasts for a few minutes or hours (e.g., dissociation during a traumatic event). Trait dissociation is viewed as an integral aspect of personality. Dissociative symptoms occur in patients but also in the general population, like you and me. Therefore, dissociation has commonly been conceptualized as ranging on a continuum, from nonsevere manifestations of daydreaming to more severe disturbances typical of dissociative disorders (Bernstein & Putnam, 1986). The dissociative disorders include:

1. Dissociative Amnesia (extensive forgetting typically associated with highly aversive events);

2. Dissociative Fugue (short-lived reversible amnesia for personal identity, involving unplanned travel or "bewildered wandering." Dissociative fugue is not viewed as a separate disorder but is a feature of some, but not all, cases of dissociative amnesia);

3. Depersonalization/Derealization Disorder (feeling as though one is an outside observer of one's body); and

4. Dissociative Identity Disorder (DID; experiencing two or more distinct identities that recurrently take control over one's behavior) (American Psychiatric Association, 2000).

Although the concept of dissociation lacks a generally accepted definition, the Structural Clinical Interview for DSM-IV Dissociative Disorders (SCID-D) (Steinberg, 2001) assesses five symptom clusters that encompass key features of the dissociative disorders. These clusters are also found in the DSM-5:

1. depersonalization,

2. derealization,

3. dissociative amnesia,

4. identity confusion, and

5. identity alteration.

Those experiencing depersonalization report "dreamlike feelings" and that their bodies, feelings, emotions, and behaviors are not their own. [Image: Janine, https://goo.gl/MDpyRG, CC BY-NC-ND 2.0, https://goo.gl/62XJAl]

Depersonalization refers to a "feeling of detachment or estrangement from one's self." Imagine that you are outside of your own body, looking at yourself from a distance as though you were looking at somebody else. Maybe you can also imagine what it would be like if you felt like a robot, deprived of all feelings. These are examples of depersonalization. Derealization is defined as "an alteration in the perception of one's surroundings so that a sense of reality of the external world is lost" (Steinberg, 2001, p. 101). Imagine that the world around you seems as if you are living in a movie, or looking through a fog. These are examples of derealization. Dissociative amnesia does not refer to permanent memory loss, similar to the erasure of a computer disk, but rather to the hypothetical disconnection of memories from conscious inspection (Steinberg, 2001). Thus, the memory is still there somewhere, but you cannot reach it. Identity confusion is defined by Steinberg as "… thoughts and feelings of uncertainty and conflict a person has related to his or her identity" (Steinberg, 2001, p. 101), whereas identity alteration describes the behavioral acting out of this uncertainty and conflict (Bernstein & Putnam, 1986).

Dissociative disorders are not as uncommon as you would expect. Several studies in a variety of patient groups show that dissociative disorders are prevalent in a 4%–29% range (Ross, Anderson, Fleischer, & Norton, 1991; Sar, Tutkun, Alyanak, Bakim, & Baral, 2000; Tutkun et al., 1998. For reviews see: Foote, Smolin, Kaplan, Legatt, & Lipschitz, 2006; Spiegel et al., 2011). Studies generally find a much lower prevalence in the general population, with rates in the order of 1%–3% (Lee, Kwok, Hunter, Richards, & David, 2010; Rauschenberger & Lynn, 1995; Sandberg & Lynn, 1992). Importantly, dissociative symptoms are not limited to the dissociative disorders. Certain diagnostic groups, notably patients with borderline personality disorder, posttraumatic stress disorder (PTSD), obsessive-compulsive disorder (Rufer, Fricke, Held, Cremer, & Hand, 2006), and schizophrenia (Allen & Coyne, 1995; Merckelbach, à Campo, Hardy, & Giesbrecht, 2005; Yu et al., 2010) also display heightened levels of dissociation.

Measuring dissociation

The Dissociative Experiences Scale (DES) (Bernstein & Putnam, 1986; Carlson & Putnam, 2000; Wright & Loftus, 1999) is the most widely used self-report measure of dissociation. A self-report measure is a type of psychological test in which a person completes a survey or questionnaire with or without the help of an investigator. This scale measures dissociation with items such as (a) "Some people sometimes have the experience of feeling as though they are standing next to themselves or watching themselves do something, and they actually see themselves as if they were looking at another person" and (b) "Some people find that sometimes they are listening to someone talk, and they suddenly realize that they did not hear part or all of what was said."

The DES is suitable only as a screening tool. When somebody scores a high level of dissociation on this scale, this does not necessarily mean that he or she is suffering from a dissociative disorder. It does, however, give an indication to investigate the symptoms more extensively. This is usually done with a structured clinical interview, called the Structured Clinical Interview for DSM-IV Dissociative Disorders (Steinberg, 1994), which is performed by an experienced clinician. With the publication of the new DSM-5 there has been an updated version of this instrument.

Dissociation and Trauma

The most widely held perspective on dissociative symptoms is that they reflect a defensive response to highly aversive events, mostly trauma experiences during the childhood years (Bremner, 2010; Spiegel et al., 2011; Spitzer, Vogel, Barnow, Freyberger, & Grabe, 2007).

One prominent interpretation of the origins of dissociative disorders is that they are the direct result of exposure to traumatic experiences. We will refer to this interpretation as the posttraumatic model (PTM). According to the PTM, dissociative symptoms can best be understood as mental strategies to cope with or avoid the impact of highly aversive experiences (e.g., Spiegel et al., 2011). In this view, individuals rely on dissociation to escape from painful memories (Gershuny & Thayer, 1999). Once they have learned to use this defensive coping mechanism, it can become automatized and habitual, even emerging in response to minor stressors (Van der Hart & Horst, 1989). The idea that dissociation can serve a defensive function can be traced back to Pierre Janet (1899/ 1973), one of the first scholars to link dissociation to psychological trauma (Hacking, 1995).

The PTM casts the clinical observation that dissociative disorders are linked to a trauma history in straightforward causal terms, that is, one *causes* the other (Gershuny & Thayer, 1999). For example, Vermetten and colleagues (Vermetten, Schmahl, Lindner, Loewenstein, & Bremner, 2006) found that the DID patients in their study all suffered from posttraumatic stress disorder and concluded that DID should be conceptualized as an extreme form of early-abuse–related posttraumatic stress disorder (Vermetten et al., 2006).

Causality and evidence

The empirical evidence that trauma *leads to* dissociative symptoms is the subject of intense debate (Kihlstrom, 2005; Bremner, 2010; Giesbrecht, Lynn, Lilienfeld & Merckelbach, 2010). Three limitations of the PTM will be described below.

First, the majority of studies reporting links between self-reported trauma and dissociation are based on cross-sectional designs. This means that the data are collected at one point in time. When analyzing this type of data, one can only state whether scoring high on a particular questionnaire (for example, a trauma questionnaire) is indicative of also scoring high on another questionnaire (for example, the DES). This makes it difficult to state if one thing led to another, and therefore if the relation between the two is *causal*. Thus, the data that these designs yield do not allow for strong causal claims (Merckelbach & Muris, 2002).

Second, whether somebody has experienced a trauma is often established using a questionnaire that the person completes himself or herself. This is called a self-report measure. Herein lies the problem. Individuals suffering from dissociative symptoms typically have high fantasy proneness. This is a character trait to engage in extensive and vivid fantasizing. The tendency to fantasize a lot may increase the risk of exaggerating or understating self-reports of traumatic experiences (Merckelbach et al., 2005; Giesbrecht, Lynn, Lilienfeld, & Merckelbach, 2008).

Third, high dissociative individuals report more cognitive failures than low dissociative individuals. Cognitive failures are everyday slips and lapses, such as failing to notice signposts on the road, forgetting appointments, or bumping into people. This can be seen, in part, in the DSM-5 criteria for DID, in which people may have difficulty recalling everyday events as well as those that are traumatic. People who frequently make such slips and lapses often mistrust their own cognitive capacities. They also tend to overvalue the hints and cues provided by others (Merckelbach, Horselenberg, & Schmidt, 2002; Merckelbach, Muris, Rassin, & Horselenberg, 2000). This makes them vulnerable to suggestive information, which may distort self-reports, and thus limits conclusions that can be drawn from studies that rely solely on self-reports to investigate the trauma-dissociation link (Merckelbach & Jelicic, 2004).

Most important, however, is that the PTM does not tell us *how* trauma produces dissociative symptoms. Therefore, workers in the field have searched for other explanations. They proposed that due to their dreamlike character, dissociative symptoms such as derealization, depersonalization, and absorption are associated with sleep-related experiences. They further noted that sleep-related experiences can explain the relation between highly aversive events and dissociative symptoms (Giesbrecht et al., 2008; Watson, 2001). In the following paragraph, the relation between dissociation and sleep will be discussed.

Dissociation and Sleep

A little history

Those who have fallen asleep in class or on the bus have likely experienced those "micro-dreams" – that moment or two where reality kind of blends in with your dreams. For a long time, scientists thought dissociative disorders were simply this confusion of waking and dreaming states. [Image: kooklanekookla, https://goo.gl/Cn3xul, CC BY 2.0, https://goo.gl/BRvSA7]

Researchers (Watson, 2001) have proposed that dissociative symptoms, such as absorption, derealization, and depersonalization originate from sleep. This idea is not entirely new. In the 19th century, double consciousness (or *dédoublement*), the historical precursor of dissociative identity disorder (DID; formerly known as multiple personality disorder), was often described as "somnambulism," which refers to a state of sleepwalking. Patients suffering from this disorder were referred to as "somnambules" (Hacking, 1995). Many 19th-century scholars believed that these patients were switching between a "normal state" and a "somnambulistic state." Hughlings Jackson, a well-known English neurologist from this era, viewed dissociation as the uncoupling of normal consciousness, which would result in what he termed "the dreamy state" (Meares, 1999). Interestingly, a century later, Levitan (1967) hypothesized that "depersonalization is a compromise state between dreaming and waking" (p.157). Arlow (1966) observed that the dissociation between the "experiencing self" and the "observing self" serves as the basis of depersonalized states, emphasizing its occurrence, especially in dreams. Likewise, Franklin (1990) considered dreamlike thoughts, the amnesia one usually has for dreams, and the lack of orientation of time, place, and person during dreams to be strikingly similar to the amnesia DID patients often report for their traumas. Related, Barrett (1994, 1995) described the similarity between dream characters and "alter personalities" in DID, with respect to cognitive and sensory abilities, movement, amnesia, and continuity with normal waking. The many similarities between dreaming states and dissociative symptoms are also a recurrent theme in the more recent clinical literature (e.g., Bob, 2004).

Sleep problems in patients with dissociative disorders

Anecdotal evidence supports the idea that sleep disruptions are linked to dissociation. For example, in patients with depersonalization, symptoms are worst when they are tired (Simeon & Abugel, 2006). Interestingly, among participants who report memories of childhood sexual abuse, experiences of sleep paralysis typically are accompanied by raised levels of dissociative symptoms (McNally & Clancy, 2005; Abrams, Mulligan, Carleton, & Asmundson, 2008).

Patients with mood disorders, anxiety disorders, schizophrenia, and borderline personality disorder—conditions with relatively high levels of dissociative symptoms—as a rule exhibit sleep abnormalities. Recent research points to fairly specific relationships between certain sleep complaints (e.g., insomnia, nightmares) and certain forms of psychopathology (e.g., depression, posttraumatic stress disorder) (Koffel & Watson, 2009).

Studying the relationship between dissociation and sleep

In the general population, both dissociative symptoms and sleep problems are highly prevalent. For example, 29 percent of American adults report sleep problems (National Sleep Foundation, 2005). This allows researchers to study the relationship between dissociation and sleep not only in patients but also in the general population. In a pioneering study, Watson (2001) showed that dissociative symptoms—measured by the DES—are linked to self-reports of vivid dreams, nightmares, recurrent dreams, and other unusual sleep phenomena. This relationship has been studied extensively ever since, leading to three important statements.

First, Watson's (2001) basic findings have been reproduced time and again. This means that the same results (namely that dissociation and sleep problems are related) have been found in lots of different studies, using different groups, and different materials. All lead to the conclusion that unusual sleep experiences and dissociative symptoms are linked.

Second, the connection between sleep and dissociation is specific. It seems that unusual sleep phenomena that are difficult to control, including nightmares and waking dreams, are related to dissociative symptoms, but lucid dreaming—dreams that are controllable—are only weakly related to dissociative symptoms. For example, dream recall frequency was related to dissociation (Suszek & Kopera, 2005). Individuals who reported three or more nightmares over a three-week period showed higher levels of dissociation compared to individuals reporting two nightmares or less (Levin & Fireman, 2002), and a relation was found between dream intensity and dissociation (Yu et al., 2010).

Third, the sleep-dissociation link is apparent not only in general population groups—people such as you and me—but also in patient groups. Accordingly, one group of researchers reported nightmare disorder in 17 out of 30 DID patients (Agargun et al., 2003). They also found a 27.5% prevalence of nocturnal dissociative episodes in patients with dissociative disorders (Agargun et al., 2001). Another study investigated a group of borderline personality disorder patients and found that 49% of them suffered from nightmare disorder. Moreover, the patients with nightmare disorder displayed higher levels of dissociation than patients not suffering from nightmare disorder (Semiz, Basoglu, Ebrinc, & Cetin, 2008). Additionally, Ross (2011) found that patients suffering from DID reported higher rates of sleepwalking compared to a group of psychiatric outpatients and a sample from the general population.

To sum up, there seems to be a strong relationship between dissociative symptoms and unusual sleep experiences that is evident in a range of phenomena, including waking dreams, nightmares, and sleepwalking.

Inducing and reducing sleep problems

Sleep problems can be induced in healthy participants by keeping them awake for a long duration of time. This is called sleep deprivation. If dissociative symptoms are fueled by a labile sleep-wake cycle, then sleep loss would be expected to intensify dissociative symptoms. Some evidence that this might work was already found in 2001, when soldiers who underwent a U.S. Army survival training, which included sleep deprivation, showed increases in dissociative symptoms (Morgan et al., 2001). Other researchers conducted a study that tracked 25 healthy volunteers during one day and one night of sleep loss. They found that dissociative symptoms increased substantially after one night of sleep loss (Giesbrecht, Smeets, Leppink, Jelicic, & Merckelbach, 2007).

To further examine the causal link between dissociative experiences and sleep, we (van der Kloet, Giesbrecht, Lynn, Merckelbach, & de Zutter, 2011) investigated the relationship between unusual sleep experiences and dissociation in a patient group at a private clinic. They completed questionnaires upon arrival at the clinic and again when they departed eight weeks later. During their stay, they followed a strict program designed to improve sleep problems. And it worked! In most patients, sleep quality was improved after eight weeks. We found a robust link between sleep experiences and dissociative symptoms and determined that sleep *normalization* was accompanied by a *reduction* in dissociative symptoms.

An exciting interpretation of the link between dissociative symptoms and unusual sleep phenomena (see also, Watson, 2001) may be this: A disturbed sleep–wake cycle may lead to dissociative symptoms. However, we should be cautious. Although studies support a causal arrow leading from sleep disruption to dissociative symptoms, the associations between sleep and dissociation may be more complex. For example, causal links may be bi-directional, such that dissociative symptoms may lead to sleep problems and vice versa, and other psychopathology may interfere in the link between sleep and dissociative symptoms (van der Kloet et al., 2011).

Implications and Conclusions

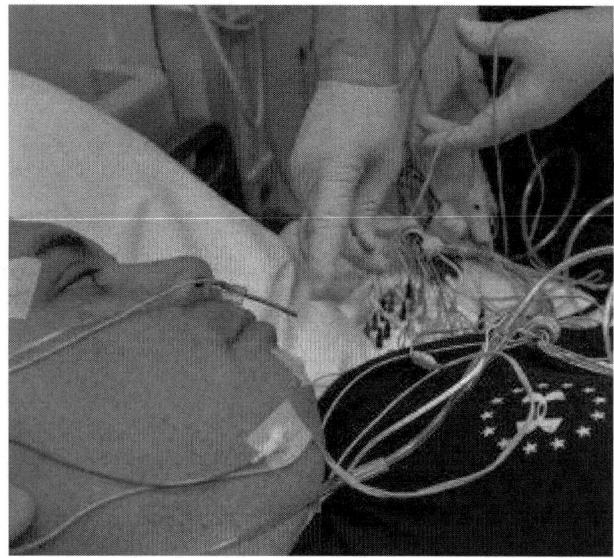

No longer are dissociative disorders untreatable illnesses. With the new methods developed by researchers, there is hope for curing or at least improving the lives of those with this debilitating disorder. [Image: CC0 Public Domain, https://goo.gl/m25gce]

The sleep-dissociation model offers a fresh and exciting perspective on dissociative symptoms. This model may seem remote from the PTM. However, both models can be integrated in a single conceptual scheme in which traumatic childhood experiences may lead to disturbed sleep patterns, which may be the final common pathway to dissociative symptoms. Accordingly, the sleep-dissociation model may explain both: (a) how traumatic experiences disrupt the sleep–wake cycle and increase vulnerability to dissociative symptoms, and (b) why dissociation, trauma, fantasy proneness, and cognitive failures overlap.Future studies can also discern what characteristic sleep disruptions in the sleep–wake cycle are most reliably related to dissociative disorders, and then establish training programs, including medication regimens, to address these problems. This would constitute an entirely novel and exciting approach to the treatment of dissociative symptoms.

In closing, the sleep-dissociation model can serve as a framework for studies that address a wide range of fascinating questions about dissociative symptoms and disorders. We now have good reason to be confident that research on sleep and dissociative symptoms will inform psychiatry, clinical science, and psychotherapeutic practice in meaningful ways in the years to come.

Outside Resources

Article: Extreme Dissociative Fugue: A life, Interrupted – A recent case of extreme dissociative fugue. The article is particularly powerful as it relates the story of a seemingly typical person, a young teacher, who suddenly experiences a dissociative fugue.

http://www.nytimes.com/2009/03/01/nyregion/thecity/01miss.html?_r=0

Book: Schreiber, F. R. (1973). *Sybil*. Chicago: Regnery.

Film: Debate Persists Over Diagnosing Mental Health Disorders, Long After 'Sybil'. This short film would be useful to provide students with perspectives on the debate over diagnoses. It could be used to introduce the debate and provide students with evidence to argue for or against the diagnosis.

http://www.nytimes.com/2014/11/24/us/debate-persists-over-diagnosing-mental-health-disorders-long-after-sybil.html

Structured Clinical Interview for DSM-5 (SCID-5)

https://www.appi.org/products/structured-clinical-interview-for-dsm-5-scid-5

Video: Depiction of the controversy regarding the existence of DID and show you some debate between

clinicians and researchers on the topics of brain imaging, recovered memories, and false memories. False memory syndrome.

- https://youtu.be/K4NZ7_Hn-rI

Video: Patient Switching on Command and in Brain Scanner – This eight-minute video depicts the controversy regarding the existence of DID and relates some of the debate between clinicians and researchers on the topics of brain imaging, recovered memories, and false memories.

- https://youtu.be/zhM0xp5vXqY

Discussion Questions

1. Why are dissociation and trauma related to each other?
2. How is dissociation related to sleep problems?
3. Are dissociative symptoms induced or merely increased by sleep disturbances?
4. Do you have any ideas regarding treatment possibilities for dissociative disorders?
5. Does DID really exist?

Vocabulary

Amnesia

The loss of memory.

Anxiety disorder

A group of diagnoses in the Diagnostic and Statistical Manual of Mental Disorders (DSM-IV-TR) classification system where anxiety is central to the person's dysfunctioning. Typical symptoms include excessive rumination, worrying, uneasiness, apprehension, and fear about future uncertainties either based on real or imagined events. These symptoms may affect both physical and psychological health. The anxiety disorders are subdivided into panic disorder, specific phobia, social phobia, posttraumatic stress disorder, obsessive-compulsive disorder, and generalized anxiety disorder.

Borderline Personality Disorder

This personality disorder is defined by a chronic pattern of instability. This instability manifests itself in interpersonal relationships, mood, self-image, and behavior that can interfere with social functioning or work. It may also cause grave emotional distress.

Cognitive failures

Every day slips and lapses, also called absentmindedness.

Consciousness

The quality or state of being aware of an external object or something within oneself. It has been defined as the ability to experience or to feel, wakefulness, having a sense of selfhood, and the executive control system of the mind.

Cross-sectional design

Research method that involves observation of all of a population, or a representative subset, at one specific point in time.

Defensive coping mechanism

An unconscious process, which protects an individual from unacceptable or painful ideas, impulses, or memories.

DES

Dissociative Experiences Scale.

DID

Dissociative identity disorder, formerly known as multiple personality disorder, is at the far end of the dissociative disorder spectrum. It is characterized by at least two distinct, and dissociated personality states. These personality states – or 'alters' – alternately control a person's behavior. The sufferer therefore experiences significant memory impairment for important information not explained by ordinary forgetfulness.

Dissociation

A disruption in the usually integrated function of consciousness, memory, identity, or perception of the environment.

Fantasy proneness

The tendency to extensive fantasizing or daydreaming.

General population

A sample of people representative of the average individual in our society.

Insomnia

A sleep disorder in which there is an inability to fall asleep or to stay asleep as long as desired. Symptoms also include waking up too early, experience many awakenings during the night, and not feeling rested during the day.

Lucid dreams

Any dream in which one is aware that one is dreaming.

Mood disorder

A group of diagnoses in the Diagnostic and Statistical Manual of Mental Disorders (DSM-IV-TR) classification system where a disturbance in the person's mood is the primary dysfunction. Mood disorders include major depressive disorder, bipolar disorder, dysthymic and cyclothymic disorder.

Nightmares

An unpleasant dream that can cause a strong negative emotional response from the mind, typically fear or horror, but also despair, anxiety, and great sadness. The dream may contain situations of danger, discomfort, psychological or physical terror. Sufferers usually awaken in a state of distress and may be unable to return to sleep for a prolonged period of time.

Obsessive-Compulsive Disorder

This anxiety disorder is characterized by intrusive thoughts (obsessions), by repetitive behaviors (compulsions), or both. Obsessions produce uneasiness, fear, or worry. Compulsions are then aimed at reducing the associated anxiety. Examples of compulsive behaviors include excessive washing or cleaning; repeated checking; extreme hoarding; and nervous rituals, such as switching the light on and off a certain number of times when entering a room. Intrusive thoughts are often sexual, violent, or religious in nature…

Prevalence

The number of cases of a specific disorder present in a given population at a certain time.

PTM

Post-traumatic model of dissociation.

Recurrent dreams

The same dream narrative or dreamscape is experienced over different occasions of sleep.

Schizophrenia

This mental disorder is characterized by a breakdown of thought processes and emotional responses. Symptoms include auditory hallucinations, paranoid or bizarre delusions, or disorganized speech and thinking. Sufferers from this disorder experience grave dysfunctions in their social functioning and in work.

SCID-D

Structural Clinical Interview for DSM-IV Dissociative Disorders.

Self-report measure

A type of psychological test in which a person fills out a survey or questionnaire with or without the help of an investigator.

Sleep deprivation

A sufficient lack of restorative sleep over a cumulative period so as to cause physical or psychiatric symptoms and affect routine performances of tasks.

Sleep paralysis

Sleep paralysis occurs when the normal paralysis during REM sleep manifests when falling asleep or awakening, often accompanied by hallucinations of danger or a malevolent presence in the room.

Sleep-wake cycle

A daily rhythmic activity cycle, based on 24-hour intervals, that is exhibited by many organisms.

State

When a symptom is acute, or transient, lasting from a few minutes to a few hours.

Trait

When a symptom forms part of the personality or character.

Trauma

An event or situation that causes great distress and disruption, and that creates substantial, lasting damage to the psychological development of a person.

Vivid dreams

A dream that is very clear, where the individual can remember the dream in great detail.

References

- Abrams, M. P., Mulligan, A. D., Carleton, R. N., & Asmundson, G. J. G. (2008). Prevalence and correlates of sleep paralysis in adults reporting childhood sexual abuse. *Journal of Anxiety Disorders, 22,* 1535–1541.

- Agargun, M. Y., Kara H., Ozer, O. A., Selvi, Y., Kiran, U., & Ozer, B. (2003). Clinical importance of nightmare disorder in patients with dissociative disorders. *Psychiatry Clinical Neuroscience, 57,*

575–579.

- Agargun, M. Y., Kara, H., Ozer, O. A., Semiz, U., Selvi, Y., Kiran, U., & Tombul, T. (2001). Characteristics of patients with nocturnal dissociative disorders. *Sleep and Hypnosis, 3*, 131–134.

- Allen, J. G., & Coyne, L. (1995). Dissociation and the vulnerability to psychotic experiences. *Journal of Nervous and Mental Disease, 183*, 615–622.

- American Psychiatric Association. (2013). *Diagnostic and statistical manual of mental disorders: DSM-5.*Washington, D.C: American Psychiatric Association.

- American Psychiatric Association. (2000). *Diagnostic and statistical manual of mental disorders (text revision).*Washington, DC: Author.

- Arlow, J. (1966). Depersonalization and derealization. In: R. Loewenstein, L. M. Newman, M. Schur, & A. J. Solnit (Eds.), *Psychoanalysis–A general psychology* (pp. 456–478). New York, NY: International Universities Press, Inc.

- Barrett, D. (1995). The dream character as a prototype for the multiple personality "alter." *Dissociation, 8*, 61-68.

- Barrett, D. (1994). Dreaming as a normal model for multiple personality disorder. In S.J. Lynn & J.W. Rhue (Eds.), *Dissociation: Clinical and theoretical perspectives* (pp. 123–135). New York, NY: Guilford Press.

- Bernstein, E., & Putnam, F. W. (1986). Development, reliability, and validity of a dissociation scale. Journal of *Nervous and Mental Disease, 174*, 727–735.

- Bob, P. (2004). Dissociative processes, multiple personality, and dream functions. *American Journal of Psychotherapy, 58*, 139-149.

- Bremner, J. D. (2010). Cognitive processes in dissociation: Comment on Giesbrecht et al. (2008). *Psychological Bulletin, 136*, 1–6.

- Bremner, J. D., & Brett, E. (1997). Trauma-related dissociative states and long-term psychopathology in posttraumatic stress disorder. *Journal of Trauma and Stress, 10*, 37–49.

- Carlson, E. B., & Putnam, F. W. (2000). DES-II. *Psychoanalytic Inquiry, 20*, 361–366.

- Foote, B., Smolin, Y., Kaplan, M., Legatt, M.E., & Lipschitz, D. (2006). Prevalence of dissociative disorders in psychiatric outpatients. *American Journal of Psychiatry, 163*, 623–629.

- Franklin, J. (1990). Dreamlike thought and dream mode processes in the formation of personalities in MPD. *Dissociation, 3*, 70–80.

- Gershuny, B. S., & Thayer, J. F. (1999). Relations among psychological trauma, dissociative phenomena, and trauma-related distress: A review and integration. *Clinical Psychology Review, 19*, 631–657.

- Giesbrecht, T., Lynn, S. J., Lilienfeld, S. O., & Merckelbach, H. (2010). Cognitive processes, trauma, and dissociation—Misconceptions and misrepresentations: Reply to Bremner (2010). *Psychological Bulletin, 136*, 7–11.

- Giesbrecht, T., Lynn, S. J., Lilienfeld, S. O., & Merckelbach, H. (2008). Cognitive processes in dissociation: An analysis of core theoretical assumptions. *Psychological Bulletin, 134*, 617–647.

- Giesbrecht, T., Smeets, T., Leppink, J., Jelicic, M., & Merckelbach, H. (2007). Acute dissociation after 1 night of sleep loss. *Journal of Abnormal Psychology, 116*, 599–606.

- Hacking, I. (1995). *Rewriting the soul: Multiple personality and the sciences*. Princeton, NJ: Princeton University Press.

- Kihlstrom, J. F. (2005). Dissociative disorders. *Annual Review of Clinical Psychology, 10*, 1–27.

- Koffel, E., & Watson, D. (2009). The two-factor structure of sleep complaints and its relation to depression and anxiety. *Journal of Abnormal Psychology, 118*, 183–194.

- Lee, W. E., Kwok, C. H. T., Hunter, E. C. M., Richards, M. & David, A. S. (2010). Prevalence and childhood antecedents of depersonalization syndrome in a UK birth cohort. *Social Psychiatry and Psychiatric Epidemiology,* (in press).

- Levin, R., & Fireman, G. (2002). Nightmare prevalence, nightmare distress, and self-reported psychological disturbance. *Sleep, 25*, 205–212.

- Levitan, H. L. (1967). Depersonalization and the dream. *The Psychoanalytic Quaterly, 36*, 157-171.

- McNally, R. J., & Clancy, S. A. (2005). Sleep paralysis in adults reporting repressed, recovered, or continuous memories of childhood sexual abuse. *Journal of Anxiety Disorders, 19*, 595–602.

- Meares, R. (1999). The contribution of Hughlings Jackson to an understanding of dissociation. *American Journal of Psychiatry, 156*, 1850–1855.

- Merckelbach, H., & Jelicic, M. (2004). Dissociative symptoms are related to endorsement of vague trauma items. *Comprehensive Psychiatry, 45*, 70–75.

- Merckelbach, H., & Muris, P. (2002). The causal link between self-reported trauma and dissociation: A critical review. *Behaviour Research and Therapy, 39*, 245–254.

- Merckelbach, H., Horselenberg, R., & Schmidt, H. (2002). Modeling the connection between self-reported trauma and dissociation in a student sample. *Personality and Individual Differences, 32*, 695–705.

- Merckelbach, H., Muris, P., Rassin, E., & Horselenberg, R. (2000). Dissociative experiences and interrogative suggestibility in college students. *Personality and Individual Differences, 29*, 1133–1140.

- Merckelbach, H., à Campo, J. A., Hardy, S., & Giesbrecht, T. (2005). Dissociation and fantasy proneness in psychiatric patients: A preliminary study. *Comprehensive Psychiatry, 46*, 181–185.

- Morgan, C. A., Hazlett, G., Wang, S., Richardson, E. G., Schnurr, P., & Southwick, S. M. (2001). Symptoms of dissociation in humans experiencing acute, uncontrollable stress: A prospective investigation. *American Journal of Psychiatry, 158*, 1239–1247.

- National Sleep Foundation. (2005). 2005 *Sleep in America poll*. Washington DC: Author.

- Rauschenberg, S.L., Lynn, S.J. (1995). Fantasy proneness, DSM-III-r axis I psychopathology and dissociation. *Journal of Abnormal Psychology, 104*, 373-380.

- Ross, C. A. (2011). Possession experiences in Dissociative Identity Disorder: A preliminary study. *Journal of Trauma & Dissociation, 12*, 393–400.

- Ross, C. A., Anderson, G., Fleisher, W. P., & Norton, G. R. (1991). The frequency of Multiple Personality Disorder among psychiatric-inpatients. *American Journal of Psychiatry, 148*, 1717–1720.

- Rufer, M., Fricke, S., Held, D., Cremer, J., & Hand, I. (2006). Dissociation and symptom dimensions of obsessive-compulsive disorder—A replication study. *European Archives of Psychiatry and Clinical Neuroscience, 256*, 146–150.

- Sandberg, D., & Lynn, S.J. (1992). Dissociative experiences, psychopathology and adjustment, and child and adolescent maltreatment in female college students. *Journal of Abnormal Psychology, 101*, 717–723.

- Sar, V., Tutkun, H., Alyanak, B., Bakim, B., & Baral, I. (2000). Frequency of dissociative disorders among psychiatric outpatients in Turkey. *Comprehensive Psychiatry, 41*, 216-222.

- Schreiber, F. R. (1973). *Sybil*. Chicago, IL: Regnery.

- Semiz, U. B., Basoglu, C., Ebrinc, S., & Cetin, M. (2008). Nightmare disorder, dream anxiety, and subjective sleep quality in patients with borderline personality disorder. *Psychiatry and Clinical Neurosciences, 62*, 48–55.

- Simeon, D., & Abugel, J. (2006). *Feeling unreal: Depersonalization disorder and the loss of the self.* New York, NY: Oxford University Press.

- Spiegel, D., Loewenstein, R. J., Lewis-Fernandez, R., Sar, V., Simeon, D., Vermetten, E., Cardena, E., & Dell, P. F. (2011). Dissociative disorders in DSM-5. *Depression and Anxiety, 28*, 824–852.

- Spitzer, C., Vogel, M., Barnow, S., Freyberger, H. J., & Grabe, H. J. (2007). Psychopathology and alexithymia in severe mental illness: The impact of trauma and posttraumatic stress symptoms. *European Archives of Psychiatry and Clinical Neuroscience, 257*, 191–196

- Steinberg, M. (2001). *The stranger in the mirror: Dissociation—the hidden epidemic.* New York, NY: Harper Collins Publishers, Inc.

- Steinberg, M. (1994). *Structured Clinical Interview for DSM-IV Dissociative Disorders* (SCID-D) (p. 96). Washington, DC: American Psychiatric Press.

- Suszek, H., & Kopera, M. (2005). Altered states of consciousness, dissociation, and dream recall. *Perceptual Motor Skills, 100*, 176–178.

- Thigpen, C. H., & Cleckley, H. (1957). *The Three Faces of Eve.* New York, NY: McGraw-Hill.

- Tutkun, H., Sar, V., Yargic, L. I., Ozpulat, T., Yanik, M., & Kiziltan, E. (1998). Frequency of dissociative disorders among psychiatric inpatients in a Turkish university clinic. *American Journal of Psychiatry, 155*, 800–805.

- Van der Hart, O., & Horst, R. (1989). The dissociation theory of Pierre Janet. *Journal of Traumatic*

Stress, 2, 2–11.

- Van der Kloet, D., Giesbrecht, T., Lynn, S.J., Merckelbach, & de Zutter, A. (2011). Sleep normalization and decrease in dissociative experiences: Evaluation in an inpatient sample. *Journal of Abnormal Psychology,* Online First Publication, August 15, 2011. doi: 10.1037/a0024781

- Vermetten, E., Schmahl, C., Lindner, S., Loewenstein, R.J. & Bremner, J.D. (2006). Hippocampal and amygdalar volumes in dissociative identity disorder. *American Journal of Psychiatry, 163,* 630–636.

- Watson, D. (2001). Dissociations of the night: Individual differences in sleep-related experiences and their relation to dissociation and schizotypy. *Journal of Abnormal Psychology, 110,* 526–535.

- Wright, D. B., & Loftus, E.F. (1999). Measuring dissociation: Comparison of alternative forms of the Dissociative Experiences Scale. *American Journal of Psychology, 112,* 497–519.

- Yu, J. H., Ross, C. A., Keyes, B. B., Li, Y., Dai, Y. F., Zhang, T. H., Wang, L. L., Fang, Q., & Xiao, Z. P. (2010). Dissociative disorders among Chinese inpatients diagnosed with schizophrenia. *Journal of Trauma and Dissociation, 11,* 358–372.

Mood Disorders

Everyone feels down or euphoric from time to time, but this is different from having a mood disorder such as major depressive disorder or bipolar disorder. Mood disorders are extended periods of depressed, euphoric, or irritable moods that in combination with other symptoms cause the person significant distress and interfere with his or her daily life, often resulting in social and occupational difficulties. In this module, we describe major mood disorders, including their symptom presentations, general prevalence rates, and how and why the rates of these disorders tend to vary by age, gender, and race. In addition, biological and environmental risk factors that have been implicated in the development and course of mood disorders, such as heritability and stressful life events, are reviewed. Finally, we provide an overview of treatments for mood disorders, covering treatments with demonstrated effectiveness, as well as new treatment options showing promise.

Learning Objectives

- Describe the diagnostic criteria for mood disorders.
- Understand age, gender, and ethnic differences in prevalence rates of mood disorders.
- Identify common risk factors for mood disorders.
- Know effective treatments of mood disorders.

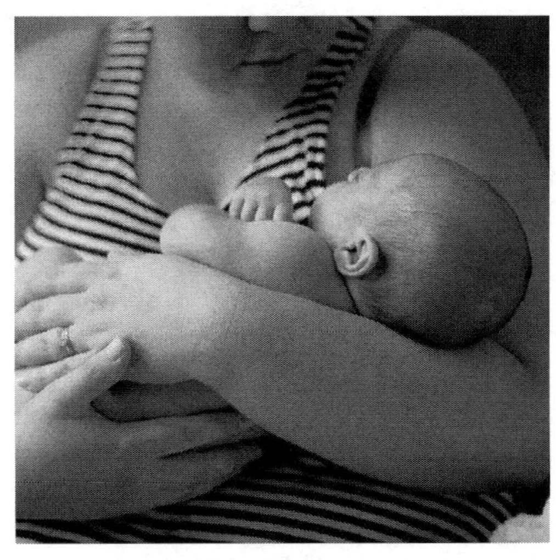

Perinatal depression following child birth afflicts about 5% of all mothers. An unfortunate social stigma regarding this form of depression compounds the problem for the women who suffer its effects. [Image: CC0 Public Domain]

The actress Brooke Shields published a memoir titled Down Came the Rain: My Journey through Postpartum Depression in which she described her struggles with depression following the birth of her daughter. Despite the fact that about one in 20 women experience depression after the birth of a baby (American Psychiatric Association [APA], 2013), postpartum depression—recently renamed "perinatal depression"—continues to be veiled by stigma, owing in part to a widely held expectation that motherhood should be a time of great joy. In an opinion piece in the New York Times, Shields revealed that entering motherhood was a profoundly overwhelming experience for her. She vividly describes experiencing a sense of "doom" and "dread" in response to her newborn baby. Because motherhood is conventionally thought of as a joyous event and not associated with sadness and hopelessness, responding to a newborn baby in this way can be shocking to the new mother as well as those close to her. It may also involve a great deal of shame for the mother, making her reluctant to divulge her experience to others, including her doctors and family.

Feelings of shame are not unique to perinatal depression. Stigma applies to other types of depressive and bipolar disorders and contributes to people not always receiving the necessary support and treatment for these disorders. In fact, the World Health Organization ranks both major depressive disorder (MDD) and bipolar disorder (BD) among the top 10 leading causes of disability worldwide. Further, MDD and BD carry a high risk of suicide. It is estimated that 25%–50% of people diagnosed with BD will attempt suicide at least once in their lifetimes (Goodwin & Jamison, 2007).

What Are Mood Disorders?

Mood Episodes

Everyone experiences brief periods of sadness, irritability, or euphoria. This is different than having a mood disorder, such as MDD or BD, which are characterized by a constellation of symptoms that causes people significant distress or impairs their everyday functioning.

Major Depressive Episode

A major depressive episode (MDE) refers to symptoms that co-occur for at least two weeks and cause significant distress or impairment in functioning, such as interfering with work, school, or relationships. Core symptoms include feeling down or depressed or experiencing anhedonia—loss of interest or pleasure in things that one typically enjoys. According to the fifth edition of the *Diagnostic and Statistical Manual* (*DSM-5;* APA, 2013), the criteria for an MDE require five or more of the following nine symptoms, including one or both of the first two symptoms, for most of the day, nearly every day:

1. depressed mood

2. diminished interest or pleasure in almost all activities

3. significant weight loss or gain or an increase or decrease in appetite

4. insomnia or hypersomnia

5. psychomotor agitation or retardation

6. fatigue or loss of energy

7. feeling worthless or excessive or inappropriate guilt

8. diminished ability to concentrate or indecisiveness

9. recurrent thoughts of death, suicidal ideation, or a suicide attempt

These symptoms cannot be caused by physiological effects of a substance or a general medical condition (e.g., hypothyroidism).

Manic or Hypomanic Episode

The core criterion for a manic or hypomanic episode is a distinct period of abnormally and persistently euphoric, expansive, or irritable mood and persistently increased goal-directed activity or energy. The mood disturbance must be present for one week or longer in mania (unless hospitalization is required) or four days or longer in hypomania. Concurrently, at least three of the following symptoms must be present in the context of euphoric mood (or at least four in the context of irritable mood):

1. inflated self-esteem or grandiosity

2. increased goal-directed activity or psychomotor agitation

3. reduced need for sleep

4. racing thoughts or flight of ideas

5. distractibility

6. increased talkativeness

7. excessive involvement in risky behaviors

Manic episodes are distinguished from hypomanic episodes by their duration and associated impairment; whereas manic episodes must last one week and are defined by a significant impairment in functioning, hypomanic episodes are shorter and not necessarily accompanied by impairment in functioning.

Mood Disorders

Unipolar Mood Disorders

Two major types of unipolar disorders described by the *DSM-5* (APA, 2013) are major depressive disorder and persistent depressive disorder (PDD; dysthymia). MDD is defined by one or more MDEs, but no history of manic or hypomanic episodes. Criteria for PDD are feeling depressed most of the day for more days than not, for at least two years. At least two of the following symptoms are also required to meet criteria for PDD:

1. poor appetite or overeating

2. insomnia or hypersomnia

3. low energy or fatigue

4. low self-esteem

5. poor concentration or difficulty making decisions

6. feelings of hopelessness

Like MDD, these symptoms need to cause significant distress or impairment and cannot be due to the effects of a substance or a general medical condition. To meet criteria for PDD, a person cannot be without symptoms for more than two months at a time. PDD has overlapping symptoms with MDD. If someone meets criteria for an MDE during a PDD episode, the person will receive diagnoses of PDD and MDD.

Bipolar Mood Disorders

Bipolar disorders are characterized by cycles of high energy and depression. [Image: Brett Whaley, https://goo.gl/ k4HTR7, CC BY-NC 2.0, https://goo.gl/ VnKlK8]

Three major types of BDs are described by the *DSM-5* (APA, 2013). Bipolar I Disorder (BD I), which was previously known as manic-depression, is characterized by a single (or recurrent) manic episode. A depressive episode is not necessary but commonly present for the diagnosis of BD I. Bipolar II Disorder is characterized by single (or recurrent) hypomanic episodes and depressive episodes. Another type of BD is cyclothymic disorder, characterized by numerous and alternating periods of hypomania and depression, lasting at least two years. To qualify for cyclothymic disorder, the periods of depression cannot meet full diagnostic criteria for an MDE; the person must experience symptoms at least half the time with no more than two consecutive symptom-free months; and the symptoms must cause significant distress or impairment.

> ### Box 1. Specifiers
>
> Both MDEs and manic episodes can be further described using standardized tags based on the timing of, or other symptoms that are occurring during, the mood episode, to increase diagnostic specificity and inform treatment. Psychotic features is specified when the episodes are accompanied by delusions (rigidly held beliefs that are false) or hallucinations (perceptual disturbances that are not based in reality). Seasonal pattern is specified when a mood episode occurs at the same time of the year for two consecutive years—most commonly occurring in the fall and winter. Peripartum onset is specified when a mood episode has an onset during pregnancy or within four weeks of the birth of a child. Approximately 3%–6% of women who have a child experience an MDE with peripartum onset (APA, 2013). This is less frequent and different from the baby blues or when women feel transient mood symptoms usually within 10 days of giving birth, which are experienced by most women (Nolen-Hoeksema & Hilt, 2009).

It is important to note that the *DSM-5* was published in 2013, and findings based on the updated manual will be forthcoming. Consequently, the research presented below was largely based on a similar, but not identical, conceptualization of mood disorders drawn from the *DSM-IV* (APA, 2000).

How Common Are Mood Disorders? Who Develops Mood Disorders?

Depressive Disorders

In a nationally representative sample, lifetime prevalence rate for MDD is 16.6% (Kessler, Berglund, Demler, Jin, Merikangas, & Walters, 2005). This means that nearly one in five Americans will meet the criteria for MDD during their lifetime. The 12-month prevalence—the proportion of people who meet criteria for a disorder during a 12-month period—for PDD is approximately 0.5% (APA, 2013).

Although the onset of MDD can occur at any time throughout the lifespan, the average age of onset is mid-20s, with the age of onset decreasing with people born more recently (APA, 2000). Prevalence of MDD among older adults is much lower than it is for younger cohorts (Kessler, Birnbaum, Bromet, Hwang, Sampson, & Shahly,

2010). The duration of MDEs varies widely. Recovery begins within three months for 40% of people with MDD and within 12 months for 80% (APA, 2013). MDD tends to be a recurrent disorder with about 40%–50% of those who experience one MDE experiencing a second MDE (Monroe & Harkness, 2011). An earlier age of onset predicts a worse course. About 5%–10% of people who experience an MDE will later experience a manic episode (APA, 2000), thus no longer meeting criteria for MDD but instead meeting them for BD I. Diagnoses of other disorders across the lifetime are common for people with MDD: 59% experience an anxiety disorder; 32% experience an impulse control disorder, and 24% experience a substance use disorder (Kessler, Merikangas, & Wang, 2007).

Women experience two to three times higher rates of MDD than do men (Nolen-Hoeksema & Hilt, 2009). This gender difference emerges during puberty (Conley & Rudolph, 2009). Before puberty, boys exhibit similar or higher prevalence rates of MDD than do girls (Twenge & Nolen-Hoeksema, 2002). MDD is inversely correlated with socioeconomic status (SES), a person's economic and social position based on income, education, and occupation. Higher prevalence rates of MDD are associated with lower SES (Lorant, Deliege, Eaton, Robert, Philippot, & Ansseau, 2003), particularly for adults over 65 years old (Kessler et al., 2010). Independent of SES, results from a nationally representative sample found that European Americans had a higher prevalence rate of MDD than did African Americans and Hispanic Americans, whose rates were similar (Breslau, Aguilar-Gaxiola, Kendler, Su, Williams, & Kessler, 2006). The course of MDD for African Americans is often more severe and less often treated than it is for European Americans, however (Williams et al., 2007). Native Americans have a higher prevalence rate than do European Americans, African Americans, or Hispanic Americans (Hasin, Goodwin, Stinson & Grant, 2005). Depression is not limited to industrialized or western cultures; it is found in all countries that have been examined, although the symptom presentation as well as prevalence rates vary across cultures (Chentsova-Dutton & Tsai, 2009).

Bipolar Disorders

Adolescents experience a higher incidence of bipolar spectrum disorders than do adults. Making matters worse, those who are diagnosed with BD at a younger age seem to suffer symptoms more intensely than those with adult onset. [Image: CC0 Public Domain]

The lifetime prevalence rate of bipolar spectrum disorders in the general U.S. population is estimated at approximately 4.4%, with BD I constituting about 1% of this rate (Merikangas et al., 2007). Prevalence estimates, however, are highly dependent on the diagnostic procedures used (e.g., interviews vs. self-report) and whether or not sub-threshold forms of the disorder are included in the estimate. BD often co-occurs with other psychiatric disorders. Approximately 65% of people with BD meet diagnostic criteria for at least one additional psychiatric disorder, most commonly anxiety disorders and substance use disorders (McElroy et al., 2001). The co-occurrence of BD with other psychiatric disorders is associated with poorer illness course, including higher rates of suicidality (Leverich et al., 2003). A recent cross-national study sample of more than 60,000 adults from 11 countries, estimated the worldwide prevalence of BD at 2.4%, with BD I constituting 0.6% of this rate (Merikangas et al., 2011). In this study, the prevalence of BD varied somewhat by country. Whereas the United States had the highest lifetime prevalence (4.4%), India had the lowest (0.1%). Variation in prevalence rates was not necessarily related to SES, as in the case of Japan, a high-income country with a very low prevalence rate of BD (0.7%).

With regard to ethnicity, data from studies not confounded by SES or inaccuracies in diagnosis are limited, but available reports suggest rates of BD among European Americans are similar to those found among African Americans (Blazer et al., 1985) and Hispanic Americans (Breslau, Kendler, Su, Gaxiola-Aguilar, & Kessler, 2005). Another large community-based study found that although prevalence rates of mood disorders were similar across ethnic groups, Hispanic Americans and African Americans with a mood disorder were more likely to remain persistently ill than European Americans (Breslau et al., 2005). Compared with European Americans with BD, African Americans tend to be underdiagnosed for BD (and over-diagnosed for schizophrenia) (Kilbourne, Haas, Mulsant, Bauer, & Pincus, 2004; Minsky, Vega, Miskimen, Gara, & Escobar, 2003), and Hispanic Americans with BD have been shown to receive fewer psychiatric medication prescriptions and specialty treatment visits (Gonzalez et al., 2007). Misdiagnosis of BD can result in the underutilization of treatment or the utilization of inappropriate treatment, and thus profoundly impact the course of illness.

As with MDD, adolescence is known to be a significant risk period for BD; mood symptoms start by adolescence in roughly half of BD cases (Leverich et al., 2007; Perlis et al., 2004). Longitudinal studies show that those diagnosed with BD prior to adulthood experience a more pernicious course of illness relative to those with adult onset, including more episode recurrence, higher rates of suicidality, and profound social, occupational, and economic repercussions (e.g., Lewinsohn, Seeley, Buckley, & Klein, 2002). The prevalence of BD is substantially lower in older adults compared with younger adults (1% vs. 4%) (Merikangas et al., 2007).

What Are Some of the Factors Implicated in the Development and Course of Mood Disorders?

Mood disorders are complex disorders resulting from multiple factors. Causal explanations can be attempted at various levels, including biological and psychosocial levels. Below are several of the key factors that contribute to onset and course of mood disorders are highlighted.

Depressive Disorders

Research across family and twin studies has provided support that genetic factors are implicated in the development of MDD. Twin studies suggest that familial influence on MDD is mostly due to genetic effects and that individual-specific environmental effects (e.g., romantic relationships) play an important role, too. By contrast, the contribution of shared environmental effect by siblings is negligible (Sullivan, Neale & Kendler, 2000). The mode of inheritance is not fully understood although no single genetic variation has been found to increase the risk of MDD significantly. Instead, several genetic variants and environmental factors most likely contribute to the risk for MDD (Lohoff, 2010).

One environmental stressor that has received much support in relation to MDD is stressful life events. In particular, severe stressful life events—those that have long-term consequences and involve loss of a significant relationship (e.g., divorce) or economic stability

Romantic relationships can affect mood as in the case of divorce or the death of a spouse. [Image: CC0 Public Domain]

(e.g., unemployment) are strongly related to depression (Brown & Harris, 1989; Monroe et al., 2009). Stressful life events are more likely to predict the first MDE than subsequent episodes (Lewinsohn, Allen, Seeley, & Gotlib, 1999). In contrast, minor events may play a larger role in subsequent episodes than the initial episodes (Monroe & Harkness, 2005).

Depression research has not been limited to examining reactivity to stressful life events. Much research, particularly brain imagining research using functional magnetic resonance imaging (fMRI), has centered on examining neural circuitry—the interconnections that allow multiple brain regions to perceive, generate, and encode information in concert. A meta-analysis of neuroimaging studies showed that when viewing negative stimuli (e.g., picture of an angry face, picture of a car accident), compared with healthy control participants, participants with MDD have greater activation in brain regions involved in stress response and reduced activation of brain regions involved in positively motivated behaviors (Hamilton, Etkin, Furman, Lemus, Johnson, & Gotlib, 2012).

Other environmental factors related to increased risk for MDD include experiencing early adversity (e.g., childhood abuse or neglect; Widom, DuMont, & Czaja, 2007), chronic stress (e.g., poverty) and interpersonal factors. For example, marital dissatisfaction predicts increases in depressive symptoms in both men and women. On the other hand, depressive symptoms also predict increases in marital dissatisfaction (Whisman & Uebelacker, 2009). Research has found that people with MDD generate some of their interpersonal stress (Hammen, 2005). People with MDD whose relatives or spouses can be described as critical and emotionally overinvolved have higher relapse rates than do those living with people who are less critical and emotionally overinvolved (Butzlaff & Hooley, 1998).

People's attributional styles or their general ways of thinking, interpreting, and recalling information have also been examined in the etiology of MDD (Gotlib & Joormann, 2010). People with a pessimistic attributional style tend to make internal (versus external), global (versus specific), and stable (versus unstable) attributions to negative events, serving as a vulnerability to developing MDD. For example, someone who when he fails an exam thinks that it was his fault (internal), that he is stupid (global), and that he will always do poorly (stable) has a pessimistic attribution style. Several influential theories of depression incorporate attributional styles (Abramson, Metalsky, & Alloy, 1989; Abramson Seligman, & Teasdale, 1978).

Bipolar Disorders

Although there have been important advances in research on the etiology, course, and treatment of BD, there remains a need to understand the mechanisms that contribute to episode onset and relapse. There is compelling evidence for biological causes of BD, which is known to be highly heritable (McGuffin, Rijsdijk, Andrew, Sham, Katz, & Cardno, 2003). It may be argued that a high rate of heritability demonstrates that BD is fundamentally a biological phenomenon. However, there is much variability in the course of BD both within a person across time and across people (Johnson, 2005). The triggers that determine how and when this genetic vulnerability is expressed are not yet understood; however, there is evidence to suggest that psychosocial triggers may play an important role in BD risk (e.g., Johnson et al., 2008; Malkoff-Schwartz et al., 1998).

In addition to the genetic contribution, biological explanations of BD have also focused on brain function. Many of the studies using fMRI techniques to characterize BD have focused on the processing of emotional stimuli based on the idea that BD is fundamentally a disorder of emotion (APA, 2000). Findings show that regions of the brain thought to be involved in emotional processing and regulation are activated differently in people with BD relative to healthy controls (e.g., Altshuler et al., 2008; Hassel et al., 2008; Lennox, Jacob, Calder, Lupson, & Bullmore, 2004).

However, there is little consensus as to whether a particular brain region becomes more or less active in response to an emotional stimulus among people with BD compared with healthy controls. Mixed findings are in part due to samples consisting of participants who are at various phases of illness at the time of testing (manic, depressed, inter-episode). Sample sizes tend to be relatively small, making comparisons between subgroups difficult. Additionally, the use of a standardized stimulus (e.g., facial expression of anger) may not elicit a sufficiently strong response. Personally engaging stimuli, such as recalling a memory, may be more effective in inducing strong emotions (Isacowitz, Gershon, Allard, & Johnson, 2013).

Within the psychosocial level, research has focused on the environmental contributors to BD. A series of studies show that environmental stressors, particularly severe stressors (e.g., loss of a significant relationship), can adversely impact the course of BD. People with BD have substantially increased risk of relapse (Ellicott, Hammen, Gitlin, Brown, & Jamison, 1990) and suffer more depressive symptoms (Johnson, Winett, Meyer, Greenhouse, & Miller, 1999) following a severe life stressor. Interestingly, positive life events can also adversely impact the course of BD. People with BD suffer more manic symptoms after life events involving attainment of a desired goal (Johnson et al., 2008). Such findings suggest that people with BD may have a hypersensitivity to rewards.

Evidence from the life stress literature has also suggested that people with mood disorders may have a circadian vulnerability that renders them sensitive to stressors that disrupt their sleep or rhythms. According to social zeitgeber theory (Ehlers, Frank, & Kupfer, 1988; Frank et al., 1994), stressors that disrupt sleep, or that disrupt the daily routines that entrain the biological clock (e.g., meal times) can trigger episode relapse. Consistent with this theory, studies have shown that life events that involve a disruption in sleep and daily routines, such as overnight travel, can increase bipolar symptoms in people with BD (Malkoff-Schwartz et al., 1998).

What Are Some of the Well-Supported Treatments for Mood Disorders?

Depressive Disorders

There are many treatment options available for people with MDD. First, a number of antidepressant medications are available, all of which target one or more of the neurotransmitters implicated in depression.The earliest antidepressant medications were monoamine oxidase inhibitors (MAOIs). MAOIs inhibit monoamine oxidase, an enzyme involved in deactivating dopamine, norepinephrine, and serotonin. Although effective in treating depression, MAOIs can have serious side effects. Patients taking MAOIs may develop dangerously high blood pressure if they take certain drugs (e.g., antihistamines) or eat foods containing tyramine, an amino acid commonly found in foods such as aged cheeses, wine, and soy sauce. Tricyclics, the second-oldest class of antidepressant medications, block the reabsorption of norepinephrine, serotonin, or dopamine at synapses, resulting in their increased availability. Tricyclics are most effective for treating vegetative and somatic symptoms of depression. Like MAOIs, they have serious side effects, the

A number of medications are effective in treating mood disorders. Meditation, exercise, counseling and other therapies also show effectiveness for some disorders. [Image: CC0 Public Domain]

most concerning of which is being cardiotoxic. Selective serotonin reuptake inhibitors (SSRIs; e.g., Fluoxetine) and serotonin and norepinephrine reuptake inhibitors (SNRIs; e.g., Duloxetine) are the most recently introduced antidepressant medications. SSRIs, the most commonly prescribed antidepressant medication, block the reabsorption of serotonin, whereas SNRIs block the reabsorption of serotonin and norepinephrine. SSRIs and SNRIs have fewer serious side effects than do MAOIs and tricyclics. In particular, they are less cardiotoxic, less lethal in overdose, and produce fewer cognitive impairments. They are not, however, without their own side effects, which include but are not limited to difficulty having orgasms, gastrointestinal issues, and insomnia.

Other biological treatments for people with depression include electroconvulsive therapy (ECT), transcranial magnetic stimulation (TMS), and deep brain stimulation. ECT involves inducing a seizure after a patient takes muscle relaxants and is under general anesthesia. ECT is viable treatment for patients with severe depression or who show resistance to antidepressants although the mechanisms through which it works remain unknown. A common side effect is confusion and memory loss, usually short-term (Schulze-Rauschenbach, Harms, Schlaepfer, Maier, Falkai, & Wagner, 2005). Repetitive TMS is a noninvasive technique administered while a patient is awake. Brief pulsating magnetic fields are delivered to the cortex, inducing electrical activity. TMS has fewer side effects than ECT (Schulze-Rauschenbach et al., 2005), and while outcome studies are mixed, there is evidence that TMS is a promising treatment for patients with MDD who have shown resistance to other treatments (Rosa et al., 2006). Most recently, deep brain stimulation is being examined as a treatment option for patients who did not respond to more traditional treatments like those already described. Deep brain stimulation involves implanting an electrode in the brain. The electrode is connected to an implanted neurostimulator, which electrically stimulates that particular brain region. Although there is some evidence of its effectiveness (Mayberg et al., 2005), additional research is needed.

Several psychosocial treatments have received strong empirical support, meaning that independent investigations have achieved similarly positive results—a high threshold for examining treatment outcomes. These treatments include but are not limited to behavior therapy, cognitive therapy, and interpersonal therapy. Behavior therapies focus on increasing the frequency and quality of experiences that are pleasant or help the patient achieve mastery. Cognitive therapies primarily focus on helping patients identify and change distorted automatic thoughts and assumptions (e.g., Beck, 1967). Cognitive-behavioral therapies are based on the rationale that thoughts, behaviors, and emotions affect and are affected by each other. Interpersonal Therapy for Depression focuses largely on improving interpersonal relationships by targeting problem areas, specifically unresolved grief, interpersonal role disputes, role transitions, and interpersonal deficits. Finally, there is also some support for the effectiveness of Short-Term Psychodynamic Therapy for Depression (Leichsenring, 2001). The short-term treatment focuses on a limited number of important issues, and the therapist tends to be more actively involved than in more traditional psychodynamic therapy.

Bipolar Disorders

Patients with BD are typically treated with pharmacotherapy. Antidepressants such as SSRIs and SNRIs are the primary choice of treatment for depression, whereas for BD, lithium is the first line treatment choice. This is because SSRIs and SNRIs have the potential to induce mania or hypomania in patients with BD. Lithium acts on several neurotransmitter systems in the brain through complex mechanisms, including reduction of excitatory (dopamine and glutamate) neurotransmission, and increasing of inhibitory (GABA) neurotransmission (Lenox & Hahn, 2000). Lithium has strong efficacy for the treatment of BD (Geddes, Burgess, Hawton, Jamison, & Goodwin, 2004). However, a number of side effects can make lithium treatment difficult for patients to tolerate. Side effects include impaired cognitive function (Wingo, Wingo, Harvey, & Baldessarini, 2009), as well as physical symptoms such as nausea, tremor, weight gain, and fatigue (Dunner, 2000). Some of these side effects can improve with continued use; however, medication noncompliance remains an ongoing concern in the treatment of patients with BD. Anticonvulsant medications (e.g., carbamazepine, valproate) are also commonly used to treat patients with BD, either alone or in conjunction with lithium.

There are several adjunctive treatment options for people with BD. Interpersonal and social rhythm therapy (IPSRT; Frank et al., 1994) is a psychosocial intervention focused on addressing the mechanism of action posited in social *zeitgeber* theory to predispose patients who have BD to relapse, namely sleep disruption. A growing body of literature provides support for the central role of sleep dysregulation in BD (Harvey, 2008). Consistent with this literature, IPSRT aims to increase rhythmicity of patients' lives and encourage vigilance in maintaining a stable rhythm. The therapist and patient work to develop and maintain a healthy balance of activity and stimulation such that the patient does not become overly active (e.g., by taking on too many projects) or inactive (e.g., by avoiding social contact). The efficacy of IPSRT has been demonstrated in that patients who received this treatment show reduced risk of episode recurrence and are more likely to remain well (Frank et al., 2005).

Conclusion

Everyone feels down or euphoric from time to time. For some people, these feelings can last for long periods of time and can also co-occur with other symptoms that, in combination, interfere with their everyday lives. When people experience an MDE or a manic episode, they see the world differently. During an MDE, people often feel hopeless about the future, and may even experience suicidal thoughts. During a manic episode, people often behave in ways that are risky or place them in danger. They may spend money excessively or have unprotected sex, often expressing deep shame over these decisions after the episode. MDD and BD cause significant problems for people at school, at work, and in their relationships and affect people regardless of gender, age, nationality, race, religion, or sexual orientation. If you or someone you know is suffering from a mood disorder, it is important to seek help. Effective treatments are available and continually improving. If you have an interest in mood disorders, there are many ways to contribute to their understanding, prevention, and treatment, whether by engaging in research or clinical work.

Outside Resources

Books: Recommended memoirs include A Memoir of Madness by William Styron (MDD); Noonday Demon: An Atlas of Depression by Andrew Solomon (MDD); and An Unquiet Mind: A Memoir of Moods and Madness by Kay Redfield (BD).
Web: Visit the Association for Behavioral and Cognitive Therapies to find a list of the recommended therapists and evidence-based treatments.
http://www.abct.org
Web: Visit the Depression and Bipolar Support Alliance for educational information and social support options.
http://www.dbsalliance.org/

Discussion Questions

1. What factors might explain the large gender difference in the prevalence rates of MDD?

2. Why might American ethnic minority groups experience more persistent BD than European Americans?

3. Why might the age of onset for MDD be decreasing over time?

4. Why might overnight travel constitute a potential risk for a person with BD?

5. What are some reasons positive life events may precede the occurrence of manic episode?

Vocabulary

Anhedonia

Loss of interest or pleasure in activities one previously found enjoyable or rewarding.

Attributional style

The tendency by which a person infers the cause or meaning of behaviors or events.

Chronic stress

Discrete or related problematic events and conditions which persist over time and result in prolonged activation of the biological and/or psychological stress response (e.g., unemployment, ongoing health difficulties, marital discord).

Early adversity

Single or multiple acute or chronic stressful events, which may be biological or psychological in nature (e.g., poverty, abuse, childhood illness or injury), occurring during childhood and resulting in a biological and/or psychological stress response.

Grandiosity

Inflated self-esteem or an exaggerated sense of self-importance and self-worth (e.g., believing one has special powers or superior abilities).

Hypersomnia

Excessive daytime sleepiness, including difficulty staying awake or napping, or prolonged sleep episodes.

Psychomotor agitation

Increased motor activity associated with restlessness, including physical actions (e.g., fidgeting, pacing, feet tapping, handwringing).

Psychomotor retardation

A slowing of physical activities in which routine activities (e.g., eating, brushing teeth) are performed in an unusually slow manner.

Social zeitgeber

Zeitgeber is German for "time giver." Social zeitgebers are environmental cues, such as meal times and interactions with other people, that entrain biological rhythms and thus sleep-wake cycle regularity.

Socioeconomic status (SES)

A person's economic and social position based on income, education, and occupation.

Suicidal ideation

Recurring thoughts about suicide, including considering or planning for suicide, or preoccupation with suicide.

References

- Abramson, L. Y, Seligman, M. E. P., & Teasdale, J. (1978). Learned helplessness in humans: Critique and reformulation. *Journal of Abnormal Psychology, 87*, 49–74. doi: 10.1037/0021-843X.87.1.49

- Abramson, L. Y., Metalsky, G. I., & Alloy, L. B. (1989). Hopelessness depression: A theory-based subtype of depression. *Psychological Review, 96*, 358–373. doi: 10.1037/0022-3514.56.3.431

- Altshuler, L., Bookheimer, S., Townsend, J., Proenza, M. A., Sabb, F., Mintz, J., & Cohen, M. S.

(2008). Regional brain changes in bipolar I depression: A functional magnetic resonance imaging study. *Bipolar Disorders, 10*, 708–717. doi: 10.1111/j.1399-5618.2008.00617.x

- American Psychiatric Association. (2013). *Diagnostic and statistical manual of mental disorders* (5th ed.). Washington, DC: Author.

- American Psychiatric Association. (2000). *Diagnostic and statistical manual of mental disorders* (4th ed., text rev.). Washington, DC: Author.

- Beck, A. T. (1967). *Depression: Clinical, experimental, and theoretical aspects.* New York, NY: Hoeber.

- Blazer, D., George, L. K., Landerman, R., Pennybacker, M., Melville, M. L., Woodbury, M., et al. (1985). Psychiatric disorders. A rural/urban comparison. *Archives of General Psychiatry, 42*, 651–656. PMID: 4015306. doi: 10.1001/archpsyc.1985.01790300013002

- Breslau, J., Aguilar-Gaxiola, S., Kendler, K. S., Su, M., Williams, D., & Kessler, R. C. (2006). Specifying race-ethnic differences in risk for psychiatric disorder in a US national sample. *Psychological Medicine, 36*, 57–68. doi: 10.1017/S0033291705006161

- Breslau, J., Kendler, K. S., Su, M., Gaxiola-Aguilar, S., & Kessler, R. C. (2005). Lifetime risk and persistence of psychiatric disorders across ethnic groups in the United States. *Psychological Medicine, 35*, 317–327. doi: 10.1017/S0033291704003514

- Brown, G. W., & Harris, T. O. (1989). *Life events and illness.* New York, NY: Guilford Press.

- Butzlaff, R. L., & Hooley, J. M. (1998). Expressed emotion and psychiatric relapse: A meta-analysis. *Archives of General Psychiatry, 55*, 547–552. doi: 10.1001/archpsyc.55.6.547

- Chentsova-Dutton, Y. E., & Tsai, J. L. (2009). Understanding depression across cultures. In I. H. Gotlib & C.L. Hammen (Eds.), *Handbook of depression* (2nd ed., pp. 363–385). New York, NY: Guilford Press.

- Conley, C. S., & Rudolph, K. D. (2009). The emerging sex difference in adolescent depression: Interacting contributions of puberty and peer stress. *Development and Psychopathology, 21*, 593–620. doi: 10.1017/S0954579409000327

- Dunner, D. L. (2000). Optimizing lithium treatment. *Journal of Clinical Psychiatry, 61*(S9), 76–81.

- Ehlers, C. L., Frank, E., & Kupfer, D. J. (1988). Social zeitgebers and biological rhythms: a unified approach to understanding the etiology of depression. *Archives of General Psychiatry, 45*, 948–952. doi: 10.1001/archpsyc.1988.01800340076012

- Ellicott, A., Hammen, C., Gitlin, M., Brown, G., & Jamison, K. (1990). Life events and the course of bipolar disorder. *American Journal of Psychiatry, 147*, 1194–1198.

- Frank, E., Kupfer, D. J., Ehlers, C. L., Monk, T., Cornes, C., Carter, S., et al. (1994). Interpersonal and social rhythm therapy for bipolar disorder: Integrating interpersonal and behavioral approaches. *Behavior Therapy, 17*, 143–149.

- Frank, E., Kupfer, D. J., Thase, M. E., Mallinger, A. G., Swartz, H. A., Fagiolini, A. M., et al. (2005).

Two-year outcomes for interpersonal and social rhythm therapy in individuals with bipolar I disorder. *Archives of General Psychiatry, 62*, 996–1004. doi: 10.1001/archpsyc.62.9.996

- Geddes, J. R., Burgess, S., Hawton, K., Jamison, K., & Goodwin, G. M. (2004). Long-term lithium therapy for bipolar disorder: systematic review and meta-analysis of randomized controlled trials. *American Journal of Psychiatry, 161*, 217–222. doi: 10.1176/appi.ajp.161.2.217

- Gonzalez, J. M., Perlick, D. A., Miklowitz, D. J., Kaczynski, R., Hernandez, M., Rosenheck, R. A., et al. (2007). Factors associated with stigma among caregivers of patients with bipolar disorder in the STEP-BD study. *Psychiatric Services, 58*, 41–48. doi: 10.1176/appi.ps.58.1.41

- Goodwin, F. K., & Jamison, K. R. (2007). *Manic-depressive illness: Bipolar disorders and recurrent depression*. New York, NY: Oxford University Press.

- Gotlib, I. H., & Joormann, J. (2010). Cognition and depression: Current status and future directions. *Annual Review of Clinical Psychology, 6*, 285–312. doi: 10.1146/annurev.clinpsy.121208.131305

- Hamilton, J. P., Etkin, A., Furman, D. F., Lemus, M. G., Johnson, R. F., & Gotlib, I. H. (2012). Functional neuroimaging of major depressive disorder: A meta-analysis and new integration of baseline activation and neural response data. *American Journal of Psychiatry, 169*, 693–703.

- Hammen, C. (2005). Stress and depression. *Annual Review of Clinical Psychology, 1*, 293–319. doi: 10.1146/annurev.clinpsy.1.102803.143938

- Harvey, A. G. (2008). Sleep and Circadian Rhythms in Bipolar Disorder: Seeking synchrony, harmony and regulation. *American Journal of Psychiatry, 165*, 820–829. doi: 10.1176/appi.ajp.2008.08010098

- Hasin, D. S., Goodwin, R. D., Sintson, F. S., & Grant, B. F. (2005). Epidemiology of major depressive disorder: Results from the National Epidemiological Survey on Alcoholism and Related Conditions. *Archives of General Psychiatry, 62*, 1097–1106. doi: 10.1001/archpsyc.62.10.1097

- Hassel, S., Almeida, J. R., Kerr, N., Nau, S., Ladouceur, C. D., Fissell, K., et al. (2008). Elevated striatal and decreased dorsolateral prefrontal cortical activity in response to emotional stimuli in euthymic bipolar disorder: No associations with psychotropic medication load. *Bipolar Disorders, 10*, 916–927. doi: 10.1111/j.1399-5618.2008.00641.x

- Isaacowitz, D. M., Gershon, A., Allard, E. S., & Johnson, S. L. (2013). Emotion in aging and bipolar disorder: Similarities, differences and lessons for further research. *Emotion Review, 5*, 312–320. doi: 10.1177/1754073912472244

- Johnson, S. L. (2005). Mania and dysregulation in goal pursuit: A review. *Clinical Psychology Review, 25*, 241–262. doi: 10.1016/j.cpr.2004.11.002

- Johnson, S. L., Cueller, A. K., Ruggero, C., Winett-Perlman, C., Goodnick, P., White, R., et al. (2008). Life events as predictors of mania and depression in bipolar I disorder. *Journal of Abnormal Psychology, 117*, 268–277. doi: 10.1037/0021-843X.117.2.268

- Johnson, S. L., Winett, C. A., Meyer, B., Greenhouse, W. J., & Miller, I. (1999). Social support and the course of bipolar disorder. *Journal of Abnormal Psychology, 108*, 558–566. doi: 10.1037/

0021-843X.108.4.558

- Kessler, R. C., Berglund, P., Demler, O., Jim, R., Merikangas, K. R., & Walters, E. E. (2005). Lifetime prevalence and age-of-onset distributions of DSM-IV disorders in the National Comorbidity Survey Replication. *Archives of General Psychiatry, 62*, 593–602. doi: 10.1001/archpsyc.62.6.593

- Kessler, R. C., Birnbaum, H., Bromet, E., Hwang, I., Sampson, N., & Shahly, V. (2010). Age differences in major depression: Results from the National Comorbidity Surveys Replication (NCS-R). *Psychological Medicine, 40*, 225–237. doi: 10.1017/S0033291709990213

- Kessler, R. C., Merikangas, K. R., & Wang, P. S. (2007). Prevalence, comorbidity, and service utilization for mood disorders in the United States at the beginning of the 21st century. *Annual Review of Clinical Psychology, 3*, 137–158. doi: 10.1146/annurev.clinpsy.3.022806.091444

- Kilbourne, A. M., Haas, G. L., Mulsant, B. H., Bauer, M. S., & Pincus, H. A. (2004) Concurrent psychiatric diagnoses by age and race among persons with bipolar disorder. *Psychiatric Services, 55*, 931–933. doi: 10.1176/appi.ps.55.8.931

- Leichsenring, F. (2001). Comparative effects of short-term psychodynamic psychotherapy and cognitive-behavioral therapy in depression: A meta-analytic approach. *Clinical Psychology Review, 21*, 401–419. doi: 10.1016/S0272-7358(99)00057-4

- Lennox, B. R., Jacob, R., Calder, A. J., Lupson, V., & Bullmore, E. T. (2004). Behavioural and neurocognitive responses to sad facial affect are attenuated in patients with mania. *Psychological Medicine, 34*, 795–802. doi: 10.1017/S0033291704002557

- Lenox, R. H., & Hahn C. G. (2000). Overview of the mechanism of action of lithium in the brain: fifty-year update. *Journal of Clinical Psychiatry, 61* (S9), 5–15.

- Leverich, G. S., Altshuler, L. L., Frye, M. A., Suppes, T., Keck, P. E. Jr, McElroy, S. L., et al. (2003). Factors associated with suicide attempts in 648 patients with bipolar disorder in the Stanley Foundation Bipolar Network. *Journal of Clinical Psychiatry, 64*, 506–515. doi: 10.4088/JCP.v64n0503

- Leverich, G. S., Post, R. M., Keck, P. E. Jr, Altshuler, L. L., Frye, M. A., Kupka, R. W., et al. (2007). The poor prognosis of childhood-onset bipolar disorder. *Journal of Pediatrics, 150*, 485–490. PMID: 17452221. doi: 10.1016/j.jpeds.2006.10.070

- Lewinsohn, P. M., Allen, N. B., Seeley, J. R., & Gotlib, I. H. (1999). First onset versus recurrence of depression: differential processes of psychosocial risk. *Journal of Abnormal Psychology, 108*, 483–489. doi: 10.1037/0021-843X.108.3.483

- Lewinsohn, P. M., Seeley, J. R., Buckley, M. E., & Klein, D. N. (2002). Bipolar disorder in adolescence and young adulthood. *Child & Adolescent Psychiatric Clinics of North America, 11*, 461–475. doi: 10.1016/S1056-4993(02)00005-6

- Lohoff, F. W. (2010). Overview of genetics of major depressive disorder. *Current Psychiatry Reports, 12*, 539–546. doi: 10.1007/s11920-010-0150-6

- Lorant, V., Deliege, D., Eaton, W., Robert, A., Philippot, P., & Ansseau, A. (2003). Socioeconomic inequalities in depression: A meta-analysis. *American Journal of Epidemiology, 157*, 98–112. doi: 10.1093/aje/kwf182

• Malkoff-Schwartz, S., Frank, E., Anderson, B. P., Sherrill, J. T., Siegel, L., Patterson, D., et al. (1998). Stressful life events and social rhythm disruption in the onset of manic and depressive bipolar episodes: a preliminary investigation. *Archives of General Psychiatry, 55*, 702–707. doi: 10.1001/archpsyc.55.8.702

• Mayberg, H. S., Lozano, A. M., Voon, V., McNeely, H. E., Seminowixz, D., Hamani, C., Schwalb, J. M., & Kennedy, S. H. (2005). Deep brain stimulation for treatment-resistant depression. *Neuron, 45*, 651–660. doi: 10.1016/j.neuron.2005.02.014

• McElroy, S. L., Altshuler, L. L., Suppes, T., Keck, P. E. Jr, Frye, M. A., Denicoff, K. D., et al. (2001). Axis I psychiatric comorbidity and its relationship to historical illness variables in 288 patients with bipolar disorder. *American Journal of Psychiatry, 158*, 420–426. doi: 10.1176/appi.ajp.158.3.420

• McGuffin, P., Rijsdijk, F., Andrew, M., Sham, P., Katz, R., Cardno, A. (2003). The heritability of bipolar affective disorder and the genetic relationship to unipolar depression. *Archives of General Psychiatry, 60,* 497–502. doi: 10.1001/archpsyc.60.5.497

• Merikangas, K. R., Akiskal, H. S., Angst, J., Greenberg, P. E., Hirschfeld, R. M., Petukhova, M., et al. (2007). Lifetime and 12-month prevalence of bipolar spectrum disorder in the National Comorbidity Survey replication. *Archives of General Psychiatry, 64*, 543–552. doi: 10.1001/archpsyc.64.5.543

• Merikangas, K. R., Jin, R., He, J. P., Kessler, R. C., Lee, S., Sampson, N. A., et al. (2011). Prevalence and correlates of bipolar spectrum disorder in the world mental health survey initiative. *Archives of General Psychiatry, 68*, 241–251. doi: 10.1001/archgenpsychiatry.2011.12

• Minsky, S., Vega, W., Miskimen, T., Gara, M., & Escobar, J. (2003). Diagnostic patterns in Latino, African American, and European American psychiatric patients. *Archives of General Psychiatry, 60,* 637–644. doi: 10.1001/archpsyc.60.6.637

• Monroe, S. M., & Harkness, K. L. (2011). Recurrence in major depression: A conceptual analysis. *Psychological Review, 118*, 655–674. doi: 10.1037/a0025190

• Monroe, S. M., & Harkness, K. L. (2005). Life stress, the "Kindling" hypothesis, and the recurrence of depression: Considerations from a life stress perspective. *Psychological Review, 112*, 417–445. doi: 10.1037/0033-295X.112.2.417

• Monroe, S.M., Slavich, G.M., Georgiades, K. (2009). The social environment and life stress in depression. In Gotlib, I.H., Hammen, C.L (Eds.) *Handbook of depression* (2nd ed., pp. 340-360). New York, NY: Guilford Press.

• Nolen-Hoeksema, S., & Hilt, L. M. (2009). Gender differences in depression. In I. H. Gotlib & Hammen, C. L. (Eds.), *Handbook of depression* (2nd ed., pp. 386–404). New York, NY: Guilford Press.

• Perlis, R. H., Miyahara, S., Marangell, L. B., Wisniewski, S. R., Ostacher, M., DelBello, M. P., et al. (2004). Long-term implications of early onset in bipolar disorder: data from the first 1000 participants in the systematic treatment enhancement program for bipolar disorder (STEP-BD). *Biological Psychia-*

try, 55, 875–881. PMID: 15110730. doi: 10.1016/j.pscychresns.2007.10.003

- Rosa, M. A., Gattaz, W. F., Pascual-Leone, A., Fregni, F., Rosa, M. O., Rumi, D. O., … Marcolin, M. A. (2006). Comparison of repetitive transcranial magnetic stimulation and electroconvulsive therapy in unipolar non-psychotic refractory depression: a randomized, single-blind study. *International Journal of Neuropsychopharmacology, 9*, 667–676. doi: 10.1017/S1461145706007127

- Schulze-Rauschenbach, S. C., Harms, U., Schlaepfer, T. E., Maier, W., Falkai, P., & Wagner, M. (2005). Distinctive neurocognitive effects of repetitive transcranial magnetic stimulation and electroconvulsive therapy in major depression. *British Journal of Psychiatry, 186*, 410–416. doi: 10.1192/bjp.186.5.410

- Shields, B. (2005). *Down Came the Rain: My Journey Through Postpartum Depression*. New York: Hyperion.

- Sullivan, P., Neale, M. C., & Kendler, K. S. (2000). Genetic epidemiology of major depression: Review and meta-analysis. *American Journal of Psychiatry, 157*, 1552–1562. doi: 10.1176/appi.ajp.157.10.1552

- Twenge, J. M., & Nolen-Hoeksema, S. (2002). Age, gender, race, SES, and birth cohort differences on the Children's Depression Inventory: A meta-analysis. *Journal of Abnormal Psychology, 111*, 578–588. doi: 10.1037/0021-843X.111.4.578

- Whisman, M. A., & Uebelacker, L. A. (2009). Prospective associations between marital discord and depressive symptoms in middle-aged and older adults. *Psychology and Aging, 24*, 184–189. doi: 10.1037/a0014759

- Widom, C. S., DuMont, K., & Czaja, S. J. (2007). A prospective investigation of major depressive disorder and comorbidity in abused and neglected children grown up. *Archives of General Psychiatry, 64*, 49–56. doi: 10.1001/archpsyc.64.1.49

- Williams, D. R., Gonzalez, H. M., Neighbors, H., Nesse, R., Abelson, J. M., Sweetman, J., & Jackson, J. S. (2007). Prevalence and distribution of major depressive disorder in African Americans, Caribbean blacks, and non-Hispanic whites: Results from the National Survey of American Life. *Archives of General Psychiatry, 64*, 305–315. doi: 10.1001/archpsyc.64.3.305

- Wingo, A. P., Wingo, T. S., Harvey, P. D., & Baldessarini, R. J. (2009). Effects of lithium on cognitive performance: a meta-analysis. *Journal of Clinical Psychiatry, 70*, 1588–1597. doi: 10.4088/JCP.08r04972

CC licensed content, Shared previously

Personality Disorders

The purpose of this module is to define what is meant by a personality disorder, identify the five domains of general personality (i.e., neuroticism, extraversion, openness, agreeableness, and conscientiousness), identify the six personality disorders proposed for retention in the 5th edition of the Diagnostic and Statistical Manual of Mental Disorders (DSM-5) (i.e., borderline, antisocial, schizotypal, avoidant, obsessive-compulsive, and narcissistic), summarize the etiology for antisocial and borderline personality disorder, and identify the treatment for borderline personality disorder (i.e., dialectical behavior therapy and mentalization therapy).

Learning Objectives

- Define what is meant by a personality disorder.

- Identify the five domains of general personality.

- Identify the six personality disorders proposed for retention in DSM-5.

- Summarize the etiology for antisocial and borderline personality disorder.

- Identify the treatment for borderline personality disorder.

Introduction

Everybody has their own unique personality; that is, their characteristic manner of thinking, feeling, behaving, and relating to others (John, Robins, & Pervin, 2008). Some people are typically introverted, quiet, and withdrawn; whereas others are more extraverted, active, and outgoing. Some individuals are invariably conscientiousness, dutiful, and efficient; whereas others might be characteristically undependable and negligent. Some individuals are consistently anxious, self-conscious, and apprehensive; whereas others are routinely relaxed, self-assured, and unconcerned. Personality traits refer to these characteristic, routine ways of thinking, feeling, and relating to others. There are signs or indicators of these traits in childhood, but they become particularly evident when the person is an adult. Personality traits are integral to each person's sense of self, as they involve what people value, how they think and feel about things, what they like to do, and, basically, what they are like most every day throughout much of their lives.

There are literally hundreds of different personality traits. All of these traits can be organized into the broad dimensions referred to as the Five-Factor Model (John, Naumann, & Soto, 2008). These five broad domains are inclusive; there does not appear to be any traits of personality that lie outside of the Five-Factor Model. This even applies to traits that you may use to describe yourself. Table I provides illustrative traits for both poles of the five domains of this model of personality. A number of the traits that you see in this table may describe you. If you can think of some other traits that describe yourself, you should be able to place them somewhere in this table.

Neuroticism (Emotional Instability) fearful, apprehensive, angry, bitter, pessimistic, glum, timid, embarrassed, tempted, urgency, helpless, fragile	VS	**Emotional Stability** relaxed, unconcerned, cool, even-tempered, optimistic, self-assured, glib, shameless, controlled, restrained, clear-thinking, fearless, unflappable
Extraversion cordial, affectionate, attached, sociable, outgoing, dominant, forceful, vigorous, energetic, active, reckless, daring, high-spirited, excitement-seeking	VS	**Introversion** cold, aloof, indifferent, withdrawn, isolated, unassuming, quiet, resigned, passive, lethargic, cautious, monotonous, dull, placid, anhedonic
Openness (unconventionality) dreamer, unrealistic, imaginative, aberrant, aesthetic, self-aware, eccentric, strange, odd, peculiar, creative, permissive, broad-minded	VS	**Closedness (conventionality)** practical, concrete, uninvolved, no aesthetic interest, constricted, unaware, alexythymic, routine, predictable, habitual, stubborn, pragmatic, rigid, traditional, inflexible, dogmatic
Agreeableness gullible, naive, trusting, confiding, honest, sacrificial, giving, docile, cooperative, meek, self-effacing, humble, soft, empathetic	VS	**Antagonism** skeptical, cynical, suspicious, paranoid, cunning, manipulative, deceptive, stingy, selfish, greedy, exploitative, oppositional, combative, aggressive, confident, boastful, arrogant, tough, callous, ruthless
Conscientiousness perfectionistic, efficient, ordered, methodical, organized, rigid, reliable, dependable, workaholic, ambitious, dogged, devoted, cautious, ruminative, reflective	VS	**Disinhibition** lax, negligent, haphazard, disorganized, sloppy, casual, undependable, unethical, aimless, desultory, hedonistic, negligent, hasty, careless, rash

Table I: Illustrative traits for both poles across Five-Factor Model personality dimensions.

DSM-5 Personality Disorders

When personality traits result in significant distress, social impairment, and/or occupational impairment, they are considered to be a personality disorder (American Psychiatric Association, 2013). The authoritative manual for what constitutes a personality disorder is provided by the American Psychiatric Association's (APA) *Diagnostic and Statistical Manual of Mental Disorders* (DSM), the current version of which is DSM-5 (APA, 2013). The DSM provides a common language and standard criteria for the classification and diagnosis of mental disorders. This manual is used by clinicians, researchers, health insurance companies, and policymakers. DSM-5 includes 10 personality disorders: antisocial, avoidant, borderline, dependent, histrionic, narcissistic, obsessive-compulsive, paranoid, schizoid, and schizotypal. All 10 of these personality disorders will be included in the next edition of the diagnostic manual, DSM-5.

This list of 10 though does not fully cover all of the different ways in which a personality can be maladaptive. DSM-5 also includes a "wastebasket" diagnosis of other specified personality disorder (OSPD) and unspecified personality disorder (UPD). This diagnosis is used when a clinician believes that a patient has a personality disorder but the traits that constitute this disorder are not well covered by one of the 10 existing diagnoses. OSPD and UPD or as they used to be referred to in previous editions – PDNOS (personality disorder not otherwise specified) are often one of the most frequently used diagnoses in clinical practice, suggesting that the current list of 10 is not adequately comprehensive (Widiger & Trull, 2007).

Description

Each of the 10 DSM-5 (and DSM-IV-TR) personality disorders is a constellation of maladaptive personality traits, rather than just one particular personality trait (Lynam & Widiger, 2001). In this regard, personality disorders are "syndromes." For example, avoidant personality disorder is a pervasive pattern of social inhibition, feelings of inadequacy, and hypersensitivity to negative evaluation (APA, 2013), which is a combination of traits from introversion (e.g., socially withdrawn, passive, and cautious) and neuroticism (e.g., self-consciousness, apprehensiveness, anxiousness, and worrisome). Dependent personality disorder includes submissiveness, clinging behavior, and fears of separation (APA, 2013), for the most part a combination of traits of neuroticism (anxious, uncertain, pessimistic, and helpless) and maladaptive agreeableness (e.g., gullible, guileless, meek, subservient, and self-effacing). Antisocial personality disorder is, for the most part, a combination of traits from antagonism (e.g., dishonest, manipulative, exploitative, callous, and merciless) and low conscientiousness (e.g., irresponsible, immoral, lax, hedonistic, and rash). See the 1967 movie, *Bonnie and Clyde,* starring Warren Beatty, for a nice portrayal of someone with antisocial personality disorder.

A man holds his head in frustration as he looks down at some paperwork.

A person with an obsessive compulsive personality disorder may have a hard time relaxing, always feel under pressure, and believe that there isn't enough time to accomplish important tasks. [Image: CC0 Public Domain, https://goo.gl/m25gce]

Some of the DSM-5 personality disorders are confined largely to traits within one of the basic domains of personality. For example, obsessive-compulsive personality disorder is largely a disorder of maladaptive conscientiousness, including such traits as workaholism, perfectionism, punctilious, ruminative, and dogged; schizoid is confined largely to traits of introversion (e.g., withdrawn, cold, isolated, placid, and anhedonic); borderlinepersonality disorder is largely a disorder of neuroticism, including such traits as emotionally unstable, vulnerable, overwhelmed, rageful, depressive, and self-destructive (watch the 1987 movie, *Fatal Attraction*, starring Glenn Close, for a nice portrayal of this personality disorder); and histrionic personality disorder is largely a disorder of maladaptive extraversion, including such traits as attention-seeking, seductiveness, melodramatic emotionality, and strong attachment needs (see the 1951 film adaptation of Tennessee William's play, *Streetcar Named Desire*, starring Vivian Leigh, for a nice portrayal of this personality disorder).

It should be noted though that a complete description of each DSM-5 personality disorder would typically include at least some traits from other domains. For example, antisocial personality disorder (or psychopathy) also includes some traits from low neuroticism (e.g., fearlessness and glib charm) and extraversion (e.g., excitement-seeking and assertiveness); borderline includes some traits from antagonism (e.g., manipulative and oppositional) and low conscientiousness (e.g., rash); and histrionic includes some traits from antagonism (e.g., vanity) and low conscientiousness (e.g., impressionistic). Narcissistic personality disorder includes traits from neuroticism (e.g., reactive anger, reactive shame, and need for admiration), extraversion (e.g., exhibitionism and authoritativeness), antagonism (e.g., arrogance, entitlement, and lack of empathy), and conscientiousness (e.g., acclaim-seeking). Schizotypal personality disorder includes traits from neuroticism (e.g., social anxiousness and social discomfort), introversion (e.g., social withdrawal), unconventionality (e.g., odd, eccentric, peculiar, and aberrant ideas), and antagonism (e.g., suspiciousness).

The APA currently conceptualizes personality disorders as qualitatively distinct conditions; distinct from each other and from normal personality functioning. However, included within an appendix to DSM-5 is an alternative view that personality disorders are simply extreme and/or maladaptive variants of normal personality traits, as suggested herein. Nevertheless, many leading personality disorder researchers do not hold this view (e.g., Gunderson, 2010; Hopwood, 2011; Shedler et al., 2010). They suggest that there is something qualitatively unique about persons suffering from a personality disorder, usually understood as a form of pathology in sense of self and interpersonal relatedness that is considered to be distinct from personality traits (APA, 2012; Skodol, 2012). For example, it has been suggested that antisocial personality disorder includes impairments in identity (e.g., egocentrism), self-direction, empathy, and capacity for intimacy, which are said to be different from such traits as arrogance, impulsivity, and callousness (APA, 2012).

Validity

It is quite possible that in future revisions of the DSM some of the personality disorders included in DSM-5 and DSM-IV-TR will no longer be included. In fact, for DSM-5 it was originally proposed that four be deleted. The personality disorders that were slated for deletion were histrionic, schizoid, paranoid, and dependent (APA, 2012). The rationale for the proposed deletions was in large part because they are said to have less empirical support than the diagnoses that were at the time being retained (Skodol, 2012). There is agreement within the field with regard to the empirical support for the borderline, antisocial, and schizotypal personality disorders (Mullins-Sweat, Bernstein, & Widiger, 2012; Skodol, 2012). However, there is a difference of opinion with respect to the empirical support for the dependent personality disorder (Bornstein, 2012; Livesley, 2011; Miller, Widiger, & Campbell, 2010; Mullins-Sweat et al., 2012).

Little is known about the specific etiology for most of the DSM-5 personality disorders. Because each personality disorder represents a constellation of personality traits, the etiology for the syndrome will involve a complex interaction of an array of different neurobiological vulnerabilities and dispositions with a variety of environmental, psychosocial events. Antisocial personality disorder, for instance, is generally considered to be the result of an interaction of genetic dispositions for low anxiousness, aggressiveness, impulsivity, and/or callousness, with a tough, urban environment, inconsistent parenting, poor parental role modeling, and/or peer support (Hare, Neumann, & Widiger, 2012). Borderline personality disorder is generally considered to be the result of an interaction of a genetic disposition to negative affectivity interacting with a malevolent, abusive, and/or invalidating family environment (Hooley, Cole, & Gironde, 2012).

To the extent that one considers the DSM-5 personality disorders to be maladaptive variants of general personality structure, as described, for instance, within the Five-Factor Model, there would be a considerable body of research to support the validity for all of the personality disorders, including even the histrionic, schizoid, and paranoid. There is compelling multivariate behavior genetic support with respect to the precise structure of the Five-Factor Model (e.g., Yamagata et al., 2006), childhood antecedents (Caspi, Roberts, & Shiner, 2005), universality (Allik, 2005), temporal stability across the lifespan (Roberts & DelVecchio, 2000), ties with brain structure (DeYoung, Hirsh, Shane, Papademetris, Rajeevan, & Gray, 2010), and even molecular genetic support for neuroticism (Widiger, 2009).

Treatment

Personality disorders are relatively unique because they are often "ego-syntonic;" that is, most people are largely comfortable with their selves, with their characteristic manner of behaving, feeling, and relating to others. As a result, people rarely seek treatment for their antisocial, narcissistic, histrionic, paranoid, and/or schizoid personality disorder. People typically lack insight into the maladaptivity of their personality.

Many people with personality disorders do not seek treatment. Those with borderline personality disorder and avoidant personality disorder are exceptions. High levels of neuroticism and emotional pain may motivate them to seek help. [Image: CC0 Public Domain, https://goo.gl/m25gce]

One clear exception though is borderline personality disorder (and perhaps as well avoidant personality disorder). Neuroticism is the domain of general personality structure that concerns inherent feelings of emotional pain and suffering, including feelings of distress, anxiety, depression, self-consciousness, helplessness, and vulnerability. Persons who have very high elevations on neuroticism (i.e., persons with borderline personality disorder) experience life as one of pain and suffering, and they will seek treatment to alleviate this severe emotional distress. People with avoidant personality may also seek treatment for their high levels of neuroticism (anxiousness and self-consciousness) and introversion (social isolation). In contrast, narcissistic individuals will rarely seek treatment to reduce their arrogance; paranoid persons rarely seek treatment to reduce their feelings of suspiciousness; and antisocial people rarely (or at least willfully) seek treatment to reduce their disposition for criminality, aggression, and irresponsibility.

Nevertheless, maladaptive personality traits will be evident in many individuals seeking treatment for other mental disorders, such as anxiety, mood, or substance use. Many of the people with a substance use disorder will have antisocial personality traits; many of the people with mood disorder will have borderline personality traits. The prevalence of personality disorders within clinical settings is estimated to be well above 50% (Torgersen, 2012). As many as 60% of inpatients within some clinical settings are diagnosed with borderline personality disorder (APA, 2000). Antisocial personality disorder may be diagnosed in as many as 50% of inmates within a correctional setting (Hare et al., 2012). It is estimated that 10% to 15% of the general population meets criteria for at least one of the 10 DSM-IV-TR personality disorders (Torgersen, 2012), and quite a few more individuals are likely to have maladaptive personality traits not covered by one of the 10 DSM-5 diagnoses.

The presence of a personality disorder will often have an impact on the treatment of other mental disorders, typically inhibiting or impairing responsivity. Antisocial persons will tend to be irresponsible and negligent; borderline persons can form intensely manipulative attachments to their therapists; paranoid patients will be unduly suspicious and accusatory; narcissistic patients can be dismissive and denigrating; and dependent patients can become overly attached to and feel helpless without their therapists.

It is a misnomer, though, to suggest that personality disorders cannot themselves be treated. Personality disorders are among the most difficult of disorders to treat because they involve well-established behaviors that can be integral to a client's self-image (Millon, 2011). Nevertheless, much has been written on the treatment of personality disorder (e.g., Beck, Freeman, Davis, & Associates, 1990; Gunderson & Gabbard, 2000), and there is empirical support for clinically and socially meaningful changes in response to psychosocial and pharmacologic treatments

(Perry & Bond, 2000). The development of an ideal or fully healthy personality structure is unlikely to occur through the course of treatment, but given the considerable social, public health, and personal costs associated with some of the personality disorders, such as the antisocial and borderline, even just moderate adjustments in personality functioning can represent quite significant and meaningful change.

Nevertheless, manualized and/or empirically validated treatment protocols have been developed for only one personality disorder, borderline (APA, 2001).

Focus Topic:
Treatment of Borderline Personality Disorder

Dialectical behavior therapy (Lynch & Cuyper, 2012) and mentalization therapy (Bateman & Fonagy, 2012): Dialectical behavior therapy is a form of cognitive-behavior therapy that draws on principles from Zen Buddhism, dialectical philosophy, and behavioral science. The treatment has four components: individual therapy, group skills training, telephone coaching, and a therapist consultation team, and will typically last a full year. As such, it is a relatively expensive form of treatment, but research has indicated that its benefits far outweighs its costs, both financially and socially.

It is unclear why specific and explicit treatment manuals have not been developed for the other personality disorders. This may reflect a regrettable assumption that personality disorders are unresponsive to treatment. It may also reflect the complexity of their treatment. As noted earlier, each DSM-5 disorder is a heterogeneous constellation of maladaptive personality traits. In fact, a person can meet diagnostic criteria for the antisocial, borderline, schizoid, schizotypal, narcissistic, and avoidant personality disorders and yet have only one diagnostic criterion in common. For example, only five of nine features are necessary for the diagnosis of borderline personality disorder; therefore, two persons can meet criteria for this disorder and yet have only one feature in common. In addition, patients meeting diagnostic criteria for one personality disorder will often meet diagnostic criteria for another. This degree of diagnostic overlap and heterogeneity of membership hinders tremendously any effort to identify a specific etiology, pathology, or treatment for a respective personality disorder as there is so much variation within any particular group of patients sharing the same diagnosis (Smith & Zapolski, 2009).

Of course, this diagnostic overlap and complexity did not prevent researchers and clinicians from developing dialectical behavior therapy and mentalization therapy. A further reason for the weak progress in treatment development is that, as noted earlier, persons rarely seek treatment for their personality disorder. It would be difficult to obtain a sufficiently large group of people with, for instance, narcissistic or obsessive–compulsive disorder to participate in a treatment outcome study, one receiving the manualized treatment protocol, the other receiving treatment as usual.

Conclusions

It is evident that all individuals have a personality, as indicated by their characteristic way of thinking, feeling, behaving, and relating to others. For some people, these traits result in a considerable degree of distress and/or impairment, constituting a personality disorder. A considerable body of research has accumulated to help understand the etiology, pathology, and/or treatment for some personality disorders (i.e., antisocial, schizotypal, borderline, dependent, and narcissistic), but not so much for others (e.g., histrionic, schizoid, and paranoid). However, researchers and clinicians are now shifting toward a more dimensional understanding of personality disorders, wherein each is understood as a maladaptive variant of general personality structure, thereby bringing to bear all that is known about general personality functioning to an understanding of these maladaptive variants.

Outside Resources

Structured Clinical Interview for DSM-5 (SCID-5)
https://www.appi.org/products/structured-clinical-interview-for-dsm-5-scid-5
Web: DSM-5 website discussion of personality disorders
http://www.dsm5.org/ProposedRevision/Pages/PersonalityDisorders.aspx

Discussion Questions

1. Do you think that any of the personality disorders, or some of their specific traits, are ever good or useful to have?

2. If someone with a personality disorder commits a crime, what is the right way for society to respond? For example, does or should meeting diagnostic criteria for antisocial personality disorder mitigate (lower) a person's responsibility for committing a crime?

3. Given what you know about personality disorders and the traits that comprise each one, would you say there is any personality disorder that is likely to be diagnosed in one gender more than the other? Why or why not?

4. Do you believe that personality disorders can be best understood as a constellation of maladaptive personality traits, or do you think that there is something more involved for individuals suffering from a personality disorder?

5. The authors suggested Clyde Barrow as an example of antisocial personality disorder and Blanche Dubois for histrionic personality disorder. Can you think of a person from the media or literature who would have at least some of the traits of narcissistic personality disorder?

Vocabulary

Antisocial
A pervasive pattern of disregard and violation of the rights of others. These behaviors may be aggressive or destructive and may involve breaking laws or rules, deceit or theft.
Avoidant
A pervasive pattern of social inhibition, feelings of inadequacy, and hypersensitivity to negative evaluation.
Borderline
A pervasive pattern of instability of interpersonal relationships, self-image, and affects, and marked impulsivity.

Dependent

A pervasive and excessive need to be taken care of that leads to submissive and clinging behavior and fears of separation.

Five-Factor Model

Five broad domains or dimensions that are used to describe human personality.

Histrionic

A pervasive pattern of excessive emotionality and attention seeking.

Narcissistic

A pervasive pattern of grandiosity (in fantasy or behavior), need for admiration, and lack of empathy.

Obsessive-compulsive

A pervasive pattern of preoccupation with orderliness, perfectionism, and mental and interpersonal control, at the expense of flexibility, openness, and efficiency.

Paranoid

A pervasive distrust and suspiciousness of others such that their motives are interpreted as malevolent.

Personality

Characteristic, routine ways of thinking, feeling, and relating to others.

Personality disorders

When personality traits result in significant distress, social impairment, and/or occupational impairment.

Schizoid

A pervasive pattern of detachment from social relationships and a restricted range of expression of emotions in interpersonal settings.

Schizotypal

A pervasive pattern of social and interpersonal deficits marked by acute discomfort with, and reduced capacity for, close relationships as well as perceptual distortions and eccentricities of behavior.

References

- Allik, J. (2005). Personality dimensions across cultures. *Journal of Personality Disorders, 19,* 212–232.

- American Psychiatric Association (2012). *Rationale for the proposed changes to the personality disorders classification in DSM-5*. Retrieved from http://www.dsm5.org/ProposedRevision/Pages/PersonalityDisorders.aspx.

- American Psychiatric Association. (2013). *Diagnostic and statistical manual of mental disorders: DSM-5.*Washington, D.C: American Psychiatric Association.

- American Psychiatric Association. (2001). *Practice guidelines for the treatment of patients with borderline personality disorder.* Washington, DC: Author.

- American Psychiatric Association. (2000). Diagnostic and statistical manual of mental disorders (4th ed., text rev.) Washington, D.C: American Psychiatric Association.

- Bateman, A. W., & Fonagy, P. (2012). Mentalization-based treatment of borderline personality disorder. In T. A. Widiger (Ed.), *The Oxford handbook of personality disorders* (pp. 767–784). New York, NY: Oxford University Press.

- Beck, A. T., Freeman, A., Davis, D., and Associates (1990). *Cognitive therapy of personality disorders,* (2nd ed.). New York, NY: Guilford Press.

- Bornstein, R. F. (2012). Illuminating a neglected clinical issue: Societal costs of interpersonal dependency and dependent personality disorder. *Journal of Clinical Psychology, 68,* 766–781.

- Caspi, A., Roberts, B. W., & Shiner, R. L. (2005). Personality development: *Stability and change. Annual Review of Psychology, 56,* 453–484.

- DeYoung, C. G., Hirsh, J. B., Shane, M. S., Papademetris, X., Rajeevan, N., & Gray, J. (2010). *Testing predictions from personality neuroscience: Brain structure and the Big Five. Psychological Science, 21,* 820–828.

- Gunderson, J. G. (2010). Commentary on "Personality traits and the classification of mental disorders: Toward a more complete integration in DSM-5 and an empirical model of psychopathology." *Personality Disorders: Theory, Research, and Treatment, 1,* 119–122.

- Gunderson, J. G., & Gabbard, G. O. (Eds.), (2000). *Psychotherapy for personality disorders.* Washington, DC: American Psychiatric Press.

- Hare, R. D., Neumann, C. S., & Widiger, T. A. (2012). Psychopathy. In T. A. Widiger (Ed.), *The Oxford handbook of personality disorders* (pp. 478–504). New York, NY: Oxford University Press.

- Hooley, J. M., Cole, S. H., & Gironde, S. (2012). Borderline personality disorder. In T. A. Widiger (Ed.), *The Oxford handbook of personality disorders* (pp. 409–436). New York, NY: Oxford University Press.

- Hopwood, C. J. (2011). Personality traits in the DSM-5. *Journal of Personality Assessment, 93,* 398–405.

- John, O. P., Naumann, L. P., & Soto, C. J. (2008). Paradigm shift to the integrative Big Five trait taxonomy: History, measurement, and conceptual issues. In O. P. John, R. R. Robins, & L. A. Pervin (Eds.), *Handbook of personality. Theory and research* (3rd ed., pp. 114–158). New York, NY: Guilford Press.

- John, O. P., Robins, R. W., & Pervin, L. A. (Eds.), (2008). *Handbook of personality. Theory and Research* (3rd ed.). New York, NY: Guilford Press.

- Livesley, W. J. (2011). Confusion and incoherence in the classification of personality disorder: Commentary on the preliminary proposals for DSM-5. *Psychological Injury and Law, 3,* 304–313.

- Lynam, D. R., & Widiger, T. A. (2001). Using the five factor model to represent the DSM-IV personality disorders: An expert consensus approach. *Journal of Abnormal Psychology, 110,* 401–412.

- Lynch, T. R., & Cuper, P. F. (2012). Dialectical behavior therapy of borderline and other personality disorders. In T. A. Widiger (Ed.), *The Oxford handbook of personality disorders* (pp. 785–793). New York, NY: Oxford University Press.

- Miller, J. D., Widiger, T. A., & Campbell, W. K. (2010). Narcissistic personality disorder and the DSM-V. *Journal of Abnormal Psychology, 119*, 640–649.

- Millon, T. (2011). *Disorders of personality. Introducing a DSM/ICD spectrum from normal to abnormal* (3rd ed.). New York, NY: John Wiley & Sons.

- Mullins-Sweatt; Bernstein; Widiger. Retention or deletion of personality disorder diagnoses for DSM-5: an expert consensus approach. *Journal of personality disorders* 2012;26(5):689-703.

- Perry, J. C., & Bond, M. (2000). Empirical studies of psychotherapy for personality disorders. In J. Gunderson and G. Gabbard (Eds.), *Psychotherapy for personality disorders* (pp. 1–31). Washington DC: American Psychiatric Press.

- Roberts, B. W., & DelVecchio, W. F. (2000). The rank-order consistency of personality traits from childhood to old age: A quantitative review of longitudinal studies. *Psychological Bulletin, 126*, 3–25.

- Shedler, J., Beck, A., Fonagy, P., Gabbard, G. O., Gunderson, J. G., Kernberg, O., … Westen, D. (2010). Personality disorders in DSM-5. *American Journal of Psychiatry, 167*, 1027–1028.

- Skodol, A. (2012). Personality disorders in DSM-5. Annual *Review of Clinical Psychology, 8*, 317–344.

- Smith, G. G., & Zapolski, T. C. B. (2009). Construct validation of personality measures. In J. N. Butcher (Ed.), The *Oxford Handbook of Personality Assessment* (pp. 81–98). New York, NY: Oxford University Press.

- Torgerson, S. (2012). Epidemiology. In T. A. Widiger (Ed.), *The Oxford handbook of personality disorders* (pp. 186–205). New York, NY: Oxford University Press.

- Widiger, T. A. (2009). Neuroticism. In M. R. Leary and R.H. Hoyle (Eds.), *Handbook of individual differences in social behavior* (pp. 129–146). New York, NY: Guilford Press.

- Widiger, T. A., & Trull, T. J. (2007). Plate tectonics in the classification of personality disorder: *Shifting to a dimensional model. American Psychologist, 62*, 71–83.

- Yamagata, S., Suzuki, A., Ando, J., One, Y., Kijima, N., Yoshimura, K., … Jang, K. L. (2006). Is the genetic structure of human personality universal? A cross-cultural twin study from North America, Europe, and Asia. *Journal of Personality and Social Psychology, 90*, 987–998.

CC licensed content, Shared previously

Psychopathy

Psychopathy (or "psychopathic personality") is a topic that has long fascinated the public at large as well as scientists and clinical practitioners. However, it has also been subject to considerable confusion and scholarly debate over the years. This module reviews alternative conceptions of psychopathy that have been proposed historically, and reviews major instruments currently in use for the assessment of psychopathic tendencies in clinical and nonclinical samples. An integrative theoretic framework, the Triarchic model, is presented that provides a basis for reconciling differing historic conceptions and assessment approaches. Implications of the model for thinking about causal hypotheses of psychopathy, and for resolving longstanding points of contention in the field, are discussed.

Learning Objectives

- Learn about Cleckley's classic account of psychopathy, presented in his book The Mask of Sanity, along with other historic conceptions.

- Compare and contrast differing inventories currently in use for assessing psychopathy in differing samples (e.g., adults and younger individuals, within clinical-forensic and community settings).

- Become familiar with the Triarchic model of psychopathy and its constituent constructs of boldness, meanness, and disinhibition.

- Learn about alternative theories regarding the causal origins of psychopathy.

- Consider how longstanding matters of debate regarding the nature, definition, and origins of psychopathy can be addressed from the perspective of the Triarchic model.

Introduction

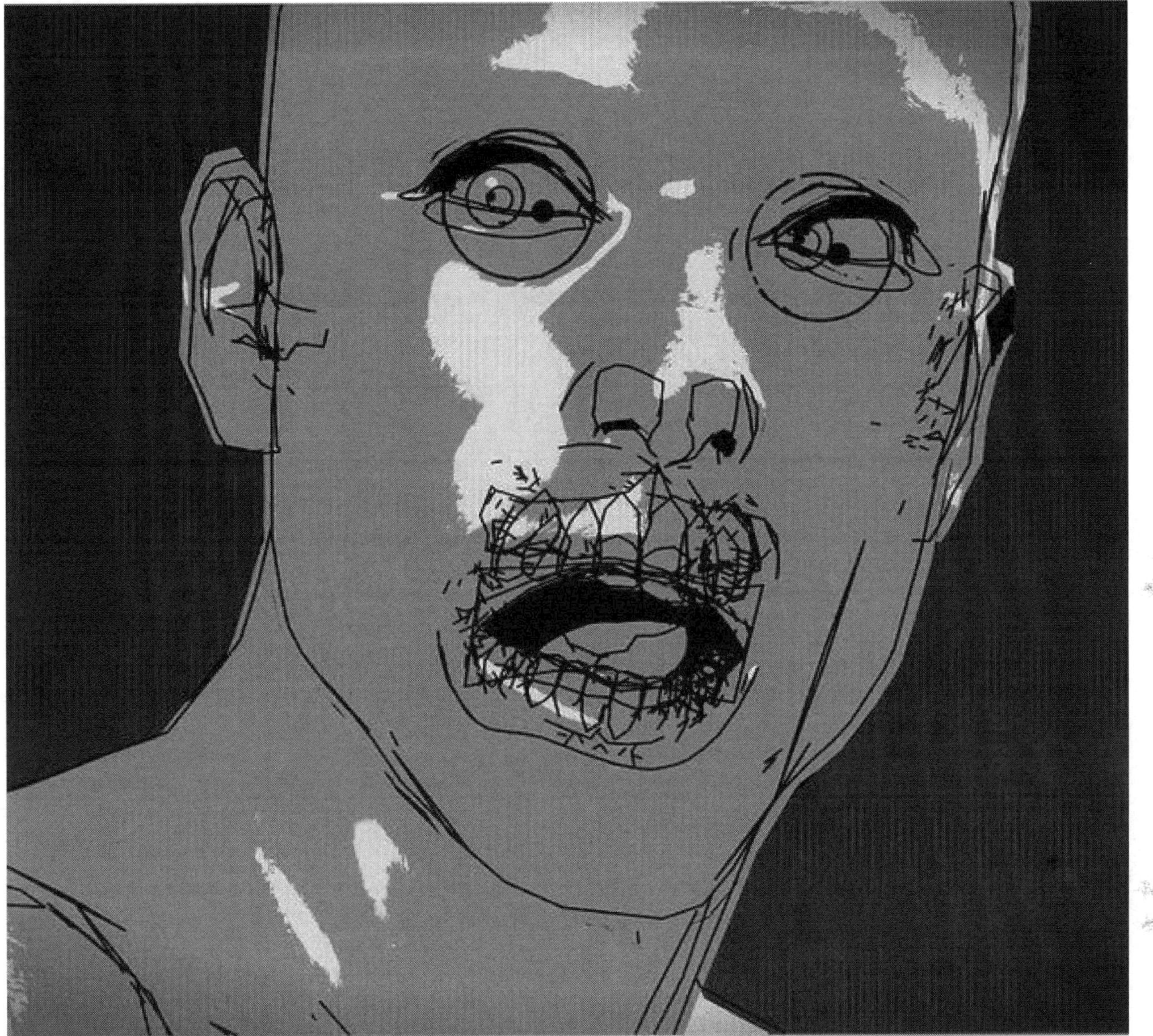

Popular media have developed the character of the psychopath into a popular genre. But often these portrayals – psychopaths as criminal monsters preying on innocent people – are misleading. [Image: CC0 Public Domain, https://goo.gl/m25gce]

For many in the public at large, the term "psychopath" conjures up images of ruthless homicidal maniacs and criminal masterminds. This impression is reinforced on an ongoing basis by depictions of psychopathic individuals in popular books and films, such as *No Country for Old Men, Silence of the Lambs,* and *Catch Me if You Can,* and by media accounts of high-profile criminals ranging from Charles Manson to Jeffrey Dahmer to Bernie Madoff. However, the concept of psychopathy ("psychopathic personality") held by experts in the mental health field differs sharply from this common public perception—emphasizing distinct dispositional tendencies as opposed to serious criminal acts of one sort or another. This module reviews historic and contemporary conceptions of psychopathy as a clinical disorder, describes methods for assessing it, and discusses how a new conceptual model can help to address key questions regarding its nature and origins that have long been debated. It will be seen from this review that the topic remains no less fascinating or socially relevant when considered from a clinical–scientific perspective.

Historic Conceptions

Early writers characterized psychopathy as an atypical form of mental illness in which rational faculties appeared normal but everyday behavior and social relationships are markedly disrupted. French physician Philippe Pinel (1806/1962) documented cases of what he called *manie sans delire* ("insanity without delirium"), in which dramatic episodes of recklessness and aggression occurred in individuals not suffering from obvious clouding of the mind. German psychiatrist Julius Koch (1888) introduced the disease-oriented term *psychopathic* to convey the idea that conditions of this type had a strong constitutional-heritable basis. In his seminal book *The Mask of Sanity*, which focused on patients committed for hospital treatment, American psychiatrist Hervey Cleckley (1941/ 1976) described psychopathy as a deep-rooted emotional pathology concealed by an outward appearance of good mental health. In contrast with other psychiatric patients, psychopathic individuals present as confident, sociable, and well adjusted. However, their underlying disorder reveals itself over time through their actions and attitudes. To facilitate identification of psychopathic individuals in clinical settings, Cleckley provided 16 diagnostic criteria distilled from his clinical case summaries, encompassing indicators of apparent psychological stability (e.g., charm and intelligence, absence of nervousness) along with symptoms of behavioral deviancy (e.g., irresponsibility, failure to plan) and impaired affect and social connectedness (e.g., absence of remorse, deceptiveness, inability to love).

Hervey Cleckley, the man who devised the original tests for psychopathy, asserted that some psychopaths may appear as well-adjusted, successful people who maintain respectable careers in fields like business and medicine. [Image: Jonna Fransa, CC0 Public Domain, https://goo.gl/m25gce]

Notably, Cleckley did not characterize psychopathic patients as inherently cruel, violent, or dangerous. Although some engaged in repetitive violent acts, more often the harm they caused was nonphysical and the product of impulsive self-centeredness as opposed to viciousness. Indeed, Cleckley's case histories included examples of "successful psychopaths" who ascended to careers as professors, medical doctors, or businessmen, along with examples of more aimless dysfunctional types. In contrast with this, other writers from Cleckley's time who were concerned with criminal expressions of psychopathy placed greater emphasis on symptoms of emotional coldness, aggression, and predatory victimization. For example, McCord and McCord (1964) described the condition in more generally pathologic terms, highlighting "guiltlessness" (lack of remorse) and "lovelessness" (lack of attachment capacity) as central defining features.

Cleckley's conception served as a referent for the diagnosis of psychopathy in the first two editions of the official American psychiatric nosology, the *Diagnostic and Statistical Manual of Mental Disorders* (DSM). However, a dramatic shift occurred in the third edition of the DSM, with the introduction of behaviorally oriented symptom definitions for most disorders to address longstanding problems of reliability. The Cleckley-oriented conception of psychopathy in prior editions was replaced by antisocial personality disorder (ASPD), defined by specific indicants of behavioral deviancy in childhood (e.g., fighting, lying, stealing, truancy) continuing into adulthood (manifested as repeated rulebreaking, impulsiveness, irresponsibility, aggressiveness, etc.). Concerns with this new conception were expressed by psychopathy experts, who noted that ASPD provided limited coverage of interpersonal-affective symptoms considered essential to psychopathy (e.g., charm, deceitfulness, selfishness, shallow affect; Hare, 1983). Nonetheless, ASPD was retained in much the same form in the fourth edition of the DSM (DSM-IV; American Psychiatric Association [APA], 2000), and remained unchanged in the fifth edition of the DSM (American Psychiatric Association, 2013). That said, the DSM-5 does include a new, dimensional-trait approach to characterizing personality pathology (Strickland, Drislane, Lucy, Krueger, & Patrick, in press).

Contemporary assessment methods

Modern approaches to the assessment of psychopathy, consisting of rating instruments and self-report scales, reflect the foregoing historic conceptions to differing degrees.

Psychopathy in adult criminal offenders

The most widely used instrument for diagnosing psychopathy in correctional and forensic settings is the Psychopathy Checklist-Revised (PCL-R; Hare, 2003), which comprises 20 items rated on the basis of interview and file-record information. The items of the PCL-R effectively capture the interpersonal-affective deficits and behavioral deviance features identified by Cleckley, but include only limited, indirect coverage of positive adjustment features. The manual for the PCL-R recommends the use of a cutoff score of 30 out of 40 for assigning a diagnosis of psychopathy. High overall PCL-R scores are correlated with impulsive and aggressive tendencies, low empathy, Machiavellianism, lack of social connectedness, and persistent violent offending. Given these correlates, and the omission of positive adjustment indicators, psychopathy as assessed by the PCL-R appears more similar to the predatory-aggressive conception of McCord and McCord than to Cleckley's conception.

Although the PCL-R was developed to index psychopathy as a unitary condition, structural analyses of its items reveal distinct *interpersonal-affective* and *antisocial deviance* subdimensions (factors). Although moderately (about .5) correlated, these factors show contrasting relations with external criterion measures. The interpersonal-affective factor relates to indices of narcissism, low empathy, and proactive aggression (Hare, 2003), and to some extent (after controlling for its overlap with the antisocial factor) adaptive tendencies such as high social assertiveness and low fear, distress, and depression (Hicks & Patrick, 2006). High scores on the antisocial deviance factor, by contrast, are associated mainly with maladaptive tendencies and behaviors, including impulsiveness, sensation seeking, alienation and mistrust, reactive aggression, early and persistent antisocial deviance, and substance-related problems.

Psychopathy in noncriminal adults

One of the key factors that the Psychopathic Personality Inventory (PPI) aims to assess is something called Fearless Dominance which includes social potency, immunity to stress, and lack of normal levels of fear. [Image: CC0 Public Domain, https://goo.gl/m25gce]

Psychopathy has most typically been assessed in noncriminal adult samples using self-report-based measures. Older measures of this type emphasized the antisocial deviancy component of psychopathy with limited coverage of inter-personal-affective features (Hare, 2003). Some newer instruments provide more balanced coverage of both. One example is the now widely used Psychopathic Personality Inventory (PPI; Lilienfeld & Andrews, 1996), which was developed to index personality dispositions embodied within historic conceptions of psychopathy. Its current revised form (PPI-R; Lilienfeld & Widows, 2005) contains 154 items, organized into eight facet scales.Like the items of the PCL-R, the subscales of the PPI cohere around two distinguishable factors: a fearless dominance (FD) factor reflecting social potency, stress immunity, and fearlessness, and a self-centered impulsivity (SCI) factor reflecting egocentricity, exploitativeness, hostile rebel-liousness, and lack of planning. However, unlike the factors of the PCL-R, the two PPI factors are uncorrelated, and thus even more distinct in their external correlates.

Scores on PPI-FD are associated with indices of positive psychological adjustment (e.g., higher well-being; lower anxiety and depression) and measures of narcissism (low) empathy, and thrill/adventure seeking (Benning, Patrick, Blonigen, Hicks, & Iacono, 2005). Given this, PPI-FD has been interpreted as capturing a more adaptive expression of dispositional fearlessness (i.e., *boldness*; see below) than the interpersonal-affective factor of the PCL-R—which can be viewed as tapping a more pathologic (antagonistic or "mean") expression of fearlessness. Scores on PPI-SCI, like Factor 2 of the PCL-R, are associated with multiple indicators of deviancy—including impulsivity and aggressiveness, child and adult antisocial behavior, substance abuse problems, heightened distress and dysphoria, and suicidal ideation.

Psychopathy in child and adolescent clinical samples

Different inventories exist for assessing psychopathic tendencies in children and adolescents. The best-known consist of rating-based measures developed, using the PCL-R as a referent, to identify psychopathic individuals among youth convicted of crimes or referred for treatment of conduct problems. The emphasis in work of this type has been on the importance of psychopathic features for predicting greater severity and persistence of conduct problems. Termed "callous-unemotional" traits, these features encompass low empathy, deficient remorse or guilt, shallow affect, and lack of concern about performance in school and other contexts (Frick & Moffitt, 2010).

One extensively researched measure for assessing psychopathic tendencies in youth is the Antisocial Process Screening Device (APSD; Frick & Marsee, 2006), used with clinic-referred children ages 6 through 13. The APSD includes 20 items completed by parents or teachers. As with the PCL-R and PPI, the items of the APSD tap two distinct factors: a Callous-Unemotional (CU) traits factor, reflecting emotional insensitivity and disregard for others; and an Impulsive/Conduct Problems (I/CP) factor, reflecting impulsivity, behavioral deviancy, and inflated self-importance. Children high on the I/CP factor alone show below-average intelligence, heightened emotional responsiveness to stressors, and angry (reactive) aggression (Frick & Marsee, 2006). By contrast, children high on both APSD factors show average or above-average intelligence, low reported levels of anxiety and nervousness, reduced reactivity to stressful events, and preference for activities entailing novelty and risk. They also learn less readily from punishment and engage in high levels of premeditated as well as reactive aggression and exhibit more persistent violent behavior across time. Given the documented importance of CU traits in moderating the expression of conduct disorder, the upcoming fifth edition of the DSM will include criteria for designating a distinct CU variant of child conduct disorder (Frick & Moffitt, 2010).

Cruelty and lack of empathy are tendencies found in those with psychopathic personality. [Image: Thomas Ricker, https://goo.gl/igmuzh, CC BY 2.0, https://goo.gl/BRvSA7]

Core ingredients of psychopathy: disinhibition, boldness, and meanness

The foregoing material highlights the fact that historic conceptions of psychopathy and available instruments for assessing it place differing emphasis on different symptomatic features. This had contributed to longstanding disagreements among scholars about what psychopathy entails and what causes it. A theoretic conceptualization formulated recently to reconcile alternative perspectives is the Triarchic model (Patrick, Fowles, & Krueger, 2009). This model conceives of psychopathy as encompassing three separable symptomatic components—disinhibition, boldness, and meanness—that can be viewed as thematic building blocks for differing conceptions of psychopathy.

Definitions

Disinhibition as described in the Triarchic model encompasses tendencies toward impulsiveness, weak behavioral restraint, hostility and mistrust, and difficulties in regulating emotion. *Meanness* entails deficient empathy, lack of affiliative capacity, contempt toward others, predatory exploitativeness, and empowerment through cruelty and destructiveness. Referents for disinhibition and meanness include the finding of distinct I/CP and CU factors in the child psychopathy literature and corresponding evidence for distinct disinhibitory and callous-aggression factors underlying impulse control (externalizing) problems in adults (Krueger, Markon, Patrick, Benning, & Kramer, 2007). The third construct in the model, *Boldness,*encompasses dominance, social assurance, emotional resiliency, and venturesomeness. Referents for this construct include the "mask" elements of Cleckley's conception, Lykken's (1995) low fear theory of psychopathy, the FD factor of the PPI, and developmental research on fearless temperament as a possible precursor to psychopathy (Patrick et al., 2009).

From the perspective of the Triarchic model, Cleckley's conception of psychopathy emphasized boldness and disinhibition, whereas criminally oriented conceptions (and affiliated measures, including the PCL-R and APSD) emphasize meanness and disinhibition more so. According to the model, individuals high in disinhibitory tendencies would warrant a diagnosis of psychopathy if also high in boldness or meanness (or both), but individuals high on only one of these tendencies would not. Individuals with differing relative elevations on these three symptomatic components would account for contrasting variants (subtypes) of psychopathy as described in the literature (Hicks, Markon, Patrick, Krueger, & Newman, 2004; Karpman, 1941; Skeem, Johansson, Andershed, Kerr, & Louden, 2007).

An inventory designed specifically to operationalize this model is the Triarchic Psychopathy Measure (TriPM; Patrick, 2010). The TriPM contains 58 items comprising three subscales that correspond to the constructs of the model (see Table 1). The items of the Disinhibition and Meanness scales (20 and 19 items, respectively) are taken from the Externalizing Spectrum Inventory (ESI; Krueger et al., 2007), a measure of problems and traits associated with externalizing psychopathology. The TriPM Boldness scale was developed to index fearless tendencies in social, affective-experiential, and activity preference domains, with reference to the FD factor of the PPI and the general factor shown to underlie differing scale measures of fear and fearlessness (Kramer, Patrick, Gasperi, & Krueger, 2012).

Although the TriPM is relatively new, promising evidence for its convergent and discriminant validity has begun to appear (e.g., Sellbom & Phillips, 2013; Strickland et al., in press; see also Venables & Patrick, 2012). Given that the inventory is freely available online, and that several foreign-language translations now exist (including Brazilian-Portuguese, Dutch, Finnish, German, Italian, Portuguese, Swedish, and Spanish), it can be expected that additional validity data will accumulate rapidly over time. Work is also being done to evaluate whether effective scale measures of the Triarchic constructs can be derived from items of other existing psychopathy inventories such as the PPI. As discussed in the last part of this section, research examining the common and distinctive correlates of these three components of psychopathy is likely to be helpful for addressing and perhaps resolving ongoing points of uncertainty and debate in the field.

TriPM Subscale	Sample Item
Boldness	32. I can get over things that would traumatize others.
	38. I can convince people to do what I want.
	47. I stay away from physical danger as much as I can. (False)
Meanness	2. How other people feel is important to me (False)
	23. I enjoy pushing people around sometimes.
	33. I've injured people to see them in pain.
Disinhibition	3. I often act on immediate needs.
	21. I have good control over myself. (False)
	56. I have had problems at work because I was irresponsible.

Table 1. Sample items from the Triarchic Psychopathy Measure (TriPM; Patrick, 2010)

Causal factors

Considerable research has been devoted over many years to investigation of causal factors in psychopathy. Existing theories are of two types: (1) theories emphasizing core deficits in emotional sensitivity or responsiveness, and (2) theories positing basic impairments in cognitive-attentional processing (Patrick & Bernat, 2009). In support of these alternative theories, differing neurobiological correlates of psychopathy have been reported. One of the most consistent entails a lack of normal enhancement of the startle blink reflex to abrupt noises occurring during viewing of aversive foreground stimuli (e.g., scary or disturbing pictorial images) as compared with neutral or pleasant stimuli (see Figure 1). This result, akin to a failure to "jump" upon hearing a trash can tip while walking alone in a dark alley, has been interpreted as reflecting a lack of normal defensive (fear) reactivity. Another fairly consistent finding involves reduced amplitude of brain potential response to intermittent target stimuli, or following incorrect responses, within cognitive performance tasks—indicative of reduced cortical-attentional processing or impaired action monitoring (Patrick & Bernat, 2009). Yet other research using functional neuroimaging has demonstrated deficits in basic subcortical (amygdala) reactivity to interpersonal distress cues (e.g., fearful human faces) in high-psychopathic individuals (Jones, Laurens, Herba, Barker, & Viding, 2009; Marsh et al., 2008).

The Triarchic model may prove to be of use for reconciling alternative causal models of psychopathy that have been proposed based on contrasting neurobiological and behavioral findings. For example, lack of startle enhancement during aversive cuing has been tied specifically to the interpersonal-affective factor of the PCL-R and the counterpart FD factor of the PPI (Figure 1)—suggesting a link to the boldness component of psychopathy. By contrast, reduced brain potential responses in cognitive tasks appear more related to impulsive-externalizing tendencies associated with the disinhibition component of psychopathy (Carlson, Thái, & McLaron, 2009; Patrick & Bernat, 2009). On the other hand, the finding of reduced subcortical response to affective facial cues has been tied to the CU traits factor of child/adolescent psychopathy, a referent for meanness in the Triarchic model. However, further research is needed to determine whether this finding reflects fear deficits common to meanness and boldness, or deficits in affiliative capacity or empathy specific to meanness.

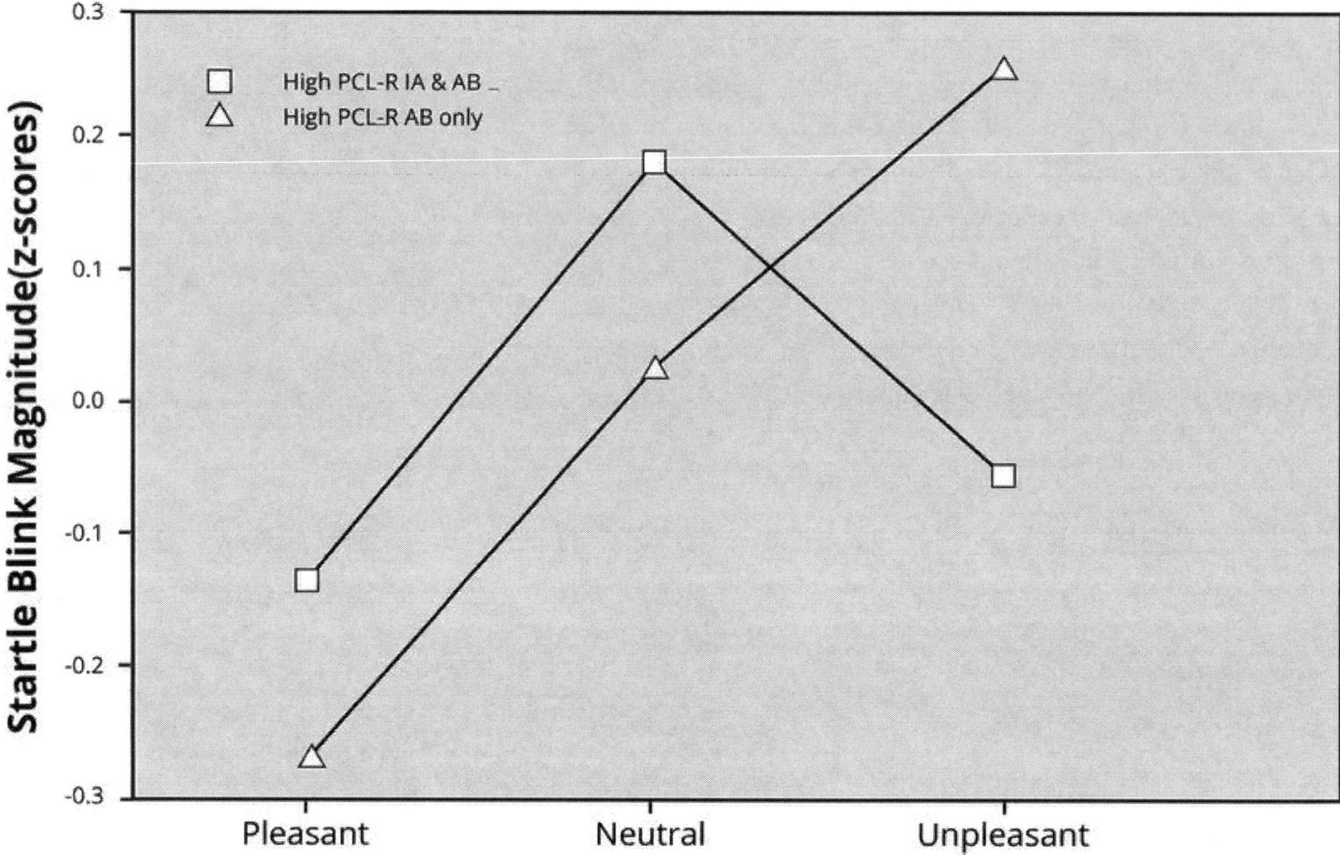

Figure 1. Evidence for lack of normal augmentation of the defensive startle reflex during viewing of aversive visual images in high-psychopathic individuals.Upper plot: Mean magnitude of startle blink responses to noise probes occurring during viewing of pleasant, neutral, and unpleasant picture stimuli in two male prisoner groups: (1) prisoners scoring high on the antisocial behavior (AB) factor of the Psychopathy Checklist-Revised (PCL-R; Hare, 2003) but not the interpersonal-affective (IA) factor (labeled "High PCL-R AB only" in the plot; n = 18), and (2) prisoners high on both factors of the PCL-R (labeled "High PCL-R IA & AB"; n = 17).

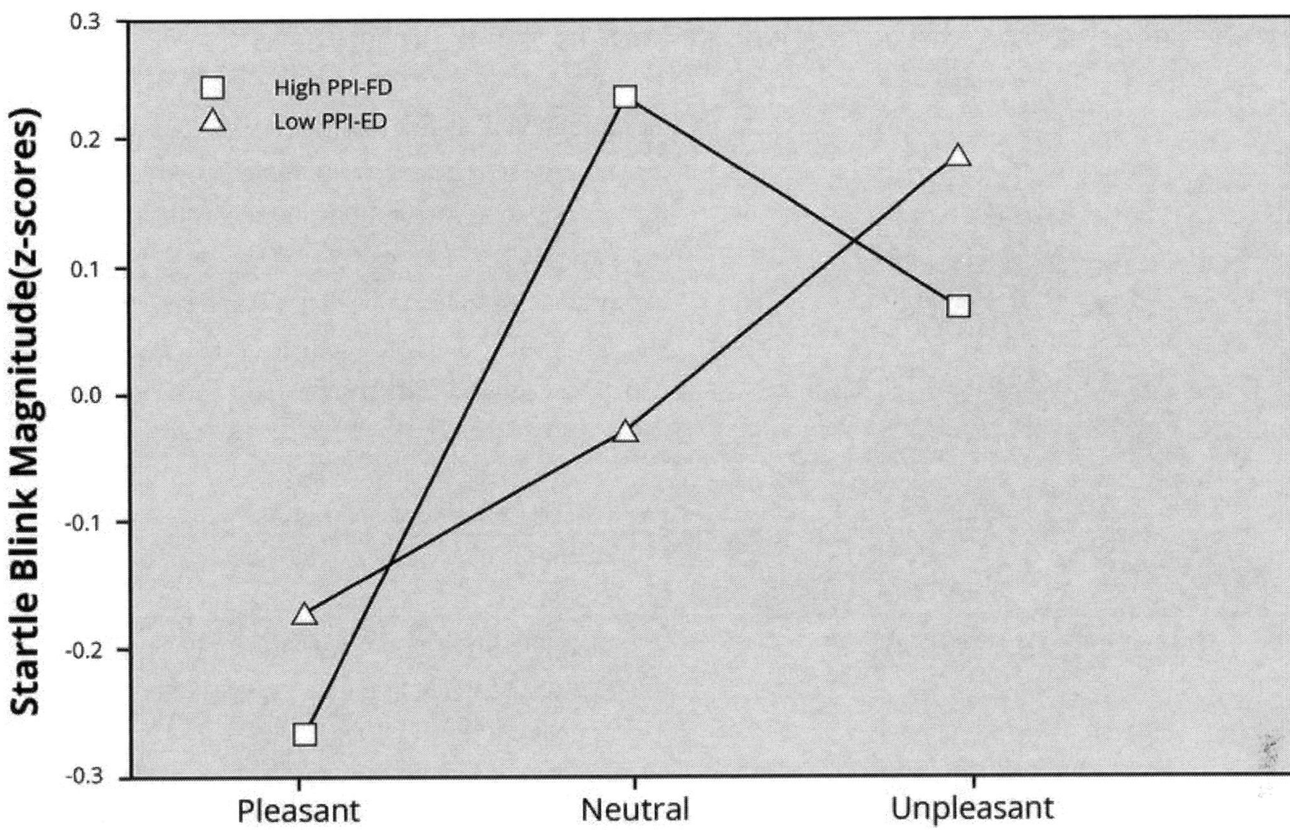

Lower plot: Mean magnitude of startle blink responses to noise probes occurring during viewing of pleasant, neutral, and unpleasant picture stimuli in two subgroups of young males from a large community sample (overall N = 307): (1) lowest 10% of scorers (n = 31) within the sample on the fearless dominance factor of the Psychopathic Personality Inventory (PPI; Lilienfeld & Andrews, 1996), labeled "Low PPI-FD" in the plot, and (2) highest 10% of scorers (n = 31) on the PPI fearless dominance factor of the PPI, labeled "High PPI-FD" in the plot. In both plots, blink means for each picture type are presented in z-score units (M = 0, SD = 1) derived by standardizing raw blink magnitude scores across trials for each individual subject. Data in the upper plot are from Patrick, Bradley, and Lang (1993); data in the lower plot are from Benning, Patrick, and Iacono (2005).

Triarchic model perspective on long-debated issues regarding psychopathy

Social psychologists classify a collection of three personality traits as the "dark triad": Machiavellianism, psychopathy, and narcissism.

As highlighted in the foregoing sections, scholars have grappled with issues of definition since psychopathy was first identified as a condition of clinical concern, and questions regarding its essential features and alternative expressions continue to be debated and studied. This final subsection discusses how some of the major issues of debate are addressed by the Triarchic model.

One key issue is whether psychological/emotional stability is characteristic or not of psychopathy. Cleckley's (1941/1976) view was that psychopathy entails a salient presentation of good mental health, and his diagnostic criteria included indicators of positive adjustment. By contrast, the dominant clinical assessment devices for psychopathy, the PCL-R and ASPD, are heavily oriented toward deviancy and include no items that are purely indicative of adjustment. From a Triarchic model standpoint, the more adaptive elements of psychopathy are embodied in its boldness facet, which entails social poise, emotional stability, and enjoyment of novelty and adventure. At the same time, high boldness is also associated with narcissistic tendencies, reduced sensitivity to the feelings of others, and risk-taking (Benning et al., 2005). Thus, the concept of boldness provides a way to think about the intriguing "mask" element of psychopathy.

Related to this, another issue is whether lack of anxiety is central to psychopathy, as Cleckley and others (e.g., Fowles & Dindo, 2009; Lykken, 1995) have emphasized. This perspective is challenged by research showing either negligible or somewhat positive associations for overall scores on the PCL-R and other psychopathy measures with anxiety. The Triarchic model helps to address this inconsistency by separating the disorder into subcomponents or facets, which relate differently to measures of trait anxiety: Boldness is correlated negatively with anxiousness (Benning et al., 2005), whereas Disinhibition and Meannness are correlated negatively and negligibly, respectively, with anxiety (Venables & Patrick, 2012). Related to this, cluster analytic studies of criminal offenders exhibiting high overall scores on the PCL-R have demonstrated one subtype characterized by low anxiety in particular, and another exhibiting high anxiety along with very high levels of impulsivity and aggression (Hicks et al., 2004; Skeem et al., 2007). The implication is that low anxiousness is central to one variant of criminal psychopathy (the bold-disinhibited, or "primary" type) but not to another variant (the "disinhibited-mean," "aggressive-externalizing," or "secondary" type).

A further key question is whether violent/aggressive tendencies are typical of psychopathic individuals and should be included in the definition of the disorder. Cleckley's (1941/1976) view was that "such tendencies should be regarded as the exception rather than as the rule" (p. 262). However, aggressiveness is central to criminally oriented conceptions of psychopathy, and the PCL-R includes an item reflecting hot-temperedness and aggression ("poor behavioral controls") along with other items scored in part based on indications of cruelty and violence. In the Triarchic model, tendencies toward aggression are represented in both the disinhibition and meanness constructs, and a "mean-disinhibited" type of psychopath clearly exists, marked by the presence of salient aggressive behavior (Frick & Marsee, 2006; Hicks et al., 2004). Thus, Cleckley's idea of aggression as ancillary to psychopathy may apply more to a variant of psychopathy that entails high boldness in conjunction with high disinhibition (Hicks et al., 2004).

Another question is whether criminal or antisocial behavior more broadly represents a defining feature of psychopathy, or a secondary manifestation (Cooke, Michie, Hart, & Clark, 2004). From the standpoint of the Triarchic model, antisocial behavior arises from the complex interplay of different "deviance-promoting" influences—including dispositional boldness, meanness, and disinhibition. However, whether approaches can be developed for classifying antisocial behaviors in ways that relate more selectively to these and other distinct influences (e.g., through reference to underlying motives, spontaneity versus premeditation) is an important topic to be addressed in future research.

Another key question is whether differing subtypes of psychopathy exist. From the perspective of the Triarchic model, alternative variants of psychopathy reflect differing configurations of boldness, meanness, and disinhibition. Viewed this way, designations such as "bold-disinhibited" and "mean-disinhibited" may prove more useful for research and clinical purposes than labels like "primary" versus "secondary" or "low anxious" versus "high anxious." An issue from this perspective is whether individuals who are high in boldness and/or meanness but low in disinhibition would qualify for a diagnosis of psychopathy. For example, should a high-bold/high-mean individual (e.g., a ruthless corporate executive, like the one portrayed by actor Michael Douglas in the film *Wall Street*; Pressman & Stone, 1987)—or an extremely mean/vicious but neither bold nor pervasively disinhibited individual, such as Russian serial murder Andrei Chikatilo (Cullen, 1993)—be considered psychopathic? Questions of this sort will need to be addressed through elaborations of existing theories in conjunction with further systematic research.

Yet another question is whether psychopathy differs in women as compared to men. Cleckley's descriptive accounts of psychopathic patients included two female case examples along with multiple male cases, and his view was that psychopathy clearly exists in women and reflects the same core deficit (i.e., absence of "major emotional accompaniments" of experience) as in men. However, men exhibit criminal deviance and ASPD at much higher rates than women (APA, 2000) and men in the population at large score higher in general on measures of psychopathy than women (Hare, 2003; Lilienfeld & Widows, 2005). From a Triarchic model perspective, these differences in prevalence may be attributable largely to differences between women and men in average levels of boldness, meanness, and disinhibition. Some supportive evidence exists for this hypothesis (e.g., findings of Hicks et al. [2007] demonstrating mediation of gender differences in ASPD symptoms by levels of externalizing proneness). Beyond this, it is important also to consider whether underlying psychopathic dispositions in men and women may be manifested differently in overt behavior (Verona & Vitale, 2006). Some intriguing evidence exists for this—including twin research findings demonstrating a genetic association between dispositional boldness (as indexed by estimated scores on PPI-FD) and a composite index of externalizing problems in male but not female participants (Blonigen, Hicks, Patrick, Krueger, Iacono, & McGue, 2005). However, more extensive research along these lines, examining all facets of the Triarchic model in relation to behavioral outcomes of differing kinds, will be required to effectively address the question of gender-moderated expression.

A final intriguing question is whether "successful" psychopaths exist. Hall and Benning (2006) hypothesized that successful psychopathy entails a preponderance of certain causal influences (resulting in particular symptomatic features) over others. Drawing on known correlates of PPI-FD (e.g., Benning et al., 2005; Ross, Benning, Patrick, Thompson, & Thurston, 2009) and theories positing separate etiologic mechanisms for differing features of psychopathy (Fowles & Dindo, 2009; Patrick & Bernat, 2009), these authors proposed that the presence of dispositional fearlessness (boldness) may be conducive to success when not accompanied by high externalizing proneness (disinhibition). For example, high-bold/low-disinhibited individuals could be expected to achieve higher success in occupations calling for leadership and/or courage because their psychopathic tendencies are manifested mainly in terms of social effectiveness, affective resilience, and venturesomeness.Data relevant to this idea come from an intriguing study by

Some aspects of the psychopathic personality could be beneficial in certain professions requiring leadership and courage. [Image: CC0 Public Domain, https://goo.gl/m25gce]

Lilienfeld, Waldman, Landfield, Rubenzer, and Faschingbauer (2012), who used personality trait ratings of former U.S. presidents provided by expert historians to estimate scores on the FD and SCI factors of the PPI (Ross et al., 2009). They found that higher estimated levels of PPI-FD (boldness) predicted higher ratings of presidential performance, persuasiveness, leadership, and crisis management ability, whereas higher estimated levels of SCI predicted adverse outcomes such as documented abuses of power and impeachment proceedings. Further research on outcomes associated with high levels of boldness and/or meanness in the absence of high disinhibition should yield valuable new insights into dispositional factors underlying psychopathy and alternative ways psychopathic tendencies can be expressed.

Outside Resources

Book: (Fictional novels or biographies/biographical novels) Capote, T. (1966). *In cold blood*. **New York, NY: Random House.**
Book: (Fictional novels or biographies/biographical novels) Highsmith, P. (1955). *The talented Mr. Ripley*. **New York, NY: Coward-McCann.**
Book: (Fictional novels or biographies/biographical novels) Kerouac, J. (1957). *On the road*. **New York, NY: Viking Press.**

Book: (Fictional novels or biographies/biographical novels) Mailer, N. (1979). *The executioner's song*. New York, NY: Little, Brown & Co.

Book: (Fictional novels or biographies/biographical novels) McMurtry, L. (1985). *Lonesome dove*. New York, NY: Simon & Schuster.

Book: (Fictional novels or biographies/biographical novels) Rule, A. (1988). *Small sacrifices*. New York, NY: Signet.

Book: (Fictional novels or biographies/biographical novels)Wolff, G. (1979). *The duke of deception*. New York, NY: Vintage.

Book: (Reference) Babiak, P., & Hare, R. D. (2006). *Snakes in suits*. New York, NY: HarperCollins.

Book: (Reference) Blair, R. J. R., Mitchell, D., & Blair, K. (2005). *The psychopath: Emotion and the brain*. Malden, MA: Blackwell.

Book: (Reference) Hare, R. D. (1993). *Without conscience*. New York, NY: Guilford Press.

Book: (Reference) Häkkänen-Nyholm, H., & Nyholm, J. (2012), *Psychopathy and law: A practitioner's guide*. New York, NY: Wiley.

Book: (Reference) Patrick, C. J. (2006). *Handbook of psychopathy*. New York, NY: Guilford Press.

Book: (Reference) Raine, A. (2013). *The anatomy of violence*. New York, NY: Random House.

Book: (Reference) Salekin, R., & Lynam, D. T. (2010). *Handbook of child and adolescent psychopathy*. New York, NY: Guilford Press.

Measure: Online home of the Triarchic Psychopathy Measure. It serves as a great resource for students who wish to look at how psychopathy is measured a little more deeply.
https://www.phenxtoolkit.org/index.php?pageLink=browse.protocoldetails&id=121601

Movie: (Facets of psychopathy – Boldness) Bigelow, K. (Producer & Director), Boal, M., Chartier, N., & Shapiro, G. (Producers). (2008). *The hurt locker*. United States: Universal Studios.

Movie: (Facets of psychopathy – Disinhibition) Felner, E. (Producer), Cox, A. (Director). (1986). *Sid and Nancy*. United States: Samuel Goldwyn.

Movie: (Facets of psychopathy – Meanness) Coen, J., Coen, E. (Producers & Directors), & Rudin, S. (Producer). (2007). *No country for old men*. United States: Miramax.

Movie: (Psychopathic criminals) Demme, J., Saraf, P., Saxon, E. (Producers), & Sena, D. (Director). (1993). *Kalifornia*. United States: Gramercy.

Movie: (Psychopathic criminals) Jaffe, S. R., Lansing, S. (Producers), & Lyn, A. (Director). (1987). *Fatal attraction*. United States: Paramount.

Movie: (Psychopathic criminals) Scorsese, M., Harris, R. A., Painten, J. (Producers), & Frears, S. (Director). (1990). *The grifters*. United States: Miramax.

Movie: (Psychopathic criminals) Ward, F., Bozman, R., Utt, K., Demme, J. (Producers), & Armitrage, G. (Director). (1990). *Miami blues*. United States: Orion.

Movie: (Psychopathic hospital patients) Wick, D., Conrad, C. (Producers), & Mangold, J. (Director). (1990). *Girl, interrupted*. United States: Columbia.

Movie: (Psychopathic hospital patients) Zaentz, S., Douglas, M. (Producers), & Forman, M. (Director). (1975). *One flew over the cuckoo's nest*. United States: United Artists.

Movie: (Psychopaths in business/politics) Bachrach, D. (Producer), & Pierson, F. (Director). (1992). *Citizen Cohn*. United States: Home Box Office.

Movie: (Psychopaths in business/politics) Pressman, E. R. (Producer), & Stone, O. (Director). (1987). *Wall Street*. **United States: 20th Century Fox.**

Web: A valuable online resource containing information of various types including detailed reference lists is Dr. Robert Hare's website on the topic of psychopathy. Dr. Hare i the person who created the PCL-R. It has a number of interesting articles to read as well as helpful psychopathy links from about the web.

http://www.hare.org/

Web: Hervey Cleckley's classic book The Mask of Sanity is no longer in print at this time, but a version authorized for nonprofit educational use by his estate can be viewed online at

http://www.quantumfuture.net/store/sanity_1.PdF

Web: The Triarchic Psychopathy Measure can be accessed online at

https://www.phenxtoolkit.org/index.php?pageLink=browse.protocoldetails&id=121601

Web: The website for the Aftermath Foundation, a nonprofit organization that provides information and support for victims and family members of psychopathic individuals, is

http://www.aftermath-surviving-psychopathy.org/

Web: The website for the Society for Scientific Study of Psychopathy. This is the major research hub for psychopathy. It has a section specifically for students that might prove especially interesting.

http://www.psychopathysociety.org/index.php?lang=en-US

Discussion Questions

1. What did Cleckley mean when he characterized psychopathy as involving a "Mask of Sanity"?

2. Compare and contrast the Psychopathy Checklist-Revised (PCL-R), the Antisocial Process Screening Device (APSD), and the Psychopathic Personality Inventory (PPI), in terms of the samples they are designed for, the way in which they are administered, and the content and factor structure of their items.

3. Identify and define the three facet constructs of the Triarchic model of psychopathy. Discuss how these facet constructs relate to the factors of the PCL-R, ASPD, and PPI. Discuss how U.S. President Teddy Roosevelt and fictional character Anton Chigurh from the film No Country for Old Men might compare in terms of scores on the three Triarchic constructs.

4. Identify alternative types of theories that have been proposed regarding the cause of psychopathy, and how these can be viewed from the perspective of the Triarchic model.

5. Identify two longstanding issues of debate regarding the nature/definition of psychopathy and how these issues are addressed by the Triarchic model.

Vocabulary

Antisocial personality disorder
Counterpart diagnosis to psychopathy included in the third through fifth editions of the Diagnostic and Statistical Manual of Mental Disorders (DSM; APA, 2000). Defined by specific symptoms of behavioral deviancy in

childhood (e.g., fighting, lying, stealing, truancy) continuing into adulthood (manifested as repeated rule-breaking, impulsiveness, irresponsibility, aggressiveness, etc.).

Psychopathy

Synonymous with psychopathic personality, the term used by Cleckley (1941/1976), and adapted from the term psychopathic introduced by German psychiatrist Julius Koch (1888) to designate mental disorders presumed to be heritable.

Triarchic model

Model formulated to reconcile alternative historic conceptions of psychopathy and differing methods for assessing it. Conceives of psychopathy as encompassing three symptomatic components: boldness, involving social efficacy, emotional resiliency, and venturesomeness; meanness, entailing lack of empathy/emotional-sensitivity and exploitative behavior toward others; and disinhibition, entailing deficient behavioral restraint and lack of control over urges/emotional reactions.

References

- American Psychiatric Association. (2013). *Diagnostic and statistical manual of mental disorders: DSM-5.*Washington, D.C: American Psychiatric Association.

- American Psychiatric Association. (2000). *Diagnostic and statistical manual of mental disorders* (4th ed., text revision). Washington, DC: Author.

- Benning, S. D., Patrick, C. J., & Iacono, W. G. (2005). Psychopathy, startle blink modulation, and electrodermal reactivity in twin men. *Psychophysiology, 42,* 753-762.

- Benning, S. D., Patrick, C. J., Blonigen, D. M., Hicks, B. M., & Iacono, W. G. (2005). Estimating facets of psychopathy from normal personality traits: A step toward community-epidemiological investigations. *Assessment, 12,* 3–18.

- Blonigen, D. M., Hicks, B. M., Patrick, C. J., Krueger, R. F., Iacono, W. G., & McGue, M. K. (2005). Psychopathic personality traits: Heritability and genetic overlap with internalizing and externalizing psychopathology. *Psychological Medicine, 35,* 637–648.

- Carlson, S. R., Thái, S., & McLaron, M. E. (2009). Visual P3 amplitude and self-reported psychopathic personality traits: Frontal reduction is associated with self-centered impulsivity. *Psychophysiology, 46,* 100–113.

- Cleckley, H. (1976). *The mask of sanity* (5th ed.). St. Louis, MO: Mosby. (Original edition published in 1941)

- Cooke, D. J., Michie, C., Hart, S. D., & Clark, D. A. (2004). Reconstructing psychopathy: Clarifying the significance of antisocial and socially deviant behavior in the diagnosis of psychopathic personality disorder. *Journal of Personality Disorders, 18,* 337–357.

- Cullen, R. (1993). *The killer department.* Birmingham, UK: Orion Media.

- Fowles, D. C., & Dindo, L. (2009). Temperament and psychopathy: A dual-pathway model. Current

Directions in *Psychological Science, 18*, 179–183.

- Frick, P. J., & Marsee, M. A. (2006). Psychopathy and developmental pathways to antisocial behavior in youth. In C. J. Patrick (Ed.), *Handbook of psychopathy* (pp. 353–374). New York, NY: Guilford Press.

- Frick, P. J., & Moffitt, T. E. (2010). *A proposal to the DSM-V Childhood Disorders and the ADHD and Disruptive Behavior Disorders Work Groups to include a specifier to the diagnosis of conduct disorder based on the presence of callous-unemotional traits*. Washington, DC: American Psychiatric Association. Retrieved from http://www.dsm5.org/Proposed Revision Attachments/Proposal for Callous and Unemotional Specifier of Conduct Disorder.pdf

- Hall, J. R., & Benning, S. D. (2006). The "successful" psychopath: Adaptive and subclinical manifestations of psychopathy in the general population. In C. J. Patrick (Ed.), *Handbook of psychopathy* (pp. 459–478). New York, NY: Guilford Press.

- Hare, R. D. (2003). *The Hare Psychopathy Checklist* (2nd ed.). Toronto, Canada: Multi-Health Systems. (Original edition published in 1991)

- Hare, R. D. (1983). Diagnosis of antisocial personality disorder in two prison populations. *American Journal of Psychiatry, 140*, 887–890.

- Hicks, B. M., & Patrick, C. J. (2006). Psychopathy and negative affectivity: Analyses of suppressor effects reveal distinct relations with trait anxiety, depression, fearfulness, and anger-hostility. *Journal of Abnormal Psychology, 115*, 276–287.

- Hicks, B. M., Blonigen, D. M., Iacono, W. G., Kramer, M., Krueger, R. F., McGue, M. K., & Patrick, C. J. (2007). Gender differences and developmental change in externalizing disorders from late adolescence to early adulthood: A longitudinal-twin study. *Journal of Abnormal Psychology, 116*, 433–447.

- Hicks, B. M., Markon, K. E., Patrick, C. J., Krueger, R. F., & Newman, J. P. (2004). Identifying psychopathy subtypes on the basis of personality structure. *Psychological Assessment, 16*, 276–288.

- Jones, A. P., Laurens, K. R., Herba, C. M., Barker, G. J., & Viding, E. (2009). Amygdala hypoactivity to fearful faces in boys with conduct problems and callous-unemotional traits. *American Journal of Psychiatry, 166*, 95–102.

- Karpman, B. (1941). On the need of separating psychopathy into two distinct clinical types: The symptomatic and the idiopathic. *Journal of Criminal Psychopathology, 3*, 112–137.

- Koch, J. L. (1888). *Kurzgefasster leitfaden der psychiatrie* [Short textbook of psychiatry]. Ravensburg, Germany: Maier.

- Kramer, M. D., Patrick, C. J., Krueger, R. F., & Gasperi, M. (2012). Delineating physiological defensive reactivity in the domain of self-report: Phenotypic and etiologic structure of dispositional fear. *Psychological Medicine, 42*, 1305–1320.

- Krueger, R. F., Markon, K. E., Patrick, C. J., Benning, S. D., & Kramer, M. (2007). Linking antisocial behavior, substance use, and personality: An integrative quantitative model of the adult externalizing spectrum. *Journal of Abnormal Psychology, 116*, 645–666.

- Lilienfeld, S. O., & Andrews, B. P. (1996). Development and preliminary validation of a self report measure of psychopathic personality traits in noncriminal populations. *Journal of Personality Assessment, 66*, 488–524.

- Lilienfeld, S. O., & Widows, M. R. (2005). *Psychopathic Personality Inventory-Revised (PPI-R) professional manual*. Odessa, FL: Psychological Assessment Resources.

- Lilienfeld, S. O., Waldman, I. D., Landfield, K., Rubenzer, S., & Faschingbauer, T. R. (2012). Psychopathic personality traits among U.S. presidents: Implications for job performance and leadership. *Journal of Personality and Social Psychology, 103*, 489–505.

- Lykken, D. T. (1995). *The antisocial personalities*. Hillsdale, NJ: Erlbaum.

- Marsh, A. A., Finger, E. C., Mitchell, D. G., Reid, M. E., Sims, C., Kosson, D. S., et al. (2008). Reduced amygdala response to fearful expressions in children and adolescents with callous-unemotional traits and disruptive behavior disorders. *The American Journal of Psychiatry, 165*, 712–720.

- McCord, W., & McCord, J. (1964). *The psychopath: An essay on the criminal mind*. Princeton, NJ: Van Nostrand.

- Patrick, C. J. (2010). *Operationalizing the Triarchic conceptualization of psychopathy: Preliminary description of brief scales for assessment of boldness, meanness, and disinhibition*. Unpublished test manual, Florida State University, Tallahassee, FL. Retrieved from https://www.phenxtoolkit.org/index.php?pageLink=browse.protocoldetails&id=121601

- Patrick, C. J., & Bernat, E. M. (2009). Neurobiology of psychopathy: A two-process theory. In: G. G. Berntson & J. T. Cacioppo (Eds.), *Handbook of neuroscience for the behavioral sciences* (pp. 1110–1131). New York, NY: John Wiley & Sons.

- Patrick, C. J., & Bernat, E. M. (2009). Neurobiology of psychopathy: A two-process theory. In: G. G. Berntson & J. T. Cacioppo (Eds.), *Handbook of neuroscience for the behavioral sciences* (pp. 1110–1131). New York, NY: John Wiley & Sons.

- Patrick, C. J., Bradley, M. M., & Lang, P. J. (1993). Emotion in the criminal psychopath: Startle reflex modulation. *Journal of Abnormal Psychology, 102*, 82-92.

- Patrick, C. J., Fowles, D. C., & Krueger, R. F. (2009). Triarchic conceptualization of psychopathy: Developmental origins of disinhibition, boldness, and meanness. *Development and Psychopathology, 21*, 913–938.

- Pinel, P. (1962). *A treatise on insanity* (D. Davis, translator). New York, NY: Hafner. (Original edition published in 1806)

- Pressman, E. R. (Producer), & Stone, O. (Director). (1987). *Wall Street*. United States: 20th Century Fox.

- Ross, S. R., Benning, S. D., Patrick, C. J., Thompson, A., & Thurston, A. (2009). Factors of the Psychopathic Personality Inventory: Criterion-related validity and relationship to the BIS/BAS and Five-

Factor models of personality. *Assessment, 16*, 71–87.

- Sellbom, M., & Phillips, T. R. (2013). An examination of the triarchic conceptualization of psychopathy in incarcerated and non-incarcerated samples. *Journal of Abnormal Psychology, 122*, 208–214.

- Skeem, J. L., Johansson, P., Andershed, H., Kerr, M., & Louden, J. E. (2007). Two subtypes of psychopathic violent offenders that parallel primary and secondary variants. *Journal of Abnormal Psychology, 116*, 395–409.

- Strickland, C. M., Drislane, L. E., Lucy, M., Krueger, R. F., & Patrick, C. J. (in press). Characterizing psychopathy using DSM-5 personality traits. *Assessment*.

- Venables, N. C., & Patrick, C. J. (2012). Validity of the Externalizing Spectrum Inventory in a criminal offender sample: Relations with disinhibitory psychopathology, personality, and psychopathic features. *Psychological Assessment, 24*, 88–100.

- Verona, E., & Vitale, J. (2006). Psychopathy in women: Assessment, manifestations, and etiology. In C. J. Patrick (Ed.), *Handbook of psychopathy* (pp. 415–436). New York, NY: Guilford Press.

CC licensed content, Shared previously

Schizophrenia Spectrum Disorders

Schizophrenia and the other psychotic disorders are some of the most impairing forms of psychopathology, frequently associated with a profound negative effect on the individual's educational, occupational, and social function. Sadly, these disorders often manifest right at time of the transition from adolescence to adulthood, just as young people should be evolving into independent young adults. The spectrum of psychotic disorders includes schizophrenia, schizoaffective disorder, delusional disorder, schizotypal personality disorder, schizophreniform disorder, brief psychotic disorder, as well as psychosis associated with substance use or medical conditions. In this module, we summarize the primary clinical features of these disorders, describe the known cognitive and neurobiological changes associated with schizophrenia, describe potential risk factors and/or causes for the development of schizophrenia, and describe currently available treatments for schizophrenia.

Learning Objectives

- Describe the signs and symptoms of schizophrenia and related psychotic disorders.
- Describe the most well-replicated cognitive and neurobiological changes associated with schizophrenia.
- Describe the potential risk factors for the development of schizophrenia.
- Describe the controversies associated with "clinical high risk" approaches to identifying individuals at risk for the development of schizophrenia.
- Describe the treatments that work for some of the symptoms of schizophrenia.

The phenomenology of schizophrenia and related psychotic disorders

Most of you have probably had the experience of walking down the street in a city and seeing a person you thought was acting oddly. They may have been dressed in an unusual way, perhaps disheveled or wearing an unusual collection of clothes, makeup, or jewelry that did not seem to fit any particular group or subculture. They may have been talking to themselves or yelling at someone you could not see. If you tried to speak to them, they may have been difficult to follow or understand, or they may have acted paranoid or started telling a bizarre story about the people who were plotting against them. If so, chances are that you have encountered an individual with schizophrenia or another type of psychotic disorder. If you have watched the movie *A Beautiful Mind* or *The Fisher King*, you have also seen a portrayal of someone thought to have schizophrenia. Sadly, a few of the individuals who have committed some of the recently highly publicized mass murders may have had schizophrenia, though most people who commit such crimes do not have schizophrenia. It is also likely that you have met people with schizophrenia without ever knowing it, as they may suffer in silence or stay isolated to protect themselves from the horrors they see, hear, or believe are operating in the outside world. As these examples begin to illustrate, psychotic disorders involve many different types of symptoms, including delusions, hallucinations, disorganized speech and behavior, abnormal motor behavior (including catatonia), and negative symptoms such anhedonia/amotivation and blunted affect/reduced speech.

Delusions are false beliefs that are often fixed, hard to change even when the person is presented with conflicting information, and are often culturally influenced in their content (e.g., delusions involving Jesus in Judeo-Christian cultures, delusions involving Allah in Muslim cultures). They can be terrifying for the person, who may remain convinced that they are true even when loved ones and friends present them with clear information that they cannot be true. There are many different types or themes to delusions.

Under Surveillance: Abstract groups like the police or the government are commonly the focus of a schizophrenic's persecutory delusions. [Image: Thomas Hawk, https://goo.gl/qsrqiR, CC BY-NC 2.0, https://goo.gl/VnKlK8]

The most common delusions are persecutory and involve the belief that individuals or groups are trying to hurt, harm, or plot against the person in some way. These can be people that the person knows (people at work, the neighbors, family members), or more abstract groups (the FBI, the CIA, aliens, etc.). Other types of delusions include grandiose delusions, where the person believes that they have some special power or ability (e.g., I am the new Buddha, I am a rock star); referential delusions, where the person believes that events or objects in the environment have special meaning for them (e.g., that song on the radio is being played *specifically* for me); or other types of delusions where the person may believe that others are controlling their thoughts and actions, their thoughts are being broadcast aloud, or that others can read their mind (or they can read other people's minds).

When you see a person on the street talking to themselves or shouting at other people, they are experiencing hallucinations. These are perceptual experiences that occur even when there is no stimulus in the outside world generating the experiences. They can be auditory, visual, olfactory (smell), gustatory (taste), or somatic (touch). The most common hallucinations in psychosis (at least in adults) are auditory, and can involve one or more voices talking about the person, commenting on the person's behavior, or giving them orders. The content of the hallucinations is frequently negative ("you are a loser," "that drawing is stupid," "you should go kill yourself") and can be the voice of someone the person knows or a complete stranger. Sometimes the voices sound as if they are coming from outside the person's head. Other times the voices seem to be coming from inside the person's head, but are not experienced the same as the person's inner thoughts or inner speech.

A painting by Craig Finn, who suffers from schizophrenia, depicting hallucinations. The painting is titled "Artistic view of how the world feels like with schizophrenia". [Image: Craig Finn, https://goo.gl/A3fyva, CC0 1.0, https://goo.gl/iRMeK3]

Talking to someone with schizophrenia is sometimes difficult, as their speech may be difficult to follow, either because their answers do not clearly flow from your questions, or because one sentence does not logically follow from another. This is referred to as disorganized speech, and it can be present even when the person is writing. Disorganized behavior can include odd dress, odd makeup (e.g., lipstick outlining a mouth for 1 inch), or unusual rituals (e.g., repetitive hand gestures). Abnormal motor behavior can include catatonia, which refers to a variety of behaviors that seem to reflect a reduction in responsiveness to the external environment. This can include holding unusual postures for long periods of time, failing to respond to verbal or motor prompts from another person, or excessive and seemingly purposeless motor activity.

Some of the most debilitating symptoms of schizophrenia are difficult for others to see. These include what people refer to as "negative symptoms" or the absence of certain things we typically expect most people to have. For example, anhedonia or amotivation reflect a lack of apparent interest in or drive to engage in social or recreational activities. These symptoms can manifest as a great amount of time spent in physical immobility. Importantly, anhedonia and amotivation do not seem to reflect a lack of enjoyment in pleasurable activities or events (Cohen & Minor, 2010; Kring & Moran, 2008; Llerena, Strauss, & Cohen, 2012) but rather a reduced drive or ability to take the steps necessary to obtain the potentially positive outcomes (Barch & Dowd, 2010). Flat affect and reduced speech (alogia) reflect a lack of showing emotions through facial expressions, gestures, and speech intonation, as well as a reduced amount of speech and increased pause frequency and duration.

In many ways, the types of symptoms associated with psychosis are the most difficult for us to understand, as they may seem far outside the range of our normal experiences. Unlike depression or anxiety, many of us may not have had experiences that we think of as on the same continuum as psychosis. However, just like many of the other forms of psychopathology described in this book, the types of psychotic symptoms that characterize disorders like schizophrenia are on a continuum with "normal" mental experiences. For example, work by Jim van Os in the Netherlands has shown that a surprisingly large percentage of the general population (10%+) experience psychotic-like symptoms, though many fewer have multiple experiences and most will not continue to experience these symptoms in the long run (Verdoux & van Os, 2002). Similarly, work in a general population of adolescents and young adults in Kenya has also shown that a relatively high percentage of individuals experience one or more psychotic-like experiences (~19%) at some point in their lives (Mamah et al., 2012; Ndetei et al., 2012), though again most will not go on to develop a full-blown psychotic disorder.

Schizophrenia is the primary disorder that comes to mind when we discuss "psychotic" disorders (see Table 1 for diagnostic criteria), though there are a number of other disorders that share one or more features with schizophrenia. In the remainder of this module, we will use the terms "psychosis" and "schizophrenia" somewhat interchangeably, given that most of the research has focused on schizophrenia. In addition to schizophrenia (see Table 1), other psychotic disorders include schizophreniform disorder (a briefer version of schizophrenia), schizoaffective disorder (a mixture of psychosis and depression/mania symptoms), delusional disorder (the experience of only delusions), and brief psychotic disorder (psychotic symptoms that last only a few days or weeks).

Schizophrenia (Lifetime prevalence about 0.3% to 0.7% [APA, 2013])
• Two or more of the following for at least 1 month: hallucinations, delusions, disorganized speech, grossly disorganized or catatonic behavior, negative symptoms. • Impairment in one or more areas of function (social, occupational, educational self-care) for a significant period of time since the onset of the illness. • Continuous signs of the illness for at least 6 months (this can include prodromal or residual symptoms, which are attenuated forms of the symptoms described above).
Schizophreniform Disorder (Lifetime prevalence similar to Schizophrenia [APA, 2013])
• The same symptoms of schizophrenia described above that are present for at least 1 month but less than 6 months.
Schizoaffective Disorder (Lifetime prevalence about 0.3% [APA, 2013])
• A period of illness where the person has both the psychotic symptoms necessary to meet criteria for schizophrenia and either a major depression or manic episode. •The person experiences either delusions or hallucinations for at least 2 weeks when they are not having a depressive or manic episode. • The symptoms that meet criteria for depressive or manic episodes are present for over half of the illness duration.
Delusional Disorder (Lifetime prevalence about 0.2% [APA, 2013])
• The presence of at least one delusion for at least a month. • The person has never met criteria for schizophrenia. • The person's function is not impaired outside the specific impact of the delusion. • The duration of any depressive or manic episodes have been brief relative to the duration of the delusion(s).
Brief Psychotic Disorder (Lifetime prevalence unclear [APA, 2013])
• One or more of the following symptoms present for at least 1 day but less than 1 month: delusions, hallucinations, disorganized speech, grossly disordered or catatonic behavior.
Attenuated Psychotic Disorder (In Section III of the [APA, 2013]-V, Lifetime presence unclear [APA, 2013])
• One or more of the following symptoms in an "attenuated" form: delusions, hallucinations, or disorganized speech. • The symptoms must have occurred at least once a week for the past month and must have started or gotten worse in the past year. • The symptoms must be severe enough to distress or disable the individual or to suggest to others that the person needs clinical help. • The person has never met the diagnostic criteria for a psychotic disorder, and the symptoms are not better attributed to another disorder, to substance use, or to a medical condition.

Table 1: Types of Psychotic Disorders (Simplified from the Diagnostic and Statistical Manual – 5th Edition (DSM-5) (APA, 2013)

The Cognitive Neuroscience of Schizophrenia

As described above, when we think of the core symptoms of psychotic disorders such as schizophrenia, we think of people who hear voices, see visions, and have false beliefs about reality (i.e., delusions). However, problems in cognitive function are also a critical aspect of psychotic disorders and of schizophrenia in particular. This emphasis on cognition in schizophrenia is in part due to the growing body of research suggesting that cognitive problems in schizophrenia are a major source of disability and loss of functional capacity (Green, 2006; Nuechterlein et al., 2011). The cognitive deficits that are present in schizophrenia are widespread and can include problems with episodic memory (the ability to learn and retrieve new information or episodes in one's life), working memory (the ability to maintain information over a short period of time, such as 30 seconds), and other tasks that require one to "control" or regulate one's behavior (Barch & Ceaser, 2012; Bora, Yucel, & Pantelis, 2009a; Fioravanti, Carlone, Vitale, Cinti, & Clare, 2005; Forbes, Carrick, McIntosh, & Lawrie, 2009; Mesholam-Gately, Giuliano, Goff, Faraone, & Seidman, 2009). Individuals with schizophrenia also have difficulty with what is referred to as "processing speed" and are frequently slower than healthy individuals on almost all tasks. Importantly, these cognitive deficits are present prior to the onset of the illness (Fusar-Poli et al., 2007) and are also present, albeit in a milder form, in the first-degree relatives of people with schizophrenia (Snitz, Macdonald, & Carter, 2006). This suggests that cognitive impairments in schizophrenia reflect part of the risk for the development of psychosis, rather than being an outcome of developing psychosis. Further, people with schizophrenia who have more severe cognitive problems also tend to have more severe negative symptoms and more disorganized speech and behavior (Barch, Carter, & Cohen, 2003; Barch et al., 1999; Dominguez Mde, Viechtbauer, Simons, van Os, & Krabbendam, 2009; Ventura, Hellemann, Thames, Koellner, & Nuechterlein, 2009; Ventura, Thames, Wood, Guzik, & Hellemann, 2010). In addition, people with more cognitive problems have worse function in everyday life (Bowie et al., 2008; Bowie, Reichenberg, Patterson, Heaton, & Harvey, 2006; Fett et al., 2011).

Some people with schizophrenia also show deficits in what is referred to as social cognition, though it is not clear whether such problems are separate from the cognitive problems described above or the result of them (Hoe, Nakagami, Green, & Brekke, 2012; Kerr & Neale, 1993; van Hooren et al., 2008). This includes problems with the recognition of emotional expressions on the faces of other individuals (Kohler, Walker, Martin, Healey, & Moberg, 2010) and problems inferring the intentions of other people (theory of mind) (Bora, Yucel, & Pantelis, 2009b). Individuals with schizophrenia who have more problems with social cognition also tend to have more negative and disorganized symptoms (Ventura, Wood, & Hellemann, 2011), as well as worse community function (Fett et al., 2011).

Some with schizophrenia suffer from difficulty with social cognition. They may not be able to detect the meaning of facial expressions or other subtle cues that most other people rely on to navigate the social world. [Image: Ralph Buckley, https://goo.gl/KuBzsD, CC BY-SA 2.0, https://goo.gl/i4GXf5]

The advent of neuroimaging techniques such as structural and functional magnetic resonance imaging and positron emission tomography opened up the ability to try to understand the brain mechanisms of the symptoms of schizophrenia as well as the cognitive impairments found in psychosis. For example, a number of studies have suggested that delusions in psychosis may be associated with problems in "salience" detection mechanisms supported by the ventral striatum (Jensen & Kapur, 2009; Jensen et al., 2008; Kapur, 2003; Kapur,

Mizrahi, & Li, 2005; Murray et al., 2008) and the anterior prefrontal cortex (Corlett et al., 2006; Corlett, Honey, & Fletcher, 2007; Corlett, Murray, et al., 2007a, 2007b). These are regions of the brain that normally increase their activity when something important (aka "salient") happens in the environment. If these brain regions misfire, it may lead individuals with psychosis to mistakenly attribute importance to irrelevant or unconnected events. Further, there is good evidence that problems in working memory and cognitive control in schizophrenia are related to problems in the function of a region of the brain called the dorsolateral prefrontal cortex (DLPFC) (Minzenberg, Laird, Thelen, Carter, & Glahn, 2009; Ragland et al., 2009). These problems include changes in how the DLPFC works when people are doing working-memory or cognitive-control tasks, and problems with how this brain region is connected to other brain regions important for working memory and cognitive control, including the posterior parietal cortex (e.g., Karlsgodt et al., 2008; J. J. Kim et al., 2003; Schlosser et al., 2003), the anterior cingulate (Repovs & Barch, 2012), and temporal cortex (e.g., Fletcher et al., 1995; Meyer-Lindenberg et al., 2001). In terms of understanding episodic memory problems in schizophrenia, many researchers have focused on medial temporal lobe deficits, with a specific focus on the hippocampus (e.g., Heckers & Konradi, 2010). This is because there is much data from humans and animals showing that the hippocampus is important for the creation of new memories (Squire, 1992). However, it has become increasingly clear that problems with the DLPFC also make important contributions to episodic memory deficits in schizophrenia (Ragland et al., 2009), probably because this part of the brain is important for controlling our use of memory.

In addition to problems with regions such as the DLFPC and medial temporal lobes in schizophrenia described above, magnitude resonance neuroimaging studies have also identified changes in cellular architecture, white matter connectivity, and gray matter volume in a variety of regions that include the prefrontal and temporal cortices (Bora et al., 2011). People with schizophrenia also show reduced overall brain volume, and reductions in brain volume as people get older may be larger in those with schizophrenia than in healthy people (Olabi et al., 2011). Taking antipsychotic medications or taking drugs such as marijuana, alcohol, and tobacco may cause some of these structural changes. However, these structural changes are not completely explained by medications or substance use alone. Further, both functional and structural brain changes are seen, again to a milder degree, in the first-degree relatives of people with schizophrenia (Boos, Aleman, Cahn, Pol, & Kahn, 2007; Brans et al., 2008; Fusar-Poli et al., 2007; MacDonald, Thermenos, Barch, & Seidman, 2009). This again suggests that that neural changes associated with schizophrenia are related to a genetic risk for this illness.

Risk Factors for Developing Schizophrenia

It is clear that there are important genetic contributions to the likelihood that someone will develop schizophrenia, with consistent evidence from family, twin, and adoption studies. (Sullivan, Kendler, & Neale, 2003). However, there is no "schizophrenia gene" and it is likely that the genetic risk for schizophrenia reflects the summation of many different genes that each contribute something to the likelihood of developing psychosis (Gottesman & Shields, 1967; Owen, Craddock, & O'Donovan, 2010). Further, schizophrenia is a very heterogeneous disorder, which means that two different people with "schizophrenia" may each have very different symptoms (e.g., one has hallucinations and delusions, the other has disorganized speech and negative symptoms). This makes it even more challenging to identify specific genes associated with risk for psychosis. Importantly, many studies also now suggest that at least some of the genes potentially associated with schizophrenia are also associated with other mental health conditions, including bipolar disorder, depression, and autism (Gejman, Sanders, & Kendler, 2011; Y. Kim, Zerwas, Trace, & Sullivan, 2011; Owen et al., 2010; Rutter, Kim-Cohen, & Maughan, 2006).

There are a number of genetic and environmental risk factors associated with higher likelihood of developing schizophrenia including older fathers, complications during pregnancy/delivery, family history of schizophrenia, and growing up in an urban environment. [Image: CC0 Public Domain]

There are also a number of environmental factors that are associated with an increased risk of developing schizophrenia. For example, problems during pregnancy such as increased stress, infection, malnutrition, and/or diabetes have been associated with increased risk of schizophrenia. In addition, complications that occur at the time of birth and which cause hypoxia (lack of oxygen) are also associated with an increased risk for developing schizophrenia (M. Cannon, Jones, & Murray, 2002; Miller et al., 2011). Children born to older fathers are also at a somewhat increased risk of developing schizophrenia. Further, using cannabis increases risk for developing psychosis, especially if you have other risk factors (Casadio, Fernandes, Murray, & Di Forti, 2011; Luzi, Morrison, Powell, di Forti, & Murray, 2008). The likelihood of developing schizophrenia is also higher for kids who grow up in urban settings (March et al., 2008) and for some minority ethnic groups (Bourque, van der Ven, & Malla, 2011). Both of these factors may reflect higher social and environmental stress in these settings. Unfortunately, none of these risk factors is specific enough to be particularly useful in a clinical setting, and most people with these "risk" factors do not develop schizophrenia. However, together they are beginning to give us clues as the neurodevelopmental factors that may lead someone to be at an increased risk for developing this disease.

An important research area on risk for psychosis has been work with individuals who may be at "clinical high risk." These are individuals who are showing attenuated (milder) symptoms of psychosis that have developed recently and who are experiencing some distress or disability associated with these symptoms. When people with these types of symptoms are followed over time, about 35% of them develop a psychotic disorder (T. D. Cannon et al., 2008), most frequently schizophrenia (Fusar-Poli, McGuire, & Borgwardt, 2012). In order to identify these individuals, a new category of diagnosis, called "Attenuated Psychotic Syndrome," was added to Section III (the section for disorders in need of further study) of the DSM-5 (see Table 1 for symptoms) (APA, 2013). However, adding this diagnostic category to the DSM-5 created a good deal of controversy (Batstra & Frances, 2012; Fusar-Poli & Yung, 2012). Many scientists and clinicians have been worried that including "risk" states in the DSM-5 would create mental disorders where none exist, that these individuals are often already seeking treatment for other problems, and that it is not clear that we have good treatments to stop these individuals from developing to psychosis. However, the counterarguments have been that there is evidence that individuals with high-risk symptoms develop psychosis at a much higher rate than individuals with other types of psychiatric symptoms, and that the inclusion of Attenuated Psychotic Syndrome in Section III will spur important research that might have clinical benefits. Further, there is some evidence that non-invasive treatments such as omega-3 fatty acids and intensive family intervention may help reduce the development of full-blown psychosis (Preti & Cella, 2010) in people who have high-risk symptoms.

Treatment of Schizophrenia

The currently available treatments for schizophrenia leave much to be desired, and the search for more effective treatments for both the psychotic symptoms of schizophrenia (e.g., hallucinations and delusions) as well as cognitive deficits and negative symptoms is a highly active area of research. The first line of treatment for schizophrenia and other psychotic disorders is the use of antipsychotic medications. There are two primary types of antipsychotic medications, referred to as "typical" and "atypical." The fact that "typical" antipsychotics helped some symptoms of schizophrenia was discovered serendipitously more than 60 years ago (Carpenter & Davis, 2012; Lopez-Munoz et al., 2005). These are drugs that all share a common feature of being a strong block of the D2 type dopamine receptor. Although these drugs can help reduce hallucinations, delusions, and disorganized speech, they do little to improve cognitive deficits or negative symptoms and can be associated with distressing motor side effects. The newer generation of antipsychotics is referred to as "atypical" antipsychotics. These drugs have more mixed mechanisms of action in terms of the receptor types that they influence, though most of them also influence D2 receptors. These newer antipsychotics are not necessarily more helpful for schizophrenia but have fewer motor side effects. However, many of the atypical antipsychotics are associated with side effects referred to as the "metabolic syndrome," which includes weight gain and increased risk for cardiovascular illness, Type-2 diabetes, and mortality (Lieberman et al., 2005).

The evidence that cognitive deficits also contribute to functional impairment in schizophrenia has led to an increased search for treatments that might enhance cognitive function in schizophrenia. Unfortunately, as of yet, there are no pharmacological treatments that work consistently to improve cognition in schizophrenia, though many new types of drugs are currently under exploration. However, there is a type of psychological intervention, referred to as cognitive remediation, which has shown some evidence of helping cognition and function in schizophrenia. In particular, a version of this treatment called Cognitive Enhancement Therapy (CET) has been shown to improve cognition, functional outcome, social cognition, and to protect against gray matter loss (Eack et al., 2009; Eack, Greenwald, Hogarty, & Keshavan, 2010; Eack et al., 2010; Eack, Pogue-Geile, Greenwald, Hogarty, & Keshavan, 2010; Hogarty, Greenwald, & Eack, 2006) in young individuals with schizophrenia. The development of new treatments such as Cognitive Enhancement Therapy provides some hope that we will be able to develop new and better approaches to improving the lives of individuals with this serious mental health condition and potentially even prevent it some day.

Outside Resources

Book: *Ben Behind His Voices: One family's journal from the chaos of schizophrenia to hope* (2011). Randye Kaye. Rowman and Littlefield.

Book: *Conquering Schizophrenia: A father, his son, and a medical breakthrough* (1997). Peter Wyden. Knopf.

Book: *Henry's Demons: Living with schizophrenia, a father and son's story* (2011). Henry and Patrick Cockburn. Scribner Macmillan.

Book: *My Mother's Keeper: A daughter's memoir of growing up in the shadow of schizophrenia* (1997). Tara Elgin Holley. William Morrow Co.

Book: *Recovered, Not Cured: A journey through schizophrenia* (2005). Richard McLean. Allen and Unwin.

Book: *The Center Cannot Hold: My journey through madness* (2008). Elyn R. Saks. Hyperion.

Book: *The Quiet Room: A journal out of the torment of madness* (1996). Lori Schiller. Grand Central Publishing.

Book: *Welcome Silence: My triumph over schizophrenia* (2003). Carol North. CSS Publishing.

Web: National Alliance for the Mentally Ill. This is an excellent site for learning more about advocacy for individuals with major mental illnesses such as schizophrenia.

http://www.nami.org/

Web: National Institute of Mental Health. This website has information on NIMH-funded schizophrenia research.

http://www.nimh.nih.gov/health/topics/schizophrenia/index.shtml

Web: Schizophrenia Research Forum. This is an excellent website that contains a broad array of information about current research on schizophrenia.

http://www.schizophreniaforum.org/

Discussion Questions

1. Describe the major differences between the major psychotic disorders.

2. How would one be able to tell when an individual is "delusional" versus having non-delusional beliefs that differ from the societal normal? How should cultural and sub-cultural variation been taken into account when assessing psychotic symptoms?

3. Why are cognitive impairments important to understanding schizophrenia?

4. Why has the inclusion of a new diagnosis (Attenuated Psychotic Syndrome) in Section III of the DSM-5 created controversy?

5. What are some of the factors associated with increased risk for developing schizophrenia? If we know whether or not someone has these risk factors, how well can we tell whether they will develop schizophrenia?

6. What brain changes are most consistent in schizophrenia?

7. Do antipsychotic medications work well for all symptoms of schizophrenia? If not, which symptoms respond better to antipsychotic medications?

8. Are there any treatments besides antipsychotic medications that help any of the symptoms of schizophrenia? If so, what are they?

Vocabulary

Alogia

A reduction in the amount of speech and/or increased pausing before the initiation of speech.

Anhedonia/amotivation

A reduction in the drive or ability to take the steps or engage in actions necessary to obtain the potentially posi-tive outcome.

Catatonia

Behaviors that seem to reflect a reduction in responsiveness to the external environment. This can include hold-ing unusual postures for long periods of time, failing to respond to verbal or motor prompts from another per-son, or excessive and seemingly purposeless motor activity.

Delusions

False beliefs that are often fixed, hard to change even in the presence of conflicting information, and often cul-turally influenced in their content.

Diagnostic criteria

The specific criteria used to determine whether an individual has a specific type of psychiatric disorder. Com-monly used diagnostic criteria are included in the Diagnostic and Statistical Manual of Mental Disorder, 5th Edition (DSM-5) and the Internal Classification of Disorders, Version 9 (ICD-9).

Disorganized behavior

Behavior or dress that is outside the norm for almost all subcultures. This would include odd dress, odd makeup (e.g., lipstick outlining a mouth for 1 inch), or unusual rituals (e.g., repetitive hand gestures).

Disorganized speech

Speech that is difficult to follow, either because answers do not clearly follow questions or because one sentence does not logically follow from another.

Dopamine

A neurotransmitter in the brain that is thought to play an important role in regulating the function of other neu-rotransmitters.

Episodic memory

The ability to learn and retrieve new information or episodes in one's life.

Flat affect

A reduction in the display of emotions through facial expressions, gestures, and speech intonation.

Functional capacity

The ability to engage in self-care (cook, clean, bathe), work, attend school, and/or engage in social relation-ships.

Hallucinations

Perceptual experiences that occur even when there is no stimulus in the outside world generating the experi-ences. They can be auditory, visual, olfactory (smell), gustatory (taste), or somatic (touch).

Magnetic resonance imaging

A set of techniques that uses strong magnets to measure either the structure of the brain (e.g., gray matter and white matter) or how the brain functions when a person performs cognitive tasks (e.g., working memory or episodic memory) or other types of tasks.

Neurodevelopmental

Processes that influence how the brain develops either in utero or as the child is growing up.

Positron emission tomography

A technique that uses radio-labelled ligands to measure the distribution of different neurotransmitter receptors in the brain or to measure how much of a certain type of neurotransmitter is released when a person is given a specific type of drug or does a particularly cognitive task.

Processing speed

The speed with which an individual can perceive auditory or visual information and respond to it.

Psychopathology

Illnesses or disorders that involve psychological or psychiatric symptoms.

Working memory

The ability to maintain information over a short period of time, such as 30 seconds or less.

References

- APA. (2013). *Diagnostic and statistical manual of mental disorders, Fifth Edition* (5th ed.). Washington, DC: American Psychiatric Association.

- Barch, D. M., & Ceaser, A. E. (2012). Cognition in schizophrenia: Core psychological and neural mechanisms. *Trends in Cognitive Science, 16*, 27–34.

- Barch, D. M., & Dowd, E. C. (2010). Goal representations and motivational drive in schizophrenia: The role of prefrontal-striatal interactions. *Schizophrenia Bulletin, 36*(5), 919–934. doi: sbq068 [pii] 10.1093/schbul/sbq068

- Barch, D. M., Carter, C. S., & Cohen, J. D. (2003). Context processing deficit in schizophrenia: Diagnostic specificity, 4-week course, and relationships to clinical symptoms. *Journal of Abnormal Psychology, 112*, 132–143.

- Barch, D. M., Carter, C. S., Macdonald, A., Sabb, F. W., Noll, D. C., & Cohen, J. D. (1999). Prefrontal cortex and context processing in medication-naive first-episode patients with schizophrenia. *Schizophrenia Research, 36*(1–3), 217–218.

- Batstra, L., & Frances, A. (2012). Diagnostic inflation: Causes and a suggested cure. *The Journal of Nervous and Mental Disease, 200*(6), 474–479. doi: 10.1097/NMD.0b013e318257c4a2

- Boos, H. B., Aleman, A., Cahn, W., Pol, H. H., & Kahn, R. S. (2007). Brain volumes in relatives of patients with schizophrenia: A meta-analysis. *Archives of General Psychiatry, 64*(3), 297–304.

- Bora, E., Fornito, A., Radua, J., Walterfang, M., Seal, M., Wood, S. J., . . . Pantelis, C. (2011). Neuroanatomical abnormalities in schizophrenia: A multimodal voxelwise meta-analysis and meta-regression analysis. *Schizophrenia Research, 127*(1–3), 46–57. doi: 10.1016/j.schres.2010.12.020

- Bora, E., Yucel, M., & Pantelis, C. (2009a). Cognitive functioning in schizophrenia, schizoaffective disorder and affective psychoses: Meta-analytic study. *The British Journal of Psychiatry: The Journal of Mental Science, 195*(6), 475–482. doi: 10.1192/bjp.bp.108.055731

- Bora, E., Yucel, M., & Pantelis, C. (2009b). Theory of mind impairment in schizophrenia: Meta-analysis. *Schizophrenia Research, 109*(1–3), 1–9. doi: 10.1016/j.schres.2008.12.020

- Bourque, F., van der Ven, E., & Malla, A. (2011). A meta-analysis of the risk for psychotic disorders among first- and second-generation immigrants. *Psychological Medicine, 41*(5), 897–910. doi: 10.1017/S0033291710001406

- Bowie, C. R., Leung, W. W., Reichenberg, A., McClure, M. M., Patterson, T. L., Heaton, R. K., & Harvey, P. D. (2008). Predicting schizophrenia patients' real-world behavior with specific neuropsychological and functional capacity measures. *Biological Psychiatry, 63*(5), 505–511. doi: 10.1016/j.biopsych.2007.05.022

- Bowie, C. R., Reichenberg, A., Patterson, T. L., Heaton, R. K., & Harvey, P. D. (2006). Determinants of real-world functional performance in schizophrenia subjects: Correlations with cognition, functional capacity, and symptoms. *The American Journal of Psychiatry, 163*(3), 418–425. doi: 10.1176/appi.ajp.163.3.418

- Brans, R. G., van Haren, N. E., van Baal, G. C., Schnack, H. G., Kahn, R. S., & Hulshoff Pol, H. E. (2008). Heritability of changes in brain volume over time in twin pairs discordant for schizophrenia. *Archives of General Psychiatry, 65*(11), 1259–1268. doi: 10.1001/archpsyc.65.11.1259

- Cannon, M., Jones, P. B., & Murray, R. M. (2002). Obstetric complications and schizophrenia: Historical and meta-analytic review. *The American Journal of Psychiatry, 159*(7), 1080–1092.

- Cannon, T. D., Cadenhead, K., Cornblatt, B., Woods, S. W., Addington, J., Walker, E., . . . Heinssen, R. (2008). Prediction of psychosis in youth at high clinical risk: A multisite longitudinal study in North America. *Archives of General Psychiatry, 65*(1), 28–37.

- Carpenter, W. T., Jr., & Davis, J. M. (2012). Another view of the history of antipsychotic drug discovery and development. *Molecular Psychiatry, 17*(12), 1168–1173. doi: 10.1038/mp.2012.121

- Casadio, P., Fernandes, C., Murray, R. M., & Di Forti, M. (2011). Cannabis use in young people: The risk for schizophrenia. *Neuroscience & Biobehavioral Reviews*. doi: S0149-7634(11)00073-X [pii] 10.1016/j.neubiorev.2011.04.007

- Cohen, A. S., & Minor, K. S. (2010). Emotional experience in patients with schizophrenia revisited: Meta-analysis of laboratory studies. *Schizophrenia Bulletin, 36*(1), 143–150. doi: 10.1093/schbul/sbn061

- Corlett, P. R., Honey, G. D., & Fletcher, P. C. (2007). From prediction error to psychosis: Ketamine as a pharmacological model of delusions. *Journal of Psychopharmacology, 21*(3), 238–252. doi: 21/3/238 [pii] 10.1177/0269881107077716

- Corlett, P. R., Honey, G. D., Aitken, M. R., Dickinson, A., Shanks, D. R., Absalom, A. R., . . . Fletcher, P. C. (2006). Frontal responses during learning predict vulnerability to the psychotogenic effects of ketamine: Linking cognition, brain activity, and psychosis. *Archives of General Psychiatry, 63*(6), 611–621. doi: 63/6/611 [pii] 10.1001/archpsyc.63.6.611

- Corlett, P. R., Murray, G. K., Honey, G. D., Aitken, M. R., Shanks, D. R., Robbins, T. W., . . . Fletcher,

P. C. (2007a). Disrupted prediction-error signal in psychosis: Evidence for an associative account of delusions. *Brain: A Journal of Neurology, 130*(Pt 9), 2387–2400. doi: 10.1093/brain/awm173

• Corlett, P. R., Murray, G. K., Honey, G. D., Aitken, M. R., Shanks, D. R., Robbins, T. W., . . . Fletcher, P. C. (2007b). Disrupted prediction-error signal in psychosis: Evidence for an associative account of delusions. *Brain, 130*(Pt 9), 2387–2400. doi: awm173 [pii] 10.1093/brain/awm173

• Dominguez Mde, G., Viechtbauer, W., Simons, C. J., van Os, J., & Krabbendam, L. (2009). Are psychotic psychopathology and neurocognition orthogonal? A systematic review of their associations. *Psychological Bulletin, 135*(1), 157–171. doi: 10.1037/a0014415

• Eack, S. M., Greenwald, D. P., Hogarty, S. S., & Keshavan, M. S. (2010). One-year durability of the effects of cognitive enhancement therapy on functional outcome in early schizophrenia. *Schizophrenia Research, 120*(1–3), 210–216. doi: S0920-9964(10)01222-3 [pii] 10.1016/j.schres.2010.03.042

• Eack, S. M., Greenwald, D. P., Hogarty, S. S., Cooley, S. J., DiBarry, A. L., Montrose, D. M., & Keshavan, M. S. (2009). Cognitive enhancement therapy for early-course schizophrenia: effects of a two-year randomized controlled trial. *Psychiatr Serv, 60*(11), 1468–1476. doi: 60/11/1468 [pii] 10.1176/appi.ps.60.11.1468

• Eack, S. M., Hogarty, G. E., Cho, R. Y., Prasad, K. M., Greenwald, D. P., Hogarty, S. S., & Keshavan, M. S. (2010). Neuroprotective effects of cognitive enhancement therapy against gray matter loss in early schizophrenia: Results from a 2-year randomized controlled trial. *Archives of General Psychiatry, 67*(7), 674–682. doi: 2010.63 [pii] 10.1001/archgenpsychiatry.2010.63

• Eack, S. M., Pogue-Geile, M. F., Greenwald, D. P., Hogarty, S. S., & Keshavan, M. S. (2010). Mechanisms of functional improvement in a 2-year trial of cognitive enhancement therapy for early schizophrenia. *Psychological Medicine*, 1–9. doi: S0033291710001765 [pii] 10.1017/S0033291710001765

• Fett, A. K., Viechtbauer, W., Dominguez, M. D., Penn, D. L., van Os, J., & Krabbendam, L. (2011). The relationship between neurocognition and social cognition with functional outcomes in schizophrenia: A meta-analysis. *Neuroscience and Biobehavioral Reviews, 35*(3), 573–588. doi: 10.1016/j.neubiorev.2010.07.001

• Fioravanti, M., Carlone, O., Vitale, B., Cinti, M. E., & Clare, L. (2005). A meta-analysis of cognitive deficits in adults with a diagnosis of schizophrenia. *Neuropsychology Review, 15*(2), 73–95. doi: 10.1007/s11065-005-6254-9

• Fletcher, P. C., Frith, C. D., Grasby, P. M., Shallice, T., Frackowiak, R. S. J., & Dolan, R. J. (1995). Brain systems for encoding and retrieval of auditory-verbal memory: An in vivo study in humans. *Brain, 118*, 401–416.

• Forbes, N. F., Carrick, L. A., McIntosh, A. M., & Lawrie, S. M. (2009). Working memory in schizophrenia: A meta-analysis. *Psychological Medicine, 39*(6), 889–905. doi: 10.1017/S0033291708004558

• Fusar-Poli, P., & Yung, A. R. (2012). Should attenuated psychosis syndrome be included in DSM-5? *Lancet, 379*(9816), 591–592. doi: 10.1016/S0140-6736(11)61507-9

• Fusar-Poli, P., McGuire, P., & Borgwardt, S. (2012). Mapping prodromal psychosis: A critical review of neuroimaging studies. *European Psychiatry: The Journal of the Association of European Psychiatrists, 27*(3), 181–191. doi: 10.1016/j.eurpsy.2011.06.006

- Fusar-Poli, P., Perez, J., Broome, M., Borgwardt, S., Placentino, A., Caverzasi, E., . . . McGuire, P. (2007). Neurofunctional correlates of vulnerability to psychosis: A systematic review and meta-analysis. *Neuroscience and Biobehavioral Reviews, 31*(4), 465–484.

- Gejman, P. V., Sanders, A. R., & Kendler, K. S. (2011). Genetics of schizophrenia: New findings and challenges. *Annual Review of Genomics and Human Genetics.* doi: 10.1146/annurev-genom-082410-101459

- Gottesman, I. I., & Shields, J. (1967). A polygenic theory of schizophrenia. *Proceedings of the National Academy of Sciences of the United States of America, 58*(1), 199–205.

- Green, M. F. (2006). Cognitive impairment and functional outcome in schizophrenia and bipolar disorder. *The Journal of Clinical Psychiatry, 67 Suppl 9,* 3–8; discussion 36–42.

- Heckers, S., & Konradi, C. (2010). Hippocampal pathology in schizophrenia. *Current Topics in Behavioral Neurosciences, 4,* 529–553.

- Hoe, M., Nakagami, E., Green, M. F., & Brekke, J. S. (2012). The causal relationships between neurocognition, social cognition, and functional outcome over time in schizophrenia: A latent difference score approach. *Psychological Medicine,* 1–13. doi: 10.1017/S0033291712000578

- Hogarty, G. E., Greenwald, D. P., & Eack, S. M. (2006). Durability and mechanism of effects of cognitive enhancement therapy. *Psychiatric Services, 57*(12), 1751–1757. doi: 57/12/1751 [pii] 10.1176/appi.ps.57.12.1751

- Jensen, J., & Kapur, S. (2009). Salience and psychosis: Moving from theory to practise. *Psychological Medicine, 39*(2), 197–198. doi: 10.1017/S0033291708003899

- Jensen, J., Willeit, M., Zipursky, R. B., Savina, I., Smith, A. J., Menon, M., . . . Kapur, S. (2008). The formation of abnormal associations in schizophrenia: Neural and behavioral evidence. *Neuropsychopharmacology: Official Publication of the American College of Neuropsychopharmacology, 33*(3), 473–479. doi: 10.1038/sj.npp.1301437

- Kapur, S. (2003). Psychosis as a state of aberrant salience: A framework linking biology, phenomenology, and pharmacology in schizophrenia. *American Journal of Psychiatry, 160*(1), 13–23.

- Kapur, S., Mizrahi, R., & Li, M. (2005). From dopamine to salience to psychosis—linking biology, pharmacology and phenomenology of psychosis. *Schizophrenia Research, 79*(1), 59–68. doi: 10.1016/j.schres.2005.01.003

- Karlsgodt, K. H., van Erp, T. G., Poldrack, R. A., Bearden, C. E., Nuechterlein, K. H., & Cannon, T. D. (2008). Diffusion tensor imaging of the superior longitudinal fasciculus and working memory in recent-onset schizophrenia. *Biological Psychiatry, 63*(5), 512–518.

- Kerr, S. L., & Neale, J. M. (1993). Emotion perception in schizophrenia: Specific deficit or further evidence of generalized poor performance? *Journal of Abnormal Psychology, 102*(2), 312–318.

- Kim, J. J., Kwon, J. S., Park, H. J., Youn, T., Kang, D. H., Kim, M. S., . . . Lee, M. C. (2003). Functional disconnection between the prefrontal and parietal cortices during working memory processing in schizophrenia: A [15O]H20 PET study. *American Journal of Psychiatry, 160,* 919–923.

- Kim, Y., Zerwas, S., Trace, S. E., & Sullivan, P. F. (2011). Schizophrenia genetics: Where next? *Schizophrenia Bulletin, 37*(3), 456–463. doi: sbr031 [pii] 10.1093/schbul/sbr031

- Kohler, C. G., Walker, J. B., Martin, E. A., Healey, K. M., & Moberg, P. J. (2010). Facial emotion perception in schizophrenia: A meta-analytic review. *Schizophrenia Bulletin, 36*(5), 1009–1019. doi: 10.1093/schbul/sbn192

- Kring, A. M., & Moran, E. K. (2008). Emotional response deficits in schizophrenia: Insights from affective science. *Schizophrenia Bulletin, 34*(5), 819–834.

- Lieberman, J. A., Stroup, T. S., McEvoy, J. P., Swartz, M. S., Rosenheck, R. A., Perkins, D. O., . . . Hsiao, J. K. (2005). Effectiveness of antipsychotic drugs in patients with chronic schizophrenia. *The New England Journal of Medicine, 353*(12), 1209–1223. doi: 10.1056/NEJMoa051688

- Llerena, K., Strauss, G. P., & Cohen, A. S. (2012). Looking at the other side of the coin: A meta-analysis of self-reported emotional arousal in people with schizophrenia. *Schizophrenia Research, 142*(1–3), 65–70. doi: 10.1016/j.schres.2012.09.005

- Lopez-Munoz, F., Alamo, C., Cuenca, E., Shen, W. W., Clervoy, P., & Rubio, G. (2005). History of the discovery and clinical introduction of chlorpromazine. Annals of *Clinical Psychiatry: Official Journal of the American Academy of Clinical Psychiatrists, 17*(3), 113–135.

- Luzi, S., Morrison, P. D., Powell, J., di Forti, M., & Murray, R. M. (2008). What is the mechanism whereby cannabis use increases risk of psychosis? *Neurotoxicity Research, 14*(2–3), 105–112. doi: 10.1007/BF03033802

- MacDonald, A. W., III, Thermenos, H. W., Barch, D. M., & Seidman, L. J. (2009). Imaging genetic liability to schizophrenia: Systematic review of FMRI studies of patients' nonpsychotic relatives. *Schizophrenia Bulletin, 35*(6), 1142–1162.

- Mamah, D., Mbwayo, A., Mutiso, V., Barch, D. M., Constantino, J. N., Nsofor, T., . . . Ndetei, D. M. (2012). A survey of psychosis risk symptoms in Kenya. *Comprehensive Psychiatry, 53*(5), 516–524. doi: 10.1016/j.comppsych.2011.08.003

- March, D., Hatch, S. L., Morgan, C., Kirkbride, J. B., Bresnahan, M., Fearon, P., & Susser, E. (2008). Psychosis and place. *Epidemiologic Reviews, 30,* 84–100. doi: 10.1093/epirev/mxn006

- Mesholam-Gately, R. I., Giuliano, A. J., Goff, K. P., Faraone, S. V., & Seidman, L. J. (2009). Neurocognition in first-episode schizophrenia: A meta-analytic review. *Neuropsychology, 23*(3), 315–336. doi: 10.1037/a0014708

- Meyer-Lindenberg, A., Poline, J., Kohn, P. D., Holt, J. L., Egan, M. F., Weinberger, D. R., & Berman, K. F. (2001). Evidence for abnormal cortical functional connectivity during working memory in schizophrenia. *American Journal of Psychiatry, 158,* 1809–1817.

- Miller, B., Messias, E., Miettunen, J., Alaraisanen, A., Jarvelin, M. R., Koponen, H., . . . Kirkpatrick, B. (2011). Meta-analysis of paternal age and schizophrenia risk in male versus female offspring. *Schizophrenia Bulletin, 37*(5), 1039–1047. doi: 10.1093/schbul/sbq011

- Minzenberg, M. J., Laird, A. R., Thelen, S., Carter, C. S., & Glahn, D. C. (2009). Meta-analysis of 41 functional neuroimaging studies of executive function in schizophrenia. *Archives of General Psychiatry, 66*(8), 811–822. doi: 10.1001/archgenpsychiatry.2009.91

- Murray, G. K., Corlett, P. R., Clark, L., Pessiglione, M., Blackwell, A. D., Honey, G., . . . Fletcher, P. C. (2008). Substantia nigra/ventral tegmental reward prediction error disruption in psychosis. *Molecular Psychiatry, 13*(3), 267–276.

- Ndetei, D. M., Muriungi, S. K., Owoso, A., Mutiso, V. N., Mbwayo, A. W., Khasakhala, L. I., . . . Mamah, D. (2012). Prevalence and characteristics of psychotic-like experiences in Kenyan youth. *Psychiatry Research, 196*(2–3), 235–242. doi: 10.1016/j.psychres.2011.12.053

- Nuechterlein, K. H., Subotnik, K. L., Green, M. F., Ventura, J., Asarnow, R. F., Gitlin, M. J., . . . Mintz, J. (2011). Neurocognitive predictors of work outcome in recent-onset schizophrenia. *Schizophrenia Bulletin, 37 Suppl 2*, S33–40. doi: 10.1093/schbul/sbr084

- Olabi, B., Ellison-Wright, I., McIntosh, A. M., Wood, S. J., Bullmore, E., & Lawrie, S. M. (2011). Are there progressive brain changes in schizophrenia? A meta-analysis of structural magnetic resonance imaging studies. *Biological Psychiatry, 70*(1), 88–96. doi: 10.1016/j.biopsych.2011.01.032

- Owen, M. J., Craddock, N., & O'Donovan, M. C. (2010). Suggestion of roles for both common and rare risk variants in genome-wide studies of schizophrenia. *Archives of General Psychiatry, 67*(7), 667–673. doi: 10.1001/archgenpsychiatry.2010.69

- Preti, A., & Cella, M. (2010). Randomized-controlled trials in people at ultra high risk of psychosis: a review of treatment effectiveness. *Schizophrenia Research, 123*(1), 30–36. doi: 10.1016/j.schres.2010.07.026

- Ragland, J. D., Laird, A. R., Ranganath, C., Blumenfeld, R. S., Gonzales, S. M., & Glahn, D. C. (2009). Prefrontal activation deficits during episodic memory in schizophrenia. *American Journal of Psychiatry, 166*(8), 863–874.

- Repovs, G., & Barch, D. M. (2012). Working memory related brain network connectivity in individuals with schizophrenia and their siblings. *Frontiers in Human Neuroscience, 6*, 137. doi: 10.3389/fnhum.2012.00137

- Rutter, M., Kim-Cohen, J., & Maughan, B. (2006). Continuities and discontinuities in psychopathology between childhood and adult life. *Journal of Child Psychology and Psychiatry, and Aallied Disciplines, 47*(3–4), 276–295. doi: 10.1111/j.1469-7610.2006.01614.x

- Schlosser, R., Gesierich, T., Kaufmann, B., Vucurevic, G., Hunsche, S., Gawehn, J., & Stoeter, P. (2003). Altered effective connectivity during working memory performance in schizophrenia: A study with fMRI and structural equation modeling. *Neuroimage, 19*(3), 751–763.

- Snitz, B. E., Macdonald, A. W., 3rd, & Carter, C. S. (2006). Cognitive deficits in unaffected first-degree relatives of schizophrenia patients: A meta-analytic review of putative endophenotypes. *Schizophrenia Bulletin, 32*(1), 179–194.

- Squire, L.R. (1992). Memory and the hippocampus: A synthesis from findings with rats, monkeys, and humans. *Psychological Review, 99,* 195–231.

- Sullivan, P. F., Kendler, K. S., & Neale, M. C. (2003). Schizophrenia as a complex trait: Evidence from a meta-analysis of twin studies. *Archives of General Psychiatry, 60*(12), 1187–1192. doi: 10.1001/archpsyc.60.12.1187

- Ventura, J., Hellemann, G. S., Thames, A. D., Koellner, V., & Nuechterlein, K. H. (2009). Symptoms as mediators of the relationship between neurocognition and functional outcome in schizophrenia: a meta-analysis. *Schizophrenia Research, 113*(2–3), 189–199. doi: 10.1016/j.schres.2009.03.035

- Ventura, J., Thames, A. D., Wood, R. C., Guzik, L. H., & Hellemann, G. S. (2010). Disorganization and reality distortion in schizophrenia: a meta-analysis of the relationship between positive symptoms and neurocognitive deficits. *Schizophrenia Research, 121*(1–3), 1–14. doi: 10.1016/j.schres.2010.05.033

- Ventura, J., Wood, R. C., & Hellemann, G. S. (2011). Symptom domains and neurocognitive functioning can help differentiate social cognitive processes in schizophrenia: A meta-analysis. *Schizophrenia Bulletin*. doi: 10.1093/schbul/sbr067

- Verdoux, H., & van Os, J. (2002). Psychotic symptoms in non-clinical populations and the continuum of psychosis. *Schizophrenia Research, 54*(1–2), 59–65.

- van Hooren, S., Versmissen, D., Janssen, I., Myin-Germeys, I., a Campo, J., Mengelers, R., . . . Krabbendam, L. (2008). Social cognition and neurocognition as independent domains in psychosis. *Schizophrenia Research, 103*(1–3), 257–265. doi: 10.1016/j.schres.2008.02.022

4. Treatment of Psychological Disorders

Therapeutic Orientations

In the past century, a number of psychotherapeutic orientations have gained popularity for treating mental illnesses. This module outlines some of the best-known therapeutic approaches and explains the history, techniques, advantages, and disadvantages associated with each. The most effective modern approach is cognitive behavioral therapy (CBT). We also discuss psychoanalytic therapy, person-centered therapy, and mindfulness-based approaches. Drug therapy and emerging new treatment strategies will also be briefly explored.

Learning Objectives

- Become familiar with the most widely practiced approaches to psychotherapy.

- For each therapeutic approach, consider: history, goals, key techniques, and empirical support.

- Consider the impact of emerging treatment strategies in mental health.

Introduction

The history of mental illness can be traced as far back as 1500 BCE, when the ancient Egyptians noted cases of "distorted concentration" and "emotional distress in the heart or mind" (Nasser, 1987). Today, nearly half of all Americans will experience mental illness at some point in their lives, and mental health problems affect more than one-quarter of the population in any given year (Kessler et al., 2005). Fortunately, a range of psychotherapies exist to treat mental illnesses. This module provides an overview of some of the best-known schools of thought in psychotherapy. Currently, the most effective approach is called Cognitive Behavioral Therapy (CBT); however, other approaches, such as psychoanalytic therapy, person-centered therapy, and mindfulness-based therapies are also used—though the effectiveness of these treatments aren't as clear as they are for CBT. Throughout this module, note the advantages and disadvantages of each approach, paying special attention to their support by empirical research.

Psychoanalysis and Psychodynamic Therapy

CBT is an approach to treating mental illness that involves work with a therapist as well as homework assignments between sessions. It has proven to be very effective for virtually all psychiatric illnesses. [Image: DFAT, https://goo.gl/bWmzaa, CC BY 2.0, https://goo.gl/BRvSA7]

The earliest organized therapy for mental disorders was psychoanalysis. Made famous in the early 20th century by one of the best-known clinicians of all time, Sigmund Freud, this approach stresses that mental health problems are rooted in unconscious conflicts and desires. In order to resolve the mental illness, then, these unconscious struggles must be identified and addressed. Psychoanalysis often does this through exploring one's early childhood experiences that may have continuing repercussions on one's mental health in the present and later in life. Psychoanalysis is an intensive, long-term approach in which patients and therapists may meet multiple times per week, often for many years.

History of Psychoanalytic Therapy

Freud initially suggested that mental health problems arise from efforts to push inappropriate sexual urges out of conscious awareness (Freud, 1895/1955). Later, Freud suggested more generally that psychiatric problems are the result of tension between different parts of the mind: the id, the superego, and the ego. In Freud's *structural model*, the id represents pleasure-driven unconscious urges (e.g., our animalistic desires for sex and aggression), while the superego is the semi-conscious part of the mind where morals and societal judgment are internalized (e.g., the part of you that automatically knows how society expects you to behave). The ego—also partly conscious—mediates between the id and superego. Freud believed that bringing unconscious struggles like these (where the id demands one thing and the superego another) into conscious awareness would relieve the stress of the conflict (Freud, 1920/1955)—which became the goal of psychoanalytic therapy.

Although psychoanalysis is still practiced today, it has largely been replaced by the more broadly defined psychodynamic therapy. This latter approach has the same basic tenets as psychoanalysis, but is briefer, makes more of an effort to put clients in their social and interpersonal context, and focuses more on relieving psychological distress than on changing the person.

Techniques in Psychoanalysis

Building on the work of Josef Breuer and others, Sigmund Freud developed psychotherapeutic theories and techniques that became widely known as psychoanalysis or psychoanalytic therapy. [Image: CC0 Public Domain, https://goo.gl/m25gce]

Psychoanalysts and psychodynamic therapists employ several techniques to explore patients' unconscious mind. One common technique is called free association. Here, the patient shares any and all thoughts that come to mind, without attempting to organize or censor them in any way. For example, if you took a pen and paper and just wrote down whatever came into your head, letting one thought lead to the next without allowing conscious criticism to shape what you were writing, you would be doing free association. The analyst then uses his or her expertise to discern patterns or underlying meaning in the patient's thoughts.

Sometimes, free association exercises are applied specifically to childhood recollections. That is, psychoanalysts believe a person's childhood relationships with caregivers often determine the way that person relates to others, and predicts later psychiatric difficulties. Thus, exploring these childhood memories, through free association or otherwise, can provide therapists with insights into a patient's psychological makeup.

Because we don't always have the ability to consciously recall these deep memories, psychoanalysts also discuss their patients' dreams. In Freudian theory, dreams contain not only *manifest* (or literal) content, but also *latent* (or symbolic) content (Freud, 1900; 1955). For example, someone may have a dream that his/her teeth are falling out—the manifest or actual content of the dream. However, dreaming that one's teeth are falling out could be a reflection of the person's unconscious concern about losing his or her physical attractiveness—the latent or metaphorical content of the dream. It is the therapist's job to help discover the latent content underlying one's manifest content through dream analysis.

In psychoanalytic and psychodynamic therapy, the therapist plays a receptive role—interpreting the patient's thoughts and behavior based on clinical experience and psychoanalytic theory. For example, if during therapy a patient begins to express unjustified anger toward the therapist, the therapist may recognize this as an act of *transference*. That is, the patient may be displacing feelings for people in his or her life (e.g., anger toward a parent) onto the therapist. At the same time, though, the therapist has to be aware of his or her own thoughts and emotions, for, in a related process, called *countertransference*, the therapist may displace his/her own emotions onto the patient.

The key to psychoanalytic theory is to have patients uncover the buried, conflicting content of their mind, and therapists use various tactics—such as seating patients to face away from them—to promote a freer self-disclosure. And, as a therapist spends more time with a patient, the therapist can come to view his or her relationship with the patient as another reflection of the patient's mind.

Advantages and Disadvantages of Psychoanalytic Therapy

Psychoanalysis was once the only type of psychotherapy available, but presently the number of therapists practicing this approach is decreasing around the world. Psychoanalysis is not appropriate for some types of patients, including those with severe psychopathology or mental retardation. Further, psychoanalysis is often expensive because treatment usually lasts many years. Still, some patients and therapists find the prolonged and detailed analysis very rewarding.

Perhaps the greatest disadvantage of psychoanalysis and related approaches is the lack of empirical support for their effectiveness. The limited research that has been conducted on these treatments suggests that they do not reliably lead to better mental health outcomes (e.g., Driessen et al., 2010). And, although there are some reviews that seem to indicate that long-term psychodynamic therapies might be beneficial (e.g., Leichsenring & Rabung, 2008), other researchers have questioned the validity of these reviews. Nevertheless, psychoanalytic theory was history's first attempt at formal treatment of mental illness, setting the stage for the more modern approaches used today.

Humanistic and Person-Centered Therapy

One of the next developments in therapy for mental illness, which arrived in the mid-20th century, is called humanistic or person-centered therapy (PCT). Here, the belief is that mental health problems result from an inconsistency between patients' behavior and their true personal identity. Thus, the goal of PCT is to create conditions under which patients can discover their self-worth, feel comfortable exploring their own identity, and alter their behavior to better reflect this identity.

History of Person-Centered Therapy

PCT was developed by a psychologist named Carl Rogers, during a time of significant growth in the movements of humanistic theory and human potential. These perspectives were based on the idea that humans have an inherent drive to realize and express their own capabilities and creativity. Rogers, in particular, believed that all people have the potential to change and improve, and that the role of therapists is to foster self-understanding in an environment where adaptive change is most likely to occur (Rogers, 1951). Rogers suggested that the therapist and patient must engage in a genuine, egalitarian relationship in which the therapist is nonjudgmental and empathetic. In PCT, the patient should experience both a vulnerability to anxiety, which motivates the desire to change, and an appreciation for the therapist's support.

The quality of the relationship between therapist and patient is of great importance in person-centered therapy. [Image: CC0 Public Domain, https://goo.gl/m25gce]

Techniques in Person-Centered Therapy

Humanistic and person-centered therapy, like psychoanalysis, involves a largely unstructured conversation between the therapist and the patient. Unlike psychoanalysis, though, a therapist using PCT takes a passive role, guiding the patient toward his or her own self-discovery. Rogers's original name for PCT was *non-directive therapy*, and this notion is reflected in the flexibility found in PCT. Therapists do not try to change patients' thoughts or behaviors directly. Rather, their role is to provide the therapeutic relationship as a platform for personal growth. In these kinds of sessions, the therapist tends only to ask questions and doesn't provide any judgment or interpretation of what the patient says. Instead, the therapist is present to provide a safe and encouraging environment for the person to explore these issues for him- or herself.

An important aspect of the PCT relationship is the therapist's unconditional positive regard for the patient's feelings and behaviors. That is, the therapist is never to condemn or criticize the patient for what s/he has done or thought; the therapist is only to express warmth and empathy. This creates an environment free of approval or disapproval, where patients come to appreciate their value and to behave in ways that are congruent with their own identity.

Advantages and Disadvantages of Person-Centered Therapy

One key advantage of person-centered therapy is that it is highly acceptable to patients. In other words, people tend to find the supportive, flexible environment of this approach very rewarding. Furthermore, some of the themes of PCT translate well to other therapeutic approaches. For example, most therapists of any orientation find that clients respond well to being treated with nonjudgmental empathy. The main disadvantage to PCT, however, is that findings about its effectiveness are mixed. One possibility for this could be that the treatment is primarily based on *unspecific treatment factors*. That is, rather than using therapeutic techniques that are specific to the patient and the mental problem (i.e., *specific treatment factors*), the therapy focuses on techniques that can be applied to anyone (e.g., establishing a good relationship with the patient) (Cuijpers et al., 2012; Friedli, King, Lloyd, & Horder, 1997). Similar to how "one-size-fits-all" doesn't really fit every person, PCT uses the same practices for everyone, which may work for some people but not others. Further research is necessary to evaluate its utility as a therapeutic approach.

Cognitive Behavioral Therapy

Although both psychoanalysis and PCT are still used today, another therapy, cognitive-behavioral therapy (CBT), has gained more widespread support and practice. CBT refers to a family of therapeutic approaches whose goal is to alleviate psychological symptoms by changing their underlying cognitions and behaviors. The premise of CBT is that thoughts, behaviors, and emotions interact and contribute to various mental disorders. For example, let's consider how a CBT therapist would view a patient who compulsively washes her hands for hours every day. First, the therapist would identify the patient's maladaptive thought: "If I don't wash my hands like this, I will get a disease and die." The therapist then identifies how this maladaptive *thought* leads to a maladaptive *emotion*: the feeling of anxiety when her hands aren't being washed. And finally, this maladaptive emotion leads to the maladaptive behavior: the patient washing her hands for hours every day.

CBT is a present-focused therapy (i.e., focused on the "now" rather than causes from the past, such as childhood relationships) that uses behavioral goals to improve one's mental illness. Often, these behavioral goals involve between-session homework assignments. For example, the therapist may give the hand-washing patient a worksheet to take home; on this worksheet, the woman is to write down every time she feels the urge to wash her hands, how she deals with the urge, and what behavior she replaces that urge with. When the patient has her next therapy session, she and the therapist review her "homework" together. CBT is a relatively brief intervention of 12 to 16 weekly sessions, closely tailored to the nature of the psychopathology and treatment of the specific mental disorder. And, as the empirical data shows, CBT has proven to be highly efficacious for virtually all psychiatric illnesses (Hofmann, Asnaani, Vonk, Sawyer, & Fang, 2012).

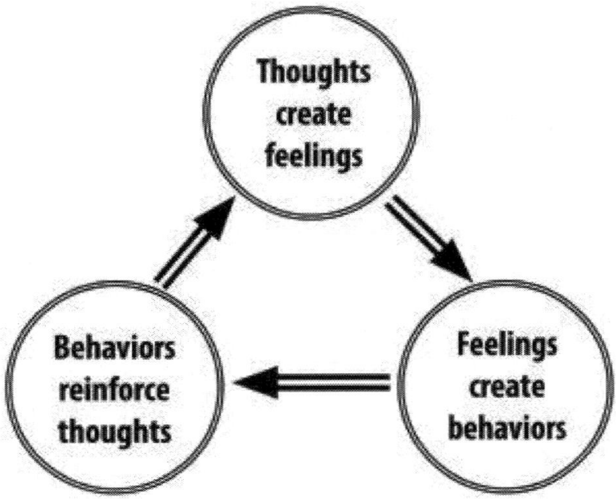

Pattern of thoughts, feelings, and behaviors addressed through cognitive-behavioral therapy.

History of Cognitive Behavioral Therapy

CBT developed from clinical work conducted in the mid-20th century by Dr. Aaron T. Beck, a psychiatrist, and Albert Ellis, a psychologist. Beck used the term automatic thoughts to refer to the thoughts depressed patients report experiencing spontaneously. He observed that these thoughts arise from three belief systems, or schemas: beliefs about the self, beliefs about the world, and beliefs about the future. In treatment, therapy initially focuses on identifying automatic thoughts (e.g., "If I don't wash my hands constantly, I'll get a disease"), testing their validity, and replacing maladaptive thoughts with more adaptive thoughts (e.g., "Washing my hands three times a day is sufficient to prevent a disease"). In later stages of treatment, the patient's maladaptive schemas are examined and modified. Ellis (1957) took a comparable approach, in what he called rational-emotive-behavioral therapy (REBT), which also encourages patients to evaluate their own thoughts about situations.

Techniques in CBT

Beck and Ellis strove to help patients identify maladaptive appraisals, or the untrue judgments and evaluations of certain thoughts. For example, if it's your first time meeting new people, you may have the automatic thought, "These people won't like me because I have nothing interesting to share." That thought itself is not what's troublesome; the appraisal (or evaluation) that it might have merit is what's troublesome. The goal of CBT is to help people make adaptive, instead of maladaptive, appraisals (e.g., "I do know interesting things!"). This technique of reappraisal, or cognitive restructuring, is a fundamental aspect of CBT. With cognitive restructuring, it is the therapist's job to help point out when a person has an inaccurate or maladaptive thought, so that the patient can either eliminate it or modify it to be more adaptive.

In addition to *thoughts*, though, another important treatment target of CBT is maladaptive *behavior*. Every time a person engages in maladaptive behavior (e.g., never speaking to someone in new situations), he or she reinforces the validity of the maladaptive thought, thus maintaining or perpetuating the psychological illness. In treatment, the therapist and patient work together to develop healthy behavioral habits (often tracked with worksheet-like homework), so that the patient can break this cycle of maladaptive thoughts and behaviors.

For many mental health problems, especially anxiety disorders, CBT incorporates what is known as exposure therapy. During exposure therapy, a patient confronts a problematic situation and fully engages in the experience instead of avoiding it. For example, imagine a man who is terrified of spiders. Whenever he encounters one, he immediately screams and panics. In exposure therapy, the man would be forced to confront and interact with spiders, rather than simply avoiding them as he usually does. The goal is to reduce the fear associated with the situation through *extinction learning,* a neurobiological and cognitive process by which the patient "unlearns" the irrational fear. For example, exposure therapy for someone terrified of spiders might begin with him looking at a cartoon of a spider, followed by him looking at pictures of real spiders, and later, him handling a plastic spider. After weeks of this incremental exposure, the patient may even be able to hold a live spider. After repeated exposure (starting small and building one's way up), the patient experiences less physiological fear and maladaptive thoughts about spiders, breaking his tendency for anxiety and subsequent avoidance.

Advantages and Disadvantages of CBT

CBT interventions tend to be relatively brief, making them cost-effective for the average consumer. In addition, CBT is an intuitive treatment that makes logical sense to patients. It can also be adapted to suit the needs of many different populations. One disadvantage, however, is that CBT does involve significant effort on the patient's part, because the patient is an active participant in treatment. Therapists often assign "homework" (e.g., worksheets for recording one's thoughts and behaviors) between sessions to maintain the cognitive and behavioral habits the patient is working on. The greatest strength of CBT is the abundance of empirical support for its effectiveness. Studies have consistently found CBT to be equally or more effective than other forms of treatment, including medication and other therapies (Butler, Chapman, Forman, & Beck, 2006; Hofmann et al., 2012). For this reason, CBT is considered a first-line treatment for many mental disorders.

Focus Topic:
Pioneers of CBT

The central notion of CBT is the idea that a person's behavioral and emotional responses are causally influenced by one's thinking. The stoic Greek philosopher Epictetus is quoted as saying, "men are not moved by things, but by the view they take of them." Meaning, it is not the event per se, but rather one's assumptions (including interpretations and perceptions) of the event that are responsible for one's emotional response to it. Beck calls these assumptions about events and situations automatic thoughts (Beck, 1979), whereas Ellis (1962) refers to these assumptions as self-statements. The cognitive model assumes that these cognitive processes cause the emotional and behavioral responses to events or stimuli. This causal chain is illustrated in Ellis's ABC model, in which A stands for the antecedent event, B stands for belief, and C stands for consequence. During CBT, the person is encouraged to carefully observe the sequence of events and the response to them, and then explore the validity of the underlying beliefs through behavioral experiments and reasoning, much like a detective or scientist.

Acceptance and Mindfulness-Based Approaches

Unlike the preceding therapies, which were developed in the 20th century, this next one was born out of age-old Buddhist and yoga practices. Mindfulness, or a process that tries to cultivate a nonjudgmental, yet attentive, mental state, is a therapy that focuses on one's awareness of bodily sensations, thoughts, and the outside environment. Whereas other therapies work to modify or eliminate these sensations and thoughts, mindfulness focuses on nonjudgmentally accepting them (Kabat-Zinn, 2003; Baer, 2003). For example, whereas CBT may actively confront and work to change a maladaptive thought, mindfulness therapy works to acknowledge and accept the thought, understanding that the thought is spontaneous and not what the person truly believes. There are two important components of mindfulness: (1) self-regulation of attention, and (2) orientation toward the present moment (Bishop et al., 2004). Mindfulness is thought to improve mental health because it draws attention away from past and future stressors, encourages acceptance of troubling thoughts and feelings, and promotes physical relaxation.

Techniques in Mindfulness-Based Therapy

One of the most important advantages of mindfulness based therapy is its level of accessibility to patients. [Image: Wayne MacPhail, https://goo.gl/aSZanf, CC BY-NC SA 2.0, https://goo.gl/TocOZF]

Psychologists have adapted the practice of mindfulness as a form of psychotherapy, generally called mindfulness-based therapy (MBT). Several types of MBT have become popular in recent years, including *mindfulness-based stress reduction* (MBSR) (e.g., Kabat-Zinn, 1982) and *mindfulness-based cognitive therapy* (MBCT) (e.g., Segal, Williams, & Teasdale, 2002).

MBSR uses meditation, yoga, and attention to physical experiences to reduce stress. The hope is that reducing a person's overall stress will allow that person to more objectively evaluate his or her thoughts. In MBCT, rather than reducing one's general stress to address a specific problem, attention is focused on one's thoughts and their associated emotions. For example, MBCT helps prevent relapses in depression by encouraging patients to evaluate their own thoughts objectively and without value judgment (Baer, 2003). Although cognitive behavioral therapy (CBT) may seem similar to this, it focuses on "pushing out" the maladaptive thought, whereas mindfulness-based cognitive therapy focuses on "not getting caught up" in it. The treatments used in MBCT have been used to address a wide range of illnesses, including depression, anxiety, chronic pain, coronary artery disease, and fibromyalgia (Hofmann, Sawyer, Witt & Oh, 2010).Mindfulness and acceptance—in addition to being therapies in their own right—have also been used as "tools" in other cognitive-behavioral therapies, particularly in dialectical behavior therapy (DBT) (e.g., Linehan, Amstrong, Suarez, Allmon, & Heard, 1991). DBT, often used in the treatment of borderline personality disorder, focuses on skills training. That is, it often employs mindfulness and cognitive behavioral therapy practices, but it also works to teach its patients "skills" they can use to correct maladaptive tendencies. For example, one skill DBT teaches patients is called *distress tolerance*—or, ways to cope with maladaptive thoughts and emotions in the moment. For example, people who feel an urge to cut themselves may be taught to snap their arm with a rubber band instead. The primary difference between DBT and CBT is that DBT employs techniques that address the symptoms of the problem (e.g., cutting oneself) rather than the problem itself (e.g., understanding the psychological motivation to cut oneself). CBT does not teach such skills training because of the concern that the skills—even though they may help in the short-term—may be harmful in the long-term, by maintaining maladaptive thoughts and behaviors.DBT is founded on the perspective of a dialectical worldview. That is, rather than thinking of the world as "black and white," or "only good and only bad," it focuses on accepting that some things can have characteristics of both "good" and "bad." So, in a case involving maladaptive thoughts, instead of teaching that a thought is entirely bad, DBT tries to help patients be less judgmental of their thoughts (as with mindfulness-based therapy) and encourages change through therapeutic progress, using cognitive-behavioral techniques as well as mindfulness exercises.

Another form of treatment that also uses mindfulness techniques is acceptance and commitment therapy (ACT) (Hayes, Strosahl, & Wilson, 1999). In this treatment, patients are taught to observe their thoughts from a detached perspective (Hayes et al., 1999). ACT encourages patients *not* to attempt to change or avoid thoughts and emotions they observe in themselves, but to recognize which are beneficial and which are harmful. However, the differences among ACT, CBT, and other mindfulness-based treatments are a topic of controversy in the current literature.

Advantages and Disadvantages of Mindfulness-Based Therapy

Two key advantages of mindfulness-based therapies are their acceptability and accessibility to patients. Because yoga and meditation are already widely known in popular culture, consumers of mental healthcare are often interested in trying related psychological therapies. Currently, psychologists have not come to a consensus on the efficacy of MBT, though growing evidence supports its effectiveness for treating mood and anxiety disorders. For example, one review of MBT studies for anxiety and depression found that mindfulness-based interventions generally led to moderate symptom improvement (Hofmann et al., 2010).

Emerging Treatment Strategies

With growth in research and technology, psychologists have been able to develop new treatment strategies in recent years. Often, these approaches focus on enhancing existing treatments, such as cognitive-behavioral therapies, through the use of technological advances. For example, *internet*-and *mobile-delivered therapies* make psychological treatments more available, through smartphones and online access. Clinician-supervised online CBT modules allow patients to access treatment from home on their own schedule—an opportunity particularly important for patients with less geographic or socioeconomic access to traditional treatments. Furthermore, smartphones help extend therapy to patients' daily lives, allowing for symptom tracking, homework reminders, and more frequent therapist contact.Another benefit of technology is cognitive bias modification. Here, patients are given exercises, often through the use of video games, aimed at changing their problematic thought processes. For

Recent improvements in video chat technology along with the proliferation of mobile devices like smartphones and tablets has made online delivery of therapy more commonplace. [Image: Noba, CC BY 2.0, https://goo.gl/BRvSA7]

example, researchers might use a mobile app to train alcohol abusers to avoid stimuli related to alcohol. One version of this game flashes four pictures on the screen—three alcohol cues (e.g., a can of beer, the front of a bar) and one health-related image (e.g., someone drinking water). The goal is for the patient to tap the healthy picture as fast as s/he can. Games like these aim to target patients' automatic, subconscious thoughts that may be difficult to direct through conscious effort. That is, by repeatedly tapping the healthy image, the patient learns to "ignore" the alcohol cues, so when those cues are encountered in the environment, they will be less likely to trigger the urge to drink. Approaches like these are promising because of their accessibility, however they require further research to establish their effectiveness.Yet another emerging treatment employs *CBT-enhancing pharmaceutical agents*. These are drugs used to improve the effects of therapeutic interventions. Based on research from animal experiments, researchers have found that certain drugs influence the biological processes known to be involved in learning. Thus, if people take these drugs while going through psychotherapy, they are better able to "learn" the techniques for improvement. For example, the antibiotic d-cycloserine improves treatment for anxiety disorders by facilitating the learning processes that occur during exposure therapy. Ongoing research in this exciting area may prove to be quite fruitful.

Pharmacological Treatments

Up until this point, all the therapies we have discussed have been talk-based or meditative practices. However, psychiatric medications are also frequently used to treat mental disorders, including schizophrenia, bipolar disorder, depression, and anxiety disorders. Psychiatric drugs are commonly used, in part, because they can be prescribed by general medical practitioners, whereas only trained psychologists are qualified to deliver effective psychotherapy. While drugs and CBT therapies tend to be almost equally effective, choosing the best intervention depends on the disorder and individual being treated, as well as other factors—such as treatment availability and comorbidity (i.e., having multiple mental or physical disorders at once). Although many new drugs have been introduced in recent decades, there is still much we do not understand about their mechanism in the brain. Further research is needed to refine our understanding of both pharmacological and behavioral treatments before we can make firm claims about their effectiveness.

Integrative and Eclectic Psychotherapy

In discussing therapeutic orientations, it is important to note that some clinicians incorporate techniques from multiple approaches, a practice known as integrative or eclectic psychotherapy. For example, a therapist may employ distress tolerance skills from DBT (to resolve short-term problems), cognitive reappraisal from CBT (to address long-standing issues), and mindfulness-based meditation from MBCT (to reduce overall stress). And, in fact, between 13% and 42% of therapists have identified their own approaches as integrative or eclectic (Norcross & Goldfried, 2005).

Conclusion

Throughout human history we have had to deal with mental illness in one form or another. Over time, several schools of thought have emerged for treating these problems. Although various therapies have been shown to work for specific individuals, cognitive behavioral therapy is currently the treatment most widely supported by empirical research. Still, practices like psychodynamic therapies, person-centered therapy, mindfulness-based treatments, and acceptance and commitment therapy have also shown success. And, with recent advances in research and technology, clinicians are able to enhance these and other therapies to treat more patients more effectively than ever before. However, what is important in the end is that people actually seek out mental health specialists to help them with their problems. One of the biggest deterrents to doing so is that people don't understand what psychotherapy really entails. Through understanding how current practices work, not only can we better educate people about how to get the help they need, but we can continue to advance our treatments to be more effective in the future.

Outside Resources

Article: A personal account of the benefits of mindfulness-based therapy
https://www.theguardian.com/lifeandstyle/2014/jan/11/julie-myerson-mindfulness-based-cognitive-therapy
Article: The Effect of Mindfulness-Based Therapy on Anxiety and Depression: A Meta-Analytic Review
https://www.ncbi.nlm.nih.gov/pmc/articles/PMC2848393/
Video: An example of a person-centered therapy session.

- https://youtu.be/4wTVbzvBH0k

Video: Carl Rogers, the founder of the humanistic, person-centered approach to psychology, discusses the position of the therapist in PCT.

- https://youtu.be/o0neRQzudzw

Video: CBT (cognitive behavioral therapy) is one of the most common treatments for a range of mental health problems, from anxiety, depression, bipolar, OCD or schizophrenia. This animation explains the basics and how you can decide whether it's best for you or not.

- https://youtu.be/9c_Bv_FBE-c

Web: An overview of the purpose and practice of cognitive behavioral therapy (CBT)
http://psychcentral.com/lib/in-depth-cognitive-behavioral-therapy/
Web: The history and development of psychoanalysis
http://www.freudfile.org/psychoanalysis/history.html

Discussion Questions

1. Psychoanalytic theory is no longer the dominant therapeutic approach, because it lacks empirical support. Yet many consumers continue to seek psychoanalytic or psychodynamic treatments. Do you think psychoanalysis still has a place in mental health treatment? If so, why?

2. What might be some advantages and disadvantages of technological advances in psychological treatment? What will psychotherapy look like 100 years from now?

3. Some people have argued that all therapies are about equally effective, and that they all affect change through common factors such as the involvement of a supportive therapist. Does this claim sound reasonable to you? Why or why not?

4. When choosing a psychological treatment for a specific patient, what factors besides the treatment's demonstrated efficacy should be taken into account?

Vocabulary

Acceptance and commitment therapy
A therapeutic approach designed to foster nonjudgmental observation of one's own mental processes.
Automatic thoughts
Thoughts that occur spontaneously; often used to describe problematic thoughts that maintain mental disorders.
Cognitive bias modification
Using exercises (e.g., computer games) to change problematic thinking habits.
Cognitive-behavioral therapy (CBT)
A family of approaches with the goal of changing the thoughts and behaviors that influence psychopathology.
Comorbidity
Describes a state of having more than one psychological or physical disorder at a given time.

Dialectical behavior therapy (DBT)

A treatment often used for borderline personality disorder that incorporates both cognitive-behavioral and mindfulness elements.

Dialectical worldview

A perspective in DBT that emphasizes the joint importance of change and acceptance.

Exposure therapy

A form of intervention in which the patient engages with a problematic (usually feared) situation without avoidance or escape.

Free association

In psychodynamic therapy, a process in which the patient reports all thoughts that come to mind without censorship, and these thoughts are interpreted by the therapist.

Integrative or eclectic psychotherapy

Also called integrative psychotherapy, this term refers to approaches combining multiple orientations (e.g., CBT with psychoanalytic elements).

Integrative or eclectic psychotherapy

Also called integrative psychotherapy, this term refers to approaches combining multiple orientations (e.g., CBT with psychoanalytic elements).

Mindfulness

A process that reflects a nonjudgmental, yet attentive, mental state.

Mindfulness-based therapy

A form of psychotherapy grounded in mindfulness theory and practice, often involving meditation, yoga, body scan, and other features of mindfulness exercises.

Person-centered therapy

A therapeutic approach focused on creating a supportive environment for self-discovery.

Psychoanalytic therapy

Sigmund Freud's therapeutic approach focusing on resolving unconscious conflicts.

Psychodynamic therapy

Treatment applying psychoanalytic principles in a briefer, more individualized format.

Reappraisal, or Cognitive restructuring

The process of identifying, evaluating, and changing maladaptive thoughts in psychotherapy.

Schema

A mental representation or set of beliefs about something.

Unconditional positive regard

In person-centered therapy, an attitude of warmth, empathy and acceptance adopted by the therapist in order to foster feelings of inherent worth in the patient.

References

- Baer, R. (2003). Mindfulness training as a clinical intervention: A conceptual and empirical review. *Clinical Psychology: Science and Practice, 10*, 125–143.

- Beck, A. T. (1979). *Cognitive therapy and the emotional disorders.* New York, NY: New American Library/Meridian.

- Bishop, S. R., Lau, M., Shapiro, S., Carlson, L., Anderson, N. D., Carmody, J., Segal, Z. V., Abbey, S., Speca, M., Velting, D., & Devins, G. (2004). Mindfulness: A proposed operational definition. *Clinical Psychology: Science and Practice, 11,* 230–241.

- Butler, A. C., Chapman, J. E., Forman, E. M., & Beck, A. T. (2006). The empirical status of cognitive behavioral therapy: A review of meta-analyses. *Clinical Psychology Review, 26,* 17–31.

- Cuijpers, P., Driessen, E., Hollon, S.D., van Oppen, P., Barth, J., & Andersson, G. (2012). The efficacy of non-directive supportive therapy for adult depression: A meta-analysis. *Clinical Psychology Review, 32,* 280–291.

- Driessen, E., Cuijpers, P., de Maat, S. C. M., Abbass, A. A., de Jonghe, F., & Dekker, J. J. M. (2010). The efficacy of short-term psychodynamic psychotherapy for depression: A meta-analysis. *Clinical Psychology Review, 30,* 25–36.

- Ellis, A. (1962). *Reason and emotion in psychotherapy.* New York, NY: Lyle Stuart.

- Ellis, A. (1957). Rational psychotherapy and individual psychology. *Journal of Individual Psychology, 13,* 38–44.

- Freud, S. (1955). *The interpretation of dreams.* London, UK: Hogarth Press (Original work published 1900).

- Freud, S. (1955). *Studies on hysteria.* London, UK: Hogarth Press (Original work published 1895).

- Freud. S. (1955). *Beyond the pleasure principle.* H London, UK: Hogarth Press (Original work published 1920).

- Friedli, K., King, M. B., Lloyd, M., & Horder, J. (1997). Randomized controlled assessment of non-directive psychotherapy versus routine general-practitioner care. *Lancet,* 350,\\n1662–1665.

- Hayes, S. C., Strosahl, K., & Wilson, K. G. (1999). *Acceptance and Commitment Therapy.* New\\nYork, NY: Guilford Press.

- Hofmann, S. G., Asnaani, A., Vonk, J. J., Sawyer, A. T., & Fang, A. (2012). The efficacy of cognitive behavioral therapy: A review of meta-analyses. *Cognitive Therapy and Research, 36,* 427–440.

- Hofmann, S. G., Sawyer, A. T., Witt, A., & Oh, D. (2010). The effect of mindfulness-based therapy on anxiety and depression: A meta-analytic review. *Journal of Consulting and Clinical Psychology, 78,* 169–183

- Kabat-Zinn J. (2003). Mindfulness-based interventions in context: Past, present, and future. *Clinical Psychology: Science and Practice, 10,* 144–156.

- Kabat-Zinn, J. (1982). An outpatient program in behavioral medicine for chronic pain patients\\nbased on the practice of mindfulness meditation: Theoretical considerations and preliminary results. *General Hospital Psychiatry, 4,* 33–47.

- Kessler, R. C., Berglund, P., Demler, O., Jin, R., Merikangas, K. R., & Walters, E. E. (2005). Lifetime prevalence and age of onset distribution of DSM-IV disorders in the National Comorbidity Survey Replication. *Archives of General Psychiatry, 62,* 593–602.

- Leichsenring, F., & Rabung, S. (2008). Effectiveness of long-term psychodynamic psychotherapy: A meta-analysis. *Journal of the American Medical Association, 300,*1551–1565.

- Linehan, M. M., Amstrong, H.-E., Suarez, A., Allmon, D., & Heard, H. L. (1991). Cognitive-behavioral treatment of chronically suicidal borderline patients. *Archives of General Psychiatry, 48,* 1060–1064.

- Nasser, M. (1987). Psychiatry in ancient Egypt. *Bulletin of the Royal College of Psychiatrists,* 11, 420-422.

- Norcross, J. C. & Goldfried, M. R. (2005). *Handbook of Psychotherapy Integration.* New York, NY: Oxford University Press.

- Rogers, C. (1951). *Client-Centered Therapy.* Cambridge, MA: Riverside Press.

- Segal, Z. V., Williams, J. M. G., & Teasdale, J. D. (2002). *Mindfulness-Based Cognitive Therapy\\nfor Depression: A New Approach to Preventing Relapse.* New York, NY: Guilford Press.

CC licensed content, Shared previously

Psychotherapy

Link to Wikipedia: https://en.wikipedia.org/wiki/Psychotherapy

Psychopharmacology

Psychopharmacology is the study of how drugs affect behavior. If a drug changes your perception, or the way you feel or think, the drug exerts effects on your brain and nervous system. We call drugs that change the way you think or feel psychoactive or psychotropic drugs, and almost everyone has used a psychoactive drug at some point (yes, caffeine counts). Understanding some of the basics about psychopharmacology can help us better understand a wide range of things that interest psychologists and others. For example, the pharmacological treatment of certain neurodegenerative diseases such as Parkinson's disease tells us something about the disease itself. The pharmacological treatments used to treat psychiatric conditions such as schizophrenia or depression have undergone amazing development since the 1950s, and the drugs used to treat these disorders tell us something about what is happening in the brain of individuals with these conditions. Finally, understanding something about the actions of drugs of abuse and their routes of administration can help us understand why some psychoactive drugs are so addictive. In this module, we will provide an overview of some of these topics as well as discuss some current controversial areas in the field of psychopharmacology.

Learning Objectives

- How do the majority of psychoactive drugs work in the brain?
- How does the route of administration affect how rewarding a drug might be?
- Why is grapefruit dangerous to consume with many psychotropic medications?
- Why might individualized drug doses based on genetic screening be helpful for treating conditions like depression?
- Why is there controversy regarding pharmacotherapy for children, adolescents, and the elderly?

Introduction

Psychopharmacology, the study of how drugs affect the brain and behavior, is a relatively new science, although people have probably been taking drugs to change how they feel from early in human history (consider the of eating fermented fruit, ancient beer recipes, chewing on the leaves of the cocaine plant for stimulant properties as just some examples). The word *psychopharmacology* itself tells us that this is a field that bridges our understanding of behavior (and brain) and pharmacology, and the range of topics included within this field is extremely broad.

Virtually any drug that changes the way you feel does this by altering how neurons communicate with each other. Neurons (more than 100 billion in your nervous system) communicate with each other by releasing a chemical (neurotransmitter) across a tiny space between two neurons (the synapse). When the neurotransmitter crosses the synapse, it binds to a postsynaptic receptor (protein) on the receiving neuron and the message may then be transmitted onward. Obviously, neurotransmission is far more complicated than this – links at the end of this module can provide some useful background if you want more detail – but the first step is understanding that virtually all psychoactive drugsinterfere with or alter how neurons communicate with each other.

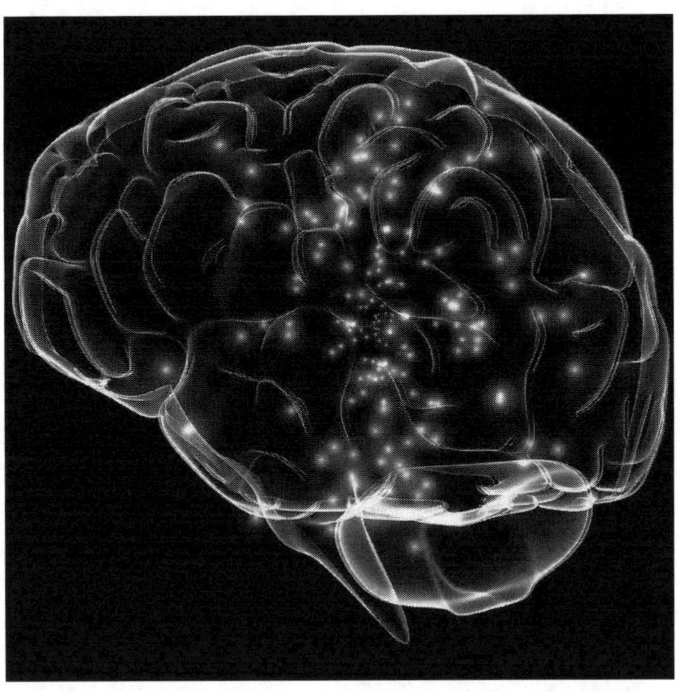

Drugs that alter our feelings and behavior do so by affecting the communication between neurons in the brain. [Image: https://goo.gl/oQCafL, CC0 Public Domain, https://goo.gl/m25gce]

There are many neurotransmitters. Some of the most important in terms of psychopharmacological treatment and drugs of abuse are outlined in Table 1. The neurons that release these neurotransmitters, for the most part, are localized within specific circuits of the brain that mediate these behaviors. Psychoactive drugs can either increase activity at the synapse (these are called agonists) or reduce activity at the synapse (antagonists). Different drugs do this by different mechanisms, and some examples of agonists and antagonists are presented in Table 2. For each example, the drug's trade name, which is the name of the drug provided by the drug company, and generic name (in parentheses) are provided.

Neurotransmitter	Abbreviation	Behaviors or Diseases Related to These Neurotransmitter
Acetylcholine	ACh	Learning and memory; Alzheimer's disease' muscle movement in the peripheral nervous system
Dopamine	DA	Reward circuits; Motor circuits involved in Parkinson's disease; Schizophrenia
Norepinephrine	NE	Arousal; Depression
Serotonin	5HT	Depression; Aggression; Schizophrenia
Glutamate	GLU	Learning; Major excitatory neurotransmitter in the brain
GABA	GABA	Anxiety disorders; Epilepsy; Major inhibitory neurotransmitter in the brain
Endogenous Opiods	Endorphins, Enkephalins	Pain; Analgesia; Reward

Table 1

A very useful link at the end of this module shows the various steps involved in neurotransmission and some ways drugs can alter this.

Table 2 provides examples of drugs and their primary mechanism of action, but it is very important to realize that drugs also have effects on other neurotransmitters. This contributes to the kinds of side effects that are observed when someone takes a particular drug. The reality is that no drugs currently available work only exactly where we would like in the brain or only on a specific neurotransmitter. In many cases, individuals are sometimes prescribed one psychotropic drug but then may also have to take additional drugs to reduce the side effects caused by the initial drug. Sometimes individuals stop taking medication because the side effects can be so profound.

Drug	Mechanism	Use	Agonist/Antagonist
L-dopa	Increase synthesis of DA	Parkinson's disease	Agonist for DA
Adderall (mixed salts amphetamine)	Increase release of DA, NE	ADHD	Agonist for DA, NE
Ritalin (methylphenidate)	Blocks removal of DA, NE, and lesser (5HT) from synapse	ADHD	Agonist for DA, NE mostly
Aricept (donepezil)	Blocks removal of ACh from synapse	Alzheimer's disease	Agonist for ACh
Prozac (fluoxetine)	Blocks removal of 5HT from synapse	Depression, obsessive compulsive disorder	Agonist 5HT
Seroquel (quetiapine)	Blocks DA and 5HT receptors	Schizophrenia, bipolar disorder	Antagonist for DA, 5HT
Revia (naltrexone)	Blocks opiod post-synaptic receptors	Alcoholism, opiod addiction	Antagonist (for opioids)

Table 2

Pharmacokinetics: What Is It – Why Is It Important?

While this section may sound more like pharmacology, it is important to realize how important pharmacokinetics can be when considering psychoactive drugs. Pharmacokinetics refers to how the body handles a drug that we take. As mentioned earlier, psychoactive drugs exert their effects on behavior by altering neuronal communication in the brain, and the majority of drugs reach the brain by traveling in the blood. The acronym ADME is often used with A standing for absorption (how the drug gets into the blood), Distribution (how the drug gets to the organ of interest – in this module, that is the brain), Metabolism (how the drug is broken down so it no longer exerts its psychoactive effects), and Excretion (how the drug leaves the body). We will talk about a couple of these to show their importance for considering psychoactive drugs.

Drug Administration

There are many ways to take drugs, and these routes of drug administration can have a significant impact on how quickly that drug reaches brain. The most common route of administration is oral administration, which is relatively slow and – perhaps surprisingly – often the most variable and complex route of administration. Drugs enter the stomach and then get absorbed by the blood supply and capillaries that line the small intestine. The rate of absorption can be affected by a variety of factors including the quantity and the type of food in the stomach (e.g., fats vs. proteins). This is why the medicine label for some drugs (like antibiotics) may specifically state foods that you should or should NOT consume within an hour of taking the drug because they can affect the rate of absorption. Two of the most rapid routes of administration include inhalation (i.e., smoking or gaseous anesthesia) and intravenous (IV) in which the drug is injected directly into the vein and hence the blood supply. Both of these routes of administration can get the drug to brain in less than 10 seconds. IV administration also has the distinction of being the most dangerous because if there is an adverse drug reaction, there is very little time to administer any antidote, as in the case of an IV heroin overdose.Why might how quickly a drug gets to the brain be important? If a drug activates the reward circuits in the brain AND it reaches the brain very quickly, the drug has a high risk for abuse and addiction. Psychostimulants like amphetamine or cocaine are examples of drugs that have high risk for abuse because they are agonists at DA neurons involved in reward AND because these drugs exist in forms that can be either smoked or injected intravenously. Some argue that cigarette smoking is one of the hardest addictions to quit, and although part of the reason for this may be that smoking gets the nicotine into the brain very quickly (and indirectly acts on DA neurons), it is a more complicated story. For drugs that reach the brain very quickly, not only is the drug very addictive, but so are the cues associated with the drug (see Rohsenow, Niaura, Childress, Abrams, & Monti, 1990). For a crack user, this could be the pipe that they use to smoke the drug. For a cigarette smoker, however, it could be something as normal as finishing dinner or waking up in the morning (if that is when the smoker usually has a cigarette). For both the crack user and the cigarette smoker, the cues associated with the drug may actually cause craving that is alleviated by (you guessed it) – lighting a cigarette or using crack (i.e., relapse). This is one of the reasons individuals that enroll in drug treatment programs, especially out-of-town programs, are at significant risk of relapse if they later find themselves in proximity to old haunts, friends, etc. But this is much *more* difficult for a cigarette smoker. How can someone avoid eating? Or avoid waking up in the morning, etc. These examples help you begin to understand how important the route of administration can be for psychoactive drugs.

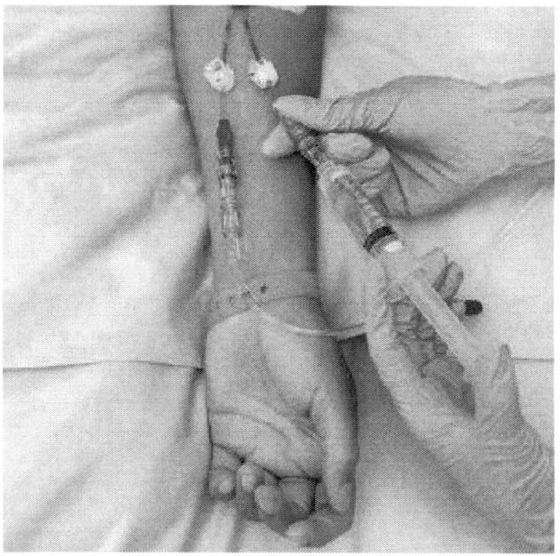

A drug delivered by IV reaches the brain more quickly than if the drug is taken orally. While rapid delivery has advantages, there are also risks involved with IV administration. [Image: Calleamanecer, https://goo.gl/OX6Yj5, CC BY-SA 3.0, https://goo.gl/eLCn2O]

Drug Metabolism

Metabolism involves the breakdown of psychoactive drugs, and this occurs primarily in the liver. The liver produces enzymes (proteins that speed up a chemical reaction), and these enzymes help catalyze a chemical reaction that breaks down psychoactive drugs. Enzymes exist in "families," and many psychoactive drugs are broken down by the same family of enzymes, the cytochrome P450 superfamily. There is not a unique enzyme for each drug; rather, certain enzymes can break down a wide variety of drugs. Tolerance to the effects of many drugs can occur with repeated exposure; that is, the drug produces less of an effect over time, so more of the drug is needed to get the same effect. This is particularly true for sedative drugs like alcohol or opiate-based painkillers. *Metabolic tolerance* is one kind of tolerance and it takes place in the liver. Some drugs (like alcohol) cause enzyme induction – an increase in the enzymes produced by the liver. For example, chronic drinking results in alcohol being broken down more quickly, so the alcoholic needs to drink more to get the same effect – of course, until so much alcohol is consumed that it damages the liver (alcohol can cause fatty liver or cirrhosis).

Recent Issues Related to Psychotropic Drugs and Metabolism

Grapefruit Juice and Metabolism

Grapefruit can interfere with enzymes in the liver that help the body to process certain drugs. [Image: CC0 Public Domain, https://goo.gl/m25gce]

Certain types of food in the stomach can alter the rate of drug absorption, and other foods can also alter the rate of drug metabolism. The most well known is grapefruit juice. Grapefruit juice suppresses cytochrome P450 enzymes in the liver, and these liver enzymes normally break down a large variety of drugs (including some of the psychotropic drugs). If the enzymes are suppressed, drug levels can build up to potentially toxic levels. In this case, the effects can persist for extended periods of time after the consumption of grapefruit juice. As of 2013, there are at least 85 drugs shown to adversely interact with grapefruit juice (Bailey, Dresser, & Arnold, 2013). Some psychotropic drugs that are likely to interact with grapefruit juice include carbamazepine (Tegretol), prescribed for bipolar disorder; diazepam (Valium), used to treat anxiety, alcohol withdrawal, and muscle spasms; and fluvoxamine (Luvox), used to treat obsessive compulsive disorder and depression. A link at the end of this module gives the latest list of drugs reported to have this unusual interaction.

Individualized Therapy, Metabolic Differences, and Potential Prescribing Approaches for the Future

Mental illnesses contribute to more disability in western countries than all other illnesses including cancer and heart disease. Depression alone is predicted to be the second largest contributor to disease burden by 2020 (World Health Organization, 2004). The numbers of people affected by mental health issues are pretty astonishing, with estimates that 25% of adults experience a mental health issue in any given year, and this affects not only the individual but their friends and family. One in 17 adults experiences a serious mental illness (Kessler, Chiu, Demler, & Walters, 2005). Newer antidepressants are probably the most frequently prescribed drugs for treating mental health issues, although there is no "magic bullet" for treating depression or other conditions. Pharmacotherapy with psychological therapy may be the most beneficial treatment approach for many psychiatric conditions, but there are still many unanswered questions. For example, why does one antidepressant help one individual yet have no effect for another? Antidepressants can take 4 to 6 weeks to start improving depressive symptoms, and we don't really understand why. Many people do not respond to the first antidepressant prescribed and may have to try different drugs before finding something that works for them. Other people just do not improve with antidepressants (Ioannidis, 2008). As we better understand why individuals differ, the easier and more rapidly we will be able to help people in distress.

One area that has received interest recently has to do with an individualized treatment approach. We now know that there are genetic differences in some of the cytochrome P450 enzymes and their ability to break down drugs. The general population falls into the following 4 categories: 1) *ultra-extensive metabolizers* break down certain drugs (like some of the current antidepressants) very, very quickly, 2) *extensive metabolizers* are also able to break down drugs fairly quickly, 3) *intermediate metabolizers* break down drugs more slowly than either of the two above groups, and finally 4) *poor metabolizers* break down drugs much more slowly than all of the other groups. Now consider someone receiving a prescription for an antidepressant – what would the consequences be if they were either an ultra-extensive metabolizer or a poor metabolizer? The ultra-extensive metabolizer would be given antidepressants and told it will probably take 4 to 6 weeks to begin working (this is true), but they metabolize the medication so quickly that it will never be effective for them. In contrast, the poor metabolizer given the same daily dose of the same antidepressant may build up such high levels in their blood (because they are not breaking the drug down), that they will have a wide range of side effects and feel really badly – also not a positive outcome. What if – instead – prior to prescribing an antidepressant, the doctor could take a blood sample and determine which type of metabolizer a patient actually was? They could then make a much more informed decision about the best dose to prescribe. There are new genetic tests now available to better individualize treatment in just this way. A blood sample can determine (at least for some drugs) which category an individual fits into, but we need data to determine if this actually is effective for treating depression or other mental illnesses (Zhou, 2009). Currently, this genetic test is expensive and not many health insurance plans cover this screen, but this may be an important component in the future of psychopharmacology.

Other Controversial Issues

Juveniles and Psychopharmacology

A recent Centers for Disease Control (CDC) report has suggested that as many as 1 in 5 children between the ages of 5 and 17 may have some type of mental disorder (e.g., ADHD, autism, anxiety, depression) (CDC, 2013). The incidence of bipolar disorder in children and adolescents has also increased 40 times in the past decade (Moreno, Laje, Blanco, Jiang, Schmidt, & Olfson, 2007), and it is now estimated that 1 in 88 children have been diagnosed with an autism spectrum disorder (CDC, 2011). Why has there been such an increase in these numbers? There is no single answer to this important question. Some believe that greater public awareness has contributed to increased teacher and parent referrals. Others argue that the increase stems from changes in criterion currently used for diagnosing. Still others suggest environmental factors, either prenatally or postnatally, have contributed to this upsurge.

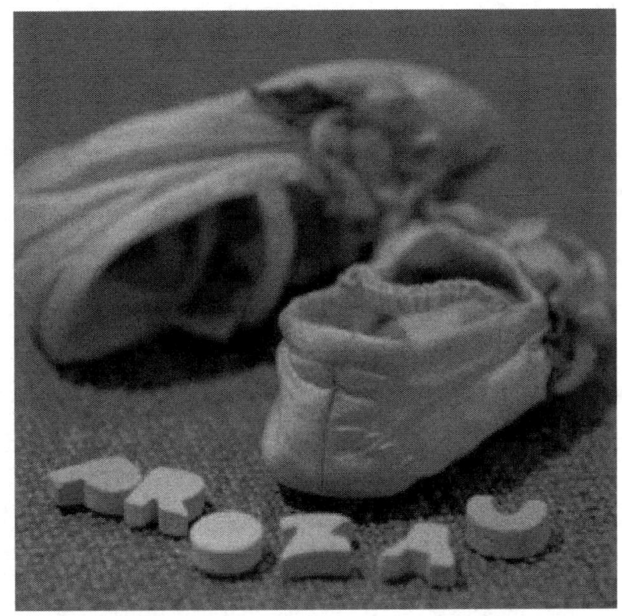

There are concerns about both the safety and efficacy of drugs like Prozac for children and teens. [Image: zaza_bj, CC BY-NC-SA 2.0, https://goo.gl/TocOZF]

We do not have an answer, but the question does bring up an additional controversy related to how we should treat this population of children and adolescents. Many psychotropic drugs used for treating psychiatric disorders have been tested in adults, but few have been tested for safety or efficacy with children or adolescents. The most well-established psychotropics prescribed for children and adolescents are the psychostimulant drugs used for treating attention deficit hyperactivity disorder (ADHD), and there are clinical data on how effective these drugs are. However, we know far less about the safety and efficacy in young populations of the drugs typically prescribed for treating anxiety, depression, or other psychiatric disorders. The young brain continues to mature until probably well after age 20, so some scientists are concerned that drugs that alter neuronal activity in the developing brain could have significant consequences. There is an obvious need for clinical trials in children and adolescents to test the safety and effectiveness of many of these drugs, which also brings up a variety of ethical questions about who decides what children and adolescents will participate in these clinical trials, who can give consent, who receives reimbursements, etc.

The Elderly and Psychopharmacology

Another population that has not typically been included in clinical trials to determine the safety or effectiveness of psychotropic drugs is the elderly. Currently, there is very little high-quality evidence to guide prescribing for older people – clinical trials often exclude people with multiple comorbidities (other diseases, conditions, etc.), which are typical for elderly populations (see Hilmer and Gnjidict, 2008; Pollock, Forsyth, & Bies, 2008). This is a serious issue because the elderly consume a disproportionate number of the prescription meds prescribed. The term polypharmacy refers to the use of multiple drugs, which is very common in elderly populations in the United States. As our population ages, some estimate that the proportion of people 65 or older will reach 20% of the U.S. population by 2030, with this group consuming 40% of the prescribed medications. As shown in Table 3 (from Schwartz and Abernethy, 2008), it is quite clear why the typical clinical trial that looks at the safety and effectiveness of psychotropic drugs can be problematic if we try to interpret these results for an elderly population.

Metabolism of drugs is often slowed considerably for elderly populations, so less drug can produce the same effect (or all too often, too much drug can result in a variety of side effects). One of the greatest risk factors for elderly populations is falling (and breaking bones), which can happen if the elderly person gets dizzy from too much of a drug. There is also evidence that psychotropic medications can reduce bone density (thus worsening the consequences if someone falls) (Brown & Mezuk, 2012). Although we are gaining an awareness about some of the issues facing pharmacotherapy in older populations, this is a very complex area with many medical and ethical questions.

Clinical Trial Subjects	Aged Patients Who Receive Drug Therapies
One drug	Drug of interest and medications
Single does	Chronic administration
No disease	Multiple diseases
No alcohol, tobacco, OTC* drugs, nutraceuticals	OTC* drugs, nutraceuticals, alcohol, tobacco, and other
20-40 years (vs 60-75 years)	65-100+ years
Caucaisians	Caucasians and minorities
Selection bias	All comers/socioeconomic basis

*OTC = Over the counter

Table 3. Characteristics if clinical trial subjects vs. actual patients. (Reprinted by permission from Schwartz & Abernethy, 2008.)

This module provided an introduction of some of the important areas in the field of psychopharmacology. It should be apparent that this module just touched on a number of topics included in this field. It should also be apparent that understanding more about psychopharmacology is important to anyone interested in understanding behavior and that our understanding of issues in this field has important implications for society.

Outside Resources

Video: Neurotransmission

- https://youtu.be/FR4S1BqdFG4

Web: Description of how some drugs work and the brain areas involved – 1

http://www.drugabuse.gov/news-events/nida-notes/2007/10/impacts-drugs-neurotransmission

Web: Description of how some drugs work and the brain areas involved – 2

http://learn.genetics.utah.edu/content/addiction/mouse/

Web: Information about how neurons communicate and the reward pathways

http://learn.genetics.utah.edu/content/addiction/rewardbehavior/

Web: National Institute of Alcohol Abuse and Alcoholism

http://www.niaaa.nih.gov/

Web: National Institute of Drug Abuse

http://www.drugabuse.gov/

Web: National Institute of Mental Health

http://www.nimh.nih.gov/index.shtml

Web: Neurotransmission

https://science.education.nih.gov/supplements/nih2/Addiction/activities/lesson2_neurotransmission.html

Web: Report of the Working Group on Psychotropic Medications for Children and Adolescents: Psychopharmacological, Psychosocial, and Combined Interventions for Childhood Disorders: Evidence Base, Contextual Factors, and Future Directions (2008):

http://www.apa.org/pi/families/resources/child-medications.pdf

Web: Ways drugs can alter neurotransmission

http://thebrain.mcgill.ca/flash/d/d_03/d_03_m/d_03_m_par/d_03_m_par.html

Discussion Questions

1. What are some of the issues surrounding prescribing medications for children and adolescents? How might this be improved?

2. What are some of the factors that can affect relapse to an addictive drug?

3. How might prescribing medications for depression be improved in the future to increase the likelihood that a drug would work and minimize side effects?

Vocabulary

Agonists

A drug that increases or enhances a neurotransmitter's effect.

Antagonist

A drug that blocks a neurotransmitter's effect.

Enzyme

A protein produced by a living organism that allows or helps a chemical reaction to occur.

Enzyme induction

Process through which a drug can enhance the production of an enzyme.

Metabolism

Breakdown of substances.

Neurotransmitter

A chemical substance produced by a neuron that is used for communication between neurons.

Pharmacokinetics

The action of a drug through the body, including absorption, distribution, metabolism, and excretion.

Polypharmacy

The use of many medications.

Psychoactive drugs

A drug that changes mood or the way someone feels.

Psychotropic drug

A drug that changes mood or emotion, usually used when talking about drugs prescribed for various mental conditions (depression, anxiety, schizophrenia, etc.).

Synapse

The tiny space separating neurons.

References

- Bailey D. G., Dresser G., & Arnold J. M. (2013). Grapefruit-medication interactions: forbidden fruit or avoidable consequences? *Canadian Medical Association Journal, 185,* 309–316.

- Brown, M. J., & Mezuk, B. (2012). Brains, bones, and aging: psychotropic medications and bone health among older adults. *Current Osteoporosis Reports, 10,* 303–311.

- Centers for Disease Control and Prevention (2011) Prevalence of autism spectrum disorders – autism and developmental disabilities monitoring network, 14 sites, United States, 2008. *Morbidity and Mortality Weekly Report 61*(SS03) 1–19.

- Centers for Disease Control and Prevention. (2013) Mental health surveillance among children – United States, 2005—2011. *Morbidity and Mortality Weekly Report 62* Suppl, 1-35.

- Hilmer, N., & Gnjidict, D. (2008). The effects of polypharmacy in older adults. *Clinical Pharmacology & Therapeutics, 85,* 86–88.

- Ioannidis, J. P. A. (2008). Effectiveness of antidepressants: an evidence myth constructed from a thousand randomized trials? *Philosophy, Ethics and Humanities in Medicine, 3,*14.

- Kessler, R. C., Chiu, W. T., Demler, O., & Walters, E. E. (2005). Prevalence, severity, and comorbidity of twelve-month DSM-IV disorders in the National Comorbidity Survey Replication (NCS-R). *Archives of General Psychiatry, 62,* 617–627.

- Moreno, C., Laje, G., Blanco, C., Jiang, H., Schmidt, A. B., & Olfson, M., (2007). National trends in the outpatient diagnosis and treatment of bipolar disorder in youth. *Archives of General Psychiatry, 64*(9), 1032–1039.

- Pollock, B. G., Forsyth, C. E., & Bies, R. R. (2008). The critical role of clinical pharmacology in geriatric psychopharmacology. *Clinical Pharmacology & Therapeutics, 85,* 89–93.

- Rohsenow, D. J., Niaura, R. S., Childress, A. R., Abrams, D. B., &, Monti, P. M. (1990). Cue reactivity in addictive behaviors: Theoretical and treatment implications. *International Journal of Addiction, 25,* 957–993.

- Schwartz, J. B., & Abernethy, D. R. (2008). Aging and medications: Past, present, future. *Clinical Pharmacology & Therapeutics, 85,* 3–10.

- World Health Organization. (2004). *Promoting mental health: concepts, emerging evidence, practice* (Summary Report). Geneva, Switzerland: Author. Retrieved from http://www.who.int/mental_health/evidence/en/promoting_mhh.pdf

- Zhou, S. F. (2009). Polymorphism of human cytochrome P450 2D6 and its clinical significance: Part II. *Clinical Pharmacokinetics, 48,* 761–804.

CC licensed content, Shared previously

5. Self Analysis (or pseudo self-analysis)

Instructions for your Clinical Case Study assignment

The purpose of this assignment is for you to demonstrate your understanding of the concepts and issues presented in this course. Your case study should be based upon yourself, and may be factual, fictional, or some mix of the two. You are NOT required to disclose any personal or sensitive information.

A large collection of fictional case studies are available for your review as you prepare to write your personal clinical case study.

A case analysis consists of several components:

- background information

    ◦ demographics

    ◦ psycho-social factors

    ◦ medical factors

    ◦ education

    ◦ family

    ◦ etc

- assessment

    ◦ methods

    ◦ instruments

- diagnosis

    ◦ using the multi-axial DSM-IV classification system

- etiology

    ◦ predisposing factors

    ◦ precipitating factors

- dynamics

    ◦ diagnosis

    ◦ presenting symptoms

    ◦ course

- treatment recommendations

    ◦ goals

    ◦ methods

- prognosis

(Here is a link to a sample case history: https://www.fmhs.auckland.ac.nz/assets/fmhs/som/psychmed/docs/writing_a_psychiatry_case_study.pdf)

Your assignment:

Part 1: Write your self analysis

- minimum length: 2000 original words
- submit to the SafeAssign drop box on or before the final day of the Module 4 discussion forums
- This assignment is graded via the rubric below.

Part 2: Discuss the analyses

- Submit to the Self-analysis discussion forum on or before the start of Module 5
- Facilitate the discussion of your self-analysis
- Be an active participant in the discussion of at least 2 other students' self-analyses
- Self-analysis dIscussions continue until the Module 5 discussion forums end.
- This forum is graded via the same discussion forum rubric used for the issue/topic discussions.

((Note: This assignment required a drop box and a "symposium" discussion forum.)

CC licensed content, Original

- (Pseudo) Self-Assessment Assignment. **Authored by**: William Pelz. **Provided by**: Herkimer College / SUNY. **Located at**: https://herkimer.open.suny.edu/webapps/blackboard/execute/content/blankPage?cmd=view&content_id=_24313_1&course_id=_794_1. **Project**: Abmormal Psychology course for Achieving the Dream. **License**: *CC BY: Attribution*

Case Studies of Fictional Characters

Major Depressive Disorder

Name: Eeyore

Source: *Winnie the Pooh* (TV Show, 1966)

Background Information

Eeyore is an older gray donkey. There are no documents indicating the exact age or specified background information, and he chooses not to share this information. Eeyore does not have an occupation. His health compared to other donkeys is slightly underweight, but slender. He chooses not to share his family background. One main difficulty Eeyore has elaborated on is his detachable tail, which seems to cause him several problems. He has indicated that his goals are to remain strong for his friends despite his lack of confidence within himself, and as a result he often feels lonely without support from others that he is close to. Some forms of coping mechanisms include trying to feel useful in the presence of others and also trying his best to find pleasure in life.

Description of the Problem

Eeyore constantly insists that his tail falls off rather frequently. Eeyore's posture typically involves a slumped head, droopy eyes, and commonly says "thanks for noticing me." Sluggish movement is also apparent, without any physical cause for movement delay. He seems to step on his tail often and fall down. Eeyore indicates that sometimes it seems that even his close friends do not need him. Around friends, he typically makes comments about his relative unimportance and travels near the back of the pack. He also stated that although he tries to force a smile, a real smile has not existed in a long time, even though others try to cheer him up. He often feels empty even when accompanied by friends. Eeyore also seems to experience a loss of energy throughout the day, although sleeping habits are not explicitly expressed.

Diagnosis

296.2x Major Depressive Disorder, Single Episode

Eeyore exhibits five symptoms of a major depressive episode, and has also experienced these for several years, therefore meeting full criteria. Criteria met include depressed mood most of the day, markedly diminished interest or pleasure in activities, fatigue or loss of energy nearly every day, feelings of worthlessness, and diminished ability to think or concentrate were indicated. Overall, Eeyore exhibits severe clinical major depression without psychotic features. Further diagnosis will be needed to determine catatonic, melancholic, or atypical features as details are limited at this point. Postpartum onset is not a factor.

Accuracy of Portrayal

Eeyore is a character that displays a relatively accurate example of major depressive disorder. One major issue with the character portrayed is his consistent involvement with a support group. A lack of interest in activities is common with this disorder, causing most persons with depression to not frequently spend time with others. This is in contrast to Eeyore, who seems to be surrounded by friends much of the time. Also, his support groups seems rather sarcastic at times, as well as exhibiting their own issues so it may be hard to diagnose if environmental factors may prolong the depression longer than it may otherwise last. Some would argue that this may be closer to a diagnosis of Dysthymia, but since Eeyore seems to exhibit more severe symptoms closer to major depression and each season of the show lasts less than two years, it is hard to fully identify a long term timespan of his disorder.

Treatment

Although various treatments exists, I would recommend cognitive behavioral therapy, and possibly electroconvulsive therapy if CBT does not work alone. Since donkeys have not been tested with medication normally given to persons suffering from depression, I would not advise any type of tricyclics, MAO inhibitors, or SSRIs be used. Regarding cognitive behavioral therapy, it is important that Eeyore first understands the relationship between events, emotions, and cognitions. As mentioned, he must first realize that if his tail falls off that he is not less of an individual. Furthermore, he must also realize that the need to be of worth can be self-induced and that he does not need to rely on others to find this feeling. Treatment would then be followed by instructing Eeyore on identifying, evaluating, and modifying automatic negative though patterns that exist. He acknowledges his feelings of worthlessness, but also having the tools to evaluate his negative thoughts as something he can control should enable him to eventually take control over his thoughts. Stress management, social skills, and activities training will then follow to give Eeyore a path to improve his well-being by being able to optimally connect with others and join in on activities that spark his interests.

Name: Anthony Soprano, Jr.

Source: The Sopranos (television series, 1999-2005)

Background Information

Anthony Soprano, Jr., referred to as A.J., is a male born on July 15, 1986 to Anthony and Carmela Soprano. The family is of Italian decent and they live in New Jersey. From a very young age, A. J. had disciplinary problems in school and a possible learning disability. After extensive testing and meeting with school counselors, he was deemed to be suffering from Attention-Deficit Hyperactivity Disorder.

It was very obvious throughout the various seasons that A. J. had a strong family history of multiple psychiatric disorders. His father was diagnosed with depression from the beginning of the series. He was on medication and would see a therapist regularly. In addition, his father had antisocial personality disorder and panic disorder without agoraphobia. His father was involved in organized crime, which caused strains on his parents' relationship. Due to these marital issues between his parents, A. J. would often act out during their period of separation and possible divorce. As A. J. got older, his father insisted on him becoming more responsible and not a failure in life. As a way to make A. J. more productive, his father got him a job at a construction site. A. J. started the job and was doing well. He met a Puerto Rican girl named Blanca at the construction site and they started dating.

The two became really close, and A. J. eventually proposed to Blanca. After some reconsideration, she decided that A. J. was not right for her and broke up with him. This is when he became depressed. A. J. continued to work at the construction site for some time, but the site of Blanca talking to other men became too much for him, so he eventually quit. Just as things seemed like they would never improve, A. J. met some childhood friends whose fathers were also in the Mafia with his father.

He started hanging out with them and seemed to be improving. He also began seeing a therapist and was prescribed Prozac. He improved to the point that he even began to take some college courses. However, these new friends turned out to be a bad influence. They were running some illegal gambling on campus and would use violence to collect money. A. J. did not seem to be affected by this, but when they badly beat up an African American student, this sent A. J. spiraling down once again.

Description of the Problem

After the breakup with Blanca, A. J. started sleeping all the time and would not come out of his room. He had a decreased appetite and anhedonia. He seemed to lack energy for quite some time. There were no suicidal ideations initially. After the African-American student incident, he again confined himself to his room and developed similar symptoms to what he was displaying after his break up with Blanca. It progressed to the point that he attempted to kill himself by tying a plastic bag around his face, wrapping a cinder block around his leg, and jumping in the pool while his parents were out of the house. Luckily, his father came home and saved him prior to there being any significant damage. A. J. was admitted to an inpatient psychiatric facility and received the therapy he needed.

Diagnosis

The diagnosis for A. J. Soprano is Major Depressive Disorder (recurrent), 296.3x. According to the DSM-IV-TR, the following are eight of nine criteria that are met for the diagnosis:

1. Depressed mood most of the day, nearly every day, as indicated by either subjective report (e.g., feels sad or empty) or observation made by others (e.g., appears tearful). NOTE: In children and adolescents, can be irritable mood.

    ◦ A. J. exhibits a depressed mood consistently for at least two weeks in both of his major depression episodes.

2. Markedly diminished interest or pleasure in all, or almost all, activities most of the day, nearly every day (as indicated by either subjective account or observation made by others)

   - A. J.'s mother noticed that he quit attending his job at the pizza parlor, even though he used to enjoy working there.

3. Significant weight loss when not dieting or weight gain (e.g., a change of more than 5% of body weight in a month), or decrease or increase in appetite nearly every day. NOTE: In children, consider failure to make expected weight gains.

   - A. J.'s mother would constantly cook different things that A. J. used to enjoy before his decrease in appetite, but none of the things she cooked seemed appealing to him.

4. Insomnia or hypersomnia nearly every day

   - A. J. could be seen sleeping throughout most of the day due to his depression.

5. Psychomotor agitation or retardation nearly every day (observable by others, not merely subjective feelings of restlessness or being slowed down)

   - This is the only criterion that does not pertain to A. J.

6. Fatigue or loss of energy nearly every day

   - A. J. appeared to be tired at all times of the day.

7. Feelings of worthlessness or excessive or inappropriate guilt (which may be delusional) nearly every day (not merely self-reproach or guilt about being sick)

   - After Blanca broke up with him, A. J. appeared to have feelings of worthlessness.

8. Diminished ability to think or concentrate, or indecisiveness, nearly every day (either by subjective account or as observed by others)

   - A. J. stopped attending his college classes due to his inability to concentrate.

9. Recurrent thoughts of death (not just fear of dying), recurrent suicidal ideation without a specific plan, or a suicide attempt or a specific plan for committing suicide.

   - A. J. actually attempts suicide, but failed to drown himself.

- Specify:

   - Longitudinal Course Specifiers (With and Without Interepisode Recovery)

A. J. displays interepisode recovery between his two major depressive episodes, making his a case of major depressive disorder, recurrent.

Accuracy of Portrayal

The average person watching A. J. on the Sopranos would receive an accurate portrayal of Major Depressive Disorder (recurrent). He displays a majority of the symptoms for the disorder in both episodes he has had. These breaks of normalcy between the two episodes are crucial in understanding major depression episodes, especially when the depression is recurrent. Major Depressive Disorder is highly heritable, so watching A. J.'s father, who also displays signs of depression, helps to understand some of the genetic influence on depression.

Treatment

Proper treatment of A. J.'s Major Depressive Disorder would, given his severe symptom levels, include beginning with antidepressant medication. Psychotherapy might also be added in A. J. case in order to increase effectiveness of treatment. It does not seem that electroconvulsive therapy would be necessary in A. J.'s case since he does not exhibit psychotic symptoms or catatonia.

CC licensed content, Shared previously

Alzheimer's Dementia

Name: Alice Howland

Source: *Still Alice* by Lisa Genova (book, 2007)

Background Information

Alice Howland is a Caucasian female who is 50 years old. She currently works as a cognitive psychology professor at Harvard University. Overall, Howland presents as a healthy 50-year-old woman. Howland is a petite woman, but not underweight. Howland remains active in her work and social life and other than leading a hectic life appears happy. Howland lives with her husband (John) and the two have three grown children, all of which live out of the home. Howland maintains many close friendships and is in a stable, long-term relationship. Howland does not have any reported drug or alcohol related history. Howland states that she may have a glass or two of wine with dinner, but the only medication she takes is a multivitamin. Howland has not had any head injuries or serious health issues. Howland's mother and sister died in a car accident when she was 18 and her father died the previous year from Cirrhosis of the liver. Howland allowed that her father was an alcoholic and that they did not have much contact over the last several years before his death.

Description of the Problem

Howland frequently exhibits disorientation and gets lost when she is only a few blocks from her home. She recognizes the building and knows that she is supposed to know how to get home, but her mind is blank. Howland frequently misplaces items and is unable to find them. At times, she replaces items and later finds the lost item. She frequently loses her train of thought, or is unable to remember significant details of her life. As a professor, she often visited other universities as a guest speaker or would present at conferences, lately, she would lose track near the middle to end of her lecture and have to refer to her notes. This was not common for Howland as she used her speeches repeatedly only making small changes that were easy to remember. Howland reports forgetting words during a lecture, she states that it is not even on the tip of her tongue; the word is just completely gone from her memory. Howland recently missed a conference in Chicago, simply because she forgot about it. Howland also states that she has to write down a detailed schedule of what time and where her classes are or she will simply forget to go teach them.

Diagnosis

Dementia of the Alzheimer's Type (294.1x)

Diagnostic criteria:

1. The development of multiple cognitive deficits manifested by both

   - (1) memory impairment (impaired ability to learn new information or to recall previously learned information)

   - (2) one (or more) of the following cognitive disturbances:

     a. aphasia (language disturbance)

     b. apraxia (impaired ability to carry out motor activities despite intact motor function)

     c. agnosia (failure to recognize or identify objects despite intact sensory function)

     d. disturbance in executive functioning (i.e. planning, organizing, sequencing, abstracting)

2. The cognitive deficits in Criteria A1 and A2 each cause significant impairment in social or occupational functioning and represent a significant decline from a previous level of functioning.

3. The course is characterized by gradual onset and continuing cognitive decline.

4. The cognitive deficits in Criteria A1 and A2 are not due to any of the following:

   - (1) other central nervous system conditions that cause progressive deficits in memory and cognition (e.g. cerebrovascular disease, Parkinson's disease, Huntington's disease, subdural hematoma, normal-pressure hydrocephalus, brain tumor)

   - (2) systemic conditions that are known to cause dementia (e.g. hypothyroidism, vitamin B12 or folic acid deficiency, niacin deficeincy, hypercalcemia, ceurosyphilis, HIV infection)

   - (3) substance-induced conditions

5. The deficits do not occur exclusively during the course of a delirium.

6. The disturbance is not better accounted for by another Axis I disorder (e.g. Major Depressive Disorder, Schizophrenia).

Howland displays impairment in recalling previous learned material and has disturbances in executive functioning. Howland is not suffering from any central nervous system conditions, systemic conditions, or substance-induced conditions. She is having difficulties at work due to her memory loss unlike her previous performance in her job. Her memory loss and confusion began gradually and steadily worsened.

- Code based on presence or absence of a clinically significant behavioral disturbance:

- ◦ 294.10 Without Behavioral Disturbance: if the cognitive disturbance is not accompanied by any clinically significant behavioral disturbance.

- ◦ 294.11 With Behavioral Disturbance: if the cognitive disturbance is accompanied by a clinically significant behavioral disturbance (e.g., wandering, agitation).

Howland does not present with any behavioral disturbances at this time.

- Specify subtype:

  - ◦ With Early Onset: if onset is at age 65 years or below

  - ◦ With Late Onset: if onset is after age 65 years

- Coding note: Also code 331.0 Alzheimer's disease on Axis III. Indicate other prominent clinical features related to the Alzheimer's disease on Axis I (e.g., 293.83 Mood Disorder Due to Alzheimer's Disease, With Depressive Features, and 310.1 Personality Change Due to Alzheimer's Disease, Aggressive Type).

Howland's diagnosis falls under the Early Onset subtype as she is only 50 years old.

Epidemiology

The prevalence rates of Dementia of Alzheimer's Type increases dramatically with increasing age, rising from .6% in males and .8% in females at age 65 to 11% in males and 14% in females by age 85. As age increases so do the prevalence rates; at age 90 the rates rise to 21% in males and 25% in females, and by age 95 the prevalence rates are as high as 36% in males and 41% in females. Unfortunately, 40%-60% are moderate to severe cases.

Howland was unaware of her extended families medical history because her mother passed at a young age and her father, to her knowledge, did not display any symptoms before his death.

Accuracy of Portrayal

Overall, the book accurately displays the course of Early Onset Alzheimer's. The high and lows of mood as the disease progresses are genuine and show the true emotions that not only a person suffering from the disease deals with, but what family members and friends deal with. The book also shows how the disease progresses, somewhat slowly at first and then a continual decline in functioning, not only mentally but also physically. The rate at which each person declines is different, but overall the beginning is gradual and then the decline seems to speed up. It does seem as if the book may have sped up the disease a bit much. The confusion and slight memory loss that progresses into complete memory loss and description of living with strangers does seem to ring true. A person with this disease must frequently feel as if she is with strangers, even when she is with her own family. The book did not go into the very late stages of the disease, at which time those with Alzheimer's physical decline is serious and require feeding tubes and most usually hospitalization or nursing home care, as they are no longer able to walk, feed themselves, or even speak.

Treatment

At this time, there are no medications available to cure Alzheimer's, only medications that seem to slow the progression. For Alice Howland the best course of treatment would include cholinesterase inhibitors during the beginning stages and an N-methyl D-aspartate (NMDA) antagonist once symptoms become more severe in nature. These medications only slow the progression of the disease, although these medications have been effective in slowing the progression of Alzheimer's in many patients. When the disease presents itself as a safety issue for Howland (forgetting that she is cooking, wandering off and getting lost or unable to take care of her personal daily needs) she needs either nursing home care or 24-hour home care. When Howland reaches the stage where she is no longer able to feed herself or walk, nursing home care is the best recourse for proper care. A healthy diet recommendation through all stages of the disease by limiting unhealthy food intake and eating healthy may help slow the progression of Alzheimer's. However, this is in combination with proper medication. As long as she is able, exercise, reading, crossword puzzles, and other mentally and physically stimulating activities may help slow the progression of the disease, however, there is not adequate research into this area.

Name: Fiona Anderson

Source: *Away From Her* (movie, 2006)

Background Information

Fiona Anderson is a Caucasian female in her late 60's/early 70's. She is fit for her age, not overweight or underweight. Fiona's family originates from Iceland, but she was raised in Canada. She is married to Grant Anderson (for 44 years) and they have no children. Fiona is currently unemployed; after Grant retired from his job as a professor, the couple moved to Brandt County, Ontario. The couple currently lives in the farmhouse that belonged to Fiona's grandparents and have lived there for 20 years. Fiona lives an active lifestyle by going on cross country skiing trips around their property with her husband. The couple will occasionally see their other married friends, but most live far away. There is no known drug or alcohol problem. Fiona has the occasional drink at home with her husband, but in no way ever appears to have had too much. There is a subject matter that has remained unresolved between Fiona and her husband; while Grant was still teaching there was speculation and rumors that he had an affair with one of his students. Fiona, instead of enraged by Grant's adultery was thankful that he did not leave her. In order to make a better life for themselves and they moved away from all the distractions. Fiona seems to have dealt with Grant's unfaithfulness and her deteriorating memory with a great deal of acceptance and dignity.

Description of the Problem

Fiona exhibits the early signs of memory loss. When she is helping put away the dishes, she forgets, pauses, puts the frying pan in the freezer, and walks away. Her memory loss then progresses to where she has to put labels on all the cabinets and drawers of what belongs where. Fiona admits that at times she forgets what words mean, like the word yellow. Fiona forgets how to say "wine" while offering her guest another glass. During her evaluation she is asked a series of questions involving mail, she answers the majority of the questions correct but then forgets where a person would take the mail to send it. Fiona becomes even more disoriented as time goes by and loses her way home and wanders off. Her husband is constantly finding things that she has left undone or forgot about, such as when she put a pot of water on to boil, then left the house. The most recent development of Fiona's memory degrading happened after she was admitted to Meadowlake, a care taking facility. After being separated from her husband for only 30 days she seemed to have lost all knowledge of their married life. She exhibited recognition of his face but not what they meant to each other or the life they shared. Fiona begins to form an attachment with a man who is in Meadowlake with her; when asked about him she states, "I like Aubrey because he doesn't confuse me."

Diagnosis

Dementia of the Alzheimer's Type (294.1x)

Diagnostic criteria:

1. The development of multiple cognitive deficits manifested by both

   - (1) memory impairment (impaired ability to learn new information or to recall previously learned information)
   - (2) one (or more) of the following cognitive disturbances:

     a. aphasia (language disturbance)

     b. apraxia (impaired ability to carry out motor activities despite intact motor function)

     c. agnosia (failure to recognize or identify objects despite intact sensory function)

     d. disturbance in executive functioning (i.e. planning, organizing, sequencing, abstracting)

2. The cognitive deficits in Criteria A1 and A2 each cause significant impairment in social or occupational functioning and represent a significant decline from a previous level of functioning.

3. The course is characterized by gradual onset and continuing cognitive decline.

4. The cognitive deficits in Criteria A1 and A2 are not due to any of the following:

   - (1) other central nervous system conditions that cause progressive deficits in memory and cognition (e.g. cerebrovascular disease, Parkinson's disease, Huntington's disease, subdural hematoma, normal-pressure hydrocephalus, brain tumor)
   - (2) systemic conditions that are known to cause dementia (e.g. hypothyroidism, vitamin B12 or folic acid deficiency, niacin deficiency, hypercalcemia, ceurosyphilis, HIV infection)
   - (3) substance-induced conditions

5. The deficits do not occur exclusively during the course of a delirium.

6. The disturbance is not better accounted for by another Axis I disorder (e.g. Major Depressive Disorder, Schizophrenia).

Fiona meets criteria for A1 and A2; the cognitive disturbances that she exhibits are aphasia, agnosia, and possible impaired ability to carry out particular motor abilities. The impairments from criteria A1 and A2 have affected her relationship with her spouse, friends, and how she interacts with others, as well as her daily activities. Fiona does not have any recorded nervous system, substance-induced, or systemic conditions that could impair her memory. Fiona's memory loss has had a continuous decline and started gradually. She is not recorded to have any other Axis I disorders.

Code based on presence or absence of a clinically significant behavioral disturbance:

- 294.10 Without Behavioral Disturbance: if the cognitive disturbance is not accompanied by any clinically significant behavioral disturbance.

- 294.11 With Behavioral Disturbance:if the cognitive disturbance is accompanied by a clinically significant behavioral disturbance (e.g., wandering, agitation).

Fiona has presented some behavioral disturbances, such as wandering the street and woods.

Accuracy of Portrayal

Overall, the movie provides an accurate portrayal of the disease and the effects it has on the person suffering from it. A person not knowing anything about Alzheimer's would learn from the movie that with time that short-term or working memory starts to diminish first. A person suffering from Alzheimer's will gradually lose more of their memory abilities, eventually impairing their long-term memory and recall. They will also learn that people with Alzheimer's can know someone one day but not know them the next. They may also repeat the same questions or statements, having no recollection of already saying them. In the movie they say Fiona is young for already having Alzheimer's, which is not entirely accurate, as she is beyond the age of 65. This puts her in the Late Onset category, which is more common than Early Onset.

Treatment

There is no current cure for Alzheimer's, but there are medications shown to help slow the progression of the disease. The Food and Drug Administration has approved two types of drugs that could help Fiona: cholinesterase inhibitors and mematine. A good diet and exercise will also help in creating a good environment for the medication to work and help Fiona stay mentally alert. It would also be beneficial to keep the mind working by taking part in any sort of puzzles that help exercise the brain. In the movie they admitted Fiona into a caretaking facility not too long after she was diagnosed with the disease. In my opinion, they could have waited longer to admit her. Her memory seemed to deteriorate faster after she was in the care of the home.

malpsych.wikispaces.com/. **License**: *CC BY-NC-SA: Attribution-NonCommercial-ShareAlike*

Mental Retardation

Name: Carla Tate

Source: *The Other Sister* (movie, 1999)

Background Information

Carla Tate is a Caucasian female around the age of 18-20 (her age was not specified.) She currently has no job, but is attending a vocational school called Bay Area Poly Technical school, and only took one class, Computer 101, which she passed. A lowered intellectual quotient (IQ) and slower processing overall characterize her mental health. No drug or alcohol usage has been reported or detected. Tate recently moved out of her parent's house and into her own apartment, although her parents pay for it. She seems to have a very healthy family structure overall. She comes from an upper socioeconomic status. She has two sisters, whom she frequently talks to, and a mother and father that are still married. Her father seems passive and very supportive to Tate. In contrast, Tate reports and it has been witnessed that Tate's mother is very controlling and overly protective. Tate complains that her mother inhibits her freedom and does not allow her to try new activities. Although this causes self-reported strain in their relationship, Tate still says she is close to her mother. Tate is very social and seems to have a positive base line of friends. Her goal is to become a veterinary assistant in the future and continue to gain freedom from her controlling mother. Her daily activities include going to her classes and spending time with her significant other and family.

Description of the Problem

Tate currently has a lowered IQ (probably around 70, although further testing would be necessary) and impaired cognitive processes. Her mother and father report that these symptoms were also present in early childhood. She also displays impaired social behaviors by violating social norms and over sharing. Tate's physical condition is very healthy. She is in her weight class for her height. She has not reported physical problems and none have been observed. Her mood is very positive and open. However, she sometimes displays rapid mood swings and quickly gets upset at what most view trivial things.

Diagnosis

Carla Tate appears to meet the criteria for mild mental retardation (317.0).

A. Significantly sub-average intellectual functioning: An IQ of approximately 70 or below on an individ-

ually administered IQ test. For infants, a clinical judgment for significantly sub-average intellectual functioning.

Although not specifically told, Tate has been diagnosed with a lowered IQ because she went to a certified school for individuals with lowered IQ.

2. Concurrent deficits or impairments in present adaptive functioning (i.e., the person's effectiveness in meeting the standards expected for his or her age by his or her cultural group) in at least two of the following areas:

1. Communication
2. Self-care
3. Home living
4. Social/interpersonal skills
5. Use of community resources
6. Self-discretion
7. Functional academic skills
8. Work
9. Leisure
10. Health
11. Safety

Tate displays a deficiency in communication when she is upset especially. Her words become slurred and rapid. She also qualifies for social and interpersonal skills impairment. Although she is an outgoing individual, she sometimes misinterprets situations. She also acts out and causes scenes in socially inappropriate places. Overall, she takes direction well, but she often misunderstands what the instructions are if they are not given to her very simplistically. Her functional academic skills are also impaired. Although Tate does attend Bay Area Poly Technical School, she struggles to keep up with the other students, and can only master basic concepts. Although no tests have been conducted, her IQ is estimated to be around 70. Tate also currently does not maintain employment at any job. Although Tate is relatively safe, there have been past reported incidences by her mother and Tate herself, of inflicting harm on other children by accident and setting accidental fires, which falls under safety. Tate does meet the criteria for mild retardation, which she has been diagnosed with and treated for in a special school, but she is relatively normally functioning in day-to-day life.

B. Onset before the age of 18

Tate's parents were alerted of her learning difficulties and social impairments around the age of 8 or 9 (no specific age was given.) She was sent to a special school soon after
because her parents felt they could not help her adequately.

C. Stable IQs from early in life to adulthood

As reported by her mother, Tate has maintained a longitudinal average of a lowered IQ from her early childhood to present.

Accuracy of Portrayal

The average person watching this movie would automatically be able to diagnose Tate as someone who is mentally retarded. However, many individuals do not understand that different levels of mental retardation exist based on IQ scores. Although mild retardation is the most common level of retardation, accounting for 65-75% of all diagnoses of mental retardation, most of the population lump all forms of mental retardation together. Another fallacy which might be correct with an everyday person watching this movie is understanding that although mentally retarded individuals are limited in some of their functions, they can become with supportive help, a very productive member of society. One possible misconception the movie might give viewers is the idea that mentally retarded individuals normally come from a higher SES and often have people to take care of their needs. However, statistically most people with a mental handicap, especially people with mild retardation, come from a low SES neighborhood. They often become homeless or wards of the state because of lack of specialized training and education.

Treatment

There is no cure for mental retardation. The goal of treatment is to maximize her potential in every area of life despite her mental condition. Special teachers and programs intervention at the youngest age possible is recommended, which she received. Tate should be trained not only in life skills and academic areas at her level, but also in social skills and self-control. Family therapy should also be conducted to help the family better understand her condition and to help her family better know what are the most effective ways of dealing with her. They should also be informed of her abilities and limitations. Tate is a highly functioning female with mental retardation, and therefore, needs less care from her family. However, because her mother is slightly controlling, it limits Tate's autonomy, which is very essential for all humans, especially for someone with mental retardation. This situation should be addressed and healthy boundaries should be agreed upon among Tate, her mother and the therapist. Autonomy will allow Tate to develop to her full potential and has shown great success in the past with other similar patients.

Name: Charles Gordon
Source: *Flowers for Algernon* (movie, 2000)

Background Information

The main character of this movie is Charlie Gordon, a mentally challenged 32-year-old man, with an IQ of 68, who works at a bakery as a delivery boy and moonlights as a janitor. He also attends the adult school for the mentally retarded at night after work. Charlie is a simple man with simple goals. One of his goals in life is for people to like him. When Charlie was little, his mother and father abandoned him shortly after they discovered that he is mentally challenged. Charlie was put in a foster home when he was merely a child. When he is old enough to make a living, he moves out and lives by himself in a deteriorated apartment in the middle of a suburban area, a place that he could afford. Isolated and alone since childhood, Charlie yearns for close relationships; as a result, it is no surprise that he wants to be liked and wanted. For example, occasionally at the work place, he would act like a clown (e.g., pretend to slip and fall, put flour on his nose, make funny faces, etc.) in hope to make his coworkers laugh because he thinks that they like him and are his "friends" but, alas, little does he knows that they are not laughing with him but at him.

One day at the adult school, his special education teacher, Ms. Kinnian –who is very impressed with his free-spirit, friendliness, and curiosity to learn –tells him about the brain-operation experiment, an experiment that promises to make people like him smart. Charlie immediately signs up for the experiment because he feels that if he is smart then maybe people would like him more. After the controversial experimental brain surgery, Charlie's IQ increases at an exponential rate, tripling his original IQ at 185. With Ms. Kinnian's guidance, Charlie also learned to read advanced level books, such as *Robinson Crusoe*, mathematical quadrants, etc., and write in comprehensive sentences, as demonstrated in his "progris riports."

Shortly after the brain-operation, Charlie explores his inner feelings and emotions, such as betrayal, jealousy, love, and pain that he never thought he had. He begins to understand the world around him. For example, after the brain surgery, he begins to understand that his coworkers aren't really his real friends after all because real "friends" would not invite you to bars and poke fun at you in front of everyone for good laughs. In addition, before the brain-surgery, he never knew he could fall in love and reciprocate his feelings. But as time goes by, his feelings for Ms. Kinnian develop. Alas, the ephemeral love between Ms. Kinnian and Charlie does not last. The movie ends with Charlie telling Ms. Kinnian goodbye the day he learns that the experiment would not work and that he would have to go back to being the mentally challenged man that he once was. Before the reversal of his intelligence, while he is still able to think and make decision, Charlie moves far away to another place to live, a place where Ms. Kinnian cannot find him.

As a man who is mentally challenged, Charlie has many difficulties and challenges in life. As you can see, his life difficulties involve deficits in intellectual abilities and functioning, such as the ability to read, write, and speak in coherence sentences. He may have learning disabilities, such as Written Expression (as demonstrated in his "progris riports"), Reading Disorder, and more. He also has difficulties in establishing interpersonal and social relationships because he does not have the ability to read facial cues and expressions. Little is known about his family mental health history. Charlie does not seem to have drug or alcohol problems. He also does not seem to have physical impairments, but mostly psychological and cognitive impairments.

Description of the Problem

Life is already hard, and life is even harder if you have Mental Retardation. As demonstrated in the movie *Flowers for Algernon*, Charlie shows significant limitations in intellectual functioning, such as not being able to read, write, and communicate coherently. He demonstrates maladaptive symptoms, such as emotional deficits and inter-personal problems. He does not seem to have sensory symptoms. His sensory modalities work fine. He can work and make a low profile and honest living as a delivery person and janitor at the bakery. He is not physically handicapped or in any way.

From the movie, Charlie is a mentally challenged man with an IQ of 68 and the symptoms that he shows qualify him for Mild Mental Retardation (MMR), which will be discussed in the diagnosis section. He is portrayed as a care-free and happy person, whose personality is almost childlike. He is not passive, placid, dependent, nor aggressive. He does not have severe nor profound mental retardation and he does not depend on anyone to dress for him or take care of him. But he does show signs of lack of communication skills, developmental delays, social and emotional deficits, impaired ability to solve or understand social problems and issues, and impaired ability in recognizing emotion in others. His academic performance is also affected by his mental delays; as a result, he goes to the adult school for the mental retarded instead of going to college. He can adapt easily at his working place, such as working as a delivery boy, janitor, and running errands, except that he does not have the capability to use a dough mixing machine, which requires the ability to follow instructions. The symptoms that Charlie has qualify him for MMR. He does not have self-injurious behaviors or stereotypical movements.

Overall, Charlie can function adequately at a slow pace environment, an environment that does not require higher order thinking and decision making abilities.

Diagnosis

Charlie Gordon meets the criteria for mild mental retardation (317.0) using the criteria from the DSM-IV-TR:

A) Significantly sub-average intellectual functioning: an IQ of approximately 70 or below on an individually administered IQ test.

Gordon has an IQ level of 68 since childhood. This qualifies him as having significantly sub-average intellectual ability.

B) Concurrent deficits or impairments in present adaptive functioning (i.e., the person's effectiveness in meeting the standards expected for his or her age by his or her culture group) in at least two of the following areas: (1) communication, (2) self-care, (3) home living, (4) social/interpersonal skills, (5) use of community resources, (6) self-direction, (7) functional academic skills, (8) work, (9) leisure, (10) health, and (11) safety.

Gordon meets more than two symptoms of the above areas. He has problems in (1) communication, (4) social/interpersonal skills, (6) self-direction, (7) functional academic skills, and (9) leisure. He does not have deficits in (3) home living, (5) use of community resources, (8) work, (10) health, and (11) safety.

C) The onset is prior to 18 years of age.

Gordon has shown signs of mental retardation since childhood. The onset must be before the age of 18; hence, he also meets this criterion.

Accuracy of Portrayal

The movie does a good job in describing someone with mental retardation, especially a man with mild mental retardation. This movie was adapted from the original novel, *Flowers for Algernon*, written by Daniel Keyes. Keyes knew what he was doing when he was writing this novel. He had worked at many mental retardation facilities and had worked as a special education teacher before he wrote this novel. With the skills and trainings that he developed, he was able to describe in details the behaviors that he had observed from his students with mental disabilities, such as how they talk, write, associate with others, and so on. A person watching this movie would not be misled but be persuaded by the information that this movie provides and how it accurately portrays someone with this mental disorder. A person watching this movie would also get to learn more about MMR and the symptoms that a person with this disorder has.

Treatment

Currently, there is no cure for mental retardation. Mental disorder are an enduring and pervasive disease (which is why it is listed on Axis II), but several empirical supported studies show that therapy, special education and training, and social skill training can help ease the symptoms of mental retardation. Mental Retardation is not an easy disorder to treat since it is related to genetic factors, such as irregular genes or genes that did not fuse together properly (i.e., Down syndrome), and environment factors (e.g., infections, chromosomal abnormalities, metabolic, and nutritional, especially for persons with low socioeconomic status [SES]). It is also important for a trained specialist to evaluate the person for co-morbidity with other disorders, such as Attention-Deficit/Hyperactivity Disorder, Mood Disorders, Pervasive Developmental Disorders, Stereotypical Movement Disorder, Down syndrome, Fragile X, and more since these disorders may also affect the diagnosis and outcomes. The prognosis depends on the severity of the disorder, such as mild, moderate, severe, and profound. The less severe the levels and the early the treatment, the better the outcomes. Many people may lead productive lives and function on their own; whereas, others need a structured environment to be most successful.

CC licensed content, Shared previously

Tourette's Disorder

Name: Lionel Essrog

Source: *Motherless Brooklyn* by Jonathan Lethem (book, 1999)

Background Information

Lionel Essrog is a Caucasian male and presumably in his mid to late thirties. Lionel Essrog is an orphan and the whereabouts of his biological parents is unknown. Essrog spent his childhood and adolescence in the St. Vincent's Home for Boys in Brooklyn, New York, which is a publicly funded boarding house for orphaned young males. The residents of St. Vincent's are required to attend public school and Essrog acquired his high school diploma but has not received any further education. Essrog currently works for a man named Frank Minna with three other of his housemates from St. Vincent's. The four of them call themselves "Minna Men" and they specialize in unconventional and frequently illegal types of jobs as provided by Frank Minna. Any familial mental health history is unknown. Essrog has no history of drug or alcohol abuse. He does not seem to have any long term goals, other than to continue working for Frank Minna. Beginning in early childhood, Essrog began experiencing compulsions which involved twitching and jerking his neck. These compulsions soon turned into various forms of motor *tics*, including incessant tapping of the metal-pipe legs of schoolroom desks and chairs as if in search of certain ringing tones, reaching for doorframes, and kneeling to grab at untied shoe laces of other classmates. One of his compulsions actually involved grabbing and kissing his fellow classmates and housemates at St. Vincent's. Because of his behavior, Essrog did not have very much social interaction with peers his age and spent a lot of time alone. Around the time he was thirteen years old, the kissing compulsion ended but was replaced with others. He was prone to tapping, whistling, tongue-clicking, winking, rapid head turns, wall stroking, and other various tics. During this time, Essrog began experiencing rapid thoughts that were becoming more and more of a compulsion to speak out loud. Many of these thoughts were echoic variations to things he heard. For example, when Essrog heard "Alfred Hitchcock" he would silently rephrase it as "Altered Houseclock". Essrog found it more and more difficult to withhold these compulsions and began exhibiting simple vocal tics by barking like a dog and chirping like a bird. While he still has the compulsion to do simple vocal tics, he also exhibits complex vocal tics as well.

Description of the Problem

Essrog currently displays simple and complex motor tics as well as simple and complex vocal tics. Examples of simple motor tics are eye blinking, nose wrinkling, neck jerking, shoulder shrugging, facial grimacing, and abdominal tensing. Complex motor tics include hand gestures, jumping, touching, pressing, stomping, facial contortions, repeatedly smelling an object, squatting, deep knee bends, retracing steps, twirling when walking, and assuming and holding unusual postures (including dystonic tics, such as holding the neck in a particular tensed position). Simple vocal tics include meaningless sounds such as throat clearing, sniffing, grunting, snorting, and chirping. Complex vocal tics more clearly involve speech and language and include the sudden, spontaneous expression of single words or phrases; speech blocking; sudden and meaningless changes in pitch, emphasis, or volume of speech; palilalia (repeating one's own sounds or words); and echolalia (repeating the last-heard sound, word, or phrase). Essrog also shows coproplalia, which is the sudden, inappropriate expression of a socially unacceptable word or phrase. Essrog describes his vocal tics as follows; "My words begin plucking at threads nervously, seeking purchase, a weak point, a vulnerable ear. It's an itch at first. Inconsequential. But that itch is soon a torrent behind a straining dam. Once I'm able to scratch that itch, it let's off the pressure in my head and I am able to concentrate". Essrog's tics cause him anxiety in social situations but the men with whom he works have learned to accept his behavior. Essrog also claims that his tics are more difficult to suppress when he is anxious or nervous.

Diagnosis

The diagnosis that seems to fit appropriately for Essrog is Tourette's Disorder (307.23)

Diagnostic Criteria for Tourette's Disorder (DSM-IV-TR)

1. Both multiple motor tics and one or more vocal tics must be present at the same time, although not necessarily concurrently

    - Essrog exhibits multiple motor and vocal tics.

2. The tics must occur many times a day nearly every day(usually in bouts) nearly everyday or intermittently over more than one year, and during this period there must not have been a tic-free period of more than three consecutive months.

    - Essrog's experiences tics everyday and has not shown any evidence of a tic-free period.

3. The onset is before age 18 years.

    - Essrog's symptoms began in early childhood. Motor tics normally develop at about $6-7$ years of age and vocal tics normally occur at after the onset of motor tics. Essrog's onset fits this criteria.

4. The disturbance must not be due to the direct physiological effects of a substance (e.g., stimulants) or general medical condition (e.g., Huntington's disease or positive encephalitis).

- ○ Essrog shows no signs of substance abuse or any symptoms of medical conditions.

Accuracy of Portrayal

Jonathan Lethem's characterization of Lionel Essrog was very accurate in the portrayal of a person diagnosed with Tourette's Disorder. The age of onset was the same as listed in the DSM-IV-TR and the description of the compulsions and tics the character exuded were also accurately portrayed when compared to the diagnostic criteria of Tourette's Disorder.

Treatment

Treatment for Essrog should include a specific kind of psychotherapy. The primary supported therapy for Tourette's Disorder is habit reversal training (HRT), commonly known now as Cognitive-Behavior Intervention for Tics (CBITS). In HRT, a person first learns to know when and where he/she is going to have a tic, followed by development of competing responses that prevent you from physically being able to perform the tic. These responses are held until the urge to tic dissipates. Over time, particularly with motor tics, the client learns that they do not need to tic to feel the release and relaxation. In many cases, Tourette's Disorder can be effectively managed. If the Tourette's Disorder is severe enough, antipsychotic medications can be helpful. These include but are not limited to Chlorpromazine, Haloperidol, and Pimozide. The severity of the tics may be exacerbated by administration of central nervous system stimulants, such as those used in the treatment for Attention-Deficit/Hyperactivity Disorder. Alternative treatments for treating Tourette's Disorder have proven to be helpful for some patients. These treatments are herbal medicines, nutritional, vitamin, and mineral supplements and behavioral therapies. It should be known that these treatments should be used as complementary and never as a substitute.

CC licensed content, Shared previously

- Abnormal Psychology: An e-text!. **Authored by**: Dr. Caleb Lack. **Located at**: http://abnormalpsych.wikispaces.com/. **License**: *CC BY-NC-SA: Attribution-NonCommercial-ShareAlike*

Specific Phobia

Name: Ronald "Ron" Billius Weasley

Source: The *Harry Potter* series by J.K. Rowling (books, 1997-2007)

Background Information:

Ron Weasley is first presented to the public audience as a young, goofy 11-year-old wizard boy. Throughout the series he transitions into a mature young adult. He attends Hogwarts School of Witchcraft and Wizardry. Overall he is an average student never going above in expectations and never going under. He is the youngest boy in the Weasley family out of Bill, Charlie, Percy, Fred, and George. He also has a younger sister Ginny, who he is very protective of. His mother, Molly, is an incredibly loving woman, taking care of her children and running a very crazy household. Her husband's name is Arthur Weasley and he works a modest job at the Ministry of Magic. The Weasley family is very rare in the wizardry world because they come from what is known as pureblood. This means that the Weasley family only have witch and wizard blood in their biological line. It is rare and often used by other Wizardry family has a way to declare dominance among their kind. The Weasleys, however, do not mistreat others and do not consider themselves to be above the rest of the wizardry population. Their good nature is one of the few things they are rich with, as there are very poor with only a modest income. They have been known to pass on handed down clothing among the children and make them handmade gifts because they cannot afford much else. They struggle finically with getting their children everything they need for school and they live in a small house that is referred to as the Burrow. Ron has a particularly difficult time dealing with the teasing that is brought on to his family because of their financial standing. He often has to defend his family to other people, especially towards Draco Malfoy, who is not afraid to bring up the handed down clothing whenever he wants to insult Ron.

Ron has two best friends at his school. They are the beautiful and very smart Hermione Granger and the ever popular boy-who-lived, Harry Potter. They have all been close since their first year in Hogwarts, when they all started battling against the evil wizard Voldemort. The relationship among these best friends, however, has often been rocky. Hermione and Ron fight constantly and as the books progress you can start to see a romantic relationship form. It is not until the final book that the audience completely knows the true feelings between these two characters. Ron and Harry instantly became best friends, but it was often hard for Ron to stand in the background of Harry's ever growing shadow. This caused a lot of tension between the two, but in the end the relationship stayed strong. The biggest problem Ron faced in his life was the financial well-being of his family. He was very lucky to have both of his parents still alive and not have to face the torment that was given to Hermione from being muggle-born. Once he completes his seven years of training at Hogwarts, Ron wants to become an Auror, who are known for catching evil wizards. He is very good at chess and likes to use strategies to help him in difficult situations. During his years in school Ron saw himself as the Head Boy and the Gryffindor Quidditch captain. Ron has difficultly dealing with certain situations and often lets his anger get the best of him. He tends to explode and lash out against others when things become too difficult to bear. The biggest weakness he faces is jealousy of those around him. He is not completely satisfied with what he has been given and normally wants what others have. This makes his relationships sometimes difficult, but over time Ron began to get over his jealousy issues.

Description of the Problem

In the second book of the Harry Potter series, *The Chamber of Secrets*, the audience becomes aware of the fact Ron is incredibly afraid of spiders. The being around them scares him immensely and the mere idea of spiders turns him into the world's biggest baby. When he is around them he begins to shake and he starts screaming at a high pitch. If he is able to form words at all, they are difficult to understand. His fear stops him in his tracks. Physiologically, his eyes get big, he has difficulty breathing, and his face sometimes turns white. His anxiety is so high in fact that he thinks the end of the world is happening and he must escape from the situation.

Diagnosis

It is very clear to see that Ron is suffering from a Specific Phobia, in particular Arachnophobia. This falls under the DSM-IV five general types of specific phobias in the animal type category.
As mentioned earlier, Ron does not even need to be in the around spiders to be afraid of them. Only mentioning them is enough to scare him and make him want the conversation shifted to a different topic.

B. Exposure to the phobic stimulus almost invariably provokes an immediate anxiety response, which may take the form of a situationally bound or situationally predisposed panic attack. Children can show affects and characteristics when it comes to specific phobias. Children can show anxiety by crying, throwing tantrums, experiencing freezing or clinging to the parent that they have the most connection to.
His level of anxiety definitely rises, as evidenced by how his voice changes, he begins sweating profusely, he starts shaking, and he does everything he can to avoid the situation.

C. The person recognizes that the fear is excessive or unreasonable.
In Ron's case his fear of spiders started long before his traumatic experience with them in *The Chamber of the Secrets*. This even may have enhanced his fear, but he knows that is fear is often the point of joke and he understands that he sometimes takes it to an extreme level of anxiety. However, the amount of teasing he gets from others does not stop his fear from being expressed.

D.The phobic situation(s) is(are) avoided, or else endured with intense anxiety or distress.
It is clear that Ron will do anything to avoid being around spiders, including using his wizardry skills on them.

E. The avoidance, anxious anticipation, or distress in the feared situation(s) interferes significantly with the person's normal routine, occupational (or academic) functioning, social activities or relationships, or there

is marked distress about having the phobia.

This does not seem like the case for Ron. He is able to conquer his fear after he builds up some esteem to do so. It is rare for him to walk away from a situation just because spiders are present, but it does require him to build up a lot of motivation in order to follow through. His normal routine is often just delayed when a spider is present or mentioned.

F. In individuals under age 18 years, the duration is at least 6 months.

Throughout the majority of the series, Ron is under the age of 18. He has had this fear of spiders in the second book when he and Harry had to go into the Forbidden Forest in order to find out if Hagrid was really opening the Chamber of Secrets. In the third book, *The Prisoner of Azkaban*, Ron and his fellow students at Hogwarts were learning how to battle of Boggarts, which turn into their biggest fear. For Ron's case it would turn into a spider since that is his biggest fear. In the seventh book, *The Deathly Hallows*, Ron is trying to destroy an evil force and it uses his fear against him by making spiders appear. In the other books, Ron's fear does not have a huge part, but it is mentioned in small sections of the book with comments explaining that his fear has been around for quite a long time. It is quite clear that every time spiders are mention that Ron's fear comes up as well. This definitely exceeds six months.

G. The phobic avoidance associated with the specific object or situation are not better accounted for by another mental disorder, such as obsessive-compulsive disorder (e.g., fear of dirt on someone with an obsession about contamination), post-traumatic stress disorder (e.g., avoidance of stimuli associated with a severe stressor), separation anxiety disorder (e.g., avoidance of school), social phobia (e.g., avoidance of social situations because of fear of embarrassment), panic disorder with agoraphobia, or panic disorder without agoraphobia.

Ron has no other signs of a mental disorder with his fear of spiders. It seems like the phobia is the only thing that is causing problems to come about in his life. He is actually quite open about his fear of spiders and it is often mentioned in the books to release tension during difficult and dramatic times.

It is very obvious that Ron is afraid of spiders. The difference between him and other individuals is that he faces his phobias despite how bad is anxiety responds. He fits the criteria and allows for a very clear and diagnosable explanation about his disorder. It is not unrealistic to place him in this category of anxiety disorders.

Accuracy of Portrayal

The portrayal of Ron does a very good job of explaining what it would feel like to live with specific phobia and for the audience presents many realistic ideas about Arachnophobia. The books give good examples about what is going on with Ron's anxiety about the spiders and why he reacts to them in the way he does. The main problem with the portrayal is that it is often used for humor in the majority of the books. There are points when the phobia is quite obvious and understood in its full meaning, but the majority of the time is spent on Ron's phobia being mentioned as a joke. For the readers, it is used as a nice little sigh of relief during the dramatic parts of this intense book series. It is important to remember that the *Harry Potter* series is mostly used for entertainment purposes and that sometimes it can over dramatic about humorous moments and complex storylines that allow for a more enjoyable read. This causes some of Ron's phobia tactics to be displayed humorously and causes it to be funny and less like a mental disorder.

Treatment

The most recommended treatment for Ron would be Behavioral Therapy. In this process exposure techniques would be used to allow Ron's anxiety levels to lower during different stages of exposure. The exposure to the spiders over a long period of time would eventually causes his anxiety levels to lower greatly. This would also cause less intensity with his fear. Ron's sessions would start with a small amount of exposure to spiders by first talking about them, showing him pictures, and being in the same room as one. The steps would increase only after Ron became comfortable with the spiders and his anxiety levels would level out. The steps would increase with exposure until Ron was able to hold a spider and not attack it or be afraid. It would also be beneficial for Ron to go through some cognitive therapy as well. This would help him identify with the truth about spiders and help him to stop thinking that they are terrible creatures. This would be important because Ron is in the magical world and his interactions are different from those in the muggle world. Ron would be able to show great improvements with his mental disorder, but he is however a stubborn red head. This might be the only thing to stop him from being successful with his treatment.

Video: Ron Weasley – A Case Study in Specific Phobia

- https://youtu.be/TMAq-p0bkL4

CC licensed content, Shared previously

- Abnormal Psychology: An e-text!. **Authored by**: Dr. Caleb Lack. **Located at**: http://abnormalpsych.wikispaces.com/. **License**: *CC BY-NC-SA: Attribution-NonCommercial-ShareAlike*

Conduct Disorder

Name: Nelson Muntz

Source: *The Simpsons* (Television series, 1989 – present)

Background Information

Nelson Muntz is a 10 year old Caucasian boy who is a student at Springfield Elementary School. Nelson is unemployed and although he is a full-time student, he is on the verge of dropping out. His health appears to be in good condition, but there was a time when he was exposed to second hand smoking. Other than that, the patient does not seem to have any physical illness. However, some problems that are observed are how he behaves towards his peers and others. Nelson is feared by many of his classmates and peers. He is known to pick fights with the "nerds" and other kids that get in his way. Nelson is known by the community as the "bad kid on the block" and "the school bully." Parents of other students, as well as school faculty, see him as a delinquent. Nelson's family consists of his father, Mr. Muntz, mother, Mrs. Muntz, grandfather, Judge Muntz, and a sister who is unnamed. Little is known about the relationship between his parents as well as his relationship with them. Currently he lives with his mom, who works at Hooters as a waitress. His father is mostly absent in his life and as the story goes, Mr. Muntz abandoned his son and wife when Nelson was really young. However, there were few times in Nelsons' life where his father does appear, such as after a football game where Nelson was the star player. Mr. Muntz came to congratulate him and invited him to have dinner at Hooters, but Nelson refused because he did not want to see his mother working there. Mrs. Muntz is known in the community as a jailbird, a prostitute, and a stripper. Mrs. Marge Simpson adopts Nelson informally. Nelson has difficulties in school when it comes to keeping up with his grades. Although he is known as a bully, there are occasions where his good nature comes out and befriends Bart Simpson and even dated Lisa Simpson. Nelson can be very disruptive and noncompliant to rules at school. He hangs out with older kids from high school, who also show no interest in education. Nelson has very little in the way of a support group, and keeping a friendship is difficult for him. Nelson can be very demanding and if he does not get what he seeks, then there will be consequences to those who get in his way. He enjoys seeing the misery of others and in many situations will laugh at their face. Nelson does not have very strong coping skills, if not any. He expresses his emotions physically by beating up someone and or by committing pranks and small crimes. There is no known history of drug or alcohol use.

Description of the Problem

Nelson Muntz displays a multitude of symptoms that are associated with Conduct Disorder. He displays anger and frustration through the act of bullying his peers. He shows no respect to authority figures and is disobedient towards them. He places no importance on school and constantly picks on the nerds and geeks that attend his school. He performs delinquent acts such as stealing, looting, vandalizing, and cheating. Nelson has made threats to other students and physically harmed them. For example, when one of his buddies stole Lisa Simpson's cupcakes, her brother went to defend her by telling Nelson's buddy to back off and soon they engage in a physical fight. Nelson, seeing Bart Simpson fighting his buddy, joins in the fight to defend his friend. Bart accidently makes Nelson's nose bleed causing Nelson to become angrier. The fight was interrupted by the school bell indicating recess was over and it was time to go back to class. Nelson, full of anger, threatens Bart and tells him to meet after school. For the next few days, after school, Nelson physically beats Bart, shoves him into a trash can and rolls him down a hill. At one point or another, Nelson has terrorized virtually everyone in Springfield. He takes great pride in seeing those he believes to be inferior to him suffer pain and is in misery; he delights in other people's pain and suffering. He shows guilt or shame about his misbehavior and often justifies his cruel actions. His close friends, who are just like him, only encourage his behavior and his parents show no concern or interest in their son's behavior.

Diagnosis

The diagnosis that is appropriate for Nelson Muntz is **Conduct Disorder (312.81).**

A. A repetitive and persistent pattern of behavior in which the basic rights of others or major age-appropriate societal norms or rules that are violated, as manifested by the presences of three (or more) of the following criteria in the past 12 months, with at least one criterion present in the past 6 months.

1. **Aggressive conduct that threatens physical harm.**

2. **Nonaggressive conduct that causes property damage.**

3. **Deceitfulness or theft.**

4. **Serious violations of rules.**

Nelson Muntz meets all three of the above criteria. His aggression has led to physical harm to others as well as to him. He has been involved in vandalism and property damage due to recklessness. He has bullied his way into getting things that are not his. He has broken many state and school laws as well as showing no obedience to authority figures.

B. To the diagnosed with Conduct Disorder an onset of at least one criterion characteristic must be displayed prior to age 10 years:

Aggression to People and Animals:

1. **Often bullies, threatens, or intimidates others.**

2. **Often initiates physical fights.**

3. **Has used a weapon that can cause serious physical harm to others.**

    a. **A bat, brick, broken bottle, knife, gun**

4. **Has been physically cruel to people.**

5. **Has been physically cruel to animals.**

6. **Has stolen while confronting a victim.**

   a. **Mugging, purse snatching, extortion, armed robbery**

7. **Has forced someone into sexual activity.**

Nelson Muntz has displayed more than one of these symptoms of Conduct Disorder prior to age 10 and currently still does. These symptoms are described above under the headline "Description of the Problem."

C. The disturbance in behavior causes clinically significant impairment in social, academic, or occupational functioning.

Nelson Muntz has no interest in school and often he is found to cheat on his assignments and exams.

D. If the individual is age 18 years or older, criteria are not met for Antisocial Personality Disorder.

Nelson Muntz is only 10 years old.

Accuracy of Portrayal

An average person watching The Simpsons would be able to come to conclusion that the character Nelson Muntz shows abnormal behaviors when compared to his peers. They will notice that his lack of a stable home does have a huge role in his delinquent behaviors. A person with an Abnormal Psychology background could easily identify Nelson's behaviors are symptoms of Conduct Disorder. The character Nelson Muntz is an accurate portrayal of how a child with Conduct Disorder behaves and acts towards others. However, in the realistic world, such symptoms are worse.

Treatment

Nelson Muntz should have a full medical examination before any treatments are given. First, Nelson's parents should be educated about the disorder as well as provided with well-established treatments. Nelson's behaviors should be modified in the class rooms as well as the play grounds. Treatments such as goal setting and developing ways to reach those goals should be taught to Nelson on a one-to-one basses. Nelson's parents need to be more involved in his life, and therefore family therapy is recommended. According to research, the optimum method seems to be an integrated approach that involves both the child and the family, within a variety of contexts throughout the child's developmental stages as well as his and his family's life. Also, when Nelson misbehaves, he should have some sort of consequences for his actions instead of encouraging his behavior, therefore, grounding or timeout should be enforced.

Delusional Disorder

Name: Marshal Edward "Teddy" Daniels (Andrew Laeddis)

Source: *Shutter Island* (movie, 2010)

Background Information

Marshal Teddy Daniels is a hard working investigator in his mid-thirties. He is a Caucasian male who seems to be highly intelligent and somewhat healthy. Teddy smokes several cigarettes a day and tends to abuse alcohol. He served in World War II and encountered many traumatic experiences at the Dachau Concentration Camp in Germany. Little is known about his family history or life situation when he was young. Teddy did, however, have a wife and three children and it is stated that his wife was emotionally unstable. Teddy is very goal orientated and spends many hours concentrating on work. His work ethic keeps him detached from family and friends. When he encounters conflict he becomes angry quickly, which interferes with his ability to control his temper. Teddy's current investigation involves the disappearance of Rachel Solando from Ashecliffe Mental Institution, located on Shutter Island.

Description of the Problem

Edward (Teddy) Daniels claims to be an investigator at Ashecliffe Mental Institution located on Shutter Island. As Teddy enters the facility with his partner, Chuck, the patients doing yard work creepily smile and wave as if they know him. Teddy asks for records of every patient on the island and is denied. He does not understand why the officials will not hand over the documents because he is well respected military personnel on a mission to discover facts about the disappearance of Rachel Solando. Teddy becomes frustrated with the institution's faculty and decides to end his mission.

A storm develops preventing Teddy to leave the island. During the storm he has delusions in which he believes patient number 67 is being kept a secret. The delusions convince him that the patient is Andrew Laeddis. He then ventures out to Ward C, which he has not been granted permission to investigate, in search of Laeddis. Upon entering Ward C, Teddy discovers George Noyce, a schizophrenic patient, who then informs Teddy about a conspiracy theory that the institution is performing lobotomies in the nearby lighthouse. Teddy begins having dreams of a little girl asking him to save her. His wife continues to appear in hallucinations, telling him that Laeddis is still in the institution and Teddy must find him and kill him.

After the storm, the institution provides Teddy with a set of dry clothes and a fresh pack of cigarettes. The clothes happen to be those that the patients wear. The lightning from the storm affects Teddy and he begins to experience migraines. The institution then provides him with headache medication. Shortly after waking up the next day he ventures out to the coast again in search for the lighthouse. Through the hallucination of meeting a former psychiatrist in a cave, he is convinced that the institution has drugged from through the pain medications and cigarettes, causing him to experience wild dreams, sleepless nights and migraines. He feels as though everyone in the institution is purposely attempting to keep him as a patient.

Teddy makes his way to the lighthouse, finding absolutely nothing unordinary. He finds his psychiatrist in a room at the top. He confronts the psychiatrist about the conspiracy theory and how he needs off of the island to report the institution to the government. The psychiatrist debriefs Teddy about his Delusional Disorder. The psychiatrist tells Teddy that he has been a patient for over two years. He explains to Teddy that he created fictional characters by using anagrams from his name, and the names of his loved ones. The psychiatrist informs Teddy that he murdered his wife after coming home to find his children floating in a pond. Teddy refuses to believe that he murdered his wife or that he had children. The psychiatrist persists in explaining that he had been trying a new type of therapy known as role-play therapy. The role-play therapy is used in hope for Teddy to realize on his own that he is Andrew Laeddis.

Teddy begins to have flash backs of the afternoon he came home and found his children dead. He realizes the little girl from his dreams is his daughter. He remembers that he killed his wife in the spring of 1952. He finally realizes that he is the lost patient, Andrew Laeddis. He realizes his partner, Chuck, is actually his specialty psychiatrist who had to be with him at all times because he is the most violent patient on Shutter Island. Teddy, now Andrew, is eligible to be released from Ashecliffe Mental Institution. He says to his specialty psychiatrist "What now? We need to find a way to get off of this island". Teddy fakes a relapse because he did not want to go out into society and possibly hurt anyone else. The officers at the institution escort Teddy to have a lobotomy to "cure" his disorder.

Diagnosis

The diagnosis for Edward Daniels is **Delusional Disorder, Mix Type (297.1)**

1. **Non-Bizarre Delusions for at least one month.**

    a. Teddy experiences non-bizarre delusions over the course of two years. The delusions are not due to Schizoaffective Disorder, nor Mood Disorder. He does not have an alcohol dependency nor is he chronically depressed.

2. **Criterion A for schizophrenia has never been met.**

    a. Teddy does not show flat inappropriate affect. He is very sociable and his delusions are not bizarre.

3. **Apart from the impact of the delusion(s) or its ramifications, functioning is not markedly impaired and behavior is not obviously odd or bizarre.**

a. Teddy is able to function normally. He is sociable and is able to properly communicate.

4. **D. If mood episodes have occurred concurrently with delusions, their total duration has been brief relative to the duration of the delusional periods.**

a. Teddy is generally in a good mood. He is not depressed or anxious. He is always looking forward to catching new hints about Rachel. He gets angry when people refuse to give him want he thinks he needs, such as case files for patients in the mental hospital.

5. **E. The disturbance is not due to the direct physiological effects of a substance (e.g., a drug of abuse, a medication) or a general medical condition.**

a. Teddy does smoke and drink however; he does not have negative episodes which develop from the substance abuse, but not alcohol dependence. He takes medications which help his migraines to go away.

6. **Specify Type**

a. **Mixed Type**

i. Delusions characteristic of more than one type.

1. **Grandiose Type**

a. Delusions which are inflated worth, power, knowledge, identity, or special relationship to a deity or famous person.

i. Teddy believes that he is a valued marshal with specialized privileges to the mental hospital. He feels that people should obey his requests.

1. **Persecutory Type**

a. Delusions that the person (or someone to whom the person is close) is being malevolently treated in some way.

i. Teddy feels that the employees of the mental institution are trying to commit him at a patient. He feels that they are controlling him by giving him special medications other than simple pain killers. Teddy is also convinced that the cigarettes the institution provides are laced with drugs to cause him to become powerless

Accuracy of Portrayal

The portrayal of Delusional Disorder was accurate throughout the film. It was not apparent until the end of the film that he was suffering from a disorder, and not an actual investigator. The delusions were believable to those who do not have a complete understanding of psychology and psychotic disorders.

Treatment

The treatment psychiatrist used in the film was ultimately performing the lobotomy. Lobotomies were accepted in the fifties as reasonable treatments for psychotic disorders. In current treatment procedures lobotomies are unethical. The lobotomy procedure is the use of an ice pick type probe which is inserted through the eye in order to dismantle the brain. This develops a calming effect on the patient.

Recent treatment used for Delusional Disorder would include both medications and psychotherapy. Medicinal treatments may involve anti-psychotics and antidepressants such as SSRI and Clomipramine. Psychotherapy treatments involve supportive therapy and cognitive therapy. The treatment used for patients must be individualized. The treatment for Andrew Laeddis should consist of cognitive therapy combined with medication.

Videos: Teddy Daniels – A Case Study in Delusional Disorder

- https://youtu.be/yZ3zpLnyz1Q
- https://youtu.be/ut2rB2PR1RA

CC licensed content, Shared previously

- Abnormal Psychology: An e-text!. **Authored by**: Dr. Caleb Lack. **Located at**: http://abnormalpsych.wikispaces.com/. **License**: *CC BY-NC-SA: Attribution-NonCommercial-ShareAlike*

Cyclothymic Disorder

Name: Dolores Price

Source: *She's Come Undone*, (book by Wally Lamb, 1992)

Background Information

The book follows Dolores through childhood, adolescence, and young adulthood. Dolores Price begins as a young girl growing up in New England. After her father leaves her and her mother, they move in with her uptight grandmother. Her mother experiences a nervous breakdown and is sent off to a mental hospital. Dolores claims it's her "nerves." Her grandmother represses everything and has difficulty speaking of her mother's mental issues. At the age of 13, Dolores is raped by her grandmother's upstairs tenant. Following the rape, Dolores' mother constantly gives her food. Throughout adolescence, Dolores continually gains weight until she weighs 257 pounds at age 18. She attempts to go to college, but ends up leaving and goes to Cape Cod to attempt suicide. After a failed attempt at drowning, she ends up in a private mental institution where she undergoes immense amounts of psychoanalytic therapy. Once released, she goes to Maine and gets a job as a grocery clerk. Now, as an adult, she marries an abusive and manipulative man. She does nothing to anger him until her grandmother's death. Because of his aversion to children, she has an abortion for him. Throughout her entire life, Dolores has issues with relationships. She had one close friend in childhood but never made many more in adolescence. Due to her weight and the rape, she kept to herself in high school. In college, she works tirelessly to please her roommate and the other girls she is around. She does the same with her husband, Dante. Her main goal is to please others around her to achieve approval. She is short and rebellious with her mother and her grandmother. She experiments with marijuana a few times but never uses any drug heavily. She drinks occasionally, but again never heavily. She has no real goals. She strives to be loved but gives up on it easily when it fails her. She strives to gain power over others at times but also gives up on that. Towards the end of the story, she simply wants a child, after obsessing over her abortion. It is incredibly hard for her to handle sexual relationships after the rape and only enjoys it sometimes with Dante. She cannot handle rejection or abandonment. The only coping skill she really has is eating, and it causes her just as much pain as the issue she aims to avoid.

Description of the Problem

Dolores' weight gain stemmed from her traumatic rape. This unnecessary weight causes her to feel extraordinarily inferior to others around her. She goes through periods of depression, believing she has harmed everyone around her. She then goes through periods of what she describes as "power." She spews vicious sarcasm at those around her and is, at times, cruel. After a lesbian encounter in college, she kills the woman's goldfish to prove she has control. She enjoys leaving her therapist upon her release from therapy. She waves the fact that a psychic has given her more help in front of his face in order to anger him. In Maine, she feels accomplished often. During these times, her job performance improves, her sexual life increases, and she cleans and cooks every day for her husband. Her depression and "power" continue after therapy. If Dante is unhappy, Dolores is unhappy. She feels useless, especially when she angers him. After her grandmother's death, Dolores leaves Dante and again becomes depressed. She says she wishes she could hold on to the power and go back in time to fix what she did to others. Dolores describes her life in sections. Her parents' divorce is one section, the rape is another section, her adolescence is one section, her college life is a section, her therapy is a section, and her adult life is a section. Throughout each section, she develops an obsession with whales. She describes a parallel between herself and whales. She craves their power and feels their hopelessness when they wash up on the beach.

Diagnosis

The diagnosis that seems most appropriate for Dolores Price is **Cyclothymic Disorder (301.13).**
Diagnostic criteria:
A. For at least 2 years, the presence of numerous periods with hypomanic symptoms and numerous periods with depressive symptoms that do not meet criteria for a Major Depressive Episode. Note; in children and adolescents, the duration must be at least 1 year.

Dolores' times of "power" contain within them hypomanic symptoms such as excessive involvement in pleasurable, yet possibly dangerous, activities. This is manifested through her increased sex drive and sexual activity with Dante the first night they met, her increased interest in sex throughout certain times in her life, and her lesbian experience with her dorm's maid. She has elevated mood and feels control over others around her. She is grandiose and believes that she will succeed in imagining her life with Dante, who is clearly abusive and unfaithful. She also exhibits grandiosity in her correspondence with her college roommate prior to moving in. She makes up stories and a completely different life in order to create a good image. She becomes highly distracted during her stay in the halfway house with an etch-a-sketch. She spends hours recreating artistic masterpieces on multiple etch-a-sketches and tunes out the rest of the world. Dolores also exhibits depressive symptoms at many times. She exhibits weight gain, not only in adolescence but later in her adult life after she moves back into her old house. She tries once to cut herself but is taken aback by the blood. She expresses feelings of inferiority and worthlessness and tries to stifle them with food. In her marriage, she is depressed when Dante is not happy. This drives her to an abortion. Even during the course of her heavy psychoanalytic therapy, she swings between depression and power. At times, she hates her therapist and wishes she could leave. At other times, she idolizes him and imagines sexual activity with him.

B. During the above 2 year period (1 year in children and adolescents), the person has not been without the symptoms in Criteria A for more than 2 months at a time

There is never a time in Dolores' life where she does not experience any of these symptoms. Even after therapy she still experiences hypomania and depression.

C. No Major Depressive Episode, Manic Episode, or Mixed Episode has been present during the first 2 years of the disturbance.

Although at one point Dolores contemplates committing suicide, she does so because she wants to feel united with the dying whales at Cape Cod. She does not sincerely want to die, she just wants to feel one in the same with something else. Her plan is disorganized and incomplete. She also never reaches full mania.

D. The symptoms in Criteria A are not better accounted for by Schizoaffective Disorder and are not superimposed on Schizophrenia, Schizophreniform Disorder, Delusional Disorder, or Psychotic Disorder Not Otherwise Specified.

Dolores exhibits no psychotic symptoms. She possesses no firmly held delusions.

E. The symptoms are not due to the direct physiological effects of a substance (e.g. a drug abuse, a medication) or a general medical conditioned (e.g. hyperthyroidism).

Her weight gain stems from her own belief in herself, not a medical condition. While she experiments with alcohol and marijuana, she has no history of substance abuse or dependence.

F. The symptoms cause clinically significant distress or impairment in social, occupational, or other important areas of functioning.

Dolores fails at almost all of her relationships. She has no friends in high school and her only friend in college was the dorm's maid. Her marriage is unsuccessful and she fails to relate to grandmother her whole life. She does not care about school so she fails in high school and drops out in college. She only manages to succeed at a job when she is in control, or in power. After she moves back to Easterly, her jobs are menial and she only works when she is experiencing hypomania.

Accuracy of Portrayal

Dolores is not a likable character by any means. She is unsympathetic, hard to relate to, and it is almost impossible to feel bad for her. She manages to ruin her relationships all on her own and she takes tragedy to an extreme. The book demonstrates the difficulty that may be faced by others who have relationships with cyclothymic individuals. It also demonstrates the impacts a mood disorder can have on every aspect of one's life. It is accurate in its depiction of the feelings that accompany cyclothymia, describing hypomania as "power" and depression as "oppressive." Dolores' mother may also have bipolar disorder, reflecting the possibility that bipolar disorder may be more common in first degree relatives. There are some inaccuracies, though. The therapy that Dolores undergoes is inaccurate. Her therapy is very psychoanalytic in nature, focusing on her mentally unstable mother and sex. Her therapist even goes as far as to pretend to be her mother. Her treatment is also only slightly effective and she still experiences cycles as she gets older. The book does not do much to describe any sort of mental disorder. Instead, it paints a picture of a woman who has lived a miserable life, caused mainly by her own hands.

Treatment

The first treatment that should be implemented for Dolores is a lifestyle change. Her extremely sedentary lifestyle would benefit from exercise and diet, which could help stabilize mood. This would have to be highly regulated in order for her to follow it and actually make the changes. Following the implementation of exercise, cognitive therapy should be used. Cognitive behavioral therapy, interpersonal therapy, or group therapy could be utilized. Due to Dolores' inability to relate well with others, cognitive behavioral therapy should be used. If therapy is ineffective, medication could be used, but only as a last result due to the health problems Dolores already has due to her weight.

https://youtu.be/sM6tQxrKKfQ

CC licensed content, Shared previously

Transvestic Fetishisim

Name: Glen
Source: *Glen or Glenda* (movie, 1953)

Background Information

Glen is a heterosexual Caucasian male and presumably in his late twenties. He appears to be in good physical heath, appropriate weight for stature and is a smoker. Glen was raised by his biological parents and has one younger sister. According to Glen his relationship with his father was strained. Glen's father wanted a son that was interested in sports and who would be a great athlete, none of which Glen was interested in. He expressed that his mother was more affectionate towards his sister and that he longed for that type of affection. He lives in the city, has a stable job, maintains friendships and has been engaged to be married for 1 year to his fiancée Barbara. Glen and Barbara have a healthly relationship displaying respect, open communication and expressions of affection. Glen has no history of drug, alcohol or other mental health issues.

Description of the Problem

Glen has a desire to dress in women's clothing (cross-dressing). He has expressed that being able to dress in clothing of the opposite sex makes him happy and more comfortable in his environment. While living at home he fulfills this desire by wearing his sister's clothing when none of his family members are at home. In order to fulfill his desire to wear women's clothing in public he wears one of his sister's dresses to a Halloween party. After Glen moves from his family residence, he finds it easier to cross-dress. He purchases more clothing but still hides them in case his family was to visit. Living alone also provides more instances to cross-dress in public. He is happy being male and has no desire to change his sexual orientation. Since his engagement to Barbara he is experiencing stress brought on by his need to dress in women's' clothing and whether or not to disclose this information to Barbara or keep it a secret. He finds support from a close friend (who is also a transvestite) who encourages him to be forthcoming and not hide his secret.

Diagnosis

DSM-IV-TR criteria
A. Over a period of at least 6 months, in a heterosexual male, recurrent, intense sexually arousing fantasies, sexual urges, or behaviors involving cross-dressing.

Glen did not meet criteria for Transvestic Fetishisim. He exhibits symptoms more associated with being a Transvestite or cross-dresser. He exhibited no recurrent, intense sexually arousing fantasies, sexual urges, or behaviors in addition to his cross-dressing.

B. The fantasies, sexual urges, or behaviors cause significant distress or impairment in social, occupational, or other important areas of functioning. It involves using nonliving objects to obtain sexual arousal.

Glen's cross-dressing created distress within himself and his relationship with Barbara. She began to see signs of difficulty or stress in Glen which create trust issue for her. Glen experiences extreme stress about the idea of telling Barbara and possible losing her because she could not understand his obsession.

Accuracy of Portrayal

Glen did not meet criteria for Transvestic Fetishisim. The movie portrayed an individual who did meet criteria for cross-dressing: A desired to wear clothing of the opposite gender in some instances to relieve stress brought about by daily encounters. The essential feature of Transvestic Fetishisim is defined as recurrent, intense sexually arousing fantasies, sexual urges, or behaviors involving cross-dressing. Glen did not exhibit any sexual urges or sexual fantasies while engaging in cross-dressing. He expressed his desire to cross-dress was only for comfort and happiness within his environment. This movie did not address any of the aforementioned criteria in regards to Transvestic Fetishisim.

Treatment

There is no empirically supported treatment for Transvestic fetishism. Two types of therapy have been utilized in an effort to treat this disorder: aversion therapy, involving electrical shock and orgasmic reorientation, an attempt to help individuals learn to respond sexually to generally acceptable stimuli. Both of these treatments were developed when little was known about the disorder and when it was less accepted. Today there is less focus on treatment of the disorder and more encouragement for societal acceptance. In cases where individuals have come in for treatment it is mainly due to others, such as spouses and /or family members requesting they seek treatment. Prognosis for this disorder is poor due to the fact that most individuals with this disorder do not want to change. Treatment that is demanded by others such as one's spouse or family members is almost always not successful.

CC licensed content, Shared previously

Gender Identity Disorder

Name: Brandon Teena (Teena Ray Brandon)
Source: *Boys Don't Cry* (movie, 1999)

Background Information

Brandon Teena is an adolescent, Caucasian female who grew up in Lincoln, Nebraska. Teena prefers to live her life as a male. She does not currently appear to have a stable and persistent means of income or employment. Teena steals because of her low social economic status and non effort to obtain an occupation. Her delinquent activity has led her to attain a juvenile record before she has reached the age of 21. Although, the whereabouts of her mother is unknown, there seems to be a distant to an almost nonexistent relationship between her and her mother. Her father died before she was born so there is absent fathering in her life from the beginning of her years. She lives with her cousin from time to time in a trailer home, yet her cousin does not support the trouble she gets into with the locals and the law. Her cousin and presumably other family members do not except her transgender choice to act as a male either. Teena mainly lives out of her travel bag with no stable, consistent place to call home. There doesn't seem to be any health concerns. There is also no evidence that there is any family mental history as well. Brandon Teena, who's legal name is Teena Brandon, has always looked like a girl, yet reported that she had always felt as guy. Cutting her hair short, wrapping up her breasts, and wearing a fake penis has in fact resembled her as looking as a male. Her past does not show any previous drug or alcoholic abuse; however, recently she has been introduced to a selected few of drugs, such as marijuana, with a group of new friends in Falls City, Nebraska. Teena's weakness appears to be females. Her goal is to have a surgical procedure to change her female sex characteristics.

Description of the Problem

Teena currently displays symptoms that indicate that she does indeed reject her identity as being a female physically. She seems to have emotional symptoms, especially when someone may mention that she is a girl and not a boy. Her cousin continued to tell her that she was a girl, that she needs to leave the girls alone, and that she needs to accept the fact that she is a lesbian. Although Teena knows that she is physically not a male, she denies being a lesbian or homosexual. Teena cross dresses and wears a fake penis and socks in her pants in order to portray body types like a male. She denies having sexual attributes such as a having a menstruation and tries to hide all of her sexual characteristics from others. She will claim to be a hermaphrodite before she claims to be a female. Teena has not ever had sexual intercourse with a male and has resisted from being touched any areas by her genitals from any of her sexual partners. Teena could pass for a male fairly easily with a short hair cut like a guy her age, male stature, and her cross dressing efforts.

Diagnosis

The diagnosis for Teena Brandon that seems to fit appropriately is **Gender Identity Disorder in Adolescents or Adults (302.85).**
A. In adolescents and adults, the disturbance is manifested by symptoms such as a stated desire to be the opposite sex, frequent dressing as the opposite sex, desire to live or be treated as the opposite sex, or the conviction that he or she has the typical feelings and reactions of the opposite sex.

Teena acted like a male and desired to be treated like a male by everyone. Teena cross dressed to look like a normal guy her age would as well. She was also very attractive to girls.

B. Persistent discomfort with his or her sex or sense of inappropriateness in the gender role of their sex. In adolescents and adults, the disturbance is manifested by symptoms such as preoccupation with getting rid of primary and secondary sex characteristics (e.g., request for hormones, surgery, or other procedures to physically alter sexual characteristics to simulate the other sex) or belief that he or she was born the wrong sex.

Teena desired to change her sexual characteristics through surgical procedures. She wrapped her breasts down in order to flatten them and wore a counterfeit penis in her underwear.

C. The disturbance is not concurrent with a physical intersex condition.

Even though Teena claimed that she was a hermaphrodite, she was full characterized and constructed as a female physically and biologically.
D. The disturbance causes clinically significant distress or impairment in social, occupational, or other important areas of functioning.

Specify if (for sexually mature individuals): Sexually attracted to males, sexually attracted to females, Sexually attracted to both, Sexually attracted to neither

Teena was a part of the low social economic status population and also did not indicate a means of trying to obtain an occupation while she continued to steal things. Teena seemed to have a hard time getting along with everyone except for her female partners.

Accuracy of Portrayal

The average person watching this movie would see a reasonably accurate portrayal of the *onset* of Gender Identity Disorder, especially since Teena Brandon denies her gender and sexual characteristics as well as being a homosexual in any part of the movie. The movie helps the portrayal of gender identity disorder in a significant way by giving good examples of all the symptoms of gender identity disorder. Because the movie portrayed true events of someone's life, most symptoms did seem neither inaccurate nor exaggerated. Teena fits the adult presentation of gender identity disorder because of her persistent frustration of her biological sex. She passed as the opposite sex by cross dressing and abstained from touching or letting female partners touching her genitalia. One may think that parental relationships were being mislabeled in the movie about gender identity disorder because the only whereabouts that were known about the parents were mentioned very briefly. The course of the disorder was also mislabeled because nothing about her childhood was revealed during the movie. If her childhood was identified during the movie, then gender dyshoria would have been prevalent in her life because research shows that children with gender dysphoria that persists into adulthood results in gender identity disorder. Teena showed to have constant discomfort with her sex as being a female which fits into the general descriptive feature of gender identity disorder. The reason why majority of people, friends, and family of Teena did not accept her sexual orientation is because there is a 1 in 100,000 occurrence opposed to 1 in 30,000 in men and men are more accepted than women. Throughout all of the details and information that was made available in the movie, the movie portrayed gender identity disorder appropriately.

Treatment

There are empirical studies that help support treatments for people who portray gender identity disorder. Psychotherapy would have been more helpful for Teena if her disorder was identified earlier. However, psychotherapy can still help Teena cope with her biological sex and behavioral patterns associated with the roles of her biological determined sex. It may reduce Teena's transsexual behavior in a very subtle way, but probably not as much because her disorder was not caught in the beginning. Another treatment that could help Teena would be hormonal therapy of surgical procedure(s). Before having any surgical procedures Teena may be given hormonal therapy in order to prevent undesired sex characteristics of the unwanted opposite sex. Various behavior therapies could help Teena by helping her to modify her behavior towards the sex she wants to be. Triadic therapy may help Teena as well. This therapy includes three differ elements; living as the desired gender, sex reassignment therapy, and hormone therapy. However, she would not have to include all of these elements into her therapy.

Name: Dil

Source: *The Crying Game* (movie, 1992)

Background Information

Dil is a young mid-twenties biracial male that prefers to live his life as a female. Dil works as a hairdresser at a salon during the day and performs as a nightclub singer at night. The bar that Dil performs at is called "The Metro". The Metro is a gay bar filled with lesbians, gays, and transsexuals. Most of the performers at The Metro are transsexual males. Dil states in the movie, that she has a blood condition that causes her to grow weak. There are several medications that she has to take for this condition. My interpretation is the blood disorder she is speaking of is HIV/AIDS. Dil does not have any family close to her. The closest, most stable relationship in her life is the bartender at the Metro. Dil is currently single because the love of her life was killed when he was a soldier in

Ireland. Dil suffers from depression and loneliness and uses alcohol to cope. She also lives a very promiscuous lifestyle in search of love and acceptance. Dil's weakness is men and she is often abused and manipulated by the men that she "loves".

Description of the Problem

Dil displays symptoms that she wants to be perceived as a female. Although she still has a penis, she wants others to perceive and treat her like a female. If a man that she potentially wants to date or "mess around with" does not perceive her as a female she gets angry. However, she also blames the man if he does not recognize that she was born a male. At first, Dil would refuse to have sex with Jimmy; instead she preferred to perform oral sex on Jimmy. This was in an effort to keep him from seeing her penis. One night, after they had been drinking, Dil decided to disrobe and show Jimmy her penis. Jimmy was shocked and he hit her. Then he proceeded to vomit in the bathroom. This further sent Dil believing he would never love and accept her for who she was. Dil seemed to get really emotional when Jimmy threatened to leave her and refused to stay with her or show any type of affection toward her. The man Dil refers to as her true love did know that she was born a male and he accepted her for who she was.

Diagnosis

The appropriate diagnosis for Dil is Gender Identity Disorder in Adolescents or Adults (302.85).

A. In adolescents and adults, the disturbance is manifested by symptoms such as a stated desire to be the opposite sex, frequent dressing as the opposite sex, desire to live or be treated as the opposite sex, or the conviction that he or she has the typical feelings and reactions of the opposite sex.

Dil was an adult male that chose to live his life as a female. Dil often stated that she was a lady and wanted to be treated as such. Mostly everyone around Dil (except Jimmy) knew that she was born a male. However, the still called her a woman and treated her like a woman. Dil dressed, talked, walked, and acted like a woman. Dil was a very emotional person and some may perceive that as acting like a woman. Most men would view Dil as a very attractive woman.

B. Persistent discomfort with his or her sex or sense of inappropriateness in the gender role of their sex. In adolescents and adults, the disturbance is manifested by symptoms such as preoccupation with getting rid of primary and secondary sex characteristics (e.g., request for hormones, surgery, or other procedures to physically alter sexual characteristics to simulate the other sex) or belief that he or she was born the wrong sex.

Dil did not speak of wanting to have surgery to change sexes; however, she never went out without a padded dress or bra to make the illusion that there were breasts there.

C. The disturbance is not concurrent with a physical intersex condition.

Dil was not a hermaphrodite, he was simply born male and wanted to live his life as a woman. He did not state that he wanted to have surgery to change his genitals but he did want others to view him as a female.

D. The disturbance causes clinically significant distress or impairment in social, occupational, or other important areas of functioning.

Specify if (for sexually mature individuals): Sexually attracted to males, sexually attracted to females, sexually attracted to both, sexually attracted to neither.

Dil lived in what seemed to be a low-income part of town; however, she worked as a hairdresser so she was able to pay her bills. She seemed to be liked by others such as her co-workers and people at the bar. Men especially found her very attractive and likeable. However, some men often took advantage of her low self-esteem and would physically abuse her. Dil was attracted to only males, especially males that told her they loved and cared about her.

Accuracy of Portrayal

The average person watching this film would not have guessed that Dil was born a male. They would have just viewed her as an attractive woman in the beginning of the movie. Most men could probably identify with the main character in being unaware that Dil was not a born female. First of all, there are many men that look for the large Adam's apple first and if they do not see it, they assume that the female was born female. Dil did not have a large Adam's apple or a deep voice; however, she did have very large hands and feet. People watching this movie could learn that not everyone that has Gender Identity Disorder, or feels that they were born in the wrong body wants to have surgery. Some choose not to undergo surgery and hormones and all of these things because of the side effects. Others choose not to have surgery because they are comfortable living as the opposite sex without making surgical changes. Dil was a person that was comfortable living as a female without seeking out surgery. The actor in this film definitely performed an accurate portrayal of Gender Identity Disorder. The emotion that was expressed throughout the film that Dil experienced seemed genuine. Anytime she felt jealous, scared or rejected that is when she would either seek attention from men or turn to alcohol.

Treatment

If I were a mental health professional and Dil walked into my office, I would first gather all of the proper background information and medical history and then proceed accordingly. One of the treatments for Gender Identity Disorder is hormones and surgery, but I do not think that would be a good fit for Dil because she has not expressed any interest in changing her biological sexual identity. Instead, I would recommend psychotherapy for Dil. I think Dil would benefit from psychotherapy because it would help her with gather and implement coping mechanisms to deal with her sexual identity. Also, empirical evidence supports that Dil would have better benefitted from psychotherapy if it was administered early in life but I think that she could still benefit from psychotherapy as an adult. The main purpose of psychotherapy in Gender Identity Disorder patients is to help them cope with their biologically determined sex and reinforce the behavioral patterns associated with those roles. However, with Dil the approach may be different because the role she is comfortable in is the role of the female. So as a professional, I would focus more on making her more comfortable with her biology and not trying to change her into becoming a male.

Generalized Anxiety Disorder

Name: Piglet

Source: *The World of Pooh* by A.A. Milne (books, 1954)

Background Information

Piglet is a young male pig and Winnie the Pooh's friend. Since he is portrayed as a baby, he is probably in the age range of 0-3 years old. Piglet does not have a job and his family history is unknown. He does not have any physical health problems but he displays characteristics of anxiety and nervousness. He stutters quite a bit and he is fearful of wind and darkness. Piglet also does not like bees or woozles (which are creatures that Piglet has not yet seen). Piglet lives in the Hundred Acre Wood with Pooh and all of the other Winnie The Pooh characters. He lives in a house in a large beech tree with a sign outside that says "Tresspassers W" which to Piglet means his Grandfather lived there and his name was "Tresspassers William". Piglet's goals are to become brave, not so timid, and to catch a heffalump (a creature that resembles an elephant).

Description of the Problem

Piglet is a very timid piglet. He shows characteristics of anxiety and he stutters. He thinks of how any situation can go wrong and he argues with himself about what he should do if a situation does go wrong. For example, while trying to catch a heffalump, Piglet thinks to himself how he can fake a headache so he will not have to face one of these creatures, in case it is fierce. Then he thinks to himself that if he fakes a headache he will be stuck in bed all morning, so he does not know what to do. These are the types of scenarios that make him anxious. He has thoughts that he creates that jump from one bad scenario to another. Piglet also shakes and blushes. His ears twitch when he is scared or nervous, which is often. He is usually very flustered.

Diagnosis

The diagnosis that would best fit Piglet is **Generalized Anxiety Disorder (300.02).**

1. **In children, to be diagnosed with Generalized Anxiety Disorder, only one of these symptoms must be present:**

(1)Restlessness or feeling keyed up or on edge

(2) Being easily fatigued

(3) Difficulty concentrating or mind going blank

(4) Irritability

(5) Muscle tension

(6) Sleep disturbance (difficulty falling or staying asleep, or restless unsatisfying sleep)

Piglet definitely shows signs of restlessness or feeling keyed up or on edge. He also has difficulty concentrating (his thoughts jump from one bad scenario to another).

1. **Excessive anxiety and worry (apprehensive expectation), occurring more days for at least six months about a number of events or activities (such as work or school performance).**

Piglet has had anxiety problems his whole life as far as we know from the books. He definitely has probably had anxiety problems for more than six months.

1. **The person finds it difficult to control their worry.**

Piglet cannot control his worry which is why he struggles with trying to be brave. He manages to live with his worry and anxiety but the thoughts are still there and he voices his worry to his friends.

1. **An unrealistic fear or worry, especially in new or unfamiliar situations.**

Piglet is afraid of the dark and wind. He has an unrealistic fear of heffalumps and woozles.

1. **The focus of the anxiety and worry is not confined to features of an Axis I disorder, e.g., the anxiety or worry is not about having a panic attack (as in panic disorder), being embarrassed in public (as in social phobia), being contaminated (as in obsessive-compulsive disorder), being away from home or close relatives (as in separation anxiety disorder), gaining weight (as in anorexia nervosa), having multiple physical complaints (as in somatization disorder), or having a serious illness (as in hypochondriasis), and the anxiety and worry do not occur exclusively during post-traumatic stress disorder.**

Piglet anxiety and worry are not due to any of the above features.

1. **The anxiety, worry, and physical symptoms cause clinically significant distress or impairment in social, occupational, or other important areas of functioning.**

Piglet's anxiety and worry does cause him clinically significant distress because he is always worrying about or is afraid of something. He shows distress from his anxiety.

1. **The disturbance is not due to the direct psychological effects of a substance (e.g., a drug of abuse, a medication) or a general medical condition (e.g., hyperthyroidism) and does not occur exclusively during a mood disorder, a psychotic disorder, or a pervasive developmental disorder.**

Piglet does not use drugs, nor does he suffer from any physical medical conditions and he does not have any of the above disorders.

Accuracy of Portrayal

The average person reading *The World of Pooh* by A.A. Milne would be exposed to an accurate portrayal of generalized anxiety disorder in Piglet. Piglet trembles, twitches, and is shaky. Piglet also has exaggerated startle responses to things that scare him. He also shows symptoms of autonomic hyperarousal, like rapid heart rate and shortness of breath. When Piglet is in stressful conditions his anxiety levels tend to elevate and worsen. This is typical of young people with generalized anxiety disorder. Children with this disorder may also show signs of being unsure of themselves. The book accurately portrays generalized anxiety disorder in Piglet.

Treatment

In treating Piglet, one would try to avoid medicines since he is a child and some of the side effects of certain medications can be suicidal thoughts in children.Starting out treating Piglet with cognitive behavioral therapy (CBT) would be optimal. CBT could help Piglet recognize his negative thoughts and try to change his thoughts to more positive thoughts that are more realistic. It would also help Piglet with relaxation techniques such as breathing exercises that could help him learn to relax better in stressful situations that cause anxiety for him. After participating in the behavioral therapy and learning relaxation techniques Piglet could better handle and manage his own anxiety. This could lead to a much happier, comfortable, and positive life. His quality of life would be better after the treatment.

CC licensed content, Shared previously

Posttraumatic Stress Disorder

Name: Nick (Nicolas)

Source: *The Deer Hunter* (movie, 1976)

Background Information

Nicolas (Nick) is a white male who seems to be in his late twenties. He lives in a small town where he has two long time friends, Michael and Steven. United States (U.S.) is still in war with Vietnam and Nick and his two friends plan to go to Vietnam War and protect their country but Steven is engaged and decides to get married before his departure to Vietnam. Nick and Michael go to Steven's marriage ceremony and seem very happy and do not seem to have any physical or psychological complication; they dance, laugh, drink and enjoy the entire night. Nick's behavior and attitude is normal and there are no observable sign of physical or mental illness associated with him. Michael is scared of going to Vietnam and very hopeless about returning back alive but Nick talks to Michael in several occasions and calms him down, promising that everything will be fine. Nick seems to be a very helpful individual in community as he lends a hand to people. Nick has a girl friend and would like to propose to her before going to Vietnam, so he proposes to his girlfriend at the end of the marriage ceremony and both decide to get married after Nick comes back from the War. After Nick's plan for marriage, he also feels bad about going to Vietnam; he is emotionally connected to his fiancée and hard for him to leave. Before Nick and his friends depart to Vietnam, they decide to go for their last deer hunt, up in the mountains close to their town. "One shot" deer hunting is Michael's favorite slang, meaning that he always wanted to catch a deer with only one shot. Michael successfully hunts a deer with only one shot and everybody enjoys the hunting that day. On the next day, they depart to Vietnam and face an unexpected battle with the Vietnamese army. It is not hard to see that they are all shocked in battle. Vietnamese soldiers attack them from all directions. After a couple of days, all three of them are taken captive in Vietnam. While captive, Nick, Michael and Steven are forced to play Russian roulette while their captors gambling on who will, or will not, blow out his brain. Russian roulette is a lethal game in which one bullet is placed in a revolver and participants (captives here) spin the cylinder, place the muzzle against their head and pull the trigger. This is a horrifying moment for Nick and his friends. Steven who is a newly married groom, shows extreme symptoms of stress and anxiety. Nick visibly disintegrates under the abuse and torture of their captors while Michael refuses to capitulate. Michael plans to free himself and his two other friends by requesting a three bullet Russian roulette game from his captors. He manages to kill the captors and runs away with Nick and Steven. An American helicopter shows up and transports Nick to army hospital, while Michael and Steven wait for the next helicopter.

Description of the Problem

While Nick is in the U.S. army hospital inside Vietnam, he displays mild symptoms of anxiety; insomnia, lack of appetite and anxiety, are among the major symptoms he displays. When a nurse comes and talks to him, he keeps staring at people who are brought to the hospital and does not talk to anyone. After about a month, he leaves the hospital and starts to have more severe symptoms of anger, especially when he is reminded of his time in Vietnam. He completely forgets that he has a fiancée or friends; he does not call his friends to see if they are still alive and seems detached from his social environment. He has a sense of a foreshortened future because he does not have a plan to go back home or do anything while he is in U.S. camp in Vietnam. Nick is very busy with his thoughts and does not communicate with his surroundings; social impairment is vivid at this point. He accidently visits a bar in that town where people gamble on playing Russian roulette. As soon as he enters the bar, he starts to have intrusive distressing recollections of the time when he was captive and forced to play this game. He experiences a high level of anxiety and anger. As he is watching a candidate place a revolver to his head, Nick grabs the revolver and passionately places it to his head and pulls the trigger. He disrupts the game and the gamblers kick him out, however on the next day as he is walking down a street, he reaches the same bar. He goes inside and sits in one of the empty seats designated for a Russian roulette player. Michael, who was more emotionally stable than Steven and Nick, shows only very mild symptoms of anxiety and goes back home. His friends and family welcome him but he goes back to Vietnam to bring Nick home. He meets Nick, however Nick does not show any emotion to him, so Michael tries to play Russian roulette with him in that bar to perhaps unfreeze Nick's memory. Nick starts to communicate with Michael a little. However, Nick dies when he pulls the trigger in front of Michael.

Diagnosis

Based on the observed symptoms, the diagnosis for Nick fits well with Post-Traumatic Stress Disorder (309.81).

A. The person has been exposed to a traumatic event in which both of the following have been present:
1. The person experienced, witnessed, or was confronted with an event or events that involved actual or threatened death or serious injury, or a threat to the physical integrity of self or others
2. The person's response involved intense fear, helplessness, or horror
Nick's symptoms certainly meet above characteristics as Nick experienced and witnessed an event in Vietnam which he was threatened to death (by the Russian roulette game). He has intense fear and feelings of hopelessness while being captive in Vietnam (Background information).
B. The traumatic event is persistently re-experienced in one (or more) of the following ways:
1. Recurrent and intrusive distressing recollections of the event, including images, thoughts, or perceptions. NOTE: In young children, repetitive play may occur in which themes or aspects of the trauma are expressed.
2. Recurrent distressing dreams of the event. NOTE: In children, there may be frightening dreams without recognizable content.
3. Acting or feeling as if the traumatic event were recurring (includes a sense of reliving the experience, illusions, hallucinations, and dissociative flashback episodes, including those that occur upon awakening or when intoxicated). NOTE: In young children, trauma-specific reenactment may occur.
4. Intense psychological distress at exposure to internal or external cues that symbolize or resemble an

aspect of the traumatic event.

5. Physiological reactivity on exposure to internal or external cues that symbolize or resemble an aspect of the traumatic event.

Nick re-experienced very intense psychological distress when he observed people who were gambling on players (playing Russian roulette) in a bar. In there, he acted as if he was a captive in Vietnam and therefore took the gun from one of the players and after he pointed the gun toward his head, pulled the trigger. So he was exposed to external cues which symbolized an aspect of the traumatic event in Vietnam. Therefore he qualifies for more than one of above conditions (3, 4 and 5).

C. Persistent avoidance of stimuli associated with the trauma and numbing of general responsiveness (not present before the trauma), as indicated by three (or more) of the following:

1. **Efforts to avoid thoughts, feelings, or conversations associated with the trauma**

2. **Efforts to avoid activities, places, or people that arouse recollections of the trauma**

3. **Inability to recall an important aspect of the trauma**

4. **Markedly diminished interest or participation in significant activities**

5. **Feeling of detachment or estrangement from others**

6. **Restricted range of affect (e.g., unable to have loving feelings)**

7. **Sense of a foreshortened future (e.g., does not expect to have a career, marriage, children, or a normal life span)**

As it was mentioned in the background information, Nick showed no interest in any activity or in friendships. He was certainly detached from his social environment and also had no feelings of love. When his friend Michael showed up to take Nick back home, Nick did not show any interest and was not passionate about his fiancé. Therefore, he met four of above conditions (4, 5, 6 and 7).

D. Persistent symptoms of increased arousal (not present before the trauma), as indicated by two (or more) of the following:

1. **Difficulty falling or staying asleep**

2. **Irritability or outbursts of anger**

3. **Difficulty concentrating**

4. **Hypervigilance**

5. **Exaggerated startle response**

Nick clearly shows outburst of anger in several scenes of the movie. He also had difficulty concentrating when his friend Michael tried to remind him of his fiancé and home. Unfortunately it was not shown in the movie whether Nick has difficulty sleeping. But his condition meets above criteria (2 and 3).

E. Duration of the disturbance (symptoms in Criteria B, C, and D) is more than one month.

Nick had above symptoms for more than one month.

F. The disturbance causes clinically significant distress or impairment in social, occupational, or other important areas of functioning.

Nick's symptoms reveal an intense social impairment as well impairment in his interpersonal relationship. Therefore his symptoms meet this criterion. Nick's condition is a representation of an acute PTSD.

Accuracy of Portrayal

Nick's symptoms were well demonstrated to portray Post Traumatic Stress Disorder (PTSD). Nick experienced intense and horrifying moments in Vietnam in which he was threatened with death through Russian roulette. He observed and watched other prisoners die. Therefore, the war portrayed an accurate condition which could be the cause of PTSD. However, this movie showed Nick revisit the bar (while he is suffering from PTSD) and playing Russian roulette over and over again. Although Nick showed intense anger toward this game, PTSD patients mostly avoid experiences that remind them of their stressful event. Therefore, this part of the movie does not accurately resemble the condition of a PTSD patient, while all other symptoms are well matched with PTSD. Overall, there was an accurate portrayal of a person's descent into PTSD.

Treatment

PTSD is highly comorbid with other anxiety problems and as such it would be beneficial to control the anxiety before starting other treatments. Therefore the primary treatment action for Nick would be to start a low dosage of an anti anxiety medication such as escitalopram (Lexapro) after a full medical examination. Once pharmaceutical treatment begins, the next level of treatment for Nick would be Prolonged Exposure (PE) therapy. This therapy will help Nick to decrease distress about his trauma and approach trauma-related thoughts, feelings, and situations that he is avoiding due to the distress. In the first part of prolonged exposure therapy, Nick needs to be educated about his disorder and common trauma reactions. This would allow Nick to learn and become more familiar about his symptoms and better understand treatment goal and process. The second part of the treatment is to train Nick how to have long breath and relax. One of the symptoms of PTSD, especially in Nick's case, is abnormal breathing habits when the patient is scared or anxious. This part of treatment will help Nick to overcome his distress by breathing differently. Real world exposure practice is the third part of this treatment in which Nick is exposed to Russian roulette game (without any bullets) over and over again. Such in vivo exposure helps Nick's trauma related distress to lessen over time. In the last part of prolonged exposure therapy, therapist should talk to Nick while he is exposed to Russian roulette game. This helps to unfreeze Nick's memory and to let him communicate about his experience and memories with therapist and not being afraid of his memories. Talking through the trauma can also help therapist to identify Nick's negative thoughts about past event and help to modify his negative thoughts, allowing him to make sense of what happened and have fewer negative thoughts about the trauma. Family therapy is also recommended for Nick since he no longer seeks any friendship and does not have any emotions for his fiancée. Family therapy can help the Nick's friends and fiancée understand what they are going through, and help them work through relationship.

Schizophrenia

Name: Nina Sayers
Source: *Black Swan* (movie, 2010)

Background Information

Nina Sayers is a Caucasian female who is presumed to be in her early to middle twenties, although her actual age is unknown. She currently works as a ballerina in a New York City ballet company whose name is undisclosed. Although there are not any known distinct physical illnesses, abnormalities, disorders, or disadvantages currently within Sayers, there are observable health concerns. The patient is visibly underweight and has serious cuts, bruises and other wounds on her feet, although both of these concerns can be attributed to her career as a dancer. However, there are also various lesions and abrasions throughout the surface of Sayers' body which cannot be attributed to anything in her current daily environment. It is speculated that these lesions could be self-inflicted. Sayers currently lives by choice with her mother. Her mother, although not diagnosed, has observable generalized anxiety disorder symptoms, as well as some neurotic personality traits. It is also observed that the mother displays a very rich sense of control over Sayers' life, such as her scheduling, room design, personal decisions, etc. Sayers appears to not have very many, if any, close friends or relatives outside of her mother. It is undisclosed whether or not Sayers has had any contact with her biological father. It is assumed that he does not actively participate in her life. Until recently, there was not any reported drug or alcohol history. However, as of late she has reported experimenting with ecstasy, a derivative of MDMA, as well as engaging in small amounts of social drinking. Her current goal is to become the principle dancer of her current ballet company. Most of her daily activities are related to improving her performance as a dancer.

Description of the Problem

Sayers currently displays a whole host of symptoms that could be indication of several disorders. The lesions and abrasions as aforementioned fit the description of self-mutilation; however, Sayers denies ever abusing herself, and frequently reports not knowing how the lesions and abrasions appeared on her body in the first place. Sayers often suffers from both visual and audio hallucinations. These hallucinations include items such as seeing feathers physically protrude from her skin, seeing and hearing paintings laughing at her, having conversations and encounters with people that never took place, and peeling off pieces of her own skin that are obviously still in tact, among many other hallucinations. She is also currently under some delusions as well. She believes that another one of her co-dancers is trying to take her starring role in the next upcoming production from her when there is not any evidence to support such a claim. She also believes that this co-dancer is sleeping with the program director, when there is no evidence to support this claim either. In general, Sayers is very convinced that various people are intentionally trying to take this acclaimed dancing role from her, or as she refers to it, her chance to be "perfect."

Diagnosis

The diagnosis for Sayers that seems to fit appropriately is **Schizophrenia, Paranoid Type (295.30)**.

1. **To be diagnosed with schizophrenia, two or more of the following characteristics must be present:**

1. Delusions
2. Hallucinations
3. Disorganized speech
4. Grossly disorganized or catatonic behavior
5. Negative symptoms, i.e., affective flattening, alogia, or avolition

Sayers definitely has both the first and second characteristics of delusions and hallucinations, as described in the section of "Description of the Problem."

1. **For a significant portion of the time since the onset of the disturbance, one or more major areas of functioning such as work, interpersonal relations, or self-care are markedly below the level achieved prior to the onset.**

The delusions and hallucinations have made both Sayers' work and personal life dysfunctional. She has been late for rehearsals and has caused a great amount of interpersonal disturbance amongst her coworkers.

1. **Continuous signs of the disturbance persist for at least 6 months. This 6-month period must include at least 1 month of symptoms that meet Criterion A and may include periods of prodromal or residual symptoms.**

The hallucinations of skin peeling and the delusion of denial of having part of her own lesions and abrasions have been present with Sayers for the majority of her life. During the last one to two month period is when her visual and auditory hallucinations have become more frequent. It is also during the last one to two month period that the persecutory delusion of having her role taken from her has become prominent. It is unknown if she has suffered from other persecutory delusions previously.

1. **Schizoaffective Disorder and Mood Disorder With Psychotic Features have been ruled out because either (1) no Major Depressive, Manic, or Mixed Episodes have occurred concurrently with the active-phase symptoms; or (2) if mood episodes have occurred during active-phase symptoms, their total duration has been brief relative to the duration of the active and residual periods.**

During observation, Sayers has not met any criteria that would indicate any of the mood disorders. Her persistent amount of dance practice may signify a possible manic episode, but since she has always spent a great deal of time practicing, it appears as if it is too consistent to be considered an episode, therefore disqualifying her from any mood disorders.

1. **The disturbance is not due to the direct physiological effects of a substance or a general medical condition.**

As previously stated, there is not any known, distinct physical illnesses, abnormalities, disorders, or disadvantages currently within Sayers that would explain her schizophrenic symptoms. She did not have any drug history until recently, but her symptoms were present long before her intake of any substance.

1. **If there is a history of Autistic Disorder or another Pervasive Developmental Disorder, the additional diagnosis of Schizophrenia is made only if prominent delusions or hallucinations are also present for at least a month.**

There is no history of either of the above listed disorders present in Sayers.
To fit the Diagnostic Criteria for 295.30 Paranoid Type, the following criteria are met:

1. **Preoccupation with one or more delusions or frequent auditory hallucinations.**

Sayers is completely preoccupied by her persistent tactile, visual, and auditory hallucinations. She is also completely preoccupied with her delusion of someone trying to take her role from her.

1. **None of the following are prominent: disorganized speech, disorganized or catatonic behavior, or flat or inappropriate affect.**

Sayers displays none of the above listed behaviors.

Accuracy of Portrayal

The average person watching this movie would see a reasonably accurate portrayal of the *onset* of Paranoid Schizophrenia, especially since Nina Sayers is in the perfect age range for onset, but not necessarily the daily experience after onset. Of course, the movie overdramatized a lot of the symptoms that the average schizophrenic would experience, but not to the point that the symptoms were so exaggerated that to make the case that she was schizophrenic was invalid if one were to make an assessment. In fact, this movie actually somewhat helps the portrayal of schizophrenia in the media, as many movies and television shows give examples of the symptoms of Dissociative Disorder as evidence of schizophrenia, which are totally inaccurate and confuse the audience as to what schizophrenia actually is. Although symptoms would not occur as rapidly as they do in Nina Sayers in most common cases of schizophrenia, it is plausible. Therefore, Black Swan is a decent portrayal of a person's descent into paranoid schizophrenia.

Treatment

To treat Sayers, after a full medical examination, it would be best to immediately start her on a mid-level dosage of an anti-psychotic, such as Vesprin. Most people with schizophrenia respond very well to current medication in comparison to people with other Axis I disorders. After pharmaceutical treatment begins and an appropriate dosage has been stabilized, it would be best to start Sayers and her mother into family therapy, as to educate and help both of them find ways to cope with this disorder, and to help Sayers' mother be more tolerant and understanding of Sayers' symptoms. Social Skill training would also be beneficial to Sayers, because as previously stated, she has no close friends or any type of social support outside of her mother. Social Skill training would also help Sayers interact more efficiently with the other people who work at the dance company, lessening interpersonal disturbances caused by her disorder.

Pathological Gambling

Name: Geoffrey Chaucer (aka Chaucer)
Source: *A Knight's Tale* (Movie, 2001)

Background Information

Geoffrey Chaucer is a male in his late 20's to early 30's. He is in good health and with no serious illnesses. We have no information from this movie about his past. This includes no information about his parents or where he is from. He announces that he is a writer for hire. He says that he has written a few poems and is known for his book "The Book of the Duchess". During the time of the movie, he acts as a writer and a herald for William. He seems to have no social ties to his past other than the people who have collected his debts. During the movie, he does start to gain close relationships with the four people he is traveling and working with. There is no evidence that he has any other vices such as drinking or drug problems throughout the movie. He has difficulty dealing with his gambling urges and knowing when to stop.

Description of the Problem

Chaucer starts the story in a very depressed mood. He is first introduced to us while he walks completely naked down a trail. He comes upon a group of men along the road. He then lies about how he has lost all of his possessions. He says that he had been robbed in a sense rather than that he had lost of his possessions to his gambling problem. To get passage to the next city he blackmails the group. He blackmails them by uncovering that the group had lied about their identities and saw that they would need forged documents that he could provide if they gave him money. After forging the documents, Chaucer presented them for authentication and had them accepted. The group offers Chaucer the job of being a herald, which he accepts. At the same time, though, he is very preoccupied with watching people gambling along the alleyway. He then immediately cuts off is conversation with William to go and gamble. This leads him to be in the same position where we had first seen: naked and with a large gambling debt. When Chaucer is unable to pay for his debts, he calls on William to get him out of the bad situation. William is given the choice of paying off Chaucer's debt or let his new friend pay for it from his hide. Chaucer admits after this that he has a problem with gambling.

Diagnosis

Based on the DSM-IV-TR criteria Chaucer fits at least eight of the ten maladaptive behaviors listed.

- **A. Persistent and recurrent maladaptive gambling behavior as indicated by five (or more) of the following:**

  - **(1) is preoccupied with gambling (e.g., preoccupied with reliving past gambling experiences, handicapping or planning the next venture, or thinking of ways to get money with which to gamble)**

When Chaucer is given a small amount of money he immediately see people gambling and is fixated his attention on them. He then says, "I must see a man about a dog" this is a cover up so that he can leave to go gamble the little cash that he had just received.

- **(2) needs to gamble with increasing amounts of money in order to achieve the desired excitement**
- **(3) has repeated unsuccessful efforts to control, cut back, or stop gambling**

Chaucer is found walking naked after losing all his possessions to gambling in the last town, he then gambles away what little money he was given in the next town.

- **(4) is restless or irritable when attempting to cut down or stop gambling**
- **(5) gambles as a way of escaping from problems or of relieving a dysphoric mood (e.g., feelings of helplessness, guilt, anxiety, depression)**

Chaucer is in a depressed state trudging (the slow, weary, depressing yet determined walk of a man) and then prays to his god to get him out of his tribulations. Then he gambles at the first opportunity to escape his current living style.

- **(6) after losing money gambling, often returns another day to get even ("chasing" one's losses)**

He had lost everything but in the next town, he bet again to try to win what he lost earlier.

- **(7) lies to family members, therapist, or others to conceal the extent of involvement with gambling**

Chaucer when asked if he had been robbed stated that he had taken an involuntary vow of poverty. This is rather than saying that he had lost all of it gambling.

- **(8) has committed illegal acts such as forgery, fraud, theft, or embezzlement to finance gambling**

Chaucer knowingly forges patents of nobility for the group to be able to compete in tournaments.

- **(9) has jeopardized or lost a significant relationship, job, or educational or career opportunity because of gambling**

Chaucer was a herald and his gambling debt he pushed off on his newly found friends almost lost him this position and their friendship.

- **(10) relies on others to provide money to relieve a desperate financial situation caused by gambling**

Chaucer loses all his positions again and tells the collectors that William can pay for his debt that he has made while gambling, later William does come and wipe out the debt.

- **B. The gambling behavior is not better accounted for by a manic episode.**
-

Accuracy of Portrayal

The portrayal of Chaucer struggling with gambling is only a small side story. With that said, it is still easy to tell that he has a problem with his ability to control his Pathological Gambling. It is demonstrated how it is affecting him and his friends in negative ways. He even goes on later in the movie to admit to his friends that he does have a gambling problem. The only flaw in the accuracy of portrayal is that once he admits to the group that he has a problem it is never a problem again in the movie. Overall this is an accurate portrayal of Pathological Gambling

Treatment

The treatment for Chaucer's Pathological Gambling is already taking place during the movie. He makes a great first step in admitting to his friends that he does have a problem and that he needed help. After his admission, he does not have any more problems with gambling. A long term goal would be to identify why he has the urge to gamble in the first place. That is because gambling is just the symptom of an underlining problem. I would look at handling his depression. His depression is seen only shortly but with the high comorbidity of pathological gambling and depression it is important to examine it. Aversion therapy can be used to treat his urges to gamble. This is done by putting him into a condition that he would usually gamble but also exposing him to something that would cause him discomfort. This is to learn self control and to overcome the illusion that they will win the next time. He should not gamble again for any reason. He should also look for support groups like Gamblers Anonymous to help him over his urges.

Video: Chaucer – A Case Study in Pathological Gambling

- https://youtu.be/xO_fKK8DdKg

Antisocial Personality Disorder

Name: The Grinch

Source: *How the Grinch Stole Christmas!* (Movie, 2000)

Background Information

The Grinch, who is bitter and cave-dwelling creature, lives on the snowy Mount Crumpits, a 10,000 foot high mountain that is north of Whoville. His age is undisclosed but he looks to be in his 40's and does not have a job. He normally spends a lot of his time being alone in his cave. The patient appears to be suffering from antisocial personality disorder with depressed mood. There was no background history on his family, as he was abandoned as a child. The Grinch was taken in by two ladies who treated him like he was their own like every other Who children with love for Christmas. He does not have any social relationship with his friends and family. The only social companion the Grinch has is his dog Max. There was no history of drug or alcohol use. The Grinch did have some life difficulties when he was a little boy being made fun of the way he looks at his school. The Grinch had no goal in his life except to stop Christmas from happening. The coping skills and weakness was to run away from his problems and leave the town, rather than facing problems.

Description of the Problem

The Grinch displays a number of problems. The Grinch was not a very happy man with life. He hated Christmas and wanted to stop it from happening. When he was little, he got irritated and aggressive at the school because he was being made fun of by the fat boy who now is the mayor of the town. The Grinch threw a fit and picked up the Christmas tree and threw it to the other side of the classroom. After that he no longer liked Christmas. Years and years later the Grinch decided that he was going to stop Christmas from happening. He decided to dress as Santa Claus and take away all the Christmas trees and presents from the people of Whoville. He failed to plan ahead to know what the consequences would be. As he went to Cindy Lou Who's house to steal their tree and present, Cindy Lou asked him why he was taking the Christmas tree. He told her that he going take the tree to his place and fix the light bulb. The Grinch did not show any remorse of what he did. He wanted Christmas to be over. He also did not care for the safety of other including his dog. His dog had to be the reindeer. The Grinch was irresponsible and thinking recklessly. He wanted everyone miserable and thought that would make him feel better.

Diagnosis

The diagnosis that seems appropriate for the Grinch is Antisocial Personality Disorder (301.7).

1. There is a pervasive pattern of disregard for and violation of the rights of others occurring since age 15 years, as indicated by three (or more) of the following:

    a. failure to conform to social norms with respect to lawful behaviors as indicated by repeatedly performing acts that are groups for arrest

        - He would have gotten big trouble for stealing all the trees and presents. Also he got in trouble by getting peoples mails in the wrong box. The Grinch did not realize there are consequences.

    b. deceitfulness, as indicated by repeated lying, use of aliases, or conning others for personal profit or pleasure

        - The Grinch lied to the little girl why he was stealing her Christmas tree and that he pretend to be a Santa.

    c. impulsive behavior or failure to plan ahead

        - He failed to plan ahead thinking he would not run into someone while stealing Christmas tree and present. The Grinch did not think what would happen if he did this.

    d. irritability and aggressiveness, as indicated by repeated physical fights or assaults

        - The Grinch was irritated by being made fun of the fat boy. He got aggressive and picked up the Christmas tree and threw it across the room,

    e. reckless disregard for safety of self or others

        - He did care for other people safety especially his dog max. He made his dog do something big than his dog can really do and that it could hurt him.

    f. consistent irresponsibility, as indicated by repeated failure to sustain consistent work behavior or honor financial obligations

        - He was being irresponsible for what he did. He wanted to make people made and not care about anyone. He was irresponsible with his dog and didn't care if his dog got hurt or not.

    g. lack of remorse, as indicated by being indifferent to or rationalizing having hurt, mistreated, or stolen from another

- The Grinch had no regrets in what he had done. He didn't regret what he did to those people. The Grinch was happy to make people unhappy and more.

2. The individual is at least age 18 years.

   - The Grinch is around in his 40's.

3. There is evidence of Conduct Disorder with onset before age 15 years.

   - The Grinch shows evidence of having conduct disorder with the onset before age 15. He first started showing symptoms around when he was 8-10 years old.

4. The occurrence of antisocial behavior is not exclusively during the course of Schizophrenia or a Manic Episode.

   - During observation, the Grinch did not meet any signs showing schizophrenia but he was showing some of the signs of having a manic episode such as increased in goal-direct activities. The Grinch was very into making everyone's Christmas miserable.

Accuracy of Portrayal

The average person watching this movie would learn quite a bit about antisocial personality disorder. They would also learn about bullying and depression. The movie did make it into fairy tale where they have happy ending for a person who has antisocial personality disorder. This is not the case in the real world with people who have that type of disorder. It does not cure them that quick. It takes time, efforts, and counseling. Though it is rare for someone who has antisocial personality disorder to seek help and get counseling. It does confuse the audience that makes them think you can cure the disorder quick when you can't. This is a movie somehow helps show people what the antisocial personality is.

Treatment

Antisocial personality disorder is one of the most difficult personality disorders to treat because people who have it tend to think there is nothing wrong with them and do not want help. It is rare for people who have antisocial personality disorder to get help. First to treat the Grinch, he needs a full medical examination to see what symptoms would come up beside antisocial personality disorder. After the full evolution, the Grinch should seek counseling to talk about his past, learn to cope what he went through, and do some social skills training. Social skilling training would help him a lot to learn how to socialize with other people. There a few medication that could help the Grinch such as with his depression he could take antidepressant medication to help improve his depressed mood, anger, impulsivity, or irritability. However, these medication do not directly treat the behavior that characterize antisocial personality disorder, they can be useful in addressing conditions that co-occur with this condition.

Video: The Grinch – A Case Study in Antisocial Personality Disorder

- https://youtu.be/rEOmeLyFbrg

Name: The Joker

Source: *The Dark Knight* (movie, 2008)

Background Information

The Joker is a disturbed and malicious villain who is the archenemy of Batman. His age is unknown but he looks to be in his late 40's to early 50's. His gender is obviously male with brown eyes, and sandy, light green hair. He does not have a "real" job, but some consider running the streets with thugs to be one of them. He spends majority of his time plotting to corrupt and destroy Batman along with bringing the city of Gotham to the ground. His overall health status is unknown, but to the naked eye, he physically looks ill along with the deep razor cuts to both sides of the mouth representing a permanent smile. Psychologically he appears to suffer from antisocial personality disorder, which is evident by his hasty behavior and lack of disregard to others. He does not have a relationship with his parents or relatives. The only social relationships he does have are those with thugs and delinquents. There is no evidence of drugs or alcohol use, although he reports that his father was an extremely abusive alcoholic, who attacked he and his mother with a blade, cutting him along the corner of his lips. The only goal in The Joker's life was to destroy Batman and everything in his path. His only coping skill and weaknesses were to see someone other than himself get hurt along with Batman. He would then vanish from sight seemingly as if he had run away from his problems, not wanting to face the consequences.

Description of the Problem

The problems The Joker displays are tremendous. To begin, he absolutely hates Batman and everything to do with justice and peace. He seems to hate everything about himself as well, considering he has to hurt others around him to feel better. His only purpose in life is to destroy Gotham for no apparent reason and to destroy Batman considering he is constantly in The Joker's way to destruction. The Joker wanted humans to understand that they were "bad" and destroyers when all the while he was the one committing crimes. The Joker expressed absolutely no empathy for his ruthless actions along with being extremely sadistic. He blatantly disregarded laws and socials norms of society as a whole, all of which are related to antisocial personality disorder.

Diagnosis

According to DSM-IV-TR criteria, the appropriate diagnosis would be Antisocial Personality Disorder (301.7)

1. There is a pervasive pattern of disregard for and violation of the rights of others occurring since age 15 years, as indicated by three (or more) of the following:

    a. Failure to conform to social norms with respect to lawful behaviors as indicated by repeatedly performing acts that are groups for arrest.

        - The Joker was constantly being arrested and reprimanded by law enforcements due to his ruthless behaviors. At times it was difficult to catch The Joker committing a crime, but once he was he was punished (for a short amount of time) he would later escape to commit more crimes.

b. Deceitfulness, as indicated by repeated lying, use of aliases, or conning other for personal profit or pleasure.

   - At one time, The Joker dressed as Bozo the clown while robbing the Gotham National City Bank. He manipulated his whole crew into robbing the bank and told them they would all split the money. However, The Joker ends up killing his crew and getting away with the money.

c. Impulsive behavior or failure to plan ahead.

   - The Joker planned seemingly impossible tasks without thinking about the consequences afterward. At one time, he tried to blow up the Gotham General Hospital. Hitting his detonator, the majority of the bombs failed to blow therefore causing him to steal a nearby city bus as a quick getaway.

d. Irritability and aggressiveness, as indicated by repeated physical fights or assaults.

   - Without a doubt The Joker was constantly fighting, assaulting, torturing, or murdering another individual. One in particular would be Batman. Batman would fight The Joker, throwing him from wall to wall and all while The Joker would be laughing hysterically.

e. Reckless disregard for safety of self or others.

   - He cared very little about his own safety considering he told Batman to run him over with his Batpod. This seemed to also be an attempted sign of sucide. Also, blowing up a hospital, violently blowing up a prison inmate, and using innocent people as police officer targets are all ways he disregarded the safety for others.

f. Consistent irresponsibility, as indicated by repeated failure to sustain consistent work behavior or honor financial obligations.

   - The Joker was never considered to have a job. However, he would steal to receive cash payments and money to support himself.

g. Lack of remorse, as indicated by being indifferent to or rationalizing having hurt, mistreated, or stolen from another.

   - The Joker never apologized for his behavior nor having any remorse for killing innocent people. He enjoyed chaos and hurting people along with himself. He still didn't feel remorse for being in jail considering that he brutally killed an inmate while there.

2. The individual is at least age 18 years.

  ◦ The Joker is in his late 40's to early 50's.

3. There is evidence of Conduct Disorder with onset before age 15 years.

  ◦ It may have taken place with his abusive father when he was younger which caused the scarring on his face. It is not known how old he was when this occurred.

4. The occurrence of antisocial behavior is not exclusively during the course of Schizophrenia or a Manic Episode.

  ◦ The Joker's behavior was constantly out of the norm. His ruthless behavior was continual for long durations of time so the presence of a Manic Episode would not be unlikely.

Accuracy of Portrayal

The average person watching the film would see that The Joker is a typical psychopath. The average person would learn the basics of antisocial personality disorder and character qualities an individual must hold in order to be classified as a psychopath. However, with antisocial personality disorder, it seems to remit by age 40 and is known to be higher among young adults than older adults. The Joker seemed to peek in his violent streaks at this age. Another inaccurate portrayal of antisocial personality disorder being used in the film was that majority of individuals suffering from antisocial personality disorders have high amounts of drug use and abuse. Drug use causes individuals to perform dysfunctional and out of the norm types of behavior. They seem to not care about the risk involved. The Joker was never seen using any types of drugs in the film. He would constantly cause harm to others on his own will without the use of mind alternating drugs. However, there were strong accuracies of portrayal. For instance, he was a male, came from an abusive childhood, had zero empathy, and performed extremely risky and ruthless behaviors. The film helped show the most extreme form of antisocial personality disorder.

Treatment

Antisocial Personality Disorder is difficult to treat, considering the fact that individuals do not believe they are in need of treatment. If a patient is taken into to counseling, there is usually a lack of improvement as the patient is usually uncooperative. The treatment that would most likely work for The Joker would be treatment in long-term structured residential settings to which he would be placed in an environment in which he cannot hurt others. If he modifies his behavior appropriately he will be able to earn privileges such as performing a non- threatening hobby of his. Since The Joker has not developed any healthy relationships in his lifetime, using psychotherapy along with behavior modification would help. Developing a relationship with a therapist would probably be beneficial for him as well. Since The Joker expressed a few signs of suicide attempts, it may be that he is suffering from depression as well. An antidepressant may help his depression and irritability. Even though antidepressants do not actually treat an individual with antisocial personality disorder, they can help with these types of comorbid conditions.

Video: The Joker – A Case Study in Antisocial Personality Disorder

- https://youtu.be/utfHPQ6TqPY

Social Phobia (Social Anxiety Disorder)

Name: Barry Egan

Source: *Punch-Drunk Love* (movie, 2002)

Background Information

Barry Egan is a Caucasian male in his early to mid-forties who lives alone in an apartment in Los Angeles, California. He is the owner of a small business that sells novelty items. Barry is not suffering from any known medical conditions or other health problems, but appears to have some mental health concerns. He is easily provoked into violent tantrums in which he punches walls, breaks windows, or destroys others personal property. He does not appear to have any alcohol or drug dependencies; in fact, he appears to drink alcohol very minimally. Barry has seven sisters, all of whom are very domineering and verbally abusive to him. Barry's sisters have tormented and ridiculed him since childhood. As an adult, his sisters are still very controlling of his life and continue to torment him with embarrassing stories from his childhood. Barry has difficulty with personal relationships and appears to be lonely. His goals include growing his business. His hobbies include finding unbelievably good deals and repairing and learning to play the harmonium. Barry can be rather naïve and trusting of others, which leads to being taken advantage of and making poor financial decisions.

Description of the Problem

Barry is currently seeking help because he feels something might be wrong and states that he "doesn't like himself," but is unsure if this is abnormal since he is uncertain how other people are. He states that he "cries a lot." Barry can be described as a socially awkward individual who does not seek out or actively engage in social activity with others. It appears that Barry has little to no family support system and that his relationship with his seven sisters relates to his low self-esteem. He constantly apologizes for things even when he did not do anything wrong, and stumbles with his speech by merging words together. Barry becomes very anxious in social situations. He endures these situations with intense anxiety and distress, which sometimes can lead to a panic attack following the interaction. Barry has a tendency to become violent when provoked with embarrassing stories from his childhood. He is known to lie and deny his actions when confronted. Barry is currently in a relationship with a woman he recently met. The relationship appears to be a positive factor in Barry's life.

Diagnosis

The diagnosis for Barry Egan is Social Phobia (300.23). According to the DSM-IV-TR the following criteria are met:

1. A marked and persistent fear of one or more social or performance situations in which the person is exposed to unfamiliar people or to possible scrutiny by others. The individual fears that he or she will act in a way (or show anxiety symptoms) that will be humiliating or embarrassing. NOTE: In children, there must be evidence of the capacity for age-appropriate social relationships with familiar people and the anxiety must occur in peer settings, not just in interactions with adults.

   - Barry shows fear in meeting new people or encountering people in unexpected situations. He showed this in several situations; for example, when he met Lena for the first time he was obviously uncomfortable and showing signs of fear and while at his sister's house he also showed a marked fear of scrutiny from his sisters.

2. Exposure to the feared social situation almost invariably provokes anxiety, which may take the form of a situationally bound or situationally predisposed panic attack. NOTE: In children, the anxiety may be expressed by crying, tantrums, freezing, or shrinking from social situations with unfamiliar people.

   - Barry's reaction to his sisters demoralizing remarks about him from the other room was a panic attack that took the form of Barry kicking out the glass at his sister's house.

3. The person recognizes that the fear is excessive or unreasonable. NOTE: In children, this feature may be absent.

   - Barry did not know exactly what was wrong with himself, but his attempt to reach out to his brother-in-law showed that he knew that something was unreasonable and that he needed help.

4. The feared social or performance situations are avoided or else endured with intense anxiety or distress.

   - Barry avoided meeting Lena at his sister's house as best he could. When his sister brought Lena to his work to introduce the two, he was extremely anxious and distressed. He started fumbling all over the place, unable to perform his job and having a hard time communicating with Lena and his sister.

5. The avoidance, anxious anticipation, or distress in the feared social or performance situation(s) interferes significantly with the person's normal routine, occupational (academic) functioning, or social activities or relationships, or there is marked distress about having the phobia.

   - Barry lived his life without much interaction with others before meeting Lena. Although he was lonely, he did not have the ability to initiate healthy interaction with others. He made a call to a 900 number as a way to engage in conversation with a woman.

6. In individuals under age 18 years, the duration is at least 6 months.

   - Even though Barry is in his forties, he has evidence of symptoms beyond 6 months. According to his sisters stories of Barry as a child, he might have been diagnosable before 18 years of age.

7. The fear or avoidance is not due to the direct psychological effects of a substance (e.g., a drug of abuse, a medication) or a general medical condition and is not better accounted for by another mental disorder (e.g., panic disorder with or without agoraphobia, separation anxiety disorder, body dysmorphic disorder, a pervasive developmental disorder, or schizoid personality disorder).

8. If a general medical condition or another mental disorder is present, the fear in Criterion A is unrelated to it, e.g., the fear is not of stuttering, trembling in Parkinson's disease, or exhibiting abnormal eating behavior in anorexia nervosa or bulimia nervosa.

   - Barry appears not to be on any medications or illegal drugs, nor does he appear to have another diagnosable mental disorder.

Specify if:

- Generalized: if the fears include most social situations (also consider the additional diagnosis of Avoidant Personality Disorder)

  - It appears that Barry works well with the other men in his company although Barry's interaction with the men is limited and somewhat awkward.

Accuracy of Portrayal

There are few portrayals of a main character with social phobia in movies and television. Barry's character in the movie gave an excellent portrayal of someone suffering from social phobia and the struggles they must face on a daily basis. The portrayal of his seven sisters gave a good indication that his upbringing was a humiliating and traumatic experience and gave insight into reasons why Barry might suffer from the disorder. Barry's relationship with Lena is less accurate to the "real-life" relationship someone with social phobia might experience. His awkward demeanor, inability to maintain eye contact, and lack of conversation skills were accurately portrayed. The manner in which the two met was also likely since Lena pursued Barry and made most of the first moves in the relationship. The inaccuracy is in the fact that Barry and Lena found love and appeared to "live happily ever after," which unfortunately does not happen for many individuals diagnosed with social phobia. In addition, Barry's love for Lena seemed to give him the courage to confront the criminals that were taking advantage of him; however, it is unlikely for someone with social phobia to be assertive or confrontational. These two factors do not exclude social phobia as a diagnosis for Barry, they are just not the norm for what one might expect for someone diagnosed with social phobia.

Treatment

Cognitive behavioral therapy is likely the most effective treatment for Barry. This treatment will help change Barry's pattern of thought about certain events by helping Barry better understand the reality of the situation and help Barry focus less on the idea that he will be embarrassed or humiliated. He will learn to identify and change his automatic negative thoughts. He will learn that everybody makes mistakes and that sometimes being embarrassed is going to happen but it will be okay. Therapy will also help give him coping strategies to change his behavior in anxiety provoking situations, as well as, giving him the skills to help manage his emotions and violent temper. Exposure therapy will help Barry learn that he can handle social situations without anxiety. Family therapy would likely not benefit Barry greatly but may help enlighten his sisters on the cause and effect their actions have on others lives. It would likely be most beneficial to meet with each sister one at a time with Barry as opposed to as a whole group.

Name: Charlie Kaufman

Source: *Adaptation* (movie, 2002)

Background Information

Charlie Kaufman is a Caucasian male in his mid-forties who lives with his twin brother Donald in an apartment they share together. He is a screenwriter who has been tasked with producing an adaptation of the book *The Orchid Thief* by Susan Orlean. Charlie appears to be suffering from some form of depression because he is constantly in doubt of his abilities to adapt the novel into a formidable screenplay, which affects his daily routines and interactions with his brother. There is no evidence of substance abuse (either drugs or alcohol), and he does not appear to be predisposed to partaking in consumption of dangerous substances. Charlie's brother Donald constantly agitates him because he is embarking on a career in screenwriting and Charlie does not approve of his methods; he is baffled when Donald sells his work for a large amount of money. Charlie appears to have trouble with starting and maintaining close personal relationships, as evidenced by his awkwardness with a former girlfriend and a waitress at a local diner he frequents. He is able to start conversations but does not know how to keep them going and is not particularly skilled at inviting other people to join him in activities.

Description of the Problem

Charlie is a socially awkward person and although he is able to start minimal conversations with strangers and acquaintances, he is very nervous and cannot seem to keep his thoughts in one particular order that would benefit the situation. His family support system seems to only come from his twin brother, who is almost completely opposite in terms of personality, social interactivity, and general comfort with life. Since a lot of his thoughts are narrated for the audience, it is apparent that he craves relationships and people to share life experiences with but cannot bring up the courage to engage anyone past initial conversations. Charlie suffers from a severe case of writer's block and takes his anger out on his brother, who is subsequently flourishing in his screenwriting endeavors. Much to the chagrin of Charlie, Donald seems to have picked up screenwriting and ran away with it and that bothers Charlie because he deems Donald an inferior screenwriter and too cliché to produce anything worthwhile. Charlie's anxiety in social situations is profound and is outlined by a fantasy he indulges in regarding the diner waitress.

Diagnosis

The diagnosis for Charlie Kaufman is Social Phobia (300.23). According to the DSM-IV-TR the following criteria are met:

1. A marked and persistent fear of one or more social or performance situations in which the person is exposed to unfamiliar people or to possible scrutiny by others. The individual fears that he or she will act in a way (or show anxiety symptoms) that will be humiliating or embarrassing. NOTE: In children, there must be evidence of the capacity for age-appropriate social relationships with familiar people and the anxiety must occur in peer settings, not just in interactions with adults.

   - Charlie shows a marked level of anxiety and fear when introduced to new people, especially in social situations. Excellent examples of these situations are when he meets a former girlfriend's new "friend," and when he is served by the waitress at the diner.

2. Exposure to the feared social situation almost invariably provokes anxiety, which may take the form of a situationally bound situationally predisposed panic attack. NOTE: In children, the anxiety may be expressed by crying, tantrums, freezing, or shrinking from social situations with unfamiliar people.

   - When Charlie meets the ex-girlfriend's "friend", it is obvious that he is speechless and cannot speak to him or the ex-girlfriend about his current situation. The waitress at the diner also causes Charlie to suffer through anxiety that freezes his conversation and makes the interaction very awkward.

3. The person recognizes that the fear is excessive or unreasonable.

   - Charlie knows that he is a socially awkward person and his continued interactions with his twin brother as well as his trip to New York to talk to Susan Orlean highlight his need to express himself in a socially acceptable way.

4. The feared social or performance situations are avoided or else endured with intense anxiety or distress.

   - On the trip to New York, Charlie ultimately avoids speaking with Susan Orlean and instead attends Robert McKee's seminars. He then has Donald imitate him and interview Susan so he does not have to face her.

5. The avoidance, anxious anticipation, or distress in the feared social or performance situation(s) interferes significantly with the person's normal routine, occupational (academic) functioning, or social activities or relationships, or there is marked distress about having the phobia.

- ◦ Charlie's avoidance behaviors and awkward social interactions severely hinder him from completing the screenplay and even render his trip to New York a waste of time and ultimate threat to his life as he is not able to talk to Susan Orlean in person.

6. In individuals under age 18 years, the duration is at least 6 months.

- ◦ Charlie is well above the age of 18, but the film seems to suggest that his problems have persisted well beyond 6 months.

7. The fear or avoidance is not due to the direct psychological effects of a substance (e.g., a drug of abuse, a medication) or a general medical condition and is not better accounted for by another mental disorder (e.g., panic disorder with or without agoraphobia, separation anxiety disorder, body dysmorphic disorder, a pervasive developmental disorder, or schizoid personality disorder.)

- ◦ Charlie's social awkwardness and anxiety due to the social situations is not accounted for with any other condition or disorder. He seems to be genuinely suffering from a social phobia and no drugs or alcohol influence his behaviors.

8. If a general medical condition or another mental disorder is present, the fear in Criterion A is unrelated to it, e.g., the fear is not of stuttering, trembling in Parkinson's disease, or exhibiting abnormal eating behavior in anorexia nervosa or bulimia nervosa.

- ◦ Charlie is not under the influence of any substances (legal or illegal), and his condition seems to be independent of any other diagnoses.

Specify if:

- • Generalized: if the fears include most social situations (also consider the additional diagnosis of Avoidant Personality Disorder.)

- ◦ Charlie is able to maintain a steady job, do excellent work, and keep relationships with coworkers and everyday acquaintances, though to a minimal extent and not without awkward social interaction.

Accuracy of Portrayal

Charlie Kaufman is an adequate representation of a person suffering from a social phobia. It is not a perfect rendition, but it covers the base areas well enough to establish a passing resemblance. The character is not completely socially awkward, as he is able to strike up a conversation a few times (which do not lead to any sort of reliable, close relationship.) Charlie's brother Donald plays a nice juxtaposition to his social anxiety and awkwardness, as evidenced by Donald's general openness and lack of social anxiety. This suggests that, as children, Charlie probably suffered greatly from witnessing his brother's easiness with social situations. A huge inaccuracy is the fact that Charlie becomes assertive and decides to fly to New York on a whim to meet with Susan Orlean. Also, his sudden insistence to check out what is going on between Susan and John Laroche is not typical of someone suffering from social phobia in any context. Although nothing good comes of these actions, the sheer fact that he pushed his social anxieties aside for those particular instances does not accurately portray someone with full blown social phobia. These are the only flaws portrayed by Charlie and the depiction is a passable example of social phobia.

Treatment

The most effective route to take with a person suffering from social phobia would be a treatment centered on cognitive behavioral therapy. This type of therapy could alter Charlie's thought processes to allow him to acclimate himself to social situations in a socially acceptable manner. Through cognitive behavioral therapy, Charlie could slowly eliminate negative thoughts attached to social situations and therefore be comfortable enough to pursue relationships outside of the scope he has become accustomed to developing his entire life. He would be able to cope with social stressors such as the inevitable times when meeting new people will not go over very well and the situations in which established relationships start to deteriorate for numerous reasons. Slowly integrating real-life situations into the therapy (exposure) would then help Charlie come to terms with the changes that would come in his life and set him on the path to being a socially normal person. If the therapy was effective, Charlie would not become a new man overnight; rather, it would probably take years and consistent dedication to the changes to see him become adaptive to social situations.

Borderline Personality Disorder

Name: Mad Hatter

Source: *Alice in Wonderland* (movies, 1951 & 2010)

Background Information

In the 1951 film

Mad Hatter appears to be Caucasian male is in his late thirties, although his age is never disclosed. He is a fictional character in Alice's dream. In the movie there are not any known physical or mental illness to be associated with the Mad Hatter, although there are visible traits to be noted for. He appears to be eccentric in his behavior and also in his appearance. He is dressed in a olive green blazer, with a green vest, aqua bow tie, beige button down shirt in which the collar is up, green pants and a large green top hat where on the side there is a 10/6 paper. He has white hair sticking out from the hat, and is rather pink in complexation throughout the movie. Prior to Alice stumbling upon them, the Mad Hatter and the Hare can be seen having a party celebrating non-birthdays (a celebration of all the other days in the year that are not one's birthday). Currently the Mad Hatter lives in the forest that is a figmentation of Alice's dream. It is unknown if the Mad Hatter has any family, although he can be seen quite often with the Hare and a little mouse. The Hare can be seen has having similar traits as the Mad Hatter; not being able to sit in one spot, interrupting others, speaking rather fast, constantly moving and appears to break teacups.

In the 2010 version

The Mad Hatter appears to be living in a forest that is part of Alice's dream, in which he lives with Mally and the Hare. He appears to be in his mid-thirties, although his age is never disclosed. He is Caucasian and dresses vibrant. He has on a rather large top hat on, which has random objects stick out of it. Under the hat can be seen his is orange hair that is rather wild. His face is painted, in which his eyes are painted an array of colors; such as blue on, orange, and brown on one eye and the other pink and orange and purple on the other eye. His whole face is painted white. He can be seen wearing a brown tattered suit that is randomly put together, in which it matches his personality perfectly. Throughout the movie, his parents and other family members are never disclosed. Although he is rather fond of the White Queen and he remains loyal to her. The Mad Hatter lost his enjoyment and became "crazy" due to the Queen of Hearts overtaking the White Queen. This happened when the Jabberwocky came and destroyed the White Queen's area and caused massive damage to her property. After that the Mad Hatter was never the same, he was no longer happy.

Description of the Problem

In the 1951 film

The Mad Hatter can be seen singing and dancing with the Hare. They are drinking tea and while dancing they continue to pour each other tea. Once they discover Alice has been watching them, they stop their dancing and signing. They run to Alice to tell her " it's *very very* rude to sit down without being invited", but quickly overcome this once she compliments them on their singing. While the Mad Hatter is talking to Alice, he has his elbow in a cup of tea, and at one point he even pours tea from the kettle down his shirt and makes the tea go into a cup. They ask Alice where she came from but never give her a chance to answer, because they become distracted by clean cups they stubble upon. While dancing with the Hare to teach Alice about what non-birthday celebration is, the Mad Hatter makes a cake appear in place of where his top hat was. At one point he dips his plate into his tea and takes a bite out of the plate. He never stays with one thing, while talking to Alice about birthdays, he insists that she drinks some tea, but as she starts to drink her tea he starts to sing "clean cup clean cup!!" Before Alice can even take a sip of her tea he has dragged her off to the other end of the table and proceeds to ask her if she would like more tea. He can hardly sit still, every few minutes; he is compelled to move down the table and has Alice and the Hare to move down with him. It is clear that the character has difficulty focusing their attention to one aspect and also has difficulty remaining in one spot. The Hatter asks her "Why is a raven like a writing desk?" but never gives Alice the chance to answer. He quickly becomes angry when she attempts to answer the question, but his attention is diverted when the White Rabbit comes exclaiming he is late. The Mad Hatter tells the White Rabbit that his watch his two days old and proceeds to destroy the White Rabbit's watch by dipping it in tea and adding an assortment of food to the watch. After placing all the food into the watch the Hare smashes the watch with his sledgehammer and the Mad Hatter and he kick out the White Rabbit.

When called to Alice's trial as a witness, it he decides to throw the Queen of Hearts a unbirthday party, but this makes the Queen happy and does not last long due to Alice seeing Chester the Cat on top of the Queen's head and the Mad Hatter running on top of the Queen to obtain Chester the Cat.

In the 2010 film

Upon seeing Alice approach him, he climbs on the table and walks across it, as he breaks plates and teacups along the way. Mally tells him that it is the wrong Alice, the Mad Hatter is positive that it is not the wrong Alice, and this is the correct one. While Alice is having tea with the Mad Hatter, the Hare and Dormouse, Chester the cat appears. While Chester is having tea, he brings up a topic that is sore for the Mad Hatter, who instantly becomes enraged in which Dormouse has to remind the Mad Hatter he needs to calm down. He is rather protective of Alice; when the guards of the Queen of Hearts come he hides her in a tea kettle. Upon making sure that Alice is safe, Mad Hatter puts her on his hat, after he had shrunk her, and takes her for a walk. While walking he starts to talk about the Jabberwocky and becomes enraged when Alice tells him that she will not slay the Jabberwocky. Talking to Alice about why she needs to slay the Jabberwocky, Mad Hatter becomes emotional, and tells Alice she has changed.

He continues to go to lengths to protect Alice; he throws his hat with her on it across the field, so the Queen of Heart's guards do not capture her, instead they capture him. He lies to the Queen and tells he has not seen Alice; when she is clearly sitting next to the Queen. Instead of answering the Queen's question, he tells her that he is thinking of things that start with M: moron, mutiny, murder and malice. He decides to charm the Queen, by tell her that he wants to make her a hat for her rather large head. Once the White Queen regained her land again, the Mad Hatter is happy. To show his happiness he does The Futterwacken Dance, which he was not able to do when the White Queen was not in power.

Diagnosis

The diagnosis the Mad Hatter seems to fit best is Borderline Personality Disorder (301.83).

1. Borderline Personality disorder is consider a pervasive pattern of instability of interpersonal relationships, self-image, and affects, and marked impulsivity beginning by early adulthood and present in a variety of contexts. This is indicated by having 5 or more of the following characteristics:

2. Being frantic to avoid abandonment, either real or imagined

3. A pattern of intense, unstable interpersonal relationships characterized by alternating between extreme variances of idealization and devaluation

   - He displays this among Mally and the Hare. He is constantly changing his mood and one minute is harsh to them, and the next minute he thinks they have the greatest idea ever. Also, he instantly he is drawn to Alice once he sees her. He goes out of his way to protect Alice from the Queen of Hearts.

4. Identity disturbance: markedly and persistently unstable self-image or sense of self

   - Although he knows he is the Mad Hatter, he does not seem like he knows this all the time. In the 2010 version the Mad Hatter saw himself as being with the White Queen, but after the Queen of Heart took over, he no longer knew who he was. He was one minute was having tea with Mally and the Hare, the next minute protecting Alice from the Queen of Hearts, and also he was someone that made hats.

5. Impulsivity in at least two areas that are potentially self-damaging (e.g., spending, sex, substance abuse, reckless driving, binge eating).

   - The Mad Hatter in the 2010 version fits this better, in that he is willing to himself at risk constantly for Alice. He takes on the Queen of Hearts' guards, he repeatedly insults them and challenges them. Although it is never disclosed, he displays a several symptoms of someone that may have substance abuse, he is quick to change his behavior, his moods are hardly stable; they vary greatly from sadness, happiness, and anger, his behavior is eccentric; he talks in riddles and is constantly moving.

6. Recurrent suicidal behavior, gestures, threats, or self-mutilating behavior

7. Affective instability due to a marked reactivity of mood (e.g., intense episodic dysphoria, irritability, or anxiety usually lasting a few hours and only rarely more than a few days)

   - He displays this GREATLY. He varies through multiple emotions, one minute he is happy then the next minute he is angry. Upon seeing Alice he drops what he is doing and decides to walk across the table to get to her. He is happy to see her because she is the right Alice and is the one that can slay the Jabberwocky. While Chester pops in for tea and brings up the topic of the Queen of Hearts taking over, Mad Hatter becomes angry instantly and cannot control his anger until Mally reminds of where he is. He displays symptoms of Attention Deficit Hyperactivity Disorder, one minute he is talking about something and his attention becomes drifted to something else. The Mad Hatter in the 1951 could qualify of Attention Deficit Hyperactivity Disorder due to his lack of being able to focus on one thing. One minute he is telling Alice to have tea but then makes everyone move down because he saw a clean cup. He is constantly over talking the Hare and Alice. His emotions are unstable; he can easy become angry but can be pacified quickly. Both of the Mad Hatters are impulsive in the sense they do something without thinking about it. For instance in the 2010 version, the Mad Hatter is quick to insult the Queen of Hearts, but is quickly able to get himself out of being killed by telling the Queen he wants to make her a hat for her big head. In the 1951 version, the Mad Hatter throws the Queen of Hearts a unbirthday party when he is on trial for Alice.

8. Chronic feelings of emptiness

   - Personally I feel like he has these feelings, and hides them by being eccentric. Reasoning for why he would have feelings of emptiness is that when the Queen of Hearts took over, he could no longer do what he loved; being with the White Queen. He is now living in a forest and displays multitudes of emotions rather rapidly. You can sense he is hiding his true feelings; depression of the White Queen no longer in charge.

9. Inappropriate, intense anger or difficulty controlling anger (e.g., frequent displays of temper, constant anger, recurrent physical fights)

   - He becomes angry instantly when Chester brings up the day of when the Queen of Hearts took over. Mally has to remind him of where he is and to control his anger.

10. Transient, stress-related paranoid ideation or severe dissociative symptoms

Accuracy of Portrayal

In a sense both Mad Hatters portray this disorder but the 2010 version does a better job of doing so. The 2010 version shows more emotion and you can see what caused him to become eccentric. His mood varies rapidly; he is quick to be impulsive and has a short attention span. He displays having other mental illness, such as depression and attention deficit hyperactivity disorder. His attention is constantly shifted between topics and is always moving. He has a hard time sitting still; he is never in one spot. The depression would be due to the Queen of

Heart coming to power. She destroyed the property that he lived on, it was the end of the world that he knew. Even though the White Queen lost her power, he still remained loyal to her. In losing the property that he lived on, and the White Queen no longer being in power, caused the Mad Hatter to be even more eccentric, psychotic.

Treatment

To treat the Mad Hatter a Diagnostic Interview for Borderline Patients would first be given. The interview looks at areas of functioning that are associated with borderline personality disorder. The four areas of functioning include Affect (chronic/major depression, helplessness, hopelessness, worthlessness, guilt, anger, anxiety, loneliness, boredom, emptiness), Cognition (odd thinking, unusual perceptions, nondelusional paranoia, quasipsychosis), Impulse action patterns (substance abuse/dependence, sexual deviance, manipulative suicide gestures, other impulsive behaviors), and Interpersonal relationships (intolerance of aloneness, abandonment, engulfment, annihilation fears, counterdependency, stormy relationships, manipulativeness, dependency, devaluation, masochism/sadism, demandingness, entitlement). The best treatment for Borderline Personality Disorder is dialectical behavior therapy; this treatment focuses on the patient building a life that balances changes and handle situations that occur in their life. Patients with Borderline Personality Disorder respond best to psychotherapy. Establishing trust between the patient and therapist is difficult to create and also maintain once established. Types of psychotherapy that can be used are cognitive-behavioral therapy, transference-focused therapy, dialectical- behavioral therapy, schema-focused therapy, and metallization-based therapy. Also it would best to place the Mad Hatter in a stable environment, and around people that have stable moods.

Video: Mad Hatter – A Case Study in Borderline Personality Disorder

- https://youtu.be/4MCymVJQKWo

Name: Ernie "Chip" Douglas "Aka" Larry Tate/Ricky Ricardo/ the Cable Guy.

Source: *Cable Guy* (Movie, 1996)

Background Information

From his reminisces, Chip grew up in a neglected home. His father was out of the picture, and his mother seemed to be some sort of cocktail waitress, or prostitute which is concluded from Chip watching a family scene on the television and saying to his mom" When am I going to get a brother to play with?," while his mother replies," Honey, that's why mommy is going to happy hour," as she leaves the house. Now in his early thirties, Chip works an eccentric cable guy who has a distinct lisp. The scene opens as Steven Kovacs waits on Chip to arrive to install his cable. It appears that Steven has waited all day on Chip. Finally, when Steven is in the shower, Chip arrives and starts banging on the door saying, "Cable guy," multiple times, and with each time getting louder and more annoyed. Finally, Steven comes to the door, upset that he was late, and Chip also becomes upset and states that he will just leave instead. After Steven asks Chip to come inside, Chip starts looking around the living room for a spot to put the cable wires. He starts talking to the walls in a sexual manner, and even displaying gestures to the walls that makes Steven uncomfortable.

Once Chip installs the cable, Steven asks him for free cable since his friend told him all he had to do was slip the cable guy a fifty-dollar bill. Chip then asks Steven to hang out with him later on yet Steven was "busy" so Chip asked again, "Well, what are you doing tomorrow?" Steven agreed and Chip exited saying "See you tomorrow pal." While hanging out, Chip takes Steven to the large satellite receiver where Chip becomes overly emotional about how people's satellite usage will expand and how you will one-day play video games with your friends in Vietnam. Afterwards, Steven asked what his name was, and Chip becomes highly emotional and explains with a dramatic monologue how it amazes him at the thought that Steven wanted to know his name, and goes on to say that his name is Ernie Douglas, but everyone calls him Chip.

After Chip incentivizes his friendship with Steven by giving gifts such as a new home theater system while having no regard for personal space or privacy, although Steven asks Chip to return it, Chip becomes upset and says that he has given him friendship and that is greater than that stuff. Chip insists on awkward social activities, including dinner at Medieval Times where Chip becomes overwhelmingly aggression by competing in jousting, and sword fighting with Steven. The next day, Chip ignorantly stumbles upon Steven and his friends playing basketball, invited himself to join them, and ruined the game by breaking the goal. The next day, Chip leaves Steven thirteen messages on his machine, and undoes his cable, so that Steven will call him. Chip arrives furious that he only calls when he needs something.

To make Steven feel better about his girlfriend problems, Chip hosts a karaoke party with all the equipment he gave to Steven and without his knowledge, hires Steven a prostitute whom he slept with that night. Outraged, Steven throws Chip out, and Chip promises he will fix it. By fixing it, Chip goes stalks Steven's girlfriend Robin with her date, and waits for him incognito in the bathroom and severely assaults her date then shows up at Robin's house and installs her free cable. After Steven tells Chip he does not want to be friends anymore, Chip calls Robin to make her paranoid about how Steven is supposedly acting and then informs the police that Steven has stolen property. Once Steven is out on bail, Chip invites himself over to Steven's parents where he instigates a game of porno password and insinuating that he slept with Robin. Infuriated, Steven punches Chip and Chip leaves. The next day, Chip kidnaps Robin, takes her to the huge satellite dish, and holds her hostage with a staple gun. Steven chases Chip and Robin up to the very top of the satellite. When the helicopter shines a light on Chip, he hallucinates that it is his mother telling him to jump. So, right as the world is waiting to hear the verdict on a huge case, Chip jumps and lands on the receiver, which knocks out the city's cable. However, Chip survives the fall and makes a mends with Steven and Robin, and as the helicopter pilot airlifts Chip away, he calls Chip pal, which starts the whole cycle over again.

Description of the Problem

Chip shows instability with personal relationships such as friendships. He becomes frantic if he believes if his friend(s) are abandoning him. He has no job, He had been fired from several cable companies in which he used different television names as his own such as Larry Tate, which is known from "I dream of Jeannie." Chip has feelings of abandonment, which stems from his neglectful childhood, where the television raised him instead of his parents. Chip has intense emotional problems such as erratic acts of aggression, violence, revenge, and dramatic emotions in terms of sobbing. Within moments, Chip can show signs that he absolutely loves his friends and then despise or hate the same friends. Chip shows signs of self-harming impulsivity such as reckless behavior including frequent trips to the large satellite dish, drinking, and hiring prostitutes. His risk of suicide behavior increased when he assumed he no longer had any friends and attempted, but failed at a suicide attempt.

Diagnosis

301.83 Borderline Personality Disorder

DSM-IV-TR criteria:

A pervasive pattern of instability of interpersonal relationships, self-image, and affects, and marked impulsivity beginning by early adulthood and present in a variety of contexts. This is indicated by having 5 or more of the following characteristics:

1. Being frantic to avoid abandonment, either real or imagined

   - Chip shows this throughout the entire movie at his multiple attempts to keep Steven as his friend, and then included Robin into the mix, and lastly the helicopter pilot.

2. A pattern of intense, unstable interpersonal relationships characterized by alternating between extreme variances of idealization and devaluation

   - Chip exhibits extreme highs and lows on how he feels about himself as a good and bad friend to Steven. Chip does this when he cooks Steven breakfast after a party the next morning (high) then feels incredibly bad at the fact that he hired a prostitute that Steven slept during the night (low). To fix the friendship, Chip goes out to make things right with Steven and Robin (high).

3. Identity disturbance: markedly and persistently unstable self-image or sense of self

   - Until Steven's friend did a background check, it was unaware. However, Chip was terminated from multiple cable companies where he had different alias from television shows such as Ricky Ricardo, and Larry Tate. Even though that Chip believes he is a great friend, he has broken into Steven's house and disrupted his privacy by wiring cameras in Steven's home and using them as blackmail.

4. Impulsivity in at least two areas that are potentially self-damaging (e.g., spending, sex, substance abuse, reckless driving, binge eating).

   - It is not real clear, however, there were scenes of him drinking alcohol and what seems to him being either drunk or drugged. In addition, by hiring the prostitute for Steven, Chip knows how to get women, whether it is through giving free cable or something else.

5. Recurrent suicidal behavior, gestures, threats, or self-mutilating behavior

- ◦ Chip displays few suicidal behaviors. However, Chip did imply that he should end his life when the police shined the light on him, and then plunged to what he thought would be his death. Chip survived the fall.

6. Affective instability due to a marked reactivity of mood (e.g., intense episodic dysphoria, irritability, or anxiety usually lasting a few hours and only rarely more than a few days)

- ◦ When Chip first met Steven to install his cable, he was very annoyed that Steven took a moment to answer the door, and then switched his mood to friendly when he asked Steven to hang out with him. Another instance occurred when Steven did not reply to Chip's 13 messages on the machine, until Steven's cable went out and then was upset at the fact that Steven only called when he needed something. Chip displayed signs of depression or dysphoria when he was telling Steven that no one ever asked his name until then.

7. Chronic feelings of emptiness

- ◦ Chip appears to feel empty from an early age as he lives in a neglectful home. There is no father present and a mother who goes out to happy hour in search of a man. In his adult age, Chip feels empty because no one takes the time to ask for his name let alone befriend him.

8. Inappropriate, intense anger or difficulty controlling anger (e.g., frequent displays of temper, constant anger, recurrent physical fights)

- ◦ Frequent temper outbursts and anger along with fights are seen throughout Chip's behavior towards Steven. Chip has temper tantrums when Steven does not want to be his friend. Chip becomes angry and vengeful when Steven says he does not want to be his friend anymore. Chip shows erratic when he plays basketball with the guys and begins to name call and play "street ball" after someone runs into him. Chip has two physical fights, one with Steven at the Medieval Times where he comes at Steven with a sword, a joust, and a mace. The second occurrence is where he waits for Robin's date in the bathroom and assaults him until he has to be rushed to the hospital.

9. Transient, stress-related paranoid ideation or severe dissociative symptoms

Accuracy of Portrayal

I believe that Chip matches most of the criteria of this disorder unquestionably if not perfectly. His uncontrollable anger issues, feelings of emptiness, unstable interpersonal relationships, and his abandonment issues seem to make him fit the criterion of this disorder. Some things that need to be addressed is the few instances of self-mutilation to himself, including impulsivity, and suicide behaviors. More examples of suicidal tendencies needed to be seen in order to accurately diagnose him with Borderline Personality Disorder. In the movie, Chip only has the one instance of self-harm, which was the attempted suicide, and although Chip portrays himself to know the prostitute, he never mentions that he himself has had personal encounter with her, nor does it ever show that Chip was sexual impulsive. With some of the criteria still uncertain, Chip does fit eight out of the nine characteristics.

Treatment

To accurately diagnose Chip with BPD, He would be given the Diagnostic Interview for Borderline Patients Test, the Structured Clinical Interview (SCID-II) and the Personality Disorder Beliefs Questionnaire (PDBQ). For treatment, the best thing available is the Dialectical behavior therapy. In this therapy, it is broken down into three focuses, which would help Chip survive and build a meaningful life by helping him to balance change and accepting his life's situations. First, life-threatening or harmful situations are addressed in Chip's life. This would include self- harm from self-mutilation or attempted suicide; each instance would be dealt with accordingly. Then, Chip would be gently pushed to experience emotions that are painful for him. Pushing Chip to experience intense emotions head-on is a type of exposure with response prevention therapy. As Chip faces his toughest emotional outbreaks with different situations, Chip's anxiety levels will eventually decrease. The decreased anxiety will allow Chip to experience those situations again only without the emotional outbreaks and anxiety. Lastly, Part three addresses living problems. Although it is unclear in the movie of Chip's living conditions, this portion of the DBT will help Chip feel complete as a person. By feeling complete, Chip would be able to deal with the feelings of "emptiness" and the imagined fears of being abandoned. Once Chip is able to cope with these feelings, he will be able to identify when these feelings are beginning and be able to recognize that they are not real. By being able to identify these feelings, Chip will be able to control his outbursts of anger and mood swings.

Video: Chip the Cable Guy – A Case Study in Borderline Personality Disorder

- https://youtu.be/1R-EdiEB1RU

CC licensed content, Shared previously

- Abnormal Psychology: An e-text!. **Authored by**: Dr. Caleb Lack. **Located at**: http://abnormalpsych.wikispaces.com/. **License**: *CC BY-NC-SA: Attribution-NonCommercial-ShareAlike*

Intermittent Explosive Disorder

Name: Matt Foley

Source: Saturday Night Live (TV series, early 1990s)

Background Information

Matt Foley is a 35 year old, male motivational speaker. Physically he is severely overweight due to his steady diet of government cheese. This may lead to high blood pressure and other health complications. He also seems to have trouble breathing normally, not just during his "rage" episodes. He doesn't speak of any interpersonal relationships, family or other, so family history and his childhood environment are unknown. Matt did admit openly that he is twice divorced and lives in a van down by the river, and he is very unsatisfied with these two facts. His social skills are very awkward. When he is around people he is loud and generally awkward, either not understanding social cues or (more likely) ignoring them. He becomes very physical with others, lifting them, invading "personal space" and so on. One episode he talked about began with shaking children to "drive his point home" that Santa wasn't real (during this episode he was being paid to dress as Santa at The Mall. At time of evaluation he had been on a coffee binge, drinking it for four hours straight. With the exception of his coffee spree there is no evidence or admittance of harder drug use. He has little to no coping skills, often reverting to yelling to relieve tension. He generally frightens people with his behavior. And while his goal in life is to not live in a van by the river (and convincing young kids that they don't want that, too) he seems unable to help himself in achieving that goal.

Description of the Problem

Matt Foley's personality is off-setting. While he can seem overly enthusiastic, it is a façade to hide his short temper. His irritability is evidenced in all his mannerisms, from his constant fidgeting to the way his voice grows louder the more irritated he becomes. He constantly has to adjust his pants and shake out his arms to get rid of his temper "tingling" in his arms. He is very short with people who think differently than he does, choosing to be verbally demeaning instead of allowing them their own opinions. This is costing him his audience when he gives speeches and not allowing him to form connections. Not being able to make positive relationships is harming his work performance and not allowing him to advance on to higher positions. Higher positions would mean a pay increase and allow him to move into a more permanent habitation (such as an apartment or a house).

His explosive nature has also led him to destroy other individual's property. While at a house for a job he annihilated a coffee table in the living room. He was sorry after the fact, but could not seem to say anything other than "whoopsie." He also once forcefully suggested he move in with another person to set them on the right path. During another episode he yelled at a mother to "shut your cake hole!" and he promptly destroyed a Christmas scene set at The Mall. Yet another episode he discussed involved him interviewing a highly respected comedian/talk show host (Conon O'Brien). The interview included Matt yelling insults, such as threatening to use the studio's curtains to "wipe (his) rear end with (them)." His episodes last about 6 minutes (specifically 5 minutes and 49 seconds) and occur sporadically.

Diagnosis

Diagnosis is Intermittent Explosive Disorder, DSM-IV 312.34. Matt clearly shows an inability to control his impulses. His episodes last less than a half hour at time and usually result in a physical altercation or destruction of property. They are also grossly uncalled for as Matt loses control "at the drop of a hat." His actions are neither planned nor used for personal gain, other than to relieve his anger. Having no history of drug abuse or suggestion of family history of mental health, it can be safely assumed that Matt is not under the influence of anything other than his own unchecked rage. That is, his actions are not accounted for by any other mental disorder or substance abuse. Since Matt is divorced he may have some unresolved anger issues, or he may have had a tense marriage where it was not unusual for him to go into episodes. Matt also says he is remorseful for the destruction of property, proving he does have a sense of what he's doing is wrong. Similar episodes have occurred before, one time involving public property at The Mall, the other involving verbal abuse during an interview with a well-known comedian Conan O'Brien.

Accuracy of Portrayal

Intermittent Explosive disorder is an impulse disorder that is specifically a lack of restraining anger and aggression. Statistically men are more likely to have IMED than women. The episodes are grossly out of proportion to the situation, be it a yelling match or breaking something. These episodes are also not accounted for by another mental disorder, drug use, or by any physiological condition (such as brain injury, dementia, Alzheimer's, and so on.). Matts episodes are short in duration (generally no longer than 20 minutes), which is consistent with the diagnosis for IMED. The breaking of the table and Christmas scene could also be accidental rather than purposeful, but it's still accounted for by his episode. His "drug use" (coffee and espresso binge) is atypical, but not unheard of. His aggressive tendencies are interfering with his life and relationships, and will continue to do so until he gets a handle on his behavior. In all these ways, Matt is a perfect example of an individual who suffers with IMED.

Treatment

As mental health professionals would agree, there are a few options for Matt Foley. Empirically supported treatment for Matt could include drug therapy such as β-Blockers, α(2)-agonists, anti-anxiety, anti-convulsion, antidepressants, antipsychotics, and mood stabilizers. Drug therapy can be used with or separate from cognitive behavioral therapy. In cognitive behavior therapy individuals identify stressors that lead to episodes and how to cope or avoid them. Other forms of treatment include social skills training, in which the individual works on improving their interpersonal skills. Although social skill training is a form of treatment it is less effective than drug and/or cognitive behavioral therapy.

Matt Foley would benefit most from the combination of drug therapy and cognitive behavior therapy. Matt would be a good candidate for β-Blockers, because they specifically block the β 1 and 2 receptors that stimulate the body into "fight or flight" mode. They would also help to lower his blood pressure, which may further help to reduce his stress and anxiety by strengthening his health. In cognitive behavior therapy he and his therapist would work specifically on ways to control his anger or use it in more constructive ways. One strategy for controlling his anger would be to record specific instances that send him into episodes. Knowing these situations would allow him and his therapist to work on ways to reduce his rage should these situations ever occur again.

Name: James Howlett (Wolverine), Logan, formerly Weapon Ten, Death, Mutate #9601, Jim Logan, Patch, Canucklehead, Emilio Garra, Weapon Chi, Weapon X, Experiment X, Agent Ten, Canada, Wildboy, Peter Richards, many others, but primarily claiming Logan as his primary name.

Source: Marvel Comics (As Wolverine, cameo) Incredible Hulk #180 (1974), (as Wolverine, fully) Incredible Hulk #181 (1974), (as Patch) Marvel Comics Presents #1 (1988), (as Weapon X) Marvel Comics Presents #72 (1991), (as Death) Astonishing X-Men #1 (1999)

Background Information

Logan is more than one hundred years of age, although he has the appearance and health of a man roughly 35-40 years of age. Born James Howlett, he was a frail boy of poor health from Alberta, Canada during the late 19th Century. He was the second son of wealthy landowners John and Elizabeth Howlet. His mother, who was institutionalized for a time following the death of her first son, John Jr., in 1897, largely neglected James. Elizabeth later committed suicide. He spent most of his early years on the estate grounds and had two playmates that lived on the Howlett estate with him: Rose, a red-headed girl who was brought in from town to be a companion to young James, and a boy nicknamed "Dog" who was the son of the groundskeeper, Thomas Logan. James assumed the name "Logan" while living incognito following a violent incident involving his companion Rose, who was consequently wrongly accused of murder. Logan is a veteran of several conflicts and wars including World War II. He has served in covert government operations working under the title Weapon X as an assassin. Logan worked as a miner in British Columbia for a time and was highly regarded as being a hard worker. He has also worked as an adventurer, instructor, bartender, bouncer, spy, government operative, mercenary, soldier, and sailor. Logan has an almost immunity to the intoxicating effects of alcohol, but no evidence of use or abuse of any other substances is apparent. Logan tends to make friends easily enough, but due to his violent and tragic past has difficulties with trust. Logan's romantic relationships are often complicated and tedious, frequently becoming situations where either his love cannot be displayed, or his love is for someone committed to someone else. Logan's difficulty with interpersonal relationships as well as his propensity toward violent outbursts often causes him to withdraw and spend a lot of time alone. This isolation often serves as a means of coping.

Description of the Problem

Logan has a strong and often forceful demeanor. He often engages in aggressive competitive behaviors, as well as being somewhat of a bully when in certain company. He seems to be tender toward women, but sees other males as either competition, or subordinates. Logan shows a generally hostile disposition, as well as a tendency to engage in aggressive forms of humor in the limited instances in which he interacts with others. When engaged in conversation, he is often abrupt and bordering on rude.

Logan's (Wolverine's) skeleton includes six retractable one-foot long bone claws, three in each arm, that are housed beneath the skin and muscle of his forearms. Logan can, at will, release these slightly curved claws through his skin beneath the knuckles on each hand. This ability coupled with Logan's short fuse and incredible physical ability often makes him dangerous.

Diagnosis

Intermittent Explosive Disorder, DSM-IV 312.34. Logan displays a number of impulsively violent outbursts, many of which last only a short time, but are extremely severe and destructive. Logan often displays violent outburst of temper, threatening others, even peers with physical harm, as well as considerable destruction of property both with his claws as well as other means. Logan is quick to anger and aggress and is often severe in his reactions to perceived threats to his safety. During one of his altercations with another male from his past, Logan inadvertently killed his childhood companion, Rose, by impaling her with his claws. One form of aggression, known as *amok*, is characterized by acute, unrestrained violence, typically associated with amnesia. This is primarily seen southeastern Asia but has also been seen in Canada and the United States. Unlike IED, *amok* does not occur frequently but in a single episode. One reason for suspecting that Logan may be suffering from this is due to two factors:

1. Logan has extreme memory loss due to having had his memories "wiped" from his consciousness after his service as Weapon-X

2. Logan possesses memories of being a Samurai in Japan. Perhaps during his travels in the Far East, he found himself in southeastern Asia.

The only reason for mentioning this is due to Logan's chronological age being much longer than that of a non-mutant human.

Accuracy of Portrayal

Being male, Logan is more at risk of having developed IED. IED is one of the impulse-control disorders that involve the inability to control impulses of anger, or rage and often results in violent physical outbursts or violent verbal attacks. Logan definitely displays these tendencies. Logan doesn't seem to have any other mental disorders such as schizophrenia, bipolar, affecting him, however during the process of "wiping" his memory, a degree of brain injury may have occurred. Logan's extremely reactive nature and his severity during his explosive episodes is often maladaptive and causes him to have to be transient in nature, drifting from location to location, rarely settling down into one specific location. His romantic relationships have been complicated by his angry outbursts as well. Enemies he has made in the past due to his mercenary work and covert government work have caused the death of at least one potential life mate.

Treatment

Since few controlled studies exist involving treatment of IED, Logan would probably benefit from cognitive behavioral therapy (CBT), helping him to identify triggers for his outbursts. Teaching him coping skills such as diaphragmic breathing, counting, and also the keeping of a stress and incident journals to help him identify what triggered specific incidents and what to do to avoid them or possibly handle them differently if a similar situation arises. Anger management and group therapy could also be effective as well. If these were unsuccessful, or only marginally effective, then the use of certain medications such as anti-convulsion, anti-anxiety, mood regulators, anti-depressants, antipsychotics, beta-blockers, alpha (2)-agonists, or phenytoin could be indicated.

Narcissistic Personality Disorder

Name: Jenna Maroney

Source: 30 Rock (Television series, mid 2000s)

Background Information

Jenna Marony is a forty-three year old woman, who was born Ystrepa Grokovitz on February 24, 1969. She grew up in Bakersfield, CA. Her father, was a burger server in suburban Santa Barbara. He dumped Jenna's mother, a dental hygienist, for another woman. Jenna still says she will "always be his little girl." After being spurned, Jenna's mother made her sit on every mall Santa's lap in Bakersfield in an attempt to find him. Jenna has a sister who urinated in one of Jenna's eyes when she was little, which causes it to not open all the way. Another sister is deceased. She did not get along with her half-sister, Courtney, who is now deceased. Upon hearing of her sister's demise, Jenna showed no obvious signs of sorrow or grief. Jenna also has a niece, who draws pictures of her Auntie Jenna. Jenna finds the pictures to be offensive, when in fact they are just childlike renderings of Jenna.

During Jenna's teen years, her mother moved what family she had left from California to Florida. Jenna attended high school on a boat, which has subsequently sunk. At the age of 16, Jenna was engaged to a congressman. She has also reportedly dated O.J. Simpson, a music producer, a sniper, a mob boss, and hinted at having been in a three-way relationship with Rosanne and Tom Arnold. Jenna's started singing at a young age, as a distraction for her mom, who was busy shoplifting. Jenna went on to study voice at Northwestern University and also at the Royal Tampa Academy of Dramatic Tricks, where she majored in playing prom queens and murdered runaways. She has been in various films and commercial, and is currently employed as an actress on a television series.

There is no history of substance use, however, there is a history of binge eating, but the episode was brief, and Jenna's eating habits have since returned to normal. Jenna is in good health, with no reported concerns.

Jenna seems to have coped with her life difficulties by becoming the "center of attention," and the center of her own universe. Abandoned by her father and used by her mother as a decoy, Jenna possibly feels unloved and rejected. Jenna's inability to empathize with others and sustain lasting relationships with are major weaknesses. She is constantly battling with someone, whether it be a co-worker, a friend or a family member. Currently, Jenna is involved with a transvestite who dresses as Jenna. In fact, Jenna met her lover while participating in a Jenna Maroney Look-Alike Contest, in which Jenna herself only placed fourth. Her new lover won the contest, and they have been intimate since that time.

Description of the Problem

Jenna does not feel she has any problems, other than not receiving the attention and recognition she feels she deserves. Her achievements are not commensurate with her desire to be "worshipped," and adored. Jenna feels she is entitled to special treatment and when this fails to occur within her career or social life, she becomes explosive and stubborn. She has an excessive need for admiration, as evidenced by her choice of careers. She seems to have no empathy regarding others, and on the rare occasions empathy is displayed by Jenna, it is not genuine empathy, but a means to an end. In other words, she fakes empathy to manipulate others, or for personal gain. Jenna repeatedly poisoned a co-worker in the hopes of dating one of the "hot" EMT workers who came to the rescue. Jenna is severely jealous of her co-star in her current television series, and is constantly looking for ways to undermine him. She dreams of unparalleled success and believes she is the most beautiful, talented woman to grace this planet. While Jenna does not see this as a problem, the rest of society fails to agree with her assessment of herself, and this causes much frustration for Jenna. Jenna reacts very unfavorably to even the slightest criticism, as she believes herself to be perfect and unique. If she is criticized, she feels that the person doing the critique, "just doesn't understand her," because they are not as special and wonderful as she.

Diagnosis

Jenna best fits the diagnostic category of Narcissistic Personality Disorder (301.81)

- A pervasive pattern of grandiosity (in fantasy or behavior), need for admiration, and lack of empathy, beginning by early adulthood and present in a variety of contexts, as indicated by five (or more) of the following:

    - has a grandiose sense of self-importance (e.g., exaggerates achievements and talents, expects to be recognized as superior without commensurate achievements)

    - is preoccupied with fantasies of unlimited success, power, brilliance, beauty, or ideal love (perfect marriage to the perfect spouse)

    - believes that he or she is "special" and unique and can only be understood by, or should associate with, other special or high-status people (or institutions)

    - requires excessive admiration

    - has a sense of entitlement, i.e., unreasonable expectations of especially favorable treatment or automatic compliance with his or her expectations ("You owe me because I'm that good")

    - is inter-personally exploitative, i.e., takes advantage of others to achieve his or her own ends

    - lacks empathy: is unwilling to recognize or identify with the feelings and needs of others

    - is often envious of others or believes that others are envious of him or her

- shows arrogant, haughty behaviors or attitudes

- Other Symptoms:

  - history of intense but short-term relationships with others; inability to make or sustain gen-uinely intimate relationships

  - a tendency to be attracted to leadership or high-profile positions or occupations

  - a pattern of alternating between unrealistic idealization of others and equally unrealistic devaluation of them

  - assessment of others in terms of usefulness

  - a need to be the center of attention or admiration in a working group or social situation

  - hypersensitivity to criticism, however mild, or rejection from others

  - an unstable view of the self that fluctuates between extremes of self-praise and self-contempt

  - preoccupation with outward appearance, "image," or public opinion rather than inner reality

  - painful emotions based on shame (dislike of who one is) rather than guilt (regret for what one has done)

Jenna qualifies for almost every single diagnostic criteria, as outlined in the Description of the Problem and her Background information. There is some overlap with Histrionic Personality Disorder, as Jenna does frequently use her sexuality to gain her desires, however, she fits more of the Narcissistic criteria than the HPD criterion.

Accuracy of Portrayal

The portrayal of narcissism in this character is fairly accurate, although there is some overlap with Histrionic Personality Disorder. One of the deciding factors whether this was NPD or HPD was the fact that Jenna falls in love with a man who dresses as her. Narcissus was also in love with himself and was forever doomed to gaze upon his reflection in a pool of water, until he died. It is said as his boat crossed over into the afterlife, he leaned over to catch on last glimpse of himself in the water. This is the epitome of Jenna. While more males than females are diagnosed with NPD, (7% for males and 4 % for females), Jenna is a prime example of a female narcissist.

Treatment

Narcissists rarely seek treatment, as their perception is that they are "better" than everyone else. If a narcissist does enter treatment, psychotherapy is the recommended course of treatment, and perhaps some group therapy. If group therapy is utilized, clear boundaries should be set as to respecting other people in the group. Prognosis poor.

Video: Jenna Maroney – A Case Study in Narcissistic Personality Disorder

- https://youtu.be/X6jT4YGjmnM

Anorexia Nervosa

Name: Giselle Vasco

Source: *Skinny* by Ibi Kaslik (book, 2004)

Background Information

Giselle Vasco is a twenty-one year old, Caucasian female of Hungarian decent. She was the first born of two daughters after her parents, Thomas and Vesla, immigrated to the United States in the early 1970's to escape the communist repression of their country. Giselle's younger sister Holly is eight years behind her in age but, much like her sister, has a very grounded and intellectual personality. They both stand approximately five feet, eleven inches tall and have a very close relationship. Giselle and Holly are both considered accomplished in their own rights, even at young ages with Giselle enrolled in medical school and Holly being acknowledged as a "stand-out athlete" at her high school. At the present time, Giselle is home from medical school, taking a leave of absence to clear her mind and regroup her life. She is working at a hospital in the mental health ward as a companion to many patients. It is described that, after her first love had left, Giselle became a callous lover who would frequently sleep around – trusting nobody with her heart. This stayed a constant until she met her current boyfriend, Solomon (Sol), who desperately loves Giselle.

Both sisters however, are plagued by the fact that their father had recently passed away due to a heart attack. In the midst of this tragic loss, both sisters struggle in the grieving and coping processes respectively. Giselle and her father always had a rocky relationship that stemmed from a time before she was even born. Thomas questioned the faithfulness of his wife in the frequent suggestions that Giselle may not be his biological daughter. This was an obstacle that was battled through from Giselle's birth up until her father's death-and even after. The relationship between the girls and their mother, however, seems to be solid.

Giselle acknowledges that when she was her sister's age (approximately 14) one of her primary focuses was to discover ways to "be smaller." It is presumed that Giselle, and the entire Vasco family for that matter, were a religious group. At one point, Giselle asks for God's forgiveness after lying to her mother about her weight at the time. Giselle also acknowledges that she would masturbate in upwards of six times a day and would drink only lemon water. In lieu of her desire to "be smaller," Vesla would frequently take Giselle to see the doctor regarding her weight, often against her wishes. There is no mention of a history of drug or alcohol use by Giselle.

Description of the Problem

As mentioned earlier, while in high school, Giselle's mother would constantly bring her to the doctor to check up on her weight. Giselle would do things like put rocks or weights in her pockets to tip the scale at 120 pounds, as opposed to the 95 that she weighed. Her lack of a proper diet surrounds her potential diagnoses. Holly describes her sister's systematical approach to the dinner table as Giselle would figure out ways to clear her plate without digesting a single bite of food (i.e. dropping food on the floor, pretending to use the restroom and flushing portions of her meal). Aside from a lack of food toward her diet, Giselle would only drink lemon water.

Sexually, Giselle is not what you would call repressed. She became very sexually ambiguous after the departure of her first love. Also, as discussed earlier, Giselle would spend much of her time locked in her room, masturbating up to six times per day.

On a relational level, Giselle and her father always struggled with the speculation the she may not be his biological daughter. We go on to discover that this is indeed true. This made it hard for them to ever truly salvage a meaningful father-daughter relationship.

Diagnosis

In my personal opinion, Giselle's diagnosis would be as follows: Axis I, Anorexia Nervosa, Binge Eating/Purging Type (307.1) and Axis IV, Problems with Primary Support Group.

Criteria needing to be met for above Axis I diagnosis as follows (from DSM IV-TR):

1. Refusal to maintain body weight at or above a minimally normal weight for age and height (e.g., weight loss leading to maintenance of body weight less than 85% of that expected; or failure to make expected weight gain during period of growth, leading to body weight less than 85% of that expected).

   - Over the course of years, Giselle would consume an insufficient diet consisting of little or no food and lemon water, putting her at a weight that was below 85 percent than expected for her height. She constantly resists the cautions of her mother and doctor in regard to her weight.

2. Intense fear of gaining weight or becoming fat, even though underweight.

   - Giselle exhibits this behavior in her everyday way of thinking. Even though she is of above average height, she intensely pursues a body weight that is unhealthy for her to maintain. Also, she takes extreme measures to ensure that her body weight stays exceedingly low and, in turn, dangerous to her general well-being.

3. Disturbance in the way in which one's body weight or shape is experienced, undue influence of body weight or shape on self-evaluation, or denial of the seriousness of the current low body weight.

   - Although she is what is considered underweight, Giselle is indifferent to this fact and yearns to continue to lose dangerous amounts of weight. She evaluates herself as being "too big" but seems to have a partial awareness that she is ill-she may not be in denial.

4. In postmenarcheal females, amenorrhea, i.e., the absence of at least three consecutive menstrual cycles. (A woman is considered to have amenorrhea if her periods occur only following hormone, e.g., estrogen, administration.)

   ◦ Symptoms of this nature were not discussed; however details about her sexual history and excessive masturbation are mentioned.

Accuracy of Portrayal

Although it may not be glaringly clear, should the average person read this book, they would find a fairly accurate portrayal of the onset and manifestation of the eating disorder Anorexia Nervosa. I say that it may not be clear, in large part, due to the fact that this work is narrated by two individuals (both sisters) as almost two different stories. Not only is Giselle's case of Anorexia a prevalent point in the novel, but so is the poor relationship between Giselle and her father as well as the family dynamic after their father's death. There were, however, some very accurate descriptions of what behaviors would be exhibited from an individual with this disorder. Her constant dilemma on how to trick those around her into believing she was eating a healthy diet is quite common in individuals with Anorexia. Giselle also references her constant hunger, although she denies it to those around her. Her cold and clammy hands as well as constant fatigue are also associated features of Anorexia that allude to her problem. With that being said, I feel that the book does an exceptional job of portraying an individual with Anorexia Nervosa.

Treatment

In treating Giselle for her disorder, the treatment team would focus their attention around two main goals: (1) To help Giselle gain weight and (2) To address Giselle's psychological and environmental issues. A major step in treatment, as in the treatment of any disorder, would be to make sure that Giselle is aware that she has a problem. The most widely used form of treatment for this disorder is family and group therapy, which cannot be utilized to its full potential should the patient not admit that he/she needs help. In Giselle's case, her sister and mother would play a very significant role in treatment. As a clinician, you would like to see Giselle's family encouraging her on a regular basis, reinforcing the fact that she looks fine the way she is (while eating a normal diet), and that it is not necessary for her to exhibit these unhealthy behaviors. More specifically, I believe that Giselle's sister Holly should be utilized as best as possible during treatment as they have always had a very strong bond and friendship. If anyone would be able to aid in "breaking through" to Giselle about her disorder, I think it would be her little sister.

Self-help groups are also successful in the treatment of those with Anorexia. Treatment for Giselle should include regular group meetings with individuals who have experienced the same negative outcomes in their lives due to the disorder. The thought here is that by discussing the topic of Anorexia among those who have it, Giselle will be afforded the opportunity to become more educated on the subject and, eventually put herself in a position where she is aware of the harm she is causing her body. Over time, between family therapy and self-help group therapy, hopefully a certain sense of cognizance will begin to develop with Giselle in regard to the harm she is causing herself-this will hopefully lead to a change in attitude and eventually behavior.

Video: Giselle Vasco – A Case Study in Anorexia Nervosa

- https://youtu.be/MVBW4l-r2OQ

CC licensed content, Shared previously

- Abnormal Psychology: An e-text!. **Authored by**: Dr. Caleb Lack. **Located at**: http://abnormalpsych.wikispaces.com/. **License**: *CC BY-NC-SA: Attribution-NonCommercial-ShareAlike*

Alcohol Abuse

Name: Lila Blewitt

Source: *Lila: An Inquiry into Morals* by Robert M. Pirsig (book, 1991)

Background Information

Lila Blewitt is a Caucasian female and presumed to be middle aged, although her actual age is unknown. She is currently riding on a sailboat with a man she met the previous night in a bar located along side a river on the East Coast. Lila does not have an occupation. In the past, Lila has been a prostitute as well as a waitress. Lila's mother was critical of her. As a child, when Lila did something good, the mother said nothing; but when she did something bad, her mother mentioned the incident repeatedly. Lila was previously married to a trucker and had a daughter. Her husband and daughter are deceased. Lila's daughter died by smothering in her blanket, and her husband died in a car accident. She likes to dress very provocatively, but with no originality.

Description of the Problem

Lila has very little direction in life, and her mental processes and conversations are very surface. She dresses overtly sexual, and believes that with enough alcohol, relations with men are reduced to pure biology where they belong. Lila does not moderate her intake of alcohol, and drinks often and to the point of complete intoxication. She takes medication called Empirin whenever she begins to sense a psychotic episode is coming on. These episodes appear to be induced by social stressors, such as disagreements or arguments. Lila also suffers from severe delusions, odd ideations, and catatonia. Lila's medication was stolen from her purse; she ended up lost in New York City and thought that taking all of her clothes off would be a good idea because then somebody would "see" her and help her. Lila's social life greatly suffers due to impulsively rapid shifts between seeing individuals as either a rescuing friend, or as an enemy out to get her. Also while she was lost in New York City, Lila ordered three rum and cokes, although she didn't end up being able to pay for them, and then thought that her childhood pet and dead husband were giving her directions on how to get back to the sailboat she had been riding on. Once back at the sailboat, Lila saw a doll floating in the river and believed it to be a human baby. Also at times, Lila's speech is highly disorganized, described by the author as "word salad."

Diagnosis

The diagnosis for Lila that seems to fit appropriately is Schizophrenia, Disorganized Type (295.10) with a comorbidity of alcohol abuse (305.00).

A. To be diagnosed with schizophrenia, two or more of the following characteristics must be present:

1. Delusions

2. Hallucinations

3. Disorganized speech

4. Grossly disorganized or catatonic behavior

5. Negative symptoms, i.e., affective flattening, alogia, or avolition

Lila displayed all of these characteristics throughout the book.

B. For a significant portion of the time since the onset of the disturbance, one or more major areas of functioning such as work, interpersonal relations, or self-care are markedly below the level achieved prior to the onset.

- Lila was unable to hold down a job, drifting through life without goals or direction. Her interpersonal relationships suffered drastically. Everywhere that she went, people would end up wanting to get and stay away from her. Lila was unable to maintain stability in her life, with no home or occupation. She had to rely on others to take care of her.

C. Continuous signs of the disturbance persist for at least 6 months. This 6-month period must include at least 1 month of symptoms that meet Criterion A and may include periods of prodromal or residual symptoms.

- The author indicated from conversations with a childhood friend of Lila's that she had suffered from the above stated symptoms throughout her adult life.

D. Schizoaffective Disorder and Mood Disorder With Psychotic Features have been ruled out because either (1) no Major Depressive, Manic, or Mixed Episodes have occurred concurrently with the active-phase symptoms; or (2) if mood episodes have occurred during active-phase symptoms, their total duration has been brief relative to the duration of the active and residual periods.

- Lila did not seem to display symptoms of mood disorders. Other than during a psychotic episode, Lila's mood remained relatively stable throughout the book. She did not display depression, but she did display catatonia. Any time that she displayed anxiety, it would be involving a break from reality.

E. The disturbance is not due to the direct physiological effects of a substance or a general medical condition.

- Lila's substance abuse involved heavy drinking, but her above symptoms were never consequences of being under the influence of alcohol at that time.

F. If there is a history of Autistic Disorder or another Pervasive Developmental Disorder, the additional diagnosis of Schizophrenia is made only if prominent delusions or hallucinations are also present for at least a month.

- There is no history of either of the above listed disorders present in Lila.

To fit the Diagnostic Criteria for 295.10 Disorganized Type, the following criteria are met:

1. Disorganized speech.

   ◦ The author would describe the way Lila conversed as being "word salad." It would make sense to Lila, but not to the listener.

2. Disorganized behavior.

   ◦ Lila got lost in New York City because she was not paying attention to the direction that she was walking in, nor the direction that she would need to later return. She also thought that it would be acceptable to take her clothes off in order to get somebody to "see" her. She often needs others to rescue her from situations that she got herself into.

3. Flat and inappropriate affect.

   ◦ During a psychotic episode, Lila's affect became completely flat. She would not speak or respond to any outside stimulus for an entire day.

To fit the diagnosis for Alcohol Abuse (305.00)

1. Recurrent substance use in situations in which it is physically hazardous and continued use despite having persistent or recurrent social or interpersonal problems caused or exacerbated by the effects of the substance

   ◦ Lila would drink to the point of being intoxicated in public places where she did not know anybody, when she did not have the money to pay for the drinks, and did not even know her own whereabouts. As a result of her behavior while intoxicated, Lila would behave inappropriately and aggressively towards others. These behaviors would cause Lila to be an outcast in her social circle.

2. The symptoms have never met the criteria for Substance Dependence for this class of substance

   ◦ Lila does not meet the criteria for Substance Dependence. Although drinking alcohol did cause Lila the above stated problems, Lila did not drink as frequently as is required to be considered dependent.

Accuracy of Portrayal

The average person reading this book would see an accurate portrayal of a person whose behavior qualifies for alcohol abuse. The author does not make Lila out to be dependent on alcohol, but he does show how Lila over-consumes alcohol to the point of causing her problems in her social life, as well as putting herself in hazardous situations. The comorbidity of her alcohol abuse with her schizophrenia is also an accurate portrayal for someone with less severe schizophrenia, occurring in episodes rather than ongoing. The book also illustrates for the reader accurately what may be going on inside the mind of a person during a schizophrenic episode as well as while abusing alcohol.

Treatment

To treat Lila's alcohol abuse, the first step would be to provide treatment for her Schizophrenia. No long term success for treatment of her alcohol abuse could occur while Lila was suffering from a psychotic disorder without treatment. Once Lila was in treatment for Schizophrenia, you would then address her alcohol abuse. Lila would have to realize and admit that she was abusing alcohol. The fact that alcohol abuse was causing social problems for Lila as well as putting herself in dangerous situations could be presented to Lila so that she would correlate alcohol abuse with its negative consequences. While her treatment for schizophrenia could involve medication, it would be important to look at possible drug interactions before prescribing her any medication to help her stop drinking. Next, Lila could start cognitive behavioral therapy to explore her emotional reaction to events in her life and her ensuing behaviors and their further consequences, while emphasizing alcohol abuse throughout this process. Last, Lila could attend Alcoholics Anonymous to learn more about alcohol abuse and to have a social environment that is supportive of her while she is learning to change her behaviors involving alcohol abuse.

Panic Disorder without Agoraphobia

Name: Tony Soprano

Source: *The Sopranos* (Television series, 1999-2005)

Background Information

Tony was born of Italian descent on August 24, 1960 and is male. At time of symptoms Tony was 39 years of age. Tony Soprano declares himself to be in the "waste management" business but is actually involved in criminal activity. The Tony is the *capo* in the Dilteo crime family. The duties included with this occupation are collecting "loans" and "persuading" people to pay back money that was "loaned" to them. These "persuasions" include physical attacks as well as other forms of violence. Tony has the added responsibility to attempt to keep peace between him and other members of the organization. Tony is in relatively good health for a man his age, but is noticeably overweight. Tony's family mental health is very stressful. Tony has stressful relationships with his wife and work associates. An especially stressful and dysfunctional relationship with the mother is also present. Tony has a history of alcohol and tobacco use. Major life difficulties include stress from work and problems from aging mother. Tony displays poor coping skills, often resorting to anger and aggression. The use of alcohol and promiscuous relationships are used as escaping behaviors.

Description of the Problem

Tony has had several episodes of fainting. The first paint attack was described by Tony as a feeling of "ginger ale in the skull". The symptoms Tony experiences during his panic attack episodes include "racing" heart, feeling faint and dizzy, chest pains, and breathing difficulties. Specific problems these symptoms are causing are increased difficulty dealing with demands from his occupation, increased stress with family responsibilities (especially issues involving the future of the Tony's aging mother). Tony is hesitant to admit he is experiencing depression but ultimately does state that he is depressed. Tony became deeply saddened by the departure of ducks he had been caring for. He came to the realization the departure of the ducks symbolized his fear of losing control of his family, job, and life in general.

Diagnosis

Diagnosis for the Tony meets criteria for Panic disorder without Agoraphobia, DSM-4 TR code 300.01. Tony has recurrent, unexpected panic attacks and shows worry about the implications of the attack (e.g. losing control). The Tony does not display characteristics of agoraphobia. The panic attacks do not appear to be due to the Tony's use of alcohol, tobacco, or any other pre-existing physical conditions.

Accuracy of Portrayal

The average person watching the portrayal of the Tony would think that panic disorder is only caused by extreme life stress and that the disorder has minimal impact on other aspects of life functioning. The main point for accuracy of portrayal included with this character is he also displays major depressive disorder. This lends to the accuracy of portrayal due to the high comorbidity between panic disorder and major depressive disorder, which is between ten to 65 percent. Also, accuracy of the portrayal comes from the recurrent and unexpected nature of the panic attacks. The inaccuracies from the portrayal include the presentation that panic attacks are only associated with highly stressful life events. Other inaccuracies are the lack of behavioral change and lack of impact on Tony's relationships and social life.

Treatment

The primary source of treatment would be cognitive behavioral therapy. CBT would focus on having Tony face behaviors and thinking patterns that sustain or trigger the panic attacks. This treatment would have Tony realistically ask themselves such questions as, "what is the worst thing that could happen?" For Tony, questions might include, "what is the worst that could happen to my business or family if something were to happen to me?" When Tony is forced to look at the worst outcome and realize that everything would go on if this outcome happened, he learns the source of his panic is less terrifying. Cognitive behavioral therapy might also be supplemented with anti-depressant medicationdue to his co-occuring depressive symptoms. The treatment that is displayed on the show for Tony is a psychoanalytic approach. The American Psychiatric Association does not acknowledge the role of intensive psychoanalytic therapies, including psychoanalysis, in the treatment of panic disorders. However, studies have shown significantly reduced panic symptoms from panic-focused psychodynamic psychotherapy (Barbara et al., 2007). More evidence must be gathered before the treatment presented in the show is recognized as a significant treatment for panic disorder.

Panic Disorder with Agoraphobia

Name: Dr. Helen Hudson

Source: *Copycat* (movie, 1995)

Background Information

Dr. Helen Hudson is a retired criminal psychologist. Her exact age is not given but she is estimated to be in her mid 40's. She is a physically healthy female without a family of her own. No family background is provided in the film. Dr. Hudson is very renowned in her field and often lectures on the subject. She testifies against and profiles serial killers. Dr. Hudson was attacked by a killer she testified against and witnessed him kill one of her police bodyguards. After he was sentenced to jail, he threatened to kill her. This triggered a deep fear and extensive amount of anxiety in Dr. Hudson. Due to her fear and anxiety, Dr. Hudson confines herself to her home and puts in premium security systems to attempt to feel safe. Because Dr. Hudson does not leave her home, her social relationships are confined to her live-in assistant and anonymous online friends she communicates with through chat rooms and games. She is a heavy drinker and takes many pills for her condition. Upon becoming homebound, Dr. Hudson retired from clinical practice and writes books to generate an income.

Description of the Problem

Dr. Hudson was extremely traumatized by her attack and the violence and death she witnessed. After the attack, Dr. Hudson not only retired from her practice but also became totally homebound to avoid contact with anyone who might be a potential serial killer. She feels she is "the pin-up girl" for serial killers. She believes they all know her and want to either impress her with their killings or want to kill her. Dr. Hudson displays perceptions of imminent danger in even simple tasks such as retrieving the newspaper from the hallway in front of her apartment door. When she does attempt to leave the apartment, even in the face of another attack, it brings on such severe panic that she almost becomes unconscious and returns to her home, even though there is an intruder inside. She has nightmares, paranoia, hyperventilates, becomes dizzy, breaks out in sweat, and sometimes will pass out from her panic symptoms. She occasionally hallucinates that she is seeing her attacker. Her panic attacks happen often enough that she keeps anti-anxiety medications in several places in her house for easy access. She has a live-in assistant to aid her in case she passes out during her attacks. Because of her alcohol and pill use, she does not trust her own thoughts or actions from time to time. She is often agitated. In severe stress situations, Dr. Hudson will sometimes laugh inappropriately. Dr. Hudson does not verbally discuss the symptoms she is feeling but she does obviously sweat during her attacks and blurred vision is implied with camera use in the film. She has a deep distrust of others and views herself as superior to others much of the time, especially police officers.

Diagnosis

The diagnosis for Dr. Helen Hudson would be Panic Disorder with Agoraphobia (300.21) and is comorbid with Post-Traumatic Stress Disorder (309.81).

DSM –IV-TR Criteria

A. Both:

1. Recurrent, unexpected panic attacks

2. At least one of the attacks has been followed by one month or more or one or more of the following:

   a. Persistent concern about having additional attacks.

   b. Worry about the implications of the attack or its consequences (e.g. losing control, having a heart attack, "going crazy")

   c. A significant change in behavior related to the attacks

- Dr. Hudson does have recurrent, unexpected attacks and has shown a drastic change in behavior.

B. The presence of agoraphobia

- Dr. Hudson does not leave her home.

C. The panic attacks are not due to the direct physiological effects of a substance (e.g. a drug of abuse, a medication) or a general medical condition (e.g. hyperthyroidism)

- Although Dr. Hudson drinks heavily, her panic is not brought on by alcohol. Instead, it is a coping mechanism that she uses to numb her thoughts or "kick in" her medications.

D. The panic attacks are not better accounted for by another mental disorder such as social phobia (e.g. occurring on exposure to a feared social situation), specific phobia (e.g. on exposure to specific phobic situation), obsessive-compulsive disorder (e.g. on exposure to dirt in someone with an obsession about contamination), post-traumatic stress disorder (e.g. in response to stimuli associated with a severe stressor), or separation anxiety disorder (e.g. in response to being away from home or close relatives).

- Dr. Hudson does display the symptoms of PTSD. It is comorbid to her panic and anxiety. She experienced a life-threatening situation and has recurrent thoughts and dreams about the experience.

Accuracy of Portrayal

The people viewing this film would get a very accurate portrayal of panic disorder with agoraphobia along with post-traumatic stress disorder. Dr. Hudson displays many of the symptoms of all three conditions. Her condition is discussed in the film so it would give the general public the appropriate labels for both panic attacks and agoraphobia. However, PTSD is not discussed and seems to be the root of her problems. It is hard to feel completely confident in this diagnosis without a discussion with the character/author. Many of the symptoms one would feel in a panic disorder need to be verbally expressed. Is she feeling the symptoms of a heart attack? Is she nauseous? Does she feel like she is choking? Do all of her thoughts stem back to her attack? Only the physical symptoms are apparent to the viewer. The agoraphobia is well displayed in the film. She very obviously suffers with the feeling she will be in a situation that will not allow her to escape and will suffer as she did when she was attacked by a killer. Post-traumatic stress disorder is comorbid in this diagnosis. Dr. Hudson's symptoms were brought on by a horrific, life-threatening event. She does have continued thoughts about this situation along with sleep disturbances from the attack.

Treatment

Dr. Helen Hudson would probably be very difficult to treat since she is a psychologist and would have been trained in and practiced treatments for her disorder. By taking an anti-depressant medication, she could hopefully reduce her agoraphobic symptoms and with a benzodiazepine she could control her panic attacks. However, beginning other therapies would a healthier way for her to overcome her issues. Hopefully the medications would not need to be a long-term solution.

Teaching Dr. Hudson some relaxation techniques would help her avoid the thought processes that lead to her panic and agoraphobic symptoms. Practicing and using diaphragmatic breathing and positive meditation when panic symptoms present themselves would be a good coping skill for her. Keeping a thought record to help her recognize what situations or thought processes bring about her attacks would also be helpful. Recognition of detrimental thought processes and the relaxation techniques might help to reduce her panic symptoms and possibly help her avoid them altogether.

Discussing the statistical data of people killed by serial killers would be a starting point in cognitive therapy for Dr. Hudson. She probably has a higher than chance probability of being targeted because she is a famous criminal psychologist and killers might try to impress her by outwitting her, but generally speaking the chance of being killed by a serial killer is low. Next, having Dr. Hudson go through some low-level fear exposures would be necessary. This would include viewing photos of serial killers and viewing documentaries about them.

Next, developing and rehearsing coping responses could be done. Here, intense imagery would be used to help Dr. Hudson imagine her darkest fears and increase her anxiety so that realistic solutions to her fears could be developed. In this case, possibly watching films of people being attacked (fictionally) and what they could have done to prevent or escape the attack.

To begin dealing with her agoraphobia, baby steps could be taken to get here to a place where she feels comfortable leaving the home. First might be opening the door to her apartment and just standing in the doorway. Second, walking out of the door and standing in the hallway. Third standing in the hall with the door to the apartment closed. These steps would continue hopefully to the point where she might even return to the convention hall in which she was attacked.

Ending Dr. Hudson's reliance on alcohol would also have to be dealt with in her therapy. She uses this as a numbing agent or as a kicker to her anti-anxiety drugs. In confronting her issues, it would be assumed she could become less reliant on these substances and live a much more normal life.

Video: Helen Hudson – A Case Study in Panic Disorder

- https://youtu.be/yn_3-x7KhGw

Obsessive-Compulsive Disorder

Character Name: Adrian Monk

Source: *Monk* (Television series, 2002-2009)

Background Information

Adrian is a 51 year old widowed male with no children. Adrian shows no signs of physical ailments or other health problems. He does not have a history of drug or alcohol abuse. He presently works for the San Francisco Police Department as a consultant in homicide cases. Adrian obsesses over high levels of order and neatness and, therefore, has trouble functioning in the outside world. He also self-reports an extensive list of phobias. These symptoms were evident in childhood, but seem to have been exacerbated by the death of his wife. His goals are to extinguish the many phobias he suffers from and to experience some level of happiness. Adrian's social circle consists of a few co-workers who are familiar with his condition.

According to Adrian, his parents were highly strict and very over-protective when he was a child. Adrian's mother has been deceased since 1994. His father abandoned the family when Adrian was 8 years old, and they have only recently begun communicating again. Mental history of the father and mother are unknown. Adrian's brother, Ambrose, suffers from agoraphobia. Ambrose has little social contact and fears leaving his home. Relationships with both his father and brother are strained, but otherwise healthy. No other family mental illness is known.

Though not a family member, an important person in Adrian's life is his assistant. This person assists Adrian in his professional life as well as his personal life. Adrian has had two consecutive assistants that have filled this role for him. This assistant is aware of Adrian's many phobias and does her best to help him avoid stressful situations. For example, she is responsible for always having anti-bacterial hand wipes available to "protect" Adrian from the germs he fears.

Description of the Problem

The greatest catalyst of Monk's behaviors seems to be the tragic death of his wife, Trudy, who was murdered in a car bombing. Adrian was previously employed by the SFPD as a homicide detective but received a psychiatric discharge after the murder of his wife. Following his wife's death, Adrian retreated to his home and refused to leave for three years. With the help of his nurse/assistant, he has reluctantly entered out into the world again, but still suffers from extreme obsessions, compulsions, and fears. Adrian has been unable to solve his wife's homicide, and this causes great emotional distress to him. He often re-visits and obsesses over the case.

Adrian self-reports that he has 312 phobias and continues to accumulate more as time goes on. These phobias range from common fears such as heights or germs to unordinary fears such as, milk or mushrooms. Adrian also suffers from phobias of dentists, sharp objects, vomiting, ladybugs, glaciers, death, snakes, crowds, fear and small spaces. These fears prohibit him from completing everyday tasks such as driving, shopping, and social interaction.

Adrian's work as a consultant for the SFPD requires him to visit crime scenes and evaluate evidence. His photographic memory is especially helpful in his line of work. However, his anxiety often prevents him from being able to use his talents. For example, he arrived at a crime scene that had a burnt out bulb in a chandelier and was unable to work until the bulb had been changed. In another instance, he was unable to work because a police officer's zipper was undone. Adrian is very intent on every aspect of his life being orderly, neat, and clean. He has a habit of cleaning household cleaning appliances, such as vacuums. Balance and symmetry are also important. While working undercover at a bank, he added his own money to every deposit so that the amounts would be whole dollars. He also declined to see a therapist with an amputated arm because he could not get over the asymmetry.

Adrian keeps a meticulous home, with everything in order at all times. He is obsessed with cleaning and cleaning products. He has established certain menus and ways of eating that he also finds organized and acceptable. For example, he will only drink a certain kind of water and cuts his pancakes into squares because he prefers the symmetry. If travel is absolutely necessary, he goes to extreme lengths to pack. Everything must be kept in sealed plastic bags and he will often pack brand new, individually wrapped bedding so he does not have to use something that someone else has used.

Diagnosis

The main diagnosis for Mr. Monk appears to be Obsessive Compulsive Disorder (300.3). This disorder is classified in the anxiety disorders. DMS criteria require that either obsessions or compulsions must be present in order to qualify for the disorder. Both do not have to be present. Adrian appears to have both obsessions and compulsions. To qualify for this disorder, the client must exhibit uncontrolled concern about specific ideas and feel compelled to repeat particular acts of series of acts. Adrian's concern over harmless objects, such as milk, and his compulsion to touch things, such as poles, makes him a candidate for Obsessive Compulsive Disorder.

Other DSM criteria include:

1. The person has recognized that the obsessions or compulsions are excessive or unreasonable

2. If another Axis I disorder is present, the content of the obsessions or compulsions is not restricted to it.

3. The obsessions or compulsions cause marked distress, are time consuming (take more than 1 hour a day), or significantly interfere with the person's normal routine, occupational (or academic) functioning, or usual social activities or relationships.

4. The disturbance s not due to the direct physiological effects of a substance or general medical condition.

Adrian fits this criterion as well. He is intelligent and sees that his behaviors are unreasonable, but is comforted by them anyway. His grooming and cleaning habits often take excessive amounts of time and go beyond what would reasonably be considered clean. He has no other known physical or mental problems that would cause his behavior. There is no history of substance abuse.

Associated features of OCD that are present in Adrian's behavior are avoidance of situations where the objects of obsessions are present, frequent doctor visits, and feelings of guilt/responsibility. Adrian also exhibits the associated features of compulsive acts in order to alleviate anxiety, excessive cleansing or grooming practices, and extreme need for symmetrical aligning of objects.

Accuracy of Portrayal

I think the portrayal of Adrian Monk is an accurate description of Obsessive Compulsive Disorder. Someone watching this series would be able to learn about the irrational fears and the difficulties that Adrian has in overcoming them despite how irrational they are. They would be able to see how his behaviors prohibit him from functioning at an optimal level. Another positive aspect of the show is that it shows Adrian as someone with a mental illness, but he is not vilified or seen as inferior. I think this helps promote the idea that having mental illness is not shameful. One possible problem with the show is how his behaviors are usually seen as quirky but still fuional. For someone suffering from OCD in real life, the consequences can be much more detrimental and debilitating. Also, although he is presented as a gloomy character, real OCD can lead to severe depression in the affected individual. Also, he seems to have more phobias than compulsions. Aside from touching poles, he does not exhibit the repetitive behaviors associated with OCD.

Treatment

Treatment for Adrian could include a prescription for an SSRI medication in order to increase his serotonin production. This could aid in the reduction of depression symptoms, anxiety symptoms, and obsessive-compulsive symptoms. In addition to medication, intense behavioral therapy, specifically exposure therapy with response prevention, is also recommended. This would involve exposing Adrian to the things he fears most (whenever practical and ethical) and compelling him to experience his anxiety until it comes down to a bearable or normal level. In Adrian's case, however, this would be very time-consuming due to the number of phobias he possesses. Due to Adrian's difficulty in establishing interpersonal relationships following his wife's death, grief counseling may also be indicated. Also, his assistant could be included in much of the therapy so that she could be reinforcing appropriate behaviors in his daily life.

Video: Adrian Monk – A Case Study in OCD

- https://youtu.be/0s6fTrSnoIw

Bipolar II Disorder

Name: Casey Roberts

Source: *Mad Love* (Movie, 1995)

Background Information

Casey Roberts is a female high school student in her late teens. Upon arriving at a new high school, she appears to be fairly normal in behavior. However, it is apparent from early on that she has almost no social relationships, or even more, a desire to have any. Aside from a relationship with her parents, who appear supportive and loving, she only has one other relationship which consumes her throughout the movie: her relationship with her boyfriend Matt. This relationship is what drives many of her actions throughout the movie. Her parents say there is no past mental health history in their families. However, they are in denial of her having an actual mental illness and attribute it to her trying to get back at them for controlling her, so the real history may not be reported. No major drug or alcohol use is apparent although casual drinking is seen throughout the movie and nicotine use, especially while in her depressed episode, is also shown. There are no outward health problems visible in Casey. She is a very intelligent girl with a very strong willed personality. However, she does not seem to care too much about asserting that intelligence towards any goals. School is in no way important to her.

Description of the Problem

Although Casey is at some points able of living and functioning normally, she has a past of suicidal behavior. As stated in the Background Information, she has little to no social relationships. However, she does appear to be a fairly friendly person. Probably the largest hindrance on her functioning is her impulsivity. She seems to think that she should do and be able to do whatever she wants when she pleases. Towards the end she also has a tendency towards thoughts that are very sporadic in nature. Casey displays much risk taking behavior without seeing any important consequences that could occur from them. She is also temperamental and very easy to irritate. Delinquent behavior is also presented in her behaviors in the form of truancy and the case of her pulling a fire alarm in the school. She also has very strong thoughts of guilt and states that as punishment for the things she has done to Matt, he should leave her. When the onset of her illness begins to be very apparent, she shows much distractibility and tends to not behave correctly in social situations. Insomnia also is presented along with strange ideas. These ideas could possibly also be symptoms of Schizophrenia such as thinking people are always watching her and out to get her. She believes that she must put cut outs of eyes up around their apartment to protect them.

Diagnosis

The diagnosis for Casey is Bipolar II Disorder (296.89). To reach that diagnosis the following must be true:

1. Presence (or history) of one or more Major Depressive Episodes.

   ◦ Within the movie there is a Major Depressive Episode. Her parents also referred back to the fact that Casey had experienced episodes before as well.

2. Presence (or history) of at least one Hypomanic Episode.

   ◦ A Hypomanic Episode was also included in the movie. Evidence on whether or not she had been through more than one episode of this before was not provided.

3. There has never been a Manic Episode or a Mixed Episode.

   ◦ Casey's symptoms were not severe enough to classify as a Manic or Mixed Episode.

4. The mood symptoms in Criteria A and B are not better accounted for by Schizoaffective Disorder and are not superimposed on Schizophrenia, Schizophreniform Disorder, Delusional Disorder, or Psychotic Disorder Not Otherwise Specified.

   ◦ Although Casey had some odd behaviors that seemed almost similar to ones that would be presented in Schizophrenia or a very similar disorder, they would not be classified as actual delusions. The inconsistencies in her behaviors seem to classify more into Bipolar Disorder.

5. The symptoms cause clinically significant distress or impairment in social, occupational, or other important areas of functioning.

   ◦ Casey's ability to form relationships was greatly affected by her symptoms. Also, distress was definitely seen within social situations. Casey was found in a bathroom with her dress off and hitting the walls and crying.

A diagnosis of a Major Depressive Episode was found by the following:

1. Must include five or more of the following over a 2-week period:

   a. Depressed mood most of the day, nearly every day, as indicated by either subjective report (e.g., feels sad or empty) or observation made by others (e.g., appears tearful). NOTE: In children and adolescents, can be irritable mood.

   b. Markedly diminished interest or pleasure in all, or almost all, activities most of the day, nearly every day (as indicated by either subjective account or observation made by others)

c. Significant weight loss when not dieting or weight gain (e.g., a change of more than 5% of body weight in a month), or decrease or increase in appetite nearly every day. NOTE: In children, consider failure to make expected weight gains.

d. Insomnia or hypersomnia nearly every day

e. Psychomotor agitation or retardation nearly every day (observable by others, not merely subjective feelings of restlessness or being slowed down)

f. Fatigue or loss of energy nearly every day

g. Feelings of worthlessness or excessive or inappropriate guilt (which may be delusional) nearly every day (not merely self-reproach or guilt about being sick)

h. Diminished ability to think or concentrate, or indecisiveness, nearly every day (either by subjective account or as observed by others)

i. Recurrent thoughts of death (not just fear of dying), recurrent suicidal ideation without a specific plan, or a suicide attempt or a specific plan for committing suicide.

- Casey presented symptoms a, d, g, and i.

2. The symptoms do not meet criteria for a Mixed Episode.

   ◦ Her symptoms were not presented as both Manic and Depressive on a nearly daily basis.

3. The symptoms cause clinically significant distress or impairment in social, occupational, or other important areas of functioning.

   ◦ Distress and impairment were definitely apparent in social situations. The example of the bathroom scene previously mentioned demonstrated this.

4. The symptoms are not due to the direct physiological effects of a substance (e.g., a drug of abuse, a medication) or a general medical condition (e.g., hypothyroidism).

   ◦ No drugs were being used besides nicotine and no other stated medical condition was present.

5. The symptoms are not better accounted for by Bereavement, i.d., after the loss of a loved one; the symptoms persist for longer than 2 months or are characterized by marked functional impairment, morbid preoccupation with worthlessness suicidal ideation, psychotic symptoms, or psychomotor retardation.

   ◦ No loved ones were lost; the symptoms had been reported for over 2 months and she had attempted suicide numerous times.

A diagnosis of a Hypomanic Episode was found according to the following:

1. A distinct period of persistently elevated, expansive, or irritable mood, lasting throughout at least 4 days, that is clearly different from the usual non-depressed mood. It is characterized as a period of increased energy that is not sufficient or severe enough to qualify as a Manic Episode.

    ◦ Casey's mood was elevated while they were traveling and she was in her Hypomanic Episode. The severity of it would not classify as a Manic Episode however.

2. During the period of mood disturbance, three (or more) of the following symptoms have persisted (four if the mood is only irritable) and have been present to a significant degree:

    a. inflated self-esteem or grandiosity

    b. decreased need for sleep (e.g., feels rested after only 3 hours of sleep)

    c. more talkative than usual or pressure to keep talking

    d. flight of ideas or subjective experience that thoughts are racing

    e. distractibility (i.e., attention too easily drawn to unimportant or irrelevant external stimuli)

    f. increase in goal-directed activity (either socially, at work or school, or sexually) or psychomotor agitation

    g. excessive involvement in pleasurable activities that have a high potential for painful consequences (e.g., engaging in unrestrained buying sprees, sexual indiscretions, or foolish business investments)

        ▪ Casey presents symptoms b, c, e, and g within her Hypomanic Episode.

3. The episode is associated with an unequivocal change in functioning that is uncharacteristic of the person when not symptomatic.

    ◦ She seemed to function almost normally when the episode was not happening. When she started presenting symptoms, her level of functioning obviously decreased.

4. The disturbance in mood and the change in functioning are observable by others.

    ◦ Like previously stated, her changes were observable.

5. The episode is not severe enough to cause marked impairment in social or occupational functioning, or to necessitate hospitalization, and there are no psychotic features.

    ◦ Her Hypomanic Episode did not strike Matt as "scary" or needing help immediately like her Depressive Episode. No hospitalization was seen as necessary.

6. The symptoms are not due to the direct physiological effects of a substance (e.g., a drug of abuse, a medication, or other treatment) or a general medical condition (e.g., hyperthyroidism).

    ◦ No drugs were being used besides nicotine and no other stated medical condition was present.

Accuracy of Portrayal

Watching the portrayal of Casey would give a person a fairly good look into Bipolar Disorder. Most people label someone as "bipolar" when really they are just having mood swings or maybe suffering from Cyclothymic Disorder. This idea of such rapid switching is not accurate. Although Casey did have her moments of sudden anger or happiness, that can be accounted for by simply an experience she had or something that was said. Simple reactions like this are very common. However, her episodes as portrayed were seen as changing over periods of time, not just in an instant, giving the watchers a pretty good insight on the disorder. In the film, Casey's mother stated that Casey suffered from depression. This may have influenced watchers to disregard her Hypomanic symptoms. Overall, the audience would get a fairly good look into the actual life of a person with Bipolar Disorder.

Treatment

When Casey arrived for treatment, a medical work up would occur to make sure the disorder was accurately diagnosed. This would also allow knowledge of the current episode, suicidal thoughts, and hopefully more family history. Casey would probably then be prescribed lithium carbonate. Because of the potency of this drug, her dosage would need to be very closely monitored. Therapy would also be a very useful tool for Casey's treatment. Cognitive behavioral therapy would be a good start to help her deal with her emotions and stress. Therapy would also help Casey to fully understand Bipolar Disorder and to know in the future when an episode may happen. Likewise, education would be essential for her parents. Helping them understand what exactly is happening with Casey and to recognize her episodes would be very beneficial.

Oppositional Defiant Disorder

Name: Stewie Griffin

Source: *Family Guy* (Television series, 1999 – Present)

Background Information

Stewie Griffin is a Caucasian male who is presumed to be one years old, although he may be four to five years old because in later episodes he attends preschool. Stewie is unemployed but shows a mastery level of physics and mechanical engineering. He has designed such things as mind control devices, weather control, fighter jets, and teleportation devices. Although there are not any known distinct physical illnesses, abnormalities, or disorders currently within Stewie Griffin, there are observable health concerns. The patient displays unprovoked hostility towards others, constant disobeying of parental rules, is extremely vengeful and vindictive, and easily loses his temper quite frequently. Stewie currently lives with his parents, Peter and Lois Griffin. Stewie's father, Peter Griffin shows observable symptoms of mild mental retardation. This is evident when he took an IQ test in one of the episodes and scored a 70. It is also observed that Stewie's parents exhibit a strong sense of control over his life, such as scheduling play dates for him to go on, toys he can/can not play with, and what/when, he can eat. Stewie exhibits strong introversion in social relationships. He does not have close relationships with anyone outside of his immediate family. This is due to the fact that Stewie sees his peers as obstacles in his path toward world domination. Because of this, he frequently kills off the lesser characters with tanks, guns, and other assorted weaponry. There have not been patterns of consistent alcohol usage by Stewie, but he has excessively used alcohol on occasion. This is particularly problematic, as any type of alcohol usage by a one year old can severely inhibit brain development. Stewie's goal is to attain world domination by first killing his mother, who he fears will stand in his way. All of Stewie's daily activities are designed to accomplish these two goals by creating weapons such as rocket launchers, engaging in violent criminal activities, carjacking, loan sharking, and forgery. Other weaknesses that Stewie displays are his stresses of infant life, such as teething and eating his vegetables.

Description of the Problem

Stewie Griffin currently displays a multitude of symptoms indicative of oppositional defiant disorder. He displays disobedient actions towards authority figures; however, Stewie believes that he is conducting himself in an appropriate manner for his own self-preservation. He also suffers from delusional behaviors such as having conversations with his stuffed teddy bear Rupert. He protects Rupert and will avenge any harm that comes Rupert's way. Stewie deliberately annoys his peers by picking on them and continuously making rude remarks about their appearance or inabilities as a person. He also shows anger and resentfulness towards his mother because he feels that he is wrongly punished for activities he is supposed to carry out for the betterment of himself and world domination. As a result of this, he is also very spiteful and vindictive. For example, in one episodes Stewie loans Brian some money and they contractually agree that payment would be made on a certain date, but Brian does not repay on that date, so Stewie beats Brian with a bat daily until he receives payment. Stewie often uses a scapegoat for his own mistakes. When his attempts to kill his mother fail, he blames her for being unfair and bitchy.

Diagnosis

The diagnosis for Stewie Griffin that fits appropriately is **Oppositional Defiant Disorder (313.81).**

A. To be diagnosed with Oppositional Defiant Disorder a pattern of negativism, hostile, and defiant behavior lasting at least 6 months during which four (or more) of the following are present:

1. Often loses temper
2. Often argues with adults
3. Often actively defies complying with adults' requests/rules
4. Often deliberately annoys people
5. Often blames others for his or her mistakes
6. Is often easily annoyed by others
7. Is often angry and resentful
8. Is often spiteful or vindictive

Stewie Griffin undoubtedly shows more than four symptoms of Oppositional Defiant Disorder, as described in the section "Description of the Problem."

B. Consider a criterion met only if the behavior occurs more frequently than is typically observed in individuals of comparable age and developmental level.

Stewie possesses the ability to talk fluently at age one and interact with people at an intimate social level that is not yet observable in the one year old population. Typical one year olds rely heavily on parental care, where Stewie is significantly more independent than his peers (e.g. taking trips to San Francisco and Rhode Island).

C. The disturbance in behavior causes clinically significant impairment in social, academic, or occupational functioning.

Stewie is significantly impaired in social functioning because he does not develop and nurture his relationships, instead he sees his peers as obstacles towards his goal that he must defeat at all costs. Because of this, he does not have any significant social relationship with anyone outside his immediate family.

D. The behaviors do not occur exclusively during the course of a Psychotic or Mood Disorder.

Characteristics of oppositional defiant disorder can be observed in the patient in all settings and instances throughout his daily activities.

E. If the individual is age 18 years or older, criteria are not met for Antisocial Personality Disorder.

The patient is between the ages of 1-4 years old.

F. There is a recurrent pattern of negativistic, defiant, disobedient, and hostile behavior towards authority figures.

Stewie is in constant confliction with how he is going to succeed in killing his mother and attaining world domination.

G. Occurs outside of normal developmental levels and leads to impairment in functioning.

Stewies behavior is clearly outside of normal development for a one year old, and this leads to impairment in functioning such as developing strategies to kill his mother and take over the world (e.g. making weapons with the purpose of carrying out these goals).

Accuracy of Portrayal

The typical person watching Family Guy would be able to reach the conclusion that the character Stewie Griffin is abnormally developing compared to his average peer. A person with an Abnormal Psychology background would be able to further determine that Stewie showed all the symptoms for Oppositional Defiant Disorder. This is a cartoon character created to break the boundaries of normal development for babies, even to represent the general helplessness of an infant through the eyes of an adult. This show helps illustrate Oppositional Defiant Disorder by successfully creating a character that exemplifies every characteristic of the disorder, and not wavering from season to season. Although Stewie is not an accurate portrayal of the average one year old, he still can be related to children suffering from this disorder. Therefore, Stewie Griffin is an accurate illustration of someone with Oppositional Defiant Disorder.

Treatment

To treat Stewie Griffin, after a full medical examination, it would be best to teach him problem-solving skills as well as parent management training. Problem solving skills would help Stewie learn to solve problems in a logical and predictable manner. The downfall with this strategy is that is time consuming and on average requires 20 sessions. Another effective way to treat Oppositional Defiant Disorder is parent management training. This allows the parents to develop and implement structured management programs at home. This is designed to improve interactions between child and parent. Parents implementing this strategy should positively reinforce good behaviors. A secondary methodology of treating Oppositional Defiant Disorder is to medicate the child using Ritalin. Research has shown children treated with Ritalin who have Oppositional Defiant Disorder, 75% of the children no longer showed symptoms of ODD.

Name: Walker Bobby and Texas Ranger "TR" Bobby

Source: *Talladega Nights: The Ballad of Ricky Bobby* (Movie, 2006)

Background Information

Walker and Texas Ranger Bobby are pre-pubescent males, with an estimated age of 11 and 7, respectively. Neither boy holds a job because of their young age. The Bobby brothers do not display any specific health issues. Walker and Texas Ranger live with both of their parents and their maternal grandfather, Chip. Their father, Ricky, is a famous racecar driver who displays some symptoms of Narcissistic personality disorder, claiming that he is "the best there is," and that he "piss[es] excellence." Their mother, Carley, does not show any observable symptoms of a mental disorder. However, she is very materialistic, markedly aggressive when provoked, and shows extreme devotion to her husband, at least until the promise of better prospect comes along (e.g., she leaves Ricky for Cal when Ricky can no longer race). In other words, their mother is a gold-digger. The family unit is still very much intact – they eat dinner together every night and attend all of Ricky's races together. While the bonds between the family are obviously very strong, Walker and Texas Ranger display many types of defiant and hostile behaviors toward authority figures. Most likely due to their lack of shock and surprise, these behaviors are not typically directed towards their parents. Rather, the Bobby brothers act out to other close adults like both of their grandfathers, Chip and Reese, and their grandmother, Lucy. In fact, the boys' mother and father seem to condone this behavior, claiming that they did not raise "sissies". Walker and Texas Ranger were never portrayed as having done illicit drugs, although they did inquire about a comment that their grandfather Reese had made about possessing marijuana. Besides the problems that they have run into at school due to behavioral issues, the boys do not possess any real life difficulties. They do not have any deeply defined goals either as they are just kids looking to enjoy themselves while they can. Due to their inconsistent and overindulgent lifestyle, Walker and Texas Ranger's coping skills are not very good. They handle less-than-perfect situations with immaturity and anger, often lashing out at whoever they believe will take it. Their weaknesses are handling new, unwanted situations (such as Sunday school) and being polite to adults.

Description of the Problem

Walker and Texas Ranger currently display a multitude of symptoms indicative of oppositional defiant disorder. They are consistently defiant and hostile, spouting out at whomever they believe deserves the criticism or hatred. These two display a constant need to argue and swear, especially to adults. They argue most often with their grandfathers, Chip and Reese, their grandmother, Lucy, and their teachers in school. There is nothing off limits for these boys. Their actions and criticisms are often unnecessary and cruel – usually just for the purpose of upsetting or annoying the adults around them.

Diagnosis

The diagnosis for the Bobby brothers that fits most appropriately is **Oppositional Defiant Disorder (313.81). To be diagnosed with Oppositional Defiant Disorder the following criteria must be met:**

1. A pattern of negativism, hostile, and defiant behavior lasting at least 6 months, during which four (or more) of the following are present:

    a. Often loses temper

    b. Often argues with adults

    c. Often actively defies or refuses to comply with adults' requests or rules

    d. Often deliberately annoys people

    e. Often blames others for his or her mistakes or misbehavior

    f. Is often touchy or easily annoyed by others

    g. Is often angry or resentful

    h. Is often spiteful or vindictive

*Note – Consider a criterion met only if the behavior occurs more frequently than is typically observed in individuals of comparable age and developmental level.

Walker and Texas Ranger meet all criteria for oppositional defiant disorder except for number 5, blaming others for mistakes or misbehavior. They constantly insulted and swore at adults, threw Chip's war medals off of a bridge to make him mad, argued with their teachers, and purposefully peed their pants and refused to take them off just to prove a point. These behaviors are more extreme than those of children at similar developmental levels. Where most children their age might only do these sorts of things once, Walker and Texas Ranger do them all of the time.

1. The disturbance in behavior causes clinically significant impairment in social, academic, or occupational functioning.

The boys do not know how to function in a social setting, repulsing most adults who come into contact with them. The boys do not seem to care what other people think of them. They say mean things, causing adults to react negatively, creating a viscious cycle of disobedience. Academic functioning, although mentioned briefly, is most likely effected. Texas Ranger, specifically, flaunted his bad behavior in the classroom.

1. The behaviors do not occur exclusively during the course of a Psychotic or Mood Disorder.

The characteristics previously described are displayed in many contexts over a lasting period of time. They are not a result of a psychotic or mood disorder.

1. Criteria are not met for Conduct Disorder, and, if the individual is age 18 years or older, criteria are not met for Antisocial Personality Disorder.

Walker and Texas Ranger are approximately 11 and 7 years old, respectively. They did not physically aggress towards others and did not commit any serious crimes.

1. Recurrent pattern of negativistic, defiant, disobedient, and hostile behavior towards authority figures.

The symptoms are constant – they do not vary from day to day. Their disobedience is only in response to authority figures.

1. Occurs outside of normal developmental levels and leads to impairment in functioning.

Most children their ages do not insult, swear, and act out this much. The quality of their interactions are severely inhibited and functioning is impaired.

Accuracy of Portrayal

The average person watching these boys would immediately recognize that there is a significant problem. Walker and Texas Ranger are on the extreme side of disobedience. Most parents would probably be able to relate the problems of these characters to those of their own children, only to a much lesser degree. They would learn that Oppositional Defiant Disorder is characterized by defiance, hostility, frequent outbursts of rage, swearing, and disobedience. The portrayal of this disorder is very accurate – the boys' behavior was consistent throughout the movie and did not waiver. Their depiction, in particular, was very extreme as their behavior was observed both at home and in school. The inaccurate aspects of the boys' portrayal would be their display of oppositional behaviors in unfamiliar territory, their lack of temper tantrums or clear frustration with difficult situations, and the ease and rapid pace of change in behavior once their grandmother decided it was time to start acting appropriately.

Treatment

In the movie, Walker and Texas Ranger's grandmother, Lucy, took things into her own hands. She established what she called, "Granny Law," and broke the boys like "wild horses" with community service, yoga, disposal of their weapons, and church attendance.

As a mental health professional, it would be best to first conduct a structured or semi-structured clinical interview to explore fully the family's history, the symptoms that pertain to ODD, and the possible co-morbid problems that can occur as a result of the disorder. The first measure of treatment that should be implemented are Problem-Solving – Skills-Training programs, which involve teaching children how to solve problems in a logical and predictable manner. The only setback of this training is that it is extremely time-consuming, requiring an average of twenty sessions. Another possible treatment is called Parent Management Training. This training teaches parents how to effectively implement contingency management programs at home, allowing both parent and child to better enjoy their interactions by learning how to praise positive behaviors, establishing schedules and sticking to them, and maintaining effective timeouts. This greatly increases awareness in the child as to what is expected of them as well as what will happen if they misbehave.

Autistic Disorder

Name: Arnie Grape

Source: *What's Eating Gilbert Grape?* (movie, 1993)

Background Information

Arnie Grape is a Caucasian male who is 17 years old and is close to turning 18. He does not go to school and spends most of his time with his older brother, Gilbert. Arnie appears to be mentally disabled or developmentally disabled. When Arnie was born, the doctor said he would be lucky if he lived to the age of 10 and when he turned 10, the doctor said he could die at anytime. He has repetitive speech, which it seems as if he is listening but then turns around, and does the same things over again. He engages in very dangerous behaviors but is not aware of how dangerous his behaviors are. For example, he climbed up the water tower in the town and was dangling off the side of the ladder laughing the entire time not knowing how serious the situation was. Arnie lives with his mother, brother, and two sisters. He is very close to his older brother because Gilbert takes care of him. His mother, Bonnie, who has not left the house in seven years, became morbidly obese and depressed when her husband committed suicide. His two sisters, Amy and Ellen, take care of the chores and do all the cooking. Arnie is very friendly to other children in his town but it does not appear that he has very many friends because they do not understand his ways of communication, although there were many children at his eighteenth birthday party. There is an instance when Arnie will not go into the basement because he said "dad is down there" and then he does a hanging motion. Arnie does not appear to take any medication or see a regular physician or psychologist. His feelings are easily hurt because he does not fully understand what people are saying to him. Arnie does not appear to have any goals other than trying to survive.

Description of the Problem

Arnie kills a grasshopper by cutting its head off in the mailbox and a little while after he kills it he gets very upset at himself and is sad that the grasshopper died. He has certain hand movements that he constantly does. He puts his hand to his mouth a certain way when he is in an uncomfortable situation. He has eye twitches and he blinks quite often. Arnie is always running off and hiding from Gilbert or climbing the water tower. Gilbert knows where Arnie is hiding but plays a game and pretends that he does not know Arnie is up in the tree and he thinks Gilbert has no idea where he is. When other people get hurt or when Arnie says mean things to others he thinks that it is very funny and usually laughs hysterically. He is arrested for climbing the water tower and when they put him in the cop car, all he is worried about is the cops turning on the lights and sirens. He is not able to take care of himself. For example, Gilbert puts Arnie in the bath and tells him that he is a big boy and can wash himself. Gilbert leaves and comes back the next morning to find Arnie still in the bathtub. Arnie repeats everything that people tell him to do and what they say in general. After the bathtub incident, Arnie is afraid of any kind of body of water. He gets very upset and starts to hurt himself when he tries to wake his mother and she never wakes up.

Diagnosis

The diagnosis for Arnie Grape that fits most appropriately is **Autistic Disorder (299.00)**. To be diagnosed with Autism Disorder criteria A, B, and C must be met:

1. **A total of six (or more) items from (1), (2), and (3), with at least two from (1), and one each from (2) and (3):**

(1) qualitative impairment in social interaction, as manifested by at least two of the following:
(a) marked impairment in the use of multiple nonverbal behaviors such as eye-to-eye gaze, facial expression, body postures, and gestures to regulate social interaction
(b) failure to develop peer relationships appropriate to developmental level
(c) a lack of spontaneous seeking to share enjoyment, interests, or achievements with other people (e.g., by a lack of showing, bringing, or pointing out objects of interest)
(d) lack of social or emotional reciprocity
(2) qualitative impairments in communication as manifested by at least one of the following:
(a) delay in, or total lack of, the development of spoken language (not accompanied by an attempt to compensate through alternative modes of communication such as gesture or mime)
(b) in individuals with adequate speech, marked impairment in the ability to initiate or sustain a conversation with others
(c) stereotyped and repetitive use of language or idiosyncratic language
(d) lack of varied, spontaneous make-believe play or social imitative play appropriate to developmental level
(3) restricted repetitive and stereotyped patterns of behavior, interests, and activities, as manifested by at least one of the following:
(a) encompassing preoccupation with one or more stereotyped and restricted patterns of interest that is abnormal either in intensity or focus
(b) apparently inflexible adherence to specific, nonfunctional routines or rituals
(c) stereotyped and repetitive motor mannerisms (e.g., hand or finger flapping or twisting, or complex whole body movements)

Arnie meets the criteria for deficits for three out of the four in section one, as described in the section of "Description of the Problem". Arnie does not meet the criteria in (c) because he was always trying to talk to people and make friends with them. Arnie meets all the criteria for section two because he repeats every word a person says to him, he is not able to carry on a conversation with anyone, and he does not seem to have any imaginative friends. He does not meet the criteria in section three listed under (b) because he does not have any specific rituals. Arnie meets the criteria for (a) and (c) because he was obsessed with taking care of a cricket and kept it in a jar and he constantly made the same hand movements when he felt uncomfortable in a situation.

B. Delays or abnormal functioning in at least one of the following areas, with onset prior to age 3 years:

1. Social interaction

2. Language as used in social communication

3. Symbolic or imaginative play

Arnie's history was not given prior to age three but one could conclude that he had delays in all three areas prior to age three.

C. The disturbance is not better accounted for by Rett's Disorder or Childhood Disintegrative Disorder.

Arnie was born with his disorder and has had it his whole life. The doctors did not expect him to live long but he did and everyone called him a miracle child.

Accuracy of Portrayal

The average person watching this movie would probably think this individual is mentally disabled. They would see that he needs a caretaker constantly, that he is not able to communicate well with others and that he is unaware of the outside world around him. These symptoms could be confused with mental retardation or a mental disability. To be specifically diagnosed with autism all the criteria above have to be met. Arnie met all the criteria so if an individual was familiar with or educated on autism they would be able to see an accurate portrayal of autism. This movie lets people see the different types of autism. The types of autism that are usually shown in the media are children who are quiet, reserved and do not talk to anyone, but Arnie was the complete opposite. He was loud, tried to speak to everyone, and was not afraid of most things. Throughout the entire movie, no one talked about Arnie's disorder nor did they label what he had been diagnosed with at birth. *What's Eating Gilbert Grape?* was an accurate portrayal of an individual with autism.

Treatment

First, a full medical and psychological evaluation would be given to Arnie. Arnie would need to be put in a stable setting. Currently he lives with his mother and siblings but his mother is unable to take care of him. He needs an individual to take care of him full time and that individual needs to be specialized in how to take care of his needs. He also needs an individual to work with him on his communication skills, yes, he is past the developmental stage of language, but having that daily practice could help him greatly with his language skills. Arnie also needs behavioral treatment therapy so that he is able to understand how to act in certain situations. He needs more support from his family, everyone needs to be interactive in his treatment and give a helping hand

***

Name: Mandy (Amanda)

Source: *Fly Away* (movie, 2011)

Background Information

Mandy is a 16-year-old Caucasian female who lives at home with her mother Jeanne. Jeanne makes sure Mandy has a consistent daily routine and tries to teach her day-to-day responsibilities. Mandy seems to be making slow progress and then other days she regresses, especially when her mother is not as attentive to her needs. Mandy's mother is a single mother who works from home to be able to provide constant care for her daughter. Her father Peter comes to visit occasionally but is not consistently there. He loves his daughter and tries to interact with her, but cannot seem to without becoming overwhelmed and angry. Mandy goes to a school for the mentally disabled;

however, she does not like the staff and is always acting out to be able to go home. She takes medication twice a day, and has doctor visits regularly. She has a difficult time coping with certain situations and does not know how to control her emotional impulses. Her mother has to hold her and tell her to breathe before she will calm down. Sometimes the outbursts are so bad there is nothing and no one that can control or sooth her. Jeanne also uses singing to calm and refocus her daughter. Mandy is very responsive to this technique and it gets her back down to a controllable level. This is the only form of positive coping shown. Mandy's weaknesses are her short temper, and violent outbursts. This makes it almost impossible for her to be out in public or in a social setting.

Description of the Problem

When a situation arises that a normal 16 year old could handle, she seems to react like a young child. Mandy repeats anything said to her, displaying echolalia. Mandy also has outbursts of aggression. Her aggressive behaviors include biting, pushing, punching, yelling, and running away from her mother. She has overly dramatic emotional swings during these outbursts, where she is very enthusiastic or very upset. While Mandy is experiencing these fits, she becomes physically abusive with objects, throwing them at walls and other objects around her. After the outbursts Mandy encounters, she feels sympathetic only to her mother. She is the only person that she will apologize to for her behavior.

In addition to the above outbursts, almost every night while she is sleeping she yells out, "Mandy's a bad girl, I hate myself!" Her mother will then have to comfort Mandy. When Mandy is in public, her emotions are erratic; she is very enthusiastic or extremely angry. She is not concerned with the reactions of people around her or how her behavior impacts others. She has no impulse control and immediately acts on how she feels. She begins to feel the need for some social interaction, but due to lack of knowledge on how to do so, she is angered by this emotion as well. Her interest in the opposite sex becomes more apparent and at one point in the film she asks her mother if she will ever get married. This shows her longing for human interaction and her capability to understand social interactions. Physically, Mandy's hands are disfigured and are constantly curled. She walks on her toes primarily, and she rocks whenever she feels anxiety.

Diagnosis

Autistic Disorder (299.00) is the criteria that Mandy fits in the DSM-IV diagnostic system. The patient must meet criteria for category A, B, and C to be diagnosed with Autistic disorder.

- **A) A total of six (or more) items from (1), (2), and (3), with at least two from (1), and one each from (2) and (3):**

    - Qualitative impairment in social interaction, as manifested by at least two of the following:

        - Impairments in social interaction may include the following:

            - Pronounced deficits in non-verbal social behavior

                - Lack of eye contact

                - Facial expressions

                - Body posturing

- Gesturing

- Lack of age-appropriate peer relationships

  - Possibly interacting with parts of people

- Absence of spontaneous attempts to share interests or pleasure with others

  - Not pointing to or showing things to others

- Lack of social/emotional reciprocity

  - Lack joint attention
  - Fail to share actively with other's activities or interests
  - Act as if unaware of the presence of others
  - Select solitary activities

- Qualitative impairments in communication including both verbal and nonverbal communication, as manifested by at least one of the following:

  - Delay or absence in spoken language

    - not compensated for by attempts to communicate nonverbally

  - Inability to converse appropriately with others regardless of the presence of speech
  - Odd, stereotyped, repetitive uses of language
  - Absence of imaginative or pretend play
  - There is also a great deal of variability in communication.

    - Ranging from the absence of expressive or receptive language to fluent speech with semantic/inappropriate social uses.
    - Echolalia is the repetition of a phrase heard in the present or the past.

      - Occurs in up to 75% of individuals with PDD who are verbal

        - This characteristic is a cardinal feature of autism.

    - Receptive language continues to impair social communication in that individuals have difficulties in understanding abstractions.

      - Echolalia and receptive language are not utilized in a functional communicative fashion by those with autism.

- Restricted and stereotyped behavioral patterns require at least one of the following criterion:

  - Restricted interests that are abnormally intense

      - Can range from cars and trains to numbers and letters

      - Inappropriately intense or odd in their content

      - Rigid adherence to routines or rituals

      - Repetitive motor mannerisms

          - Opening and closing doors

      - Preoccupation with parts of objects

          - May become overly interested in moving parts of objects

      - Compulsive behaviors

          - Lining up objects in a specific way

          - Slight alterations in routines can cause behavioral outbursts

      - Motor stereotypes

          - Hand or finger-flapping

          - Rocking

          - Spinning

      - Non-specific motor abnormalities

          - Toe walking

          - Unusual hand movements or body postures

      - Continuous course for those with autism however, school-aged children may show improvements in social, play, and communicative functioning, which ultimately can improve further intervention

- **B. Delays or abnormal functioning in at least one of the following areas, with onset prior to age 3 years:**

1. Social interaction

2. Language as used in social communication

3. Symbolic or imaginative play

- **C. The disturbance is not better accounted for by Rhett's Disorder or Childhood Disintegrative Disorder.**

There would be no difficulties in diagnosis for Mandy as being autistic. She meets criteria in A, B, and C. Pertaining to the previously stated problems, Mandy is clearly autistic.

Accuracy of Portrayal

Most people who watch the film would label Mandy as having a mental disability. The average person would not know the criterion that depicts autism. Mandy clearly can be labeled as autistic because she meets all of the above criteria. Most films that portray individuals with autism show them as quiet and socially distant. This movie shows an individual with an extreme case of autism and does a very good job showing how hard it is to live with this disorder. The movie did a good job showing the daily hassles for the family members and how it affects the individuals self esteem. People watching this film got a truthful insight on the life of an individual with autism and would learn about the disorder through the film and Mandy's character. *Fly Away* was an accurate portrayal of an individual with autism.

Treatment

First, Mandy would undergo a full medical and psychological evaluation. She would need to be put in a stable environment and be able to express some sort of responsibility and self support. Mandy lives with her mom and has a good support system but at her age Mandy needs to be able to do things on her own without some supervision and her mother is not trained properly to be able to provide that. Currently she lives with her mother. She needs to have a specialized worker that can help her but not treat her like a child. Developing her self sufficient skills will help her be able to control more of her emotional responses and better understand social interactions. She also needs an individual to work with her on her communication skills. Even though Mandy is past the developmental stage of language, but having that daily practice could help her greatly with her language skills. Mandy will also need behavioral treatment therapy so that she is able to understand how to act in certain situations and control her violent outbursts. With behavioral therapy, more developed communication skills, family support and more accountability Mandy will be able to better cope and function with her disorder.

Dysthymic Disorder

Name: Bill Dauterive, born Gillaume Fontaine de la Tour D'Haute Rive
Source: *King of the Hill* (Television series, 1997-2010)

Background Information

Bill Dauterive is a Caucasian male around the age of 42. This age estimate is based on his friends, including Hank Hill, who has been stated to be 42 years old, and that he was in the same school grade as his friends. Bill is from an upper-class family in Louisiana, around New Orleans. His family is not present very often and the only remaining relative he has is a male cousin. His self-reports of childhood hardships caused by his father could be fictitious because there is no way to verify this. He has almost no family so genetic factors are hard to account for. His cousin is in good shape and healthy. Bill is the opposite. He was told by a doctor that he would become diabetic if he did not change his lifestyle.

He was a high school athlete, nicknamed the "Billdozer". He was very popular, had many friends and even held the school touchdown record. He was drafted into the military his senior year of high school and never graduated. He has remained in the Army and is now a Sergeant barber. He is not particularly poor or wealthy. He is a simple person and does not have any extravagant tastes or interests that he has reported.

He met his wife, Lenore, at a concert. She cheated on him and subsequently they divorced. This is reportedly when the depressive symptoms began appearing. He could not heal from the divorce and claims he still loves her. He became overweight and started losing his hair. His friends Dale Gribble, Jeff Boomhauer, and Hank Hill constantly comment on his depression and try to help him. He has had this core group of friends from a young age. They all live on the same street and get together in the alley to have a beer often. Bill is obsessed with Hank's wife and believes she is the perfect picture of a woman. She is the complete opposite of Bill's ex-wife. Even though he has a core group of these 3 friends, they often make fun of him and sometimes exclude him. He has a very poor sense of hygiene and his house is often very dirty. His friends and their wives often make remarks about this.

He is in a depressive state most of the time. The only time he is out of a depressive state is when he is with a woman (who always later rejects him) or gets very involved in a project, such as an instance where he turned his home into a halfway house. He enjoyed the company and enjoyed being needed, but the occupants took advantage of him and he missed so many days at work the Army almost reported him Absent Without Leave, or AWOL. He clings to women he gets into relationships with very quickly. He will be overly dedicated to the women but they always end up taking advantage of him and ending the relationship. He perceives relationships to be more serious than they are in reality. This behavior inevitably drives them away.

Description of the Problem

Bill often states that he is depressed. This depression has lasted since his divorce, which is estimated to be 7-9 years ago. He is in a depressed state most of the time. Others describe him as very depressed and down. He has some periods of normality, but usually he is just depressed. He believes no one loves him or will love him and gets into relationships in which he is very likely to be rejected. He overeats and does not take care of himself very well. He has a very poor image of himself but does not seem to care enough to attempt to better himself.

He often speaks of his ex-wife and the divorce and of still loving her. If he is not working, he is at home eating and watching TV or in the alley having a beer with his friends. He does not do much else. His friends often remark on his bringing up of his divorce and try to set him up with women, but the women usually reject him. There have been a few relationships he has ended himself, but the majority are not his choice. His friends attempt to tell him he is too good for his ex-wife and that she is not coming back.

Bill gets particularly depressed around the holidays. He usually spends Thanksgiving with Hank Hill's family, which is very intrusive to them. He went through a period of suicidal actions and thoughts but never completed or repeated these behaviors. His friends were constantly watching him.

Diagnosis

The disorder Bill Dauterive most accurately can be diagnosed as having is Dysthymic Disorder (300.4).

A. Depressed mood for most of the day, for more days than not, as indicated either by subjective account or obser-vation by others, for at least 2 years.

Bill is self-described as being depressed a lot of the time. His friends also state that he is depressed all of the time and it has been going on for longer than 2 years. In fact, it is closer to 7 years.

B. Presence, while depressed, of two (or more) of the following:

1.   poor appetite or overeating

2.   insomnia or hypersomnia

3.   low energy or fatigue

4.   low self-esteem

5.   poor concentration or difficulty making decisions

6.   feelings of hopelessness

Bill experiences overeating, low energy and fatigue, low self-esteem, and feelings of hopelessness. Occasionally he experiences insomnia and poor concentration. Quite often his despair will lead him to overeat which leads to further low self-esteem. The symptoms seem to compound themselves. Bill's friend Hank is usually the one who makes a lot of Bill's decisions because he has difficulty doing so himself, whether everyday decisions or more meaningful decisions.

C. During the 2-year period of the disturbance, the person has never been without the symptoms in Criteria A and B for more than 2 months at a time.

Bill fits this and does not seem to reach the 2 month mark for absence of symptoms. Bill's symptoms of depression seem to be chronic. He is never out of his depressed state for longer than a few days and this is usually because he has found someone to be in a relationship with for a short time.

D. No Major Depressive Episode has been present during the first 2 years of the disturbance i.e., the disturbance is not better accounted for by chronic Major Depressive Disorder, or Major Depressive Disorder, In Partial Remission.
This is hard to account for because Bill is being seen 7 years after the onset. Since it has lasted so long, however, Dysthymic Disorder accounts for it very well.

E. There has never been a Manic Episode, a Mixed Episode, or a Hypomanic Episode, and criteria have never been met for Cyclothymic Disorder.
There has been no evidence of a hypomanic episode. The closest period would be when Bill experiences some type of normalcy does not last very long. He does not have manic episodes or even hypomanic episodes. Sometimes he is obsessive but that does not last very long and he slips back into depression, no period of normalcy is seen. He does not qualify for Cyclothymic Disorder because he does not have periods of hypomanic or manic symptoms.

F. The disturbance does not occur exclusively during the course of a chronic Psychotic Disorder, such as Schizophrenia or Delusional Disorder.
Bill does not have symptoms of a Psychotic Disorder.

G. The symptoms are not due to the direct physiological effects of a substance (e.g., a drug of abuse, a medication) or a general medical condition (e.g., hypothyroidism).
Bill does not present with any substance abuse or other medical conditions. Before the onset of Dysthymic Disorder, he was happy, popular, and content with his life. He does drink a beer in the alley with his friends nearly everyday, but it is usually just one beer. If he is feeling extremely depressed, he will drink to excess, but this is a result of his depression, not a cause.

H. The symptoms cause clinically significant distress or impairment in social, occupational, or other important areas of functioning.
This disorder impacts every portion of Bill's life. He needs to be needed, and when he is, for short periods of time, it makes him miss work; he was almost listed as AWOL on more than one occasion. In his social life, his depression causes major impairment. All his friends state that he is depressed all the time. He does not take care of himself which leads to low self-esteem. This majorly impacts his attempts at finding a date. He does not make new friends, and he only has the core group of friends he grew up with. When he attempts to meet new people, he is usually rejected and thus, he does not try very often.

Regarding etiology, Bill's Dysthymia seems to have been caused by his divorce, so the psychosocial causal factor fits. There is no way to determine if genetic factors are possible as his only living relative is a male cousin.

Accuracy of Portrayal

An average person watching Bill in King of the Hill would get a very good idea for what Dysthymic Disorder is. Bill expresses almost all of the symptoms, almost all of the time. The portrayal is accurate in that Bill exhibits almost all of the symptoms of Dysthymic Disorder, nearly all the time. Saying that Bill is depressed all of the time is not an exaggeration. In people with Major Depressive Disorder there are longer periods of normalcy, but in Dysthymic Disorder there are not long periods of normalcy. More often than not, Bill is depressed. Major Depressive Disorder is more about episodes of depression, but Dysthymic Disorder is depression nearly all of the time, and Bill exhibits this. The only inaccuracy was his period of suicidality, but this was a cry for help, not an actual wish of death. It was not repeated.

Treatment

Dysthymia has not been widely studied and this impacts research on treatment. Many findings from Major Depressive Disorder have been applied to Dysthymic Disorder, since it is often referred to as a milder form of Major Depressive Disorder.

One could begin by treating Bill with an antidepressant. After the appropriate dosage was found, he would begin psychotherapy. Bill needs to be taught about the disorder and recognize that he is not in a normal state of mind and begin to come out of it. Since he does not really have any family to speak of to attend therapy with him, his friends should accompany him because they are the individuals he sees most often. They could be shown that their comments to Bill are hurtful and need to end. If Bill's core group of friends were taught about Dysthymic Disorder they could learn ways to help Bill when he was feeling down and make him feel better about himself and the situations he finds himself in.

A therapist could use cognitive therapy to help Bill change how he sees the world and to think more optimistically. This would show Bill that not every bad thing that happens is a crisis and which events to just let go of. He needs help getting over his divorce and gaining his self-esteem back. Other recommendations that he find a hobby he likes and recommend him to someone to help him with nutritional skills, such as what to eat and what to cook.

Video: Bill Dautrieve – A Case Study in Dysthymic Disorder

- https://youtu.be/FNCYo8YkNhE

Name: Andrew Largeman

Source: *Garden State* (movie, 2004)

Background Information

Andrew is a 26 year old actor and waiter from New Jersey. He was living in Los Angeles when he got the news that his mother has passed away. Returning to New Jersey for his mother's funeral, he has to face his psychiatrist father with whom he has no relationship. When Andrew was nine years old a terrible accident occurred where he pushed his mother over a dishwasher door that left her paralyzed. This left him in a depressed and distant state. His mother was a very depressed individual too. Andrew resented the fact that he could never make her happy and that he had pushed her out of anger, leaving her paralyzed.

He appears to be very lost and detached. Drugs such as marijuana and ecstasy have been used by Andrew. He has complaints of reoccurring headaches. Andrew seems to be isolating himself from his father and others. In Los Angeles in particular, he has no friends and no desire to attain any. His general lack of attention is established when he forgets to remove the gas pump from the car when finished getting gas.

Andrew feels like he does not have a problem and for the first time has stopped taking the medication that has been prescribed to him. After meeting a female friend, Andrew feels that he can relate to her and seems less depressed when he is with her. However, this is largely just taking his mind off his problems and his symptoms are still apparent.

Gideon Largeman is Andrew's father who is a psychiatrist. After his wife's accident involving Andrew, Gideon tries to suppress a deep loathing towards his son. He blames Andrew for the accident that left his wife paralyzed. To "curb the anger" that he holds towards his son, he heavily medicates him starting at a young age to "protect him from his own feelings". He puts Andrew on Lithium that has left him in an emotionless haze for many years. He feels that when Andrew was younger he had an anger problem so he decided to place him in boarding school fallowing his mother's accident. His mother was very depressed and abusing alcohol before her accident. She died while drowning in a bath tub. This was known to be an accident and not a suicide attempt, although it was very suspect.

Description of the Problem

Andrew looks depressed and acts depressed. He zones out and lacks attention to certain important daily functions. There is not any color present in his bedroom, everything is white and sterile. He also experiences terrible dreams of being in a situation where the people around him and himself are about to die, yet he still does not or cannot show any emotion. He is just in a daze, without care of what is going on in the world around him. He has explained that he has not cried in many years. It is apparent that he isolates himself from his family and friends.

Diagnosis

The appropriate disorder after evaluating Andrew is Dysthymia Disorder (300.4)

A. Depressed mood for most of the day, for more days than not, as indicated either by subjective account or observation by others, for at least 2 years.

Andrew has indicated that he has been depressed for as far as he can remember. Before the accident that left his mother paralyzed, Andrew felt depressed by the fact that he couldn't make his mother happy. After causing his mother to be paralyzed he also become depressed and was sent to boarding school where he was isolated from his family. He shows a great amount of guilt for his mother's accident and her recent death.

B. Presence, while depressed, of two (or more) of the following:

1. Poor appetite or overeating

2. Insomnia or hypersomnia

3. Low energy or fatigue

4. Low self-esteem

5. Poor concentration or difficulty making decisions

6. Feelings of hopelessness

Andrew experiences low energy, low self-esteem, poor concentration, and feelings of hopelessness. He seems to have low energy by the way he carries himself. He is late to work, has no interest and lacks energy when talking to people. Not being to work on time seems to be a reoccurring event for Andrew, as his boss mentions his last warning before he is replaced. Andrew expresses low self-esteem by explaining that he has a "fucked up family". He blames himself for his mother's accident and remains in isolation most of the time. His concentration on important things is also lacking. He has driven away with the gas pump still attached to his car, and has occasionally not responded to his name being called. Andrew has a sense of hopelessness; he does not have hope in the fact that he can fix the relationship between his father and him.

C. During the 2-year period of the disturbance, the person has never been without the symptoms in Criteria A and B for more than 2 months at a time.

Andrew meets this by explaining that he has felt this way from at least the age of nine. Before his mother's accident he felt like he could not make her happy when she was depressed. He is also to blame for his mother's accident and has been in therapy for depression since the age of 9.

D. No Major Depressive Episode has been present during the first 2 years of the disturbance i.e., the disturbance is not better accounted for by Chronic Major Depressive Disorder, Major Depressive Disorder or in Partial Remission.

The criteria of Dysthymia are met due to the amount of time that Andrew has experienced these depressed symptoms. It is estimated that he has had these symptoms for approximately 17 years. No major depressive episode has occurred. He has successfully carried a job, and has played a major role in a film.

E. There has never been a Manic Episode, a Mixed Episode, or a Hypomanic Episode, and criteria have never been met for Cyclothymic Disorder.

It is not apparent that Andrew has had Manic, Mixed or Hypomanic Episodes. The depression seems to remain at a consistent level over the time period estimated to be depressed. He does not meet the criteria for Cyclothymic disorder because Andrew has not experienced or expressed levels of Hypomanic episodes. He also has not experienced as time period of 2 or more months were he has shown no symptoms of depression.

F. The disturbance does not occur exclusively during the course of a chronic Psychotic Disorder, such as Schizophrenia or Delusional Disorder.

Andrew shows no symptoms of a chronic Psychotic Disorder such as Schizophrenia or Delusional Disorder.

G. The symptoms are not due to the direct physiological effects of a substance (e.g., a drug of abuse, a medication) or a general medical condition (e.g., hypothyroidism).

Andrew shows no symptoms that occur from drug, or medication abuse. The lithium that Andrew has been taking is to help his depression and aggression and he shows no signs of abusing it. He has experienced some drug and alcohol use. However it appears that it is only in social situations and he expressed signs of hesitation and has refused drugs from peers.

H. The symptoms cause clinically significant distress or impairment in social, occupational, or other important areas of functioning.

Andrew's symptoms have significantly impaired his social relationship with peers, friends, co-workers and his father. He shows little interest in having friends around and has been isolating himself for a long period of time. He has no relationship with his father and other family members and has isolated himself from them as well. Andrew's job as a waiter seems to be coming to an end. He is consistently late and is on his last warning before he job position is replaced.

Early Onset – Occurred before the age of 9 and has continued through his adulthood.

Accuracy of Portrayal

When the average person watches Andrew it is obvious that he is depressed. It is also obvious that this depression has lasted a significant amount of time and has been consistent. He shows that he is suffering with depression more often than not. However, there are times where it seems as if Andrew is not depressed, such as when he is with his newest female friend. Yet, Andrew still shows apparent symptoms of depression and guilt that would categorize him with Dysthymia Disorder. One may inaccurately portray Andrew as someone who has major depressive disorder but, this is not the case. Andrew's depression has lasted more than two years and he is depressed for most of the time. They may also label him with drug abuse; however, drugs are not a consistent player in his life. He knows to refuse it and to my knowledge has done ecstasy once after pressure from peers.

Treatment

Pharmacotherapy would be the most effective treatment for Andrew's dysthymia. Andrew has been on anti-depressants and involved in therapy since the age of nine. He has been heavily medicated with Lithium prescribed by his father. From a mental health professional perspective Andrew should not be on Lithium. It is obviously not helping him or eliminating the depression he is feeling. The Lithium dosage is too high and maybe triggering some of the depression he is experiencing. Trying another form of anti-depressants and finding the correct amount needed, with the addition to psychotherapy appears to be the most effective treatment for Andrew.

Psychotherapy should be incorporated with Andrew's treatment plan once his pharmacotherapy has been correct and is showing significant results in decreasing his depression. Therapy involving his father in attempt to repair their relationship should also be in Andrew's treatment plan. This could relieve a lot of the stress and guilt built up in the both of them. Talk therapy is shown to benefit those with dysthymia. It will give him an opportunity to talk about his problems and learn ways to deal with him in a healthy manner.

Cognitive behavior therapy could also be helpful in treating Andrew's dysthymia disorder. Here he can go over and review that his behavior as a child needs to be put in the past. He needs help realizing that what has happened cannot be taken back but, instead needs to be moved on from.

Bulimia Nervosa

Name: Shelly Hunter
Source: *Hunger Point* (movie, 2003)

Background Information

Shelly Hunter is a Caucasian female currently in high school. Although her age is unknown, she is presumed to be a teenager. A first look at Hunter gives evidential proof that she is seriously underweight. This raises serious concerns about her health. Hunter lives at home with her domineering mother, Marsha, and David, her passive father. She is the younger sister of Frannie, who is away at college and also struggles with eating. Shelly has a very strenuous relationship with her mother. As a child Hunter was always very slender, but she grew up listening to her mother lecture Frannie, who was not as slender, on the importance's of being slim. Mrs. Hunter's obsessive belief that being slender is the most important thing has severely distorted Hunter's views on eating. Hunter clearly seeks approval from her mother and puts great strains on her body to reach that approval. Hunter's life is devoted to her weight. Her time is spent obsessing about being slender. She does not know how to cope with her eating disorder and her irrational views on being skinny. The eating disorder is also causing severe mental problems with Hunter. She is exhibiting signs of depression and distrust from her family.

Description of the Problem

Hunter displays the symptoms of an eating disorder. She is abnormally underweight for her age and is very unhealthy. She exhibits the characteristics of Bulimia Nervosa. She eats very little when she is in the presence of other people. Most undoubtedly when she is eating in front of her mother, she becomes very self conscious about what and how much she eats. After restraining from food intake for a period of time she then will over eat. She stuffs herself with large portions of food. After doing so she begins to feel shame and guilt for over eating. The way she deals with her guilt is to self- induce vomiting. This purging is a defense mechanism Hunter uses to cope with "disappointing" herself as well as her mother. Although it only lasts for a short while, she feels satisfied with her body after vomiting.

Diagnosis

The diagnosis for Hunter appropriately fits **Bulimia Nervosa (307.51).**

To be diagnosed with Bulimia Nervosa one or more or a combination of the following characteristics must be present:

1. Eating in a discrete period of time (e.g., within any 2-hour period), an amount of food that is definitely larger than most people would eat during a similar period of time and under similar circumstances; it is common for more than 10,000 calories to be consumed per binge.
2. An abnormal constant craving for food; a sense of a lack of control of eating during an episode (e.g., a feeling that one cannot stop eating or control what or how much one is eating).
3. Eating is usually done in secret.

Hunter displays the characteristics of 1 and 3. As described in the "Description of the Problem" she eats large portions of food alone.
B. Recurrent inappropriate, compensatory behavior in order to prevent weight gain. Such as self-induced vomiting, misuse of laxatives, diuretics, enemas, or other medications, fasting, or excessive exercise.

Hunter exhibits these compensatory behaviors in order to prevent weight gain. She fasts for a long period of time. She then will binge eat and self-induce vomiting.
C. The binge eating and inappropriate compensatory behaviors both occur on average at least twice a week for three months.

Hunter began binge eating at a very young age and continues to binge eat into her high school years.
D. Self-evaluation is unduly influenced by body shape and weight.
Hunter has a very unhealthy view about her body. She is constantly concerned with gaining weight. Even though she looks too slender and unhealthy to others, she views herself as overweight.
E. The disturbance does not occur exclusively during episodes of Anorexia Nervosa.

Hunter will eat very little for a short period of time, and then she will binge eat to self-induce vomiting.

Accuracy of Portrayal

The average person watching this movie would see an accurate portrayal of the behavioral characteristics of Bulimia Nervosa. Hunter displays the onset characteristics of someone suffering from this disorder. Someone watching this movie would learn that having an eating disorder can cause many other problems. Hunter became very untrusting and displayed signs of depression. Bulimia Nervosa took control over Hunter's life and began to affect her mentally. Therefore, the movie *Hunger Point* portrays an accurate depiction of Bulimia Nervosa.

Treatment

After fully examining Hunter it might be best to start her on some medications. To help with depression Tricyclic antidepressants or Selective Serotonin Re-Uptake Inhibitors (SSRI's) could be prescribed to elevate her mood. Vitamin and mineral supplements would be prescribed until signs of deficiency disappeared and normal eating patterns were reestablished. The vitamins would also help to treat acid reflux caused by bulimia. After Hunter's weight becomes stabilized it would be a good idea to start a behavioral therapy program. This will help to change the mindset of Hunter and her negative views about her body. This will also help to control her binge eating habits. Not only does Hunter need individual therapy, but she and her mother need family therapy. Mrs. Hunter needs therapy in order to understand that her obsessive beliefs, about being slender, caused her daughter to become diagnosed with bulimia nervosa. Communication exercises will be exhibited to help resolve conflict and re-establishing boundaries. The treatments will better help Hunter to have control over Bulimia Nervosa and to gradually overcome the disorder.

Video: Marsha & Frannie Hunter – Case Studies in Eating Disorders

- https://youtu.be/P5ZyQ_rPOwc

Name: Blair Waldorf

Source: Gossip Girl (television series, 2007-present)

Background Information

Blair Waldorf is a 16 year old female who lives in Manhattan, New York. She is a full time student, and attends a private high school. She is in good health, and her family is in good mental health. Her parents are divorced, mother in Manhattan and father in Paris. She has a great relationship with her father, but he left his family for a male model, so Blair suffers slightly with separation anxiety and depression. Her mother has very high status in Manhattan, and would do anything to keep it that way. Blair and her mother get into arguments every now and then, but no more than a normal teen and her mother. Blair is an only child. Serena is Blair's best friend and has been since they were little. Blair is snobbier of the two, and Serena keeps her grounded without going overboard. They often get into tiffs, but always end up making up. Blair's ex-boyfriend is Nate. They dated from age 5 until 16. Dealing with the breakup of her longtime lover, Blair goes a little crazy and her separation anxiety and depression shows up again. Blair drinks often, and for some reason in the world that she lives in, adults do not seem to care. She could walk into a bar and drink martinis all night, and it would be completely normal. She does not do drugs, however. Her biggest life difficulty is staying queen bee at her high school. She goes through a lot throughout the show, but staying the most popular girl in school is always her top priority. Her number one goal is to attend Yale after she graduates, and later become a trophy wife just like her mother was. Blair copes with her problems by putting other people down. She loves the fact that she is at the top of the totem pole, and she is not afraid to let anyone and everyone know it. She also often uses alcohol to cope with her problems.

Description of the Problem

During the first season of Gossip Girl, the fact that Blair had been to treatment in her past comes up a few times. Blair's eating habits are normal for the first few episodes, but after she experiences different stressors, her eating habits become abnormal again. She starts to pick at food most of the time, but binges at other times. Also, her best friend Serena and her mother started to bring up the fact that her symptoms were returning. She completely closed them off and ignored the fact that they were. Every time that she would get into a fight with Serena, her ex boyfriend, or her mother, her lack of control for eating would return. One incident that was shown on the show was that Blair had gotten into a huge fight with Serena on Thanksgiving, which caused Blair to be extremely snappy with her mother. She found out that her mother lied to her about her father coming into town for the holiday, which caused a fight with her mother as well. She was picking at her Thanksgiving meal during dinner, and when her mother told her to go pick out a dessert, she stormed off to the kitchen. She found an apple pie that she wanted to eat, but instead of just taking one piece, she stared at it for a few minutes, and binged and ate the entire pie. Immediately, she went into her bathroom and started to purposely vomit. She has always had an issue with her self-image, and the binging and purging was her solution to make herself feel better. After vomiting in her bathroom, she called Serena, and she quickly came over and let Blair cry on her shoulder. This is not the only incident that Blair had with binging and purging, but it was a very critical event to Blair's illness.

Diagnosis

The diagnosis for Blair Waldorf fits most appropriately with **Bulimia Nervosa (307.51).**
To be diagnosed with Bulimia Nervosa, you must have the following characteristics:

1. Recurrent episodes of binge eating. An episode of binge eating is characterized by the following:

    a. Eating in a discrete period of time (e.g., within any 2-hour period), an amount of food that is larger than most people would eat during a similar period of time and under similar circumstances.

    b. A sense of lack of control of eating during an episode (e.g., a feeling that one cannot stop eating or control what or how much one is eating).

Blair Waldorf displays both of these characteristics. When she has an episode, it is as if she cannot control what food she is putting into her body, or how much food she is putting into her body.

1. Recurrent inappropriate compensatory behavior in order to prevent weight gain, such as self-induced vomiting, misuse of laxatives, diuretics, or other medications, fasting, or excessive exercise.

Blair Waldorf will do whatever she thinks is necessary to prevent weight gain, and her methods of choice are self-induced vomiting and fasting.

1. The binge eating and inappropriate compensatory behaviors both occur, on average, at least once a week for three months.

The television show does not state what age Blair Waldorf started binge eating, but while she was only 16 years old, her mother discussed Blair already having gone to treatment for her Bulimia. So this must have been a problem in her life for quite a few years.

1. Self-evaluation is unduly influenced by body shape and weight.

Blair Waldorf is very self conscious of her body image and her weight. Her mother mentions a few times that she needs to watch her weight, so this may have helped lead to Blair's body image issues.

1. The disturbance does not occur exclusively during episodes of anorexia nervosa.

Blair Waldorf will eat a very small amount and continue to pick at food at every meal, until another episode of binging and purging occurs.

Accuracy of Portrayal

The average person watching Gossip Girl and watching Blair with her eating disorder would learn the behavioral characteristics of Bulimia Nervosa. Someone watching this television show would understand that it is a disorder that a person cannot necessarily always control. There can be triggers that can lead to an episode, just like any other illness. This portrayal is accurate of Bulimia Nervosa. However, the show does not show the seriousness as much as it should of this disorder. It was mislabeled in this way because it has affected Blair's mental health, so any issue in her life that leads to her showing any signs of depression will most likely lead to an episode. This is her way of dealing with problems in her life, and Gossip Girl does not show the severity of this.

Treatment

After evaluating Blair Waldorf's condition, it would be best to start her with a behavioral therapy program. She was not taught the proper way to handle her emotions and deal with problems that arise in her life, and therapy would help approach these issues. Therapy could also approach her body image issues, and help her to devise an exercise program that would make her feel more in shape and healthy. Her mother and her friends would have to help monitor her eating habits, but after understanding her condition fully and seeing that there are other ways of dealing with issues, Blair would take on a better eating schedule. Also, putting Blair on a very low dosage anti-depressant or Selective Serotonin Re-Uptake Inhibitors (SSRI's) and monitoring her progress very closely while on this medication would help a great deal. Communication exercises will also be necessary between Blair and her mother to teach them how to discuss this illness in a healthier manner. These different treatments will, in time, help Blair overcome this disorder. She will be able to talk about her feelings and problems, rather than regressing to binging and purging.

Histrionic Personality Disorder

Name: Michael Scott

Source: *The Office* (American television show, 2005-2011)

Background Information

Michael Scott is a forty-six year old Caucasian male from Scranton, Pennsylvania. Scott is the regional manager at Dunder Mifflin Inc., a local paper and printer distribution company, where he has worked for the last fifteen years. There are no known medical conditions held by Scott, though his family history is unknown. He claims to be of English, Irish, German, Scottish, and Native American descent, though this is unconfirmed, and perhaps an exaggeration. The patient's outward appearance is well put together, as he presents as a business professional, and there are no obvious health concerns. Despite his seemingly composed demeanor, Scott displays exaggerated emotions and reactions. In addition to this, romantic relationships have proven turbulent for Scott throughout his life, as he goes from one relationship to the next with the other person usually being the one to end it. He has few close friends or relatives, and tends to perceive new friendships as closer than they actually are. Scott believes his subordinates to be his family, and often times gets involved in their personal lives without their consent. His parents divorced when he was young (age unknown), and he displays clear resentment towards his stepfather and sister, whom he once didn't talk to for fifteen years. Scott has a very close relationship with his mother now, though this was not case when he was a child. Though Scott seems to be lacking in managerial style, responsibility, and delegation, he demonstrates above average sales abilities due to his personable qualities. Scott does not have a history of drug or alcohol abuse, though he will drink in social situations and when pressured to do so by coworkers.

Description of the Problem

The patient demonstrates many personality traits that could be indicative of a variety of disorders. Scott seeks attention every opportunity he gets, and this often interferes with his ability to function in his job as manager. In addition to attention-seeking, Scott often interrupts his subordinates from working to discuss his personal life. This behavior not only affects his ability to work, but it interferes with the overall productivity of the office. It is Scott's belief that he should not be seen as just a boss, but more of a close friend and even family member, to the dismay of his subordinates. This expectation of a close bond leads Scott to display rapidly shifting emotions, from exuberant and hopeful, to depressed and hopeless. There seems to be a lack of consistency in his behavior, rather a dramatic shift from extremely happy to irreversibly sad. In Scott's depressed state, he feels as if the entire office should be focused on his problem and that others' problems pale in comparison, such as his birthday being of more importance than a coworkers cancer scare. When he is happy, however, work at the office ceases to a halt, as his well-being is put before the needs of the company. In addition to his attention-seeking and rapidly shifting emotions, the patient is easily suggestible and is often the victim of pyramid schemes and persuasive coworkers. Scott also shows a pattern of theatric behavior, including different characters, voices, and personalities, in which he uses as distractions on a constant basis.

Diagnosis

The diagnosis that seems to fit most appropriately for Scott is **Histrionic Personality Disorder (301.50).**

To qualify for a diagnosis of Histrionic Personality Disorder, a person must display the following general criteria of a Personality Disorder:

A. An enduring pattern of inner experience and behavior that deviates markedly from the expectations of the individual's culture. This pattern is manifested in two (or more) of the following areas:

1. Cognition (I.e., ways of perceiving and interpreting self, other people, and events)
2. Affectivity (I.e., the range, intensity, and appropriateness of emotional response)
3. Interpersonal functioning
4. Impulse Control
Mr. Scott displays dysfunctions in many, if not all, of the above categories. His thoughts are consumed by his thinking that he is a comedian, consistently referring to his improv classes and impersonations. The affectivity displayed by the patient is continuously out of proportion to the situation, such as halting the workday for an office meeting over a minor problem, oftentimes a non-work related problem. His interpersonal and relationship functioning is severely limited, demonstrated by his lack insight into the true feelings (I.e. distain) of the people in his life. His impulse control is lacking, if not nonexistent.
B. The enduring pattern is inflexible and pervasive across a broad range of personal and social situations.
The displayed symptoms cause, and have caused, significant distress in the areas of work relationships, friendships, and romantic relationships. The observed behavior also has negative consequences in many aspects of his life, including resentment and distain from coworkers, as well as from his superiors and romantic partners.
C. The enduring pattern leads to clinically significant distress or impairment in social, occupational, or other important areas of functioning.
The inflexible nature of his symptoms clearly affects his ability to function in his day-to-day tasks. His ability to function is severely impacted by his need for attention, as he demonstrates a lack of motivation and productiveness in his occupation and social life. This enduring pattern has also led to resentment from his subordinates, who believe he is incompetent due to his emotional outbursts.
D. The pattern is stable and of long duration, and its onset can be traced back at least to adolescence or early adulthood.
Scott's symptoms have been present for at least six years, though they seem to have been present during his entire employment at Dunder Mifflin, and are pervasive in both his work and personal life. The symptoms can be traced

back to his early adulthood, as demonstrated by his lack of friendships and romantic relationships in the past. The symptoms may also be a result of early childhood experiences, as he lacked a father-figure and his mother seemingly neglected him.

E. The enduring pattern is not better accounted for as a manifestation or consequence of another mental disorder.

Although the patient demonstrates some characteristics consistent with Narcissistic Personality Disorder, he is too suggestible to fit this criteria. As those with Narcissistic PD are interpersonally exploitative, Scott demonstrates a need for immediate attention as opposed to a need for future success. Neither mood, psychotic, nor anxiety disorders better account for his symptoms.

F. The enduring pattern is not due to the direct physiological effects of a substance (e.g., a drug of abuse, a medication) or a general medical condition (e.g., head trauma).

The presenting symptoms are not the result of drugs, alcohol or head trauma.

To fit the Diagnostic Criteria for 301.50 Histrionic Type, at least five (or more) of the following criteria must be met:

1. Uncomfortable in situations in which they are not the center of attention

In many instances, such as making a coworkers wedding all about him, caring more about his superficial wound than an employee with a concussion, holding impromptu meetings to discuss his personal life, or dozens of other examples, Scott demands the attention be on him and only him. Typically in a situation in which he is not the center of attention, Scott is visibly uncomfortable and can barely sit still.

2. Interaction with others are often characterized by inappropriate sexually seductive or provocative behavior

Although Scott does not demonstrate sexually seductive behavior, he exhibits provocative behavior on a regular basis by use of inappropriate jokes or sexual advances on coworkers.

3. Displays rapid shifting and shallow expressions of emotions

Scott goes from angry, to upset, to jealous, to happy, to ecstatic very rapidly, and displays a pattern of shallow emotions. For instance, after hitting a coworker with his car, the patient displayed little remorse or genuine emotion.

4. Consistently uses physical appearance to draw attention to self

5. Has a style of speech that is excessively impressionistic and lacking in detail

6. Shows self-dramatization, theatricality, and exaggerated expression of emotion

After a superficial wound, the patient exaggerated the symptoms for the entire day, demanding the focus of that workday be on his recovery. Scott also demonstrates theatricality through use of characters, voices, and impromptu presentations.

7. Is suggestible, I.e., easily influenced by others or circumstances

Scott is highly suggestible, and has been observed to lose substantial amounts of money in pyramid schemes due to his trusting nature and easily influenced personality. The patient is so suggestible that he has participated in highly risky behaviors, such as placing his face in drying cement, from pressure from those around him.

8. Considers relationships more intimate than they actually are

In many aspects of his life, the patient demonstrates a destructive attachment style, oftentimes believing those around him are closer to him than they actually are. Scott believes the office staff to be his family, and considers a temporary employee to be his best friend after only one day of knowing him. As with his friendships, Scott's personal relationships suffer from the same overzealous attitude. While once dating a woman, Scott placed his own photo over the photo of her ex-husband, while also proposing to her after three dates.

Accuracy of portrayal

To those watching The Office, the portrayal of Michael Scott as a person with Histrionic Personality Disorder is quite good, though those with the disorder are more often females than males. Those with Histrionic Personality Disorder are known to use their body as a seductive tool, and Scott's portrayal lacks this important quality of the disorder. However, due to the differing presentation of Histrionic Personality Disorder between men and women, this trait may be unnecessary for the diagnosis. The sudden change of emotion is quite accurately portrayed, as well as the attention-seeking behavior patterns. As symptom expression is accurately portrayed, so too is the onset of symptoms. Histrionic PD is expressed most often in a person's early adult years, and those with the disorder typically come from a family history of neglect or lack of attention from the primary caregiver during pivotal developmental years. For this reason, the attention-seeking and self-centered behavior tends to manifest later in life as a result of the early experience. This symptom is accurately portrayed in the show as well. Overall, the portrayal of Michael Scott as a person with Histrionic Personality Disorder is accurate in many ways.

Treatment

The best course of treatment for Scott would be therapy. Cognitive-behavioral therapy would be beneficial in a similar way by helping him to cope with his emotional outbursts. CBT would provide Scott tools for controlling his behavior in a more systematic and structured way to be able to function more productively in the workplace. In addition to systematic planning, it is recommended that Scott be given assertiveness training to help with his propensity for taking advice from others. Behavioral rehearsals may aid in his workplace manner and help him to establish appropriate workplace behaviors. Although family counseling is not an option, it is recommended that Scott participate in relationship counseling to help establish a long-lasting, stable relationship.

Video: Michael Scott – A Case Study in Histrionic Personality Disorder

- https://youtu.be/1LLfLTsiDAo

Name: Regina George

Source: *Mean Girls* (movie, 2004)

Background Information

Regina George is a sixteen year old Caucasian female. She is a junior in high school at North Shore High School. Regina comes from a very wealthy family and does not have a job besides attending school. She is presumed to be in good health since the film did not mention any health conditions. Regina George is considered the ring leader of the meanest girl clique at North Shore High. She is the queen bee of the popular girls group that pride themselves on making each other look as hot as possible while they put others down in the process.

As previously mentioned Regina comes from a very affluent family. They live in a beautiful mansion considered to be the biggest and most lavish house out of any of the 'mean girl clique'. Regina's relationship with her parents is very twisted and abnormal. One example of this backward relationship is displayed when Regina brings her friends over and her mom insists on inserting herself into Regina and her friend's conversations. Not only does her mom think of her as her best friend but her parents allowed her take the master bedroom simply because she desired it. Regina does not have a strong relationship with either parent but drifts more toward her mother.

Regina George has a preoccupation with her looks. She is constantly talking about how she is either too fat or that she is not pretty enough and also seeks confirmation about her body and looks through others. She does not have a regular drinking problem or drug abuse issue since she is so preoccupied with her appearance and that would definitely tarnish her ideal reputation. Her obsession with her appearance would have to be one of her biggest weaknesses. With regard to her weight, she is constantly seeking new and unsearched ways of losing weight.

Description of the Problem

This patient displays many of the traits associated with a number of personality disorders, but most strongly shows symptoms of Histrionic Personality Disorder. Regina George is an attention junkie. She seeks out attention from people in every aspect of her daily life. This hunger for attention has created tension between Regina and her group of friends. Her need for attention impairs her abilities to function inside the classroom, hindering her performance in school. Regina often wears seductive clothing that most girls and women would not walk out the front door in, let alone wear to school. Another way Regina actively seeks attention is by talking about people behind their backs. In a three way phone call, she deliberately tries to sabotage one of her close friend's relationships with another close friend of hers. This attack displays her need to be needed. She felt threatened by their relationship so the only means of coping with the problem to her was by pinning two of her friends against each other. When Regina has a problem, the only way she knows to resolve it is by making someone else feel inferior. Along with these distorted coping skills, Regina displays extreme variances in her emotions. When she is happy she is through the moon happy and when she is mad she is definitely going to let someone know about it. When Regina has a problem going on in her life, she thinks that every single one of her friends must stop what they are doing and solve the problem with or for her. One example of this is shown when Regina is eating lunch, wants something else to eat, and then she says that she is really trying to lose five pounds. She is flabbergasted when the rest of the clique does not immediately pipe in to say that she is already flawless.

Diagnosis

The diagnosis that seems to fit most appropriately for Regina George is Histrionic Personality Disorder (301.50). To qualify for a diagnosis of Histrionic Personality Disorder, a person must display the following general criteria of a Personality Disorder:

A. An enduring pattern of inner experience and behavior that deviates markedly from the expectations of the individual's culture. This pattern is manifested in two (or more) of the following areas:

1. Cognition (I.e., ways of perceiving and interpreting self, other people, and events)

2. Affectivity (I.e., the range, intensity, and appropriateness of emotional response)

3. Interpersonal functioning

4. Impulse Control

Regina George has shown impairments through all of these conditions. She has shown that all that consumes her thoughts is the obsession she has with her appearance and the appearance of others. Her displayed affectivity is most often over exaggerated to the situation. Most notable was her reaction to her "friend" not inviting her to her house party: she single handedly brought the entire student body to a crippling halt by sharing a "burn book" with them. This book contained pictures and captions (written by Regina herself) about different people in their school. The pictures were not the most flattering and the captions were mean spirited and hurtful to say the least.

B. The enduring pattern is inflexible and pervasive across a broad range of personal and social situations.

Her symptoms have caused her significant turmoil in her relationships at home, school, and in her daily life. Her behavior has caused many issues in all aspects of her life, such as with friends turning against her, her family not being very supportive and the entire student body rallying against her.

C. The enduring pattern leads to clinically significant distress or impairment in social, occupational, or other important areas of functioning.

Regina's apparent inflexible nature has caused tremendous impairment among her social life as well as her occupational or school life. Regina's preoccupation with her outward appearance has left her little if any time to focus on things that really matter to people such as her character and demeanor towards others.

D. The pattern is stable and of long duration, and its onset can be traced back at least to adolescence or early adulthood.

The behaviors that Regina displays in the movie *Mean Girls* has been going on her entire life, per her mother's report. She has been the same appearance obsessed girl since she was born. This pattern of attention seeking, mean behavior escalated in middle school when she made up a rumor about a girl being a lesbian in the eighth grade.

E. The enduring pattern is not better accounted for as a manifestation or consequence of another mental disorder.

This patient does display some of the characteristics of a person with narcissistic personality disorder and perhaps even some dependent PD characteristics, but the disorder that Regina displays through the entire movie is HPD.

F. The enduring pattern is not due to the direct physiological effects of a substance (e.g., a drug of abuse, a medication) or a general medical condition (e.g., head trauma).

The symptoms are not as a result of drugs, alcohol, or any general medical condition.

To fit the Diagnostic Criteria for 301.50 Histrionic Type, at least five (or more) of the following criteria must be met:

1. Uncomfortable in situations in which they are not the center of attention

Regina George is not only uncomfortable in situations in which she is not the center of attention but she most notably does not allow herself to be in a situation where she is not the center of attention. When a new girl starts going to North Shore, and the girl is as pretty as or prettier than her, Regina makes a consorted effort to make that girl her new best friend forever.

1. Interaction with others are often characterized by inappropriate sexually seductive or provocative behavior

Regina definitely displays this behavior in every aspect of her life. She cannot even sing in the Christmas talent show without being in a midriff tube top shirt with a matching much too short skirt.

1. Displays rapid shifting and shallow expressions of emotions

Regina has an extremely wide range of shallow emotions. For example when she is confronted with an old friend (the one she spread the lesbian rumor about) she shrugs it off as if it never happened. Her ability to show no remorse and be so nonchalant about something that destroyed a young impressionable human being show her shallow expression of emotion.

1. Consistently uses physical appearance to draw attention to self

She uses her body, her beauty, and her weight to keep people focused on herself. When someone tries to shift the conversation she always finds a way to get the attention back on herself.

1. Has a style of speech that is excessively impressionistic and lacking in detail

Regina has an immature speaking style. When talking in the cafeteria she uses many words that are not even words such as 'skeeze' to describe other students.

1. Shows self-dramatization, theatricality, and exaggerated expression of emotion

In regard to her constant obsession with her weight, Regina has all of her friends focus on the things that she should be doing on her own to lose the weight. When Regina goes to a dress shop to be fitted for her prom dress and finds that she cannot fit the one she wants she has a tyrannical outburst.

1. Is suggestible, I.e., easily influenced by others or circumstances

Regina is highly suggestible especially since she does not focus on the facts. She is a person who will take a person for their word. When one of her friends tries to help her with a "weight-loss" bar she takes it without question. She is shocked to later find out that the bars she has been eating for the past few months has been the sole contributor to her slow but steady weight gain.

1. Considers relationships more intimate than they actually are

Accuracy of Portrayal

To the average person watching the movie *Mean Girls,* Regina George would seem like the typical high school bitch. She is popular, pretty, and, most of all, rich. To most laypeople they would not think to make the connection that she has histrionic personality disorder even though she does a phenomenal job portraying an individual with this disorder. Regina displays the symptom most commonly associated with having histrionic personality disorder, those being sexually seductive behaviors. Regina is sexually seductive in appropriate times such as high school girls and Halloween but most notably she is seductive at times when it is completely inappropriate. Her extreme variances and range of shallow emotions are another key symptom of histrionic personality disorder. The fact that Regina is unhappy and uncomfortable with not being the center of attention is another symptom of histrionic personality disorder. The portrayal of Regina George in the movie *Mean Girls* is an accurate portrayal a person living with histrionic personality disorder.

Treatment

The best treatment for histrionic personality disorder is through therapy. The most effective therapy treatment would be Cognitive Behavioral Therapy. Cognitive Behavioral Therapy would help Regina to be able to control her emotionality better as well as give her some tools to cope with life in a more adaptive way. Regina would benefit from CBT in that it would help her in her interpersonal relationships to be better able to make and maintain friendships.

Video: Regina George – Histrionic Personality Disorder

- https://youtu.be/9lxk5IRLysI

Attention-Deficit/Hyperactivity Disorder

Name: Bart Simpson

Source: *The Simpsons* (Television series, 1989-present)

Background Information

Bart Simpson is an eight-year-old male with no history of a mental health diagnosis. Bart has been labeled an "underachiever" by authority figures and has poor grades in school ranging from D-minus to F. Bart can be ingenious regarding things that interest him such as learning portions of the Talmud to help reunite his idol, Krusty the Clown with Krusty's father, Rabbi Krustofsky. However, this drive is absent for school-related performance. His academic achievements are behind those of his fourth-grade peers.

He has a history of consistent and sometimes significant trouble making. He also reports feelings of frustration with the narrow-minded people in his town for judging him by his problematic thoughts and actions. His relationship with his father is volatile and dysfunctional. One minute he is being strongly scolded by his father and the next him and his father bond over a collaborative prank. He once told Bart it was not okay to lose a children's miniature golf tournament and made Bart stare angrily at this opponent for 15 minutes a day. There is evidence that his father forgets his youngest daughter even exists (Bart's infant sister). Bart's mother tends to "over-mother" her children and once left the family for a brief period due to a mental breakdown. Despite this, Bart has no significant problems in the relationship with his mother. Bart enjoys skateboarding, bubble gum, Squishees from the Kwik-E-Mart, and a single-handedly bringing a homicidal TV sidekick to justice – twice.

Family Mental Health History:

Marge Simpson is Bart's mother. She is described as a happy homemaker and mother of three. Marge puts up with the antics of her husband (Homer, Bart's father) and children in good spirits, for the most part. Though, in 1992 the combined stress of her workload and family's problems caused her to have a mental breakdown. She went away to spend time at "Rancho Relaxo" before returning home to her overly-dependant family. Marge over-mothers her children and reports staying with Homer because he makes her feel needed. Marge speaks out about issues such as violence and moral hygiene. The townspeople respond with frustration for her disregard of social norms. However, she also has a history of gambling addiction. She worked to overcome this addiction but it always lingers as a possible problem.

Homer Simpson is Bart's father. Homer's father Abe raised Homer in the absence of his "radical hippie mother."

Homer has a reported low IQ of 55 accompanied by periods of forgetfulness and ignorance. A crayon was discovered to be lodged in his brain and when removed his IQ rose to 105. However, he did not like his new ability to understand reason so he had the crayon re-inserted. This returned his IQ to 55. Other contributors to his low functioning include his exposure to radioactive waste, his alcohol use, and repetitive cranial trauma. It is uncertain whether his low level of functioning can attributed to genetics or to his life events. Homer works in a nuclear power plant and has remained an entry-level employee longer than any other employee. Prior to that, he attempted other jobs on impulse. At work, he falls asleep constantly and does not perform his duties. Homer displays regular instances of explosive anger. He does not attempt to hide this in public. He is ruled by his impulses. These impulses combined with his intense rage leads him to strangle Bart on occasion. His impulses change frequently affecting his attention span. He pursues many hobbies and enterprises and then quickly changes his mind about them.

Abraham Jay "Abe" Simpson is Bart's paternal grandpa. He is a grizzled old man who is incredibly long-winded and often ignored. The stories he tells seem wildly inaccurate and often consist of events that are physically, or historically impossible. For example, he reports serving in World War I, although he was a small child at that time. He reports many confrontations with famous figures and writes letters to organizations making unreasonable requests such as asking the president to get rid of three states because there are too many and requesting that *Modern Bride Magazine* feature more people with wrinkles and toothless grins. He reports homicide attempts of Adolf Hitler via javelin throw in the 1936 Olympics. It appears that Grandpa Simpson suffers from some mental health impairment(s). Without knowing his history, it is hard to tell whether this is a lifelong disease or one that attributed to old age. If he has suffered these delusions for a long period, suffice it to say some of Bart's mental health problems could be genetically linked to his grandpa.

Bart's eight-year-old sister Lisa is a high-achieving student who is already a member of MENSA with an IQ of 159. She is smart, witty, and goal oriented. Lisa does not appear to have any limiting mental health symptoms. Bart's younger sister Maggie and two maternal aunts are also featured on the show but do not seem to have any notable mental health limitations.

Description of the Problem

Bart displays multiple symptoms that are indicators for several mental health disorders. He shows very consistent symptoms for ADHD. Several problems arise as a result of Bart being distracted by video games. Specifically, he misses important family announcements because he is so distracted by his video games. Similarly, upon getting a satellite dish, Bart and his father became so distracted by the television that he could not study for an important achievement test. During the test, Bart continued to be distracted by daydreaming about things he saw on television the night before. This resulted in him failing the test and being held back a grade. In another instance, Bart got an F on a test so the school psychiatrist recommended he repeat the fourth grade. Out of desperation to avoid being held back, he promises to study but is repeatedly distracted so did worse on the next test. For the third test, Bart tries to focus while he is studying, but is still easily distracted and is forced to slap himself continually to continue his studying. The next day, still slapping himself, he finishes the test to receive a D- allowing him to pass by one point. During another instance, Bart also spontaneously interrupts an important lecture. There are many more instances where Bart becomes distracted, leading him to fail at tasks.

Diagnosis

The most appropriate diagnosis for Bart seems to be Attention-Deficit/Hyperactivity Disorder (under code 314.0). He fits the Inattentive Type meeting the following symptoms: 1, 2, 3, 4, 6, 8. Bart displays many problems with attention and distractibility. His symptoms seem sufficient for satisfying this ADHD, Inattentive Type criteria. However, he also displays some dominant symptoms for ODD and CD. These symptoms undergo dramatic changes from episode to episode creating some difficulties in rendering a diagnosis.

Two types of <u>ADHD</u>: 1) <u>Inattentive Type, and 2) Hyperactive-Impulsive Type</u>.

- **<u>DSM-IV-TR criteria:</u>**

- **<u>Inattentive Type and Hyperactive-Impulsive Type</u>:**

  - **1. <u>Inattentive Type</u>:**

  - **Six or more of the following symptoms of inattention have been present for at least 6 months to a point that is disruptive and inappropriate for developmental level:**
    1) Often does not give close attention to details or makes careless mistakes in school-work, work, or other activities.
    2) Often has trouble keeping attention on tasks or play activities.
    3) Often does not seem to listen when spoken to directly.
    4) Often does not follow instructions and fails to finish schoolwork, chores, or duties in the workplace (not due to oppositional behavior or failure to understand instructions).
    5) Often has trouble organizing activities.
    6) Often avoids, dislikes, or doesn't want to do things that take a lot of mental effort for a long period of time (such as schoolwork or homework).
    7) Often loses things needed for tasks and activities (e.g. toys, school assignments, pencils, books, or tools).
    8) Is often easily distracted.
    9) Often forgetful in daily activities.

  - **2. <u>Hyperactive-Impulsive Type</u>:**

  - **Six or more of the following symptoms of hyperactivity-impulsivity have been present for at least 6 months to an extent that is disruptive and inappropriate for developmental level:**
    <u>Hyperactivity:</u>
    1) Often fidgets with hands or feet or squirms in seat.
    2) Often gets up from seat when remaining in seat is expected.
    3) Often runs about or climbs when and where it is not appropriate (adolescents or adults may feel very restless).

4) Often has trouble playing or enjoying leisure activities quietly.

Is often "on the go" or often acts as if "driven by a motor".

5) Often talks excessively.

Impulsiveness:

6) Often blurts out answers before questions have been finished.

7) Often has trouble waiting one's turn.

8) Often interrupts or intrudes on others (e.g., butts into conversations or games).

Accuracy of Portrayal

A viewer of the Bart Simpson character can see many accurate symptoms of ADHD, but his character has many overlapping symptoms of Oppositional Defiant Disorder and even Conduct Disorder. His problems with attention are displayed in numerous experiences. However, he also displays multiple symptoms of deceitfulness, serious violations of rules, deliberately annoys people, and often argues with adults. These symptoms are found in individuals with ODD or CD. However, Bart does not demonstrate the temper, anger, or aggressiveness problems that can also be found in ODD or CD. The Bart Simpson character does display ADHD symptoms with fair accuracy, over many different episodes but also displays the ability to effectively organize delinquent behaviors in others, which would be less likely for someone with ADHD. So, there are some inconsistencies in his character but that is to be expected for a character with such different dramatic storylines, in weekly episodes for over 20 years.

Treatment

Treatment of Bart should begin with a structured or semi-structured clinical interview discussing developmental and family history, ADHD symptoms, and symptoms of co-morbid problems. Intelligence testing, achievement testing, and reports from parents and teachers will also provide valuable insight. In light of the 2011 study by Dr. Lidy Pelsser of the ADHD Research Centre in the Netherlands, it seems appropriate to begin Bart on restricted, non-allergenic diet to eliminate allergens related to ADHD symptoms. A strictly supervised restricted elimination diet is a valuable instrument to assess whether ADHD is induced by food. This diet should be followed and monitor his symptoms closely for five weeks.

If ADHD symptoms have not drastically improved or disappeared after five weeks, the diet should be ceased and medication will be the next course of action. Medication should be used to treat Bart's core ADHD symptoms. Central nervous system (CNS) stimulants have a high success rate for ADHD. Bart would begin taking a low dose of Ritalin. It should be taken two times a day; morning before breakfast and at night before dinner. He should begin taking 6mg tablets and then can move up to 60mg a day. A combination of medication and behavior therapy will be used to treat co-occurring problems for the long term. This therapy will promote improvements in the parent-child interactions, aggressive responses, and social skills. Parent training can also provide parents with skills to effectively interact with a child with ADHD.

Video: Bart Simpson – A Case Study in ADHD

- https://youtu.be/6SMdwNa4K4U

Name: Clark Griswold

Source: *National Lampoon's Christmas Vacation* (movie, 1989)

Background Information

Clark Griswold is a forty-four year old male patriarch of a traditional middle-income family with a wife and two teenage children (one son and one daughter). Clark works as a food additive designer for a large firm. His achievement is inconsistent and fluctuates from high level (creating a new "varnish" to keep cereal crispy in milk) to minimal effort and being "invisible" to his boss. Although Clark proclaims himself as "a regular family man, trying to do what's best for his wife and kids," his actions contradict his behavior. On more than one occasion, Clark has introduced his children as "Rusty and what's-her-name". This verbal outburst demonstrates a subconscious disconnect between beliefs and actions. Clark's wife, Ellen, does not display outwardly noticeable symptoms of mental health disorder. She demonstrates a loving relationship to her husband (a.k.a "Sparky") and children, although she tends to enable the household behaviors and live in a state of denial about Clark's eccentricities until his behavior is extreme. The children both display typical teenage angst and disinterest in family situations. Both minor children have past experience with illegal substances, but do not present addictive behaviors (see National Lampoon's Vacation, 1983). Clark's cousin Eddy displays a possible genetic link to maladaptive behaviors. For example, when Clark does not receive his anticipated Christmas bonus from work, Eddy kidnaps Clark's boss. Clark displays poor coping skills and reacts abruptly and inappropriately in both public and private settings. Although he lives in constant pursuit of the ultimate family vacation, his overall achievement goals are shallow and limited to materialistic gain.

The close proximity of relatives that may or may not always get along under normal circumstances, increases tensions and exacerbates Clark's ADHD symptoms. Family support and understanding for display of symptoms is minimal and inconsistent, although time spent together is abundant. Most of Clark's outbursts or behaviors are dismissed as normal for him. As of 1989, Clark has received no official mental health diagnosis but has displayed multiple symptoms that his family normally dismisses as "part of his character." Individuals from the outside view Clark as impulsive and prone to quick outbursts. It is possible that Clark displayed symptoms before age seven but went undiagnosed due to the lack of information regarding ADHD prior to 1970. Subsequent controversy and downplay of ADHD from critics may have interfered with proper diagnosis and treatment.

Description of the Problem

Clark presents with several significant symptoms pointing to Attention-Deficit/Hyperactivity Disorder. Clark is easily distracted and demonstrates an inability to stay on task with everyday items. However, he does overindulge on items he deems important. Clark becomes so involved in his quest for the perfect family vacation and Christmas lights for the house that he misses quality family time and activities with the group. Clark has a tendency to behave in an overly energetic manner and is unable to rest or at times maintain an even temperament. He is quick to anger at even mundane situations and consistently holds extreme grudges. Furthermore, he shows inappropriate affect and significant impairment in both personal and professional settings. For example, while Christmas shopping for his wife; Clark is unable to maintain composure with the female working the counter. He also displays inappropriate affect and coping behaviors with anger towards his boss by demonstrative and abrupt outbursts.

Diagnosis

Clark's symptoms fit best with a diagnosis of Attention-Deficit/Hyperactivity Disorder (314.0) from the DSM-IV-TR, with the specific subtype of Inattentive Type best describing his symptoms. Clark meets the following symptoms for Inattentive Type: 1, 2, 3, 4, 5, 8, 9. Although he presents with symptoms for Hyperactive-Impulsive Type, he does not display the required six or more for a complete diagnosis. Clark's hyperactive and impulsive behaviors may be caused by environmental factors. The following symptoms must be met to be diagnosed with Attention-Deficit/Hyperactivity Disorder:

1. Inattentive Type:
Six or more of the following symptoms of inattention have been present for at least 6 months to a point that is disruptive and inappropriate for developmental level:

1) Often does not give close attention to details or makes careless mistakes in schoolwork, work, or other activities.

Clark overlooks specific details in personal activities with an elevated risk such as driving or home improvement. During a family trip to choose a Christmas tree, Clark became distracted by his frustration with another driver and drove the car directly parallel under the bed of a semi-truck. He was unaware of his wife's warnings to stop or that he was pulling under the truck until after the action was complete. His home improvement skills lack detail such as the time he stapled his shirt sleeve to the top floor guttering while precariously balanced on a ladder.

2) Often has trouble keeping attention on tasks or play activities.

While Christmas gift shopping for his wife, Clark was distracted by the counter attendant and unable to focus on the task at hand. He continuously rambled, stumbled on words, or changed sentence syntax by saying "hooter" instead of "hotter". Clark displayed difficulty staying on task or keeping his attention on the purpose of his trip.

3) Often does not seem to listen when spoken to directly.

Clark's daughter, Audrey continuously updated him of her "freezing" body parts during a trek to find the family Christmas tree. He remained unaware of the situation, even after his wife expressed concern that Audrey's eyes were frozen. He dismissed the problem once he realized he was being addressed.

4) Often does not follow instructions and fails to finish schoolwork, chores, or duties in the workplace (not due to oppositional behavior or failure to understand instructions).

Failed to latch the ladder placed against his house and slid down to the ground from the second floor. Clark also overlooked the directions for the "twinkling" holiday lights and was unable to change them from the constant on position.

5) Often has trouble organizing activities.

Clark forgets to bring the saw necessary to cut down the tree on the family Christmas tree trip and also manages to freeze most of his daughter's body by leading them through massive snow and freezing temperatures without adequate preparation. His son, Rusty, spends most of the time during the Christmas light installation retrieving items from various locations or untangling the jumbled mess of string lights.

6) Often avoids, dislikes, or does not want to do things that take a lot of mental effort for a long period of time (such as schoolwork or homework).

7) Often loses things needed for tasks and activities (e.g. toys, school assignments, pencils, books, or tools).

8) Is often easily distracted.

Clark asks his wife about his mother-in-law waxing her lip during a serious conversation about holiday tension. He becomes trapped in the attic and becomes distracted by the case of home movies he found while searching for warm clothing. He proceeds to watch the movies instead of trying to find a way out of the attic.

9)Often forgetful in daily activities.

Clark is easily distracted and forgets basic activities or the involvement of others.

Some symptoms that cause impairment were present before age 7 years. There has to be an onset of symptoms prior to 7 years old, but a diagnosis can occur much later.

Unable to find medical history confirming childhood diagnosis but this could be due to the lack of information regarding ADHD prior to 1970.

Some impairment from the symptoms is present in two or more settings (e.g. at school/work and at home).

Clark's behavioral problems are consistent at both home and work, with home being his largest source of symptomatic display.

There must be clear evidence of significant impairment in social, school, or work functioning.

Clark displays inappropriate affect and displays attentional deficits at work and home.

The symptoms do not happen only during the course of a Pervasive Developmental Disorder, Schizophrenia, or other Psychotic Disorder. The symptoms are not better accounted for by another mental disorder (e.g. Mood Disorder, Anxiety Disorder, Dissociative Disorder, or a Personality Disorder).

Clark's does not demonstrate the symptoms associated with other disorders to warrant a full diagnosis of Mood Disorder, Anxiety Disorder, Dissociative Disorder, or Personality Disorder. He does present with OCD like symptoms and should be observed to assure an accurate diagnosis.

Accuracy of Portrayal

Clark's ADHD oriented behavior traits are consistent over the course of each movie. His excessive talking, trouble organizing activities, trouble staying focused when spoken to directly, and forgetfulness of daily activities are just a few of the direct ADHD symptoms that Clark displays. However, He does not consistently display the passiveness normally associated with Inattentive ADHD. Clark is compliant and passive during some events, yet he is also prone to outbursts and demonstrates a quick temper. ADHD shows a high comorbidity with Oppositional Defiant Disorder (ODD) and Conduct Disorder (CD), but Clark's temper and outbursts are more likely caused by environmental and psychological factors, thereby presenting an inaccuracy in the portrayal. The average viewer watching Clark Griswold may consider his behaviors are more consistent with Obsessive-Compulsive Disorder (OCD). Clark displays an inability to curb impulses and recurrent thoughts and is prone to act according to his own volition, regardless of the outcome on others. Although these attributes illustrate OCD, they are just a few of the many symptoms of ADHD that Clark exhibits.

Treatment

The best course of treatment should begin with a structured or semi-structured clinical interview to obtain Clark's family and medical history, and pervasive symptoms pertaining to ADHD and co-morbid disorders. Empirically supported treatment includes stimulant medication to relieve core symptoms. FDA-approved medications are useful for reducing physical symptoms. Specifically, ADHD responds best to stimulant medications such as Ritalin, Cylert, and Dexedrine. Due to the severity and inability to predict side effect occurrence from Cylert, the better pharmaceutical choice is either Methylphenidate (Ritalin) or Destroamphetamine Sulfate (Dexedrine) for Clark's symptoms. Potential stimulant medication side effects include insomnia, decreased appetite, and potential dependence. Dosage is prescribed based on patient age, weight, and medical history. Clark should begin with the lowest possible dosage and gradually increase prescription strength only at the advice of a therapist or doctor. Behavior therapy is preferred as the primary treatment choice in conjunction with pharmacotherapy and can be useful for improving social skills, modifying behavioral deficits, and reducing aggression. Additionally, family support methods are vital to effective treatment plans.

Video: Clark Griswold – A Case Study in ADHD

- https://youtu.be/UL_1HiuxEes

Anorexia Nervosa

Name: Trevor Reznik

Source: *The Machinist* (movie, 2004)

Background Information

Trevor Renik is a middle aged male of Euro-Asian decent. Trevor is a blue-collar worker. Trevor works for a company, National Machine, as a welder. Trevor's work environment is not a positive or friendly one. Trevor's age and family history are not known through the film. Trevor Reznik is not a healthy individual: he smokes cigarettes, he does not sleep, he does not eat at all, and consumes large amount of caffeine. Trevor states he does not drink frequently, but is seen drinking throughout the film. Trevor is not seen eating once throughout the film, nor does he engage in any physical exercise.

Trevor is socially withdrawn and does not have any close friends or family members. The interactions with women in the beginning of the film indicate that Trevor is lonely. Trevor's interactions with women show he does not have healthy relationships with women. One is with a prostitute, Stevie, whom he is a patron of throughout the film. Another woman is a waitress, Maria, whom Trevor believes he interacts with, but is actually one of Trevor's hallucinations. Realistically, Trevor never interacted with his waitress, whom was unrecognizable to Trevor when he is not hallucinating. Trevor's work environment is a constant stressor. Trevor's boss informs Trevor he "is on his shit list". Trevor is confronted by his bosses and asked for a Urinary Analysis because they believe he "looks like shit" thus he must be on drugs. Co-workers invite him to play poker and Trevor declines, upon doing so a co-worker responds "What's wrong with you, you used to be alright" while another co-worker says "You were never alright, but you used to hang". Trevor creates a hazardous situation at work while in an induced fatigue hallucination resulting in a co-worker losing his hand due to Trevor's actions. Trevor's co-workers are hostile and aggressive towards him after the work-related accident, thus Trevor experiences persecutory delusions and referential delusions. Trevor experiences many life-stressors throughout the film such as injuring others, himself, losing his job, losing relationships, and legal issues.

Trevor is consumed by his own delusions and hallucinations, which are induced from a hit-and-run. Trevor allows his memory to torment himself and has poor coping skills. Trevor's coping technique of thought repression to handle the hit-and-run make him feel enormous amounts of guilt. The implicit guilt Trevor experiences is explicitly seen throughout the film by his sticky notes in his home. Trevor's hit-and-run provoked the negative image of self to control all aspects of his life. Trevor has no desired goals or outcomes from his life, except to answer sticky notes he leaves himself. "Who are you?" is a sticky note Trevor leaves himself to remind him to seek for whom he really is. Trevor's weaknesses are his inability to interact socially and distinguish what is actually reality. Trevor is paranoid from his hallucinations and delusions and he frequently feels as if people are following him. Trevor thoughtfully analyzes situations to "expose" plots against him, while doing so he throws himself in front of a moving car in order to get information from the police. Upon doing so, the police inform him he is committing a felony and so he runs through underground tunnels to evade pursuit. Trevor finally realizes who he is by the end of the film: he is an individual that killed a little boy by committing a hit-and-run. After realizing who he is, a "killer", Trevor turns himself into the police for the hit-and-run. The individual who he hallucinated throughout the film was himself as Ivan and Maria, the victim's mother. Trevor is able to sleep once he turns himself into the police.

Description of the Problem

The opening scene is Trevor standing in front of a mirror looking at his self then replies, "shit", in disgust while looking at his reflection. Trevor holds a negative image of himself. In this scene, Trevor's shirt is off and his underweight body is revealed. Trevor displays physical symptoms of Anorexia Nervosa such as his body weight, sunken eyes, and puffy cheeks.

Individuals who interact with an individual suffering from Anorexia Nervosa display concern for their health. This is displayed as Trevor is asked "Are you alright?" throughout the film, indicating others do not perceive him as being in an okay state. Others ask Trevor if he uses drugs throughout the film. The prostitute and waitress try to feed Trevor food in many scenes. The women say, "If you were any thinner, you wouldn't exist".

Trevor's actions of not eating and properly nourishing his body are common for individuals suffering from Anorexia Nervosa, specifically the restrictive type. Trevor orders pie at a diner he goes to but he is never seen eating the pie. Fatigue is a common sign of Anorexia Nervosa due to malnourishment. Trevor reports to always be tired, cannot sleep, nor has slept in the past year. Trevor's sexual relations are not atypical of one with Anorexia Nervosa since he is the prostitute's "best costumer".

Trevor socially withdraws, which is a symptom associated with Anorexia Nervosa. Trevor loses touch with reality and those whom interact with him call him crazy and psycho. The persecutory delusions and referential delusions may be a side effect from long-term malnutrition and dehydration. Trevor believes his coworkers are plotting against him and ends up losing his job when he behaves erratically by physically attacking his co-workers. The physical attack results in Trevor becoming short in breath, another common symptom displayed with the disorder.

Diagnosis

One possible diagnosis for Trevor Reznik from the DSM IV-TR would be **Anorexia Nervosa, Restrictive Type, (307.1)**. Trevor experiences many social and economical stressors as well, including a hostile work environment, negative co-worker interactions, social interaction non-existent, job loss, committing a hit-and-run, and a loss of relationships.

Criterion that are met for Anorexia Nervosa include:

A. Refusal to maintain body weight at or above a minimally normal weight for age and height.

Trevor was substantially under 85% of the body weight he should have maintained.

C. Disturbance in the way in which one's body weight or shape is experienced, undue influence of body shape on self-evaluation, or denial of the seriousness of the current low body weight.

Trevor was disturbed by his body image as indicated with his response to his reflection. Trevor denied the seriousness of his underweight body. He does not seem aware of his diet, weight, or health thus, in denial of his personal health.

Difficulties diagnosing Trevor Reznik include: lack of knowledge about family history, lack of personal history, lack of medical history, and lack of self-report from him.

Accuracy of Portrayal

Trevor Reznik's suffering from Anorexia Nervosa is not very apparent due to his inattentiveness about his body weight. Therefore, Anorexia Nervosa may be mislabeled in this film. Trevor never explicitly states or indicates he has a fear of gaining weight, which is typical for those whom suffer from Anorexia Nervosa. Trevor's lack of concern with his body weight is not an accurate portrayal of an individual who suffers from Anorexia Nervosa.

If an individual watching the film knows what signs and symptoms to be aware of when assessing an individual who suffers from Anorexia Nervosa, then they may be able to diagnose Trevor Reznik as having the disorder. An individual who is aware of common symptoms and signs of Anorexia Nervosa may be able to decipher Trevor's disorder as an accurate portrayal. A stressor, murdering a little boy, may have been the on-set for Anorexia Nervosa and, as such, the film does accurately depict the course typical of individuals with Anorexia Nervosa. This includes Trevor not eating, acknowledging his poor health, and holding a negative image of self. Trevor never ate food during the film. Trevor's physical symptoms were very apparent but others in the film attributed this to drug use. Trevor's fatigue, delusions, and hallucinations may be symptoms due to severe malnourishment and dehydration. Individuals who watch the film would be able to understand how one who suffers from Anorexia Nervosa lives with constant paranoia of his self-image and induced on-set of Anorexia Nervosa that may have caused the delusions and hallucinations from inadequate diet. The film is accurate because people suffering from Anorexia Nervosa do not acknowledge the pervasiveness of their disorder. Trevor never acknowledges that his poor health is due to his lifestyle.

Treatment

Treating Trevor Reznik would require him to acknowledge having the disorder, Anorexia Nervosa. The patient's willingness and acceptance of the disorder are essential for treatment to a progressive lifestyle to changing behavior. Treatment would focus on two main goals: 1) Trevor must gain weight and nourish his body with an adequate diet and 2) address Trevor's psychological and environmental stressors. An empirically supported treatment widely used is family and group therapy. Trevor lacks a support system such as family and friends who are usually the people who initiated treatment for individuals suffering from the disorder. Typically, family and friends monitor diet and exercise for individuals suffering from Anorexia Nervosa. The lack of a social support Trevor receives makes treatment difficult. Trevor would have more success in self-help groups since he lacks a family for family therapy. The self-help group meetings would allow Trevor the opportunity to interact with others suffering from Anorexia Nervosa. The self-help group meetings would enlighten Trevor about Anorexia Nervosa tremendously. In order for self-help treatments to be successful Trevor must attend the meetings regularly and change his behavior through the acquisition of new knowledge. The self-help groups may be the social support Trevor needs to overcome Anorexia Nervosa. Trevor must change his attitude, behaviors, diet, and physically exercise to live a healthy lifestyle. If Trevor avoids situations and environments that are mental triggers for his disorder he will overcome the disorder with successful treatment. Trevor's successful treatment seems unlikely and he seems vulnerable to enduring a chronic episode that will ultimately end in his body's expiration.

Video: Trevor Reznick – A Case Study in Anorexia

- https://youtu.be/CGpQurtjJ7g